EXTRAORDINARY GROUPS

The Sociology of Unconventional Life-Styles

SECOND EDITION

SECOND EDITION

EXTRAORDINARY GROUPS

The Sociology of Unconventional Life-Styles

WILLIAM M. KEPHART
University of Pennsylvania

ST. MARTIN'S PRESS
New York

Library of Congress Catalog Card Number: 81–51860

Manufactured in the United States of America.
5432
fedc
For information, write St. Martin's Press, Inc.
175 Fifth Avenue, New York, N.Y. 10010

cover design: Tom McKeveny
cover photo: Alex Webb/Magnum

cloth ISBN: 0–312–27861–6
paper ISBN: 0–312–27862–4

Acknowledgments

Excerpts from *Gypsies: The Hidden Americans* by Anne Sutherland. Copyright 1975 by the Free Press, a division of the Macmillan Company, and reprinted by permission.

Excerpts from *Oneida Community: An Autobiography, 1851–1876,* edited by Constance Noyes Robertson. Published in 1970 by Syracuse University Press and reprinted by permission.

Excerpts from *My Father's House: An Oneida Boyhood* by Pierrepoint Noyes. Published in 1966 by Peter Smith and reprinted by permission.

Excerpts from *The American Shakers* by Henri Desroche. Translated and edited by John K. Savacool. Copyright © 1971 by The University of Massachusetts Press. Les Editions de Minuit, 7 rue Bernard-Palissy, 75006 Paris—Copyright 1955. Reprinted by permission.

Excerpts from *The Latter-day Saints: The Mormons Yesterday and Today* by Robert R. Mullen. Copyright © 1966 by Robert R. Mullen and reprinted by permission of Doubleday & Company, Inc., and W. H. Allen & Company, Ltd.

Excerpts from *The Mormon Establishment* by Wallace Turner. Published in 1966 by Houghton Mifflin Company and reprinted by permission.

CONTENTS

EXTRAORDINARY GROUPS

The Sociology of Unconventional Life-Styles

SECOND EDITION

INTRODUCTION

America is a land of fascinating cultural diversity. The *Harvard Encyclopedia* contains accounts of some 125 American ethnic groups, and the list is by no means exhaustive.[1] The *Encyclopedia of American Religions* includes information on nearly 1,200 groups—an unbelievable number.[2] Indeed, it is this *tremendous range of associational groups* that sets America apart from so many other cultures.

Of this vast array, I have chosen seven for inclusion in *Extraordinary Groups.* Most of them are important in their own right. Just as a liberally educated person should have some knowledge of other times and other places, he should also have an awareness of the subcultural diversity within his own society.

But why were these particular groups chosen, rather than others? The first—and most important—reason pertains to sociological illustration. All of the groups were selected because *they illustrate major sociological principles in concrete form.*

Definition of the situation, for example, is a standard sociological concept. As W. I. Thomas, who coined the term, put it: "What men define as real is real in its consequences." And the American Gypsies provide an excellent illustration, for they have defined the *gadje* (outsiders) as a threat to their social equilibrium. In consequence, the life-style of the Gypsies (chapter one) centers on boundary maintenance. That is, except for "business" reasons, they will not associate with the *gadje.* Dating outsiders, intermarriage, participating in community activities, socializing with non-Gypsies—all such interaction is taboo. Little wonder, therefore, that some observers look upon the Gypsies as a *counterculture.*

Another example, one employing the concept of *anomie.* First used by Emile Durkheim and now a recognized part of the sociological

[1]Stephan Thernstrom, ed., *Harvard Encyclopedia of American Ethnic Groups* (Cambridge, Mass.: Harvard University Press, 1980).

[2]J. Gordon Melton, *The Encyclopedia of American Religions* (Wilmington, N.C.: Consortium Books, 1979).

vocabulary, *anomie* refers to a sense of powerlessness or worthlessness, leading eventually to a feeling of alienation. Anomic persons feel left out of the mainstream of society, and because of this belief they may feel that their very survival is at stake.

In the case of the Shakers, *anomie* was one of the reasons for joining. Group living within Shakerdom, emotional security, camaraderie, the constant presence of like-minded people, the sociality of everyday life—such things went a long way toward dispelling the *anomie* that many Shakers had found in the outside world. And as will be shown (chapter five), the Shakers carried on a successful communal experiment for more than two hundred remarkable years.

Let us look at another example. Many years ago, sociologist William F. Ogburn formulated the concept of *disappearing family functions.* It was Ogburn's contention that, in contrast to the colonial period, modern American families were characterized by a loss of certain functions—functions which had been taken over by outside agencies. Thus education, once a function of the home, had become the province of the schools. Religion had become the domain of the church. The medical function—once centered largely in the home—had been taken over by professional medical services. Recreation had similarly been taken over by outside sources. And so on.

Not all sociologists agreed with Ogburn's position; indeed, the debate has continued down to the present. For undergraduates, however, the controversy has been largely academic. After all, most students have difficulty relating to the functional family of yesteryear. The Old Order Amish, fortunately, provide a meaningful example, for the Amish family of today has changed very little since the 1700s; that is, the Ogburnian functions still remain.

There are no churches in Amishland. All religious services are held in the home. Education is still considered to be primarily a family function. Commercial amusements are forbidden, so that recreation also revolves around the home. Most important, perhaps, the economic function has been retained, with the Amish raising their own food, building their own homes, making most of their own clothes, and the like. In brief, the Amish family is largely a self-sustaining economic unit. What better way of presenting Ogburn's point of view than with a living example?

One final illustration. As used by sociologists, the term *primary group* refers to a small, face-to-face group whose members share experiences, confide in one another, evidence mutual understanding, and so on. These primary-group needs, as they are called, are deep-seated. They are characteristic of human beings everywhere. In most societies, the basic primary group is the family, and insofar as the personality structure of children is concerned, sociologists feel that the family has a lasting influence.

It stands to reason, therefore, that any culture or subculture which attempts to eliminate the family must provide an alternative social mechanism for the satisfaction of primary-group needs. The Oneida Community is a good case in point. In their effort to create a utopian society, the Oneidans dispensed entirely with marriage, family, and parental child rearing. All males were permitted to have sex relations with all females, and all children were reared communally. In fact, undue affection between parents and children—or between a particular man and woman—was severely censured. And since the Oneida Community lasted for some fifty years, with a total membership running well into the hundreds, the methods used to promote group solidarity were obviously effective.

Oneidans were all housed under one roof—the Mansion House—a building designed specifically to promote feelings of togetherness. Members ate in a common dining hall and held meetings in a communal meeting hall. Activities such as smoking, drinking, and card playing were prohibited, since they were felt to be individualistic or antigroup. Conversely, musical presentations, theatricals, and other group activities were strongly encouraged.

In their day-to-day living, Oneidans totally rejected the concept of private property. They shared their material possessions, their wealth, their mates, and their children. Members held both a common economic philosophy and a common theology. So strong was their we-feeling that the Oneidans were able to satisfy the aforementioned primary-group needs in spite of their large size.

Other conceptual examples could be given: *relative deprivation* among the Amish; *alienation* on the part of Father Divine's followers; *formal and informal social control* among the Gypsies; *culture conflict* on the part of the Mormons. *Conspicuous consumption; level of aspiration; cultural theme; manifest* and *latent function; charisma; reference group behavior; folkways* and *mores; sex-role behavior; ethnocentrism. . . .*

Every chapter in *Extraordinary Groups* contains a series of sociological concepts around which are woven the threads and cultural fabric of the group in question.

The second reason for choosing these particular groups was their diversity. The Shakers were strictly a stay-at-home group, for whom travel was largely prohibited. Gypsies, on the other hand, may well be the world-champion travelers. The Old Order Amish are a rural group; the Father Divine movement is urban. The Oneida Community practiced "free love"; the Shakers were celibate. The Hutterites adhere to a system of strict economic communism, while the Mormons believe just as strongly in free enterprise.

The third and final reason for choosing these particular groups was simply that *they are interesting.* This I know from personal experience. I was born and raised in Philadelphia—only a stone's throw from Father Divine's headquarters—and on a number of occasions I was able to meet this remarkable man and talk with his followers. My association with Mother Divine—one that I also value—continues.

My undergraduate days were spent in the heart of Amishland (Franklin and Marshall College, Lancaster, Pennsylvania), and both my fascination and conversations with this quaint group have continued ever since. My interest in the Oneida Community also goes back many years; in fact, I was fortunate enough to have interviewed several of the surviving members (now deceased), as well as their descendants.

I have likewise enjoyed my talks with the Shakers—there are only a handful left—and with Theodore Johnson, director of the Shaker Museum and Library at Sabbathday Lake, Maine. The Mormons have been most cooperative, and I have yet to ask a question that was not answered fully and patiently.

I wish I could state that I enjoyed my relationship with the Gypsies, but—no pun intended—it was not in the cards. Both physically and conversationally, Gypsies are elusive. A good many of my interviews were out-and-out failures. That I was able to unearth as much as I did was due to a relatively small number of cooperative interviewees, much patience (nearly two years!), and some invaluable fieldwork on the part of previous investigators.

For the most part, sociological principles are not difficult to learn. The trick is to make them *meaningful.* It is hoped that a perusal of the following "extraordinary groups" will indeed result in a meaningful grasp of the subject matter. Also—who knows—a consideration of these groups may make us feel a little less smug about our own way of life.

ONE

THE GYPSIES

The Gypsies are an incredible people; in fact, the more one studies them the more incredible they become! On the dust jacket of Peter Maas' controversial and widely read *King of the Gypsies,* for example, the following statement appears:

> There are perhaps a million or more Gypsies in the United States—nobody knows exactly how many, not even the government. They no longer live in horse-drawn caravans on dusty roads; they live in cities, drive cars, have telephones and credit cards. Yet they do not go to school, neither read nor write, don't pay taxes, and keep themselves going by means of time-honored ruses and arrangements.
>
> Gypsies themselves recognize the contrast they make, and they are proud of it. "All right," one old Gypsy woman said, "it's true that we steal with our hands, but you Americans—*you* steal with your pencils."[1]

Given the nature of publishers' blurbs, can this statement be true? The answer is complicated, and each of the above points requires some explanation.

It is true that no one knows how many Gypsies there are in the United States, although the million figure is probably on the high side. Estimates vary from 100,000 to one million, with the real figure probably being in the area of 500,000.[2] The United States has one of the largest, if not the largest, Gypsy populations of any country.

Although 500,000 seems a reasonable estimate, it is unlikely that the real figure will ever be known. The fact of the matter is that Gypsies move about so much, have so many different names and aliases, and are generally so secretive that it is often difficult to pinpoint the numbers for a given city let alone for the nation at large.

Gypsies live in cities and drive cars? Indeed they do. They are not

[1]Peter Maas, *King of the Gypsies* (New York: Viking, 1975).

[2]Ian Hancock, "Gypsies," in Stephan Thernstrom, ed., *Harvard Encyclopedia of American Ethnic Groups* (Cambridge, Mass.: Harvard University Press, 1980), p. 441.

likely to be found on farms or in the suburbs. They will not be found on the water. They are urban dwellers—towns and cities—and they reside in nearly all of the fifty states. At the same time, Gypsies are, and always have been, great travelers. They may be the greatest travelers the world has ever known. (In England, the terms "Gypsy" and "Traveler" are often used interchangeably.) As we shall see, traveling serves as an integral part of the Gypsy life-style.

As for the cars, Gypsies not only drive them but sometimes make their living repairing them. The days of the horse-drawn wagons and caravans have long since gone, but Gypsies—as is their wont—have adapted remarkably well to motorized transportation. Indeed, despite the fact that they are a low-income group, Gypsies often drive Cadillacs.

Gypsies do not go to school? Not very often—and not for very long. They feel that formal education is not germane to their way of life and that the American school system would tend to "de-Gypsyize" their youngsters. Both claims are at least partially true, and the subject will be discussed later.

Gypsies neither read nor write? True. A large proportion of them are functionally illiterate. They cannot even read or write their own language, Romany, for it is a spoken rather than a written tongue. The literacy situation is improving, but so far progress has been slow. In spite of their self-imposed linguistic handicap, however, Gypsies have made a remarkable adaptation to their environment.

Gypsies do not pay taxes? Some observers would reply: "Not if they can help it." And it is true that many Gypsies do not pay property taxes because they have no taxable property. They often prefer to rent rather than to buy a dwelling-place. Also, many Gypsies work irregularly and have low-paying jobs, and the magnitude of their income tax payments is problematical. A fair number are on welfare. On the other hand, at least some Gypsies are moving into white-collar occupations, and their tax payments are probably commensurate with those of other white-collar workers.

Gypsies keep themselves going by means of time-honored ruses and arrangements? A complicated question, surely, but then the Gypsies are a complicated people. As is true of all ethnic groups, there are honest Gypsies and there are dishonest Gypsies. Unfortunately, however, many Gypsies continue to hold to the belief that all *gadje*[3] (non-Gypsies) are "fair game." And sometimes this belief does culminate in ruses and petty swindles.

[3]Most Gypsy terms have a variety of spellings. In the present account, spelling has been adapted to fit the pronunciation.

On the other side of the ledger, Gypsy attitudes toward the *gadje* have been shaped in part by the *gadje* themselves. As will be shown, Gypsies have not been met with open arms by the various host countries. On the contrary, they have experienced near-universal prejudice and discrimination. Social distance studies in several countries, including the United States, simply confirm the obvious; namely, that Gypsies rank at the absolute bottom of the scale.[4]

Through it all, the Gypsies have survived. Gypsies always survive. If they haven't exactly flourished, they have in many ways given a very good account of themselves. It is not easy to be a Gypsy. As one writer put it: "Only the fit need apply."[5] It is hoped that in the following pages the full implications of this statement will become clear.

Who Are the Gypsies?

Like so many other aspects of Gypsy life, their origins are draped in mystery. The word "Gypsy" derives from "Egyptian," for the Gypsies were mistakenly thought to have originated in Egypt. This was a belief that they themselves did little to discourage. In fact, some Gypsies still believe in their Egyptian origins, although it has now been rather well established that their original homeland was India. (Romany, the Gypsy language, has its roots in Sanskrit.)

Exactly when the Gypsies left India—or what their status was—is still being debated. They have been variously described as being descended from the Criminal and Wandering Tribes, as being deported prisoners of war, and as being "a loose federation of nomadic tribes, possibly outside the Indian caste system entirely."[6] Rishi contends that "the majority of Gypsies, before migrating from India, formed a vital part of the upper strata of the Indian population, such as the Rajputs, Kshatriyas, and Jats."[7]

Whatever their class or caste origins, it seems likely that the proto-Gypsies left India at different times, perhaps during the first few centuries A.D. By the fifth century, they seem to have settled in and around Persia and Syria. And although their early migration patterns are anything but clear, Gypsies were reported in Southeastern Europe (Greece, Hungary, Rumania, Serbia) by the 1300s, and in Western

[4]Cited in Matt Salo and Sheila Salo, *The Kalderash in Eastern Canada* (Ottawa: National Museums of Canada, 1977), p. 17.

[5]Rena C. Gropper, *Gypsies in the City* (Princeton, N.J.: Darwin, 1975), p. 189.

[6]Donald Kenrick and Grattan Puxon, *The Destiny of Europe's Gypsies* (New York: Basic Books, 1972), pp. 13–14.

[7]P. W. R. Rishi, "Roma Preserves Hindu Mythology," *Roma* (January 1977): 13.

Europe (France, Germany, Italy, Holland, Switzerland, Spain) by the 1400s.[8] Today there are Gypsies in practically every European country. They are also well established in North Africa, the Near East, South America, the United States, and Canada.

The term "Gypsy," incidentally, is not a Romany term. Gypsies refer to themselves as "Rom." (In the present account, the two terms will be used interchangeably.) And while there is much physical variation, the Rom tend to have dark hair, dark eyes, and medium to dark complexions. On the whole, they are of average or a little below average height. Several writers have noticed that Gypsies have a tendency toward obesity as they age.

(Some groups who are often thought of as Gypsies are not in fact true Gypsies, or Rom. These would include the Tinkers of Ireland and Scotland and the Taters of Norway.[9] The Irish Tinkers, for example, are of Celtic origin, and they speak Shelte, a Celtic dialect.[10] In the present account, we are concerned only with the Rom.)

As they spread throughout Europe, Gypsies came to be—above all else—travelers. "A Gypsy who does not keep on the move," wrote Block just prior to World War II, "is not a Gypsy."[11] Actually, there have always been large numbers of sedentary Gypsies, or *Sinte.* Acton reports that in Yugoslavia there is currently a town of some thirty thousand Gypsies.[12]

Nevertheless, *Sinte* or no *Sinte,* it was the horse-drawn wagons and gaily decorated caravans that seemed to strike a responsive chord in people of all ages. Jan Yoors, author of one of the most widely read books on Gypsy life, ran away as a young boy and lived for many years with a Gypsy group.[13] Webb, another writer, states that

> for as long as I can remember, Gypsies have fascinated me. These dark-skinned strangers, indifferent to the rest of the world, mysterious in their comings and goings, traveling the roads with parades of highly

[8]See Gropper, *Gypsies in the City,* pp. 1–16.

[9]Frederik Barth, "The Social Organization of a Pariah Group in Norway," in Farnham Rehfisch, ed., *Gypsies, Tinkers, and Other Travelers* (New York: Academic Press, 1975), pp. 285–99.

[10]Bettina Barnes, "Irish Traveling People"; George Gmelch, "The Effects of Economic Change on Irish Traveler Sex Roles and Marriage Patterns"; and A. Rehfisch and F. Rehfisch, "Scottish Travelers or Tinkers," in Rehfisch, *Gypsies,* pp. 231–83.

[11]Martin Block, *Gypsies: Their Life and Their Customs* (New York: Appleton-Century, 1939), p. 1.

[12]Thomas Acton, *Gypsy Politics and Social Change* (London and Boston: Routledge & Kegan Paul, 1974), p. 228.

[13]Jan Yoors, *The Gypsies* (New York: Simon and Schuster, 1967), p. 86.

> colored raggedness, fired my imagination. . . . I was curious about them and wanted to know more. But nobody, it seemed, could tell me more.[14]

The Rom themselves seemed captivated by the caravan style of life. Indeed, some still talk about the good old (premotorized) days. Whether, in fact, caravan life was all that good can be debated. Yoors himself writes as follows:

> One year, for the first time, I stayed with the Rom throughout the winter. Lying half awake in the cold stillness of the long nights in Pulika's huge wagon, I heard the snapping noise of the nails in the boards as they creaked under the effect of the severe frost. The windows had been covered up with boards, old overcoats and army blankets, straw or pieces of tar paper, but the wind blasted through cracks too many to fill.
>
> The dogs whimpered all night. The drinking water froze in the buckets, and washing in the morning became an ordeal. Hands chapped, lips cracked and bled. The men ceased to shave. The small children cried bitterly when they were put outside and chased away from the wagons near which they had wanted to relieve themselves. Clothes could not be washed. The air inside the wagons was thick and unbreathable, mixed with the coal fumes from the red-hot stove, from which small children had to be kept away.
>
> During the winter months, not enough dead wood could be gathered outside to keep the fires going all day and part of the night, so the Rom were forced to buy, beg, or steal coal.[15]

No combination of elements, however, could dampen the Gypsy spirit—or their fondness for bright colors, especially greens, yellows, and reds.[16] As one Gypsy remarked to Sandford, "I wear bright beads and bright colors because we're a bright race. We don't like anything drab."[17]

The Gypsy Paradox With their unusual life-style, there is no doubt that Gypsies have held a real fascination for the *gadje,* almost irrespective of the country involved. Novels, plays, songs, and operettas have portrayed—and often glorified—the romantic wanderings of the Gypsy vagabond. Popular pieces like "Gypsy Love Song" and "Play Gypsy, Dance Gypsy" have become part of the worldwide musical repertoire.

Yet side by side with the attraction and fascination has come harassment and persecution. This is the Gypsy paradox: attraction on

[14]G. E. C. Webb, *Gypsies: The Secret People* (London: Herbert Jenkins, 1960), pp. 9, 14.

[15]Yoors, *Gypsies,* p. 86.

[16]Block, *Gypsies,* p. 130.

[17]Jeremy Sandford, *Gypsies* (London: Secker & Warburg, 1973), p. 13.

the one hand, persecution on the other. The climax of persecution came during World War II, when the Nazis murdered between 250,000 and 500,000 Rom. Moreover, the extermination took place without the Gypsies even being given a reason!

Despite worldwide persecution, however, the Gypsies have managed to survive. Gypsies always survive. As Gropper puts it:

> For 500 years Gypsies have succeeded in being themselves against all odds, fiercely maintaining their identity in spite of persecution, prejudice, hatred, and cultural forces compelling them to change. We may have something to learn from them on how to survive in a drastically changing world.[18]

The Modern Period Following World War II, urbanization and industrialization—together with population expansion—literally cramped the Gypsies' life-style. There was less and less room on the modern highway for horse-drawn caravans. Camping sites became harder to find, and the open countryside seemed to shrink. But—as always—the Gypsies adapted. Travel continued, albeit on a reduced scale. Caravans and wagons were replaced by automobiles, trucks, campers, and trailers. Somehow, by one method or another, the Rom managed to get by. And they did so without sacrificing their group identity or their freedom.

"Freedom," however, was not maintained without a price, for prejudice and harassment continued. Gypsy nomads were often hounded from one locale to another. The *Sinte* or sedentary Rom—who came to outnumber the nomads—were also met by hostility and discrimination. Sandford notes, for example, that "No Gypsies Allowed" signs were routinely posted in public places.[19]

The issue was hardly one-sided. From the view of local authorities, Gypsies were using community services without paying their share of the taxes. Indeed, in many cases they were not paying any taxes at all! Additionally, the Rom were dirty, they would not use indoor toilets, they lied, they cheated, and they stole. Sometimes the charges were true; often they were unfounded. (Interestingly, the Rom have rarely been accused of crimes of violence.)

Fortunately, the Gypsies also had friends and supporters, and in a number of countries efforts were made to set up camping sites, establish housing facilities, provide legal assistance, and otherwise improve the lot of the Rom. By the 1970s, a number of national and international committees and councils had been organized—with Gypsy representation. The purpose of these groups has been not only

[18]Gropper, *Gypsies in the City,* p. 1.
[19]Sandford, *Gypsies,* p. 6.

to protect the interests of the Rom but to dispel stereotypes, combat false portrayals in the media, and act as a clearinghouse for information about Gypsies.

When all is said and done, however, there is no doubt that the Rom continue to have problems. According to Dodds, the idea of their having a carefree, romantic life is a myth. In reality, "the Gypsy's life is one of perpetual insecurity."[20]

And yet . . . Contrast the foregoing statement with the following, by Clebert: "Gypsies themselves are Lords of the Earth. . . . All real Gypsies are united in their love of freedom, and in their eternal flight from the bonds of civilization, in their desire to be their own masters, and in their contempt for what we pompously call the 'consequences.' "[21]

Which of the two views is correct? Perhaps both are. In some ways, the Rom do indeed have a difficult life. Their relationship with the *gadje* often takes on the appearance of an interminable contest. At the same time, Gypsies show little inclination to assimilate. They are demonstrably proud that they are Gypsies, an attitude that is unlikely to change.

How many Gypsies are there in the world today? Estimates vary from five to ten million, with the latter figure probably being closer to the truth. (More than half are in Eastern Europe.) There is general —though not unanimous—agreement that the Rom are divided into four tribes or nations *(natsiyi):* the Lowara, Machwaya, Kalderasha, and Churara. While there are linguistic and cultural differences among the four *natsiyi,* surprisingly little has been written on this score.

The United States The first Gypsies to come to what is now the United States arrived in Virginia, Georgia, New Jersey, and Louisiana during the 1600s, although their fate remains unknown.[22] It is known that these early arrivals had been deported from various European countries—hardly an auspicious beginning. Significant numbers of the Rom, however, did not enter the United States until the 1880s and after.[23]

Up until the 1930s, the Rom followed their traditional traveling and camping patterns, replete with horse-drawn vehicles and colorful caravans. By the 1930s, though—as was true in Europe—the caravan had generally given way to motorized transportation.

[20]Norman Dodds, *Gypsies, Didikois, and Other Travelers* (London: Johnson, 1976), p. 16.

[21]Jean-Paul Clebert, *The Gypsies* (London: Vista, 1963), pp. xvii–xix.

[22]Hancock, "Gypsies," p. 441.

[23]Gropper, *Gypsies in the City,* p. 18.

The Depression of the 1930s saw another significant event insofar as the Gypsies were concerned: the election of Franklin Roosevelt and the introduction of large-scale relief and welfare programs. To take advantage of the situation, the Rom began to flock to the large cities, such as Chicago and New York.[24]

The extent to which they stayed in the cities—and later in the smaller towns—depended on such things as economic opportunities, welfare practices, and degree of police harassment. And since all three of these factors changed from time to time, the Gypsy population in a given city often fluctuated. Nevertheless, the Rom were in the cities to stay, and today there are a reported ten thousand in Chicago and fifteen thousand in Los Angeles. While they reside in nearly all the states, the largest Gypsy concentrations are to be found in New York, Virginia, Illinois, Texas, and Massachusetts, and on the Pacific Coast.[25] Although Romany practices in other countries will be alluded to from time to time, our primary concern in the following pages will be with the American Gypsies.

Difficulties in Studying the Rom

> If you ask a dozen Gypsies the same question, you will probably get a dozen different answers. If you ask one Gypsy the same question a dozen times, you will still probably get a dozen different answers.
> *Anon*

Although there are many versions, this adage contains more than a little truth. Gypsies live—and always have lived—in alien cultures. The boundaries between Rom and *gadje* are sharp, and the Rom have every intention of maintaining the sharpness. Deception, avoidance, misrepresentation, and lying are part of the Gypsies' arsenal, and they have had hundreds of years to perfect and embellish their defenses. In many ways, investigating the Rom is like trying to penetrate a secret society. As Evans-Pritchard observes:

> I am sure that it is much easier to enter into a primitive Melanesian or African community than that of the Gypsies. The Melanesian or African has not had to build his barricades as the Gypsies have had to do. . . . Gypsies have been for centuries living in societies in which they have not belonged.[26]

[24]Ibid., p. 20.

[25]Hancock, "Gypsies," p. 441.

[26]E. E. Evans-Pritchard, quoted in Elwood Trigg, *Gypsy Demons and Divinities* (Secaucus, N.J.: Citadel, 1973), p. x.

Perhaps the most formidable obstacle the researcher has to face is the avoidance syndrome. The Rom ordinarily do not mingle with the *gadje;* in fact, except for a possible visit to a fortune-teller, most Americans never come into contact with a Gypsy. Almost certainly they never see the inside of a Romany dwelling. Researchers face much the same problem. The fact that they are accredited university personnel means little to the Rom. Generally speaking, Gypsies have no intention of divulging their life-style and customs to social scientists or to anybody else.

Fortunately, we have some excellent American field studies such as those by Anne Sutherland[27] and Rena C. Gropper.[28] Both of these investigators are not only trained observers but spent several years among the Rom, learning the language and achieving a fair degree of acceptance. And even they experienced difficulties! Sutherland writes that

> the first Gypsy I met was a young woman of my own age who smiled at me, talking soothingly and ingratiatingly, but when I asked to speak with her father, she lunged at me, grabbing my face with her fingernails, screaming and cursing, "WHAT DO YOU WANT?"
>
> The second Gypsy I talked with vehemently denied that he was a Gypsy (what better technique for not answering questions), and the third feigned imbecility, mumbling to herself and staring wildly into space. . . .
>
> It soon became clear that these are people who, through centuries of experience in avoiding the prying questions of curious outsiders, have perfected their techniques of evasion to an effortless art. They delight in deceiving the *gadje,* mostly for a good reason, but sometimes just for the fun of it or to keep in practice![29]

Although avoidance and deception serve as major impediments in studying the Rom, there are other difficulties involved—difficulties that make it hard to *generalize* about Gypsy life. To begin with, all four *natsiyi* or tribes are represented in the United States: the Lowara, Machwaya, Kalderasha, and Churara. Customs and practices that apply to one group might or might not apply to the others. (Actually, the Kalderasha and the Machwaya are by far the most numerous of the *natsiyi* in the United States, and most of the American studies have been done on these two groups. Little is known about the Churara, and there are relatively few Lowara in this country.)

[27] Anne Sutherland, *Gypsies: The Hidden Americans* (New York: Free Press, 1975).
[28] Gropper, *Gypsies in the City.*
[29] Sutherland, *Hidden Americans,* p. 21.

Practices of the Rom also vary depending on their mobility patterns. Some Gypsies have lived in the same domicile for many years. Others move about constantly. Still others travel as the mood strikes them. And customs and life-style vary somewhat from one group to another.

Even if all Rom followed similar travel practices, their social structure would be difficult to analyze. Gypsies live in extended families *(familiyi),* which form part of a larger kinship or cognatic group called the *vitsa.* (The *vitsi,* in turn, are affiliated with one of the four tribes, or *natsiyi:* Lowara, Machwaya, Kalderasha, and Churara.) The point is that various Gypsy customs may vary from one *familia* to the next, and from one *vitsa* to the next, making it hard, again, to generalize.

In addition to these kinship and tribal affiliations, Gypsies in a given area often form themselves into economic units called *kumpaniyi.* A *kumpania* is a loose association formed for the purpose of organizing the labor force, parceling out jobs, and so forth. *Wortacha* are much smaller economic units, such as those involving friends, brothers, or father-son partnerships.

A final factor complicates the study of American Rom: their customs often depend on their country of origin. The Romnichals (English Gypsies), for instance, differ from the Boyash (Rumanian), and both groups differ from the Arxentina (Gypsies from Argentina and Brazil).

In brief, American Rom do not present a uniform culture pattern. Because of their kinship structure, their social and economic organization, their geographical mobility, and their nationality differences, it would be difficult to generalize about Gypsies even if they were cooperative—which they are not!

Even the "cooperative" Gypsies pose a problem for the researcher. The Rom often have a working knowledge of their own particular group—and no other. Relatively few Gypsies have anything like a world view or a historical picture of their own people.

Still and all, our fund of knowledge is growing. Perhaps the wonder of it is that we know as much about Romany life as we do!

Marimé

Central to any understanding of the Rom is their concept of *marimé.* It is *marimé* that is the key to their avoidance of the *gadje,* and it is *marimé* that serves as a powerful instrument of social control.

Marimé means defilement or pollution, and as used by the Gypsies it is both an object and a concept. And since there is really no comparable term used by non-Gypsies, it is sometimes difficult for the latter to comprehend the meaning. *"Marimé,"* writes Miller, "extends to all areas of Rom life, underwriting a hygienic attitude toward the world. . . . Lines are drawn between Gypsy and non-Gypsy, the clean and the unclean, health and disease, the good and the bad, all of which are made obvious and visible through the offices of ritual avoidance."[30]

The most striking aspects of *marimé* have to do with the demarcation of the human body. The upper parts, particularly the head and the mouth, are looked upon as pure and clean. The lower portions, especially the genital and anal regions, are considered *marimé.* As the Rom see it, the upper and lower halves of the body must not "mix" in any way, and objects that come into contact with one half must not come into contact with the other.

There are countless examples of this hygienic-ritualistic separation. Ronald Lee, who is himself a Gypsy, writes that

> you can't wash clothes, dishes, and babies in the same pan, and every Gypsy has his own eating utensils, towels, and soap. Other dishes and utensils are set aside for guests, and still others for pregnant women. Certain towels are for the face, and others for the nether regions—and there are different colored soaps in the sink, each with an allotted function.[31]

Marimé apparently originated in the early caravan period, when —for hygienic purposes—it was imperative that certain areas of the camp be set aside for cooking, cleaning, washing, taking care of body functions, and the like. Also, within the close confines of the wagons and tents, it was important that rules pertaining to sex be carefully spelled out and enforced. As is so often the case, however, over the years the various hygienic and sexual taboos proliferated. Miller notes, for example, that at the present time:

> Items that come into contact with the upper portions of the body are separately maintained and washed in running water or special basins. These items would include soap, towels, razors and combs, clothes, pillows, furniture like the backs of chairs and the tops of tables, tablecloths, aprons, sinks, utensils, and, of course, food itself, which is prepared, served, and eaten with the greatest consideration for ritual quality. . . .

[30]Carol Miller, "American Rom and the Ideology of Defilement," in Rehfisch, *Gypsies,* p. 41.

[31]Ronald Lee, *Goddam Gypsy: An Autobiographical Novel* (Montreal: Tundra, 1971), pp. 29–30.

> Any contact between the lower half of the body, particularly the genitals, which are conceptually the ultimate source of *marimé,* and the upper body is forbidden. The inward character of the genitals, especially the female genitalia—which are associated with the mysteries of blood and birth—make them consummately impure. Items that have contact with this area are carefully segregated because they contain a dangerous threat to the status of pure items and surfaces. The most dreadful contact, of course, would be between the genitals and the oral cavity.[32]

Gropper states that "a woman is *marimé* during and after childbirth, and during her monthly period. . . . A *marimé* woman may not cook or serve food to men. She may not step over anything belonging to a man or allow her skirts to touch his things. Women's clothing must be washed separately from men's."[33]

Even such a natural phenomenon as urination may cause difficulties for the Rom. "One old lady called off a visit to a friend because she was indisposed and felt it would be too embarrassing to urinate frequently. Men often go outside to urinate rather than do so in their own homes, especially if guests are present."[34]

Interestingly and—given their conception of *marimé*—quite logically, Gypsy women attach shame to the legs rather than the breasts. Sutherland points out that it is shameful for a woman to have too much leg exposed, and that women who wear short skirts are expected to cover them with a sweater when they sit. On the other hand:

> Women use their brassieres as their pocketbooks, and it is quite common for a man, whether he be the husband, son, father, or unrelated, to reach into her brassiere to get cigarettes or money. When women greet each other after a certain absence, they squeeze each other's breasts. They will also squeeze the breasts to show appreciation of a witty story or joke.[35]

Marimé* vs. *Melalo Mention should be made of the distinction between *marimé* and *melalo. Marimé* is pollution or defilement, as just described. *Melalo* simply means dirty, or as Lee describes it, "dirty with honest dirt."[36] Someone who has not had a bath would be *melalo,* but not *marimé.* Hands that are dirty because of manual labor would be *melalo* rather than *marimé*—although they would be *marimé* if they had touched the genitals.

[32]Miller, "American Rom," p. 42. See also Trigg, *Gypsy Demons,* p. 64.
[33]Gropper, *Gypsies in the City,* pp. 92–93.
[34]Sutherland, *Hidden Americans,* p. 266.
[35]Ibid., p. 264.
[36]Lee, *Goddam Gypsy,* p. 244.

(In actual practice, Gypsies tend to wash their hands many times a day—because they may have touched any number of objects or organs that are *marimé.* Miller states that "a working Rom also washes his face and hands whenever he feels his luck leaving him during the day; he washes again upon returning from his work.")[37]

The distinction between *marimé* and *melalo* explains why a Gypsy domicile often appears dirty to a non-Gypsy—and vice versa! Some of the Romany dwelling places I have been in, for example, are anything but spic and span. Food scraps, cigarette butts, paper, wrappings—all may be thrown on the floor, presumably to be swept out later. Such a condition is not *marimé* so long as the proper rules of body hygiene, food preparation, and so forth are followed. As one writer puts it: "Americans tend to be shocked at visible dirt, but Gypsies abhor invisible pollution."[38]

The *Gadje*: Definition of the Situation Not all of the *natsiyi* follow the same rules and procedures regarding *marimé.* There are also some variations among family groups within the same *natsia.* (The Salos note that families who follow a strict observance pattern have a higher status than those who tend to be lax.)[39] But there is one point on which all true Rom are agreed: the *gadje* are *marimé.* Miller writes as follows:

> The *gadje* are conceived as a different race whose main value is economic, and whose *raison d'être* is to trouble the Rom. The major offense of the *gadje,* the one offense that the Rom can never forgive, is their propensity to defilement. *Gadje* confuse the critical distinction between the pure and the impure. They are observed in situations which the Rom regard as compromising: forgetting to wash in public bathrooms; eating with the fork that they rescued from the floor of the restaurant; washing face towels and tablecloths with underwear at the laundromat; relaxing with their feet resting on the top of the table.
>
> Because they do not protect the upper half of the body, the *gadje* are construed as *marimé* all over, head to foot. This condition, according to Rom belief, invites and spreads contagious disease. Rom tend to think of all illness and physical disability as communicable, and treat them accordingly.[40]

Since the *gadje* are *marimé,* relations with them are severely limited. In fact, Sutherland states that "interaction with the *gadje* is restricted to economic exploitation and political manipulation. Social

[37]Miller, "American Rom," p. 47.
[38]Gropper, *Gypsies in the City,* p. 91.
[39]Salo and Salo, *Kalderash,* p. 115.
[40]Miller, "American Rom," pp. 45–46.

relations in the sense of friendship, mutual aid, and equality are not appropriate."[41] The same author goes on to say that

> not only the person of non-Gypsies but items that come into contact with them are *marimé.* Any time a Rom is forced to use *gadje* places or to be in contact with large numbers of *gadje* (for example, in a job, hospital, welfare office, school), he is in constant danger of pollution. Public toilets are particularly *marimé* places, and some Rom go to the extent of using paper towels to turn faucets and open doors.[42]

Many years ago, W. I. Thomas—one of the founding fathers of sociology—hit upon the concept *definition of the situation.* Stated simply, this means that a social situation is whatever it is defined to be by the participants. In Thomas' own words, "What men define as real is real in its consequences."[43] The point is that the Gypsies have defined the *gadje* as a threat to their social equilibrium, and they are acting accordingly.

For example, the Rom ordinarily do not eat in *gadje* homes. Even in restaurants, they tend to avoid utensils, often preferring to eat with their hands.[44] Nor do they like to invite the *gadje* to their own homes. If they do—say, for political purposes—the *gadje* are given dishes and utensils that have been specially washed and kept separate.

Needless to say, Gypsies are prohibited from dating, marrying, or having sex relations with the *gadje,* even though all three of the prohibitions are occasionally broken. In fact, the Rom show a certain tolerance for a Gypsy male who marries a non-Gypsy female, particularly if the latter is given instructions in proper cleanliness. The Gypsy female, however, who is having relations with a *gadjo* is considered *marimé.* As long as she continues in the sexual relationship, she is treated as a social outcast.

Consciousness of Kind The question may be asked: Do not the various rules and prohibitions involved in *marimé* impose a hardship on the Rom? In one sense, the answer is yes. The urban world, the Gypsies' major habitat, is perceived as "pervasively *marimé,* filled with items and surfaces that are subject to use and re-use by careless *gadje,* polluted, diseased, and therefore dangerous."[45] To avoid the danger, the Rom must take any number of daily precautions—and there is no doubt that these precautions are time-consuming and

[41]Sutherland, *Hidden Americans,* p. 258.
[42]Ibid., p. 259.
[43]W. I. Thomas, *The Child in America* (New York: Knopf, 1928), p. 31.
[44]Sutherland, *Hidden Americans,* p. 259.
[45]Miller, "American Rom," p. 47.

burdensome. Little wonder, as Miller points out, that "the home is the final bastion of defense against defilement, and the only place that the Rom feel altogether at ease."[46]

At the same time, *marimé* serves an important sociological function. Franklin Giddings, another of the early pioneers of sociology, developed a concept which he called *consciousness of kind.* The concept, a relatively simple one, refers to the tendency of people with a similar outlook to associate with one another. To Giddings, the idea that "birds of a feather flock together" explained a good deal about human society. As it turned out, society is more complex than Giddings imagined, and consciousness of kind has limited applicability as an explanatory concept. To anyone who has had experience with Gypsies, however, it is apparent that the concept has special relevance. The fact that the Rom have a similar outlook and philosophy regarding the natural order serves as a powerful, binding force.

Nowhere is the Gypsies' consciousness of kind more apparent than in their attitude toward the *gadje.* The belief that the latter are *marimé* not only binds the Rom together but acts as an ever-present sustainer of pride and self-respect. It must be remembered that Gypsies are a low-status group, and solidifying elements such as morale and esprit de corps are extremely important.

> Categories of thought that rank the *gadje* as inferior to the Rom in the many attributes associated with purity and health have an obvious significance to pride and self-respect. . . . Despite demeaning life circumstances, which include frequent and irritating inequalities, morale is maintained at a favorable level.
>
> When a Romni is arrested for telling fortunes, or a family is forced to move because the landlord has discovered that ten children, instead of the two or three expected, are living in one house, the aggravation can be lessened by a counter offensive of verbal abuse in Romany concerning the appearance of the skin, the odor, moral character, and personal habits of the *gadje.*[47]

Some Gypsiologists believe that the rules pertaining to *marimé* are softening. The Salos, in their study of Canadian Rom, found this to be the case.[48] In most areas of the United States, *marimé* is still a potent force. When I asked an older Gypsy woman whether she felt that *marimé* was diminishing in strength, she shrugged and said, "Maybe. I hope not. Some of the young kids don't know it, but it's what holds us together."

[46]Ibid.
[47]Ibid., p. 46.
[48]Salo and Salo, *Kalderash,* pp. 128–29.

Family and Social Organization

Gypsies have a unique form of social organization, and even experienced observers have difficulty unraveling the various kinship and community networks. It will simplify matters, however, if two points are kept in mind:

1. Gypsies are not loners. Their lives are spent in the company of other Gypsies. In most of their communities, there are no single-person households, and no households of childless newlywed couples.[49]

2. The Rom are living in an alien culture, and they have no intention of assimilating. They are intensely aware of their position, and they are determined to maintain a clear boundary between the *gadje* and themselves. Their social organization is designed to enhance the process of boundary maintenance.

The *Familia* The heart of Gypsy culture is the *familia.* As Yoors states: "The inner cohesion and solidarity of the Gypsy community lies in the strong family ties—which are their basic and only constant unit."[50]

The *familia,* however, is much larger and more complex than our own nuclear family. Whereas the latter is generally thought of as a husband-wife-children unit, the *familia* includes spouses, unmarried children, married sons and their wives and children, plus other assorted relatives and adopted youngsters. And since Gypsy couples often have six or more children, the *familia* may easily total thirty to forty members.[51] By the same token, since in many ways the Gypsy world is a man's world, the male head of the *familia* may wield considerable power.

The *familia,* then, appears to be an extended family, but it is actually more than that: it is a *functional extended family.* Members live together (or close by); they often work together; they trust and protect one another; they celebrate holidays together; they take care of the sick and the aged; they bury the dead. The *familia,* in brief, is close to being a self-sufficient unit. One of the few functions it does not perform is that of matrimony, since marriages between first cousins are frowned upon.

Although the Rom believe in private property and free enterprise, ownership is often thought of in terms of the *familia* rather than the

[49]Ibid., p. 39.

[50]Yoors, *Gypsies,* p. 5.

[51]For an interesting discussion of the *familia,* see Gropper, *Gypsies in the City,* pp. 60–66.

individual. Traditionally, as Clebert notes, "the essential nucleus of the Gypsy organization is the family. Authority is held by the father. . . . property belongs to the family and not to the individual. But the family is not limited to the father, mother, and children. It includes aunts, uncles, and cousins."[52]

The *familia* is particularly effective as a *supportive institution.* Whether the problem is economic, social, political, or medical, the various family members unite in their efforts to provide aid. Should a police official, social worker, inspector, tax collector, or any other unwelcome *gadjo* appear on the scene, the intruder will be met with formidable—and generally effective—opposition. Should a family member fall ill, the *familia* will spare no expense in obtaining professional help, especially if it is a serious illness.

As hospital personnel can attest, a full-blown *familia* on the premises creates something of a problem. The Salos write that "illness, especially a terminal illness, requires the supportive presence at the hospital of the entire extended family. Hospitals often balk at the consequent waiting-room crowds."[53]

The very structure of the *familia,* of course, creates some problems —housing and otherwise. Landlords do not take kindly to rentals involving a dozen or more persons. Noise, sanitation disposal, complaints by neighbors—all must be reckoned with. Also, by virtue of its size the *familia* is cumbersome. It is one thing for a Gypsy couple to pack up and move; it is quite another for a large *familia* to "hit the road." And since the Rom obviously like to travel, the extended family presents a mobility problem.

(In an earlier period—during the days of the wagons and caravans —the *familia* probably made a better adaptation. Married sons and their families could sleep in adjoining tents, and the entire group could be packed and on the road in a remarkably short time.)

The *familia* has functional as well as structural problems. Disagreements and conflicts are bound to occur. Jealousies do arise. Living arrangements are sometimes felt to be unsatisfactory. In her study of Philadelphia Gypsies, Coker found that

> there is constant slandering; rumors are started, and attacks and counter-attacks are made. Most of the rumors involve sex. Some reflect on the morals of young girls, implying that they are dating non-Gypsy men, or, as a particularly vicious accusation, that they are going out with Negroes.[54]

[52]Clebert, *Gypsies,* p. 129.

[53]Salo and Salo, *Kalderash,* p. 19.

[54]Gulbun Coker, "Romany Rye in Philadelphia: A Sequel," *Southwestern Journal of Anthropology,* 22 (1966): 98. See also Gropper, *Gypsies in the City,* pp. 60–66.

Despite the problems involved, the Rom show few signs of abandoning the *familia*. On the contrary, they seem to thrive on it! In some cases, the size of the extended family has been reduced. In others, the married sons may form their own households. Nevertheless, the *familia* continues to be the center of the Gypsy world. As long as the *gadje* are seen in an adversary context, the *familia* will remain the Gypsies' principal bastion of security.

The *Vitsa* Whereas the *familia* can be thought of as an extended family, the *vitsa* is a cognatic kin group made up of a number of *familiyi*. Some Gypsiologists refer to the *vitsa* as a clan or a band, but the important point is that the Rom think of it as a *unit of identity.* Members of the highly publicized Bimbalesti *vitsa,* for example, would identify with one another—feel a kindred relationship—even though they might all come together very infrequently.

Vitsi vary in size from a few *familiyi* to a hundred or more households. Members of a smaller *vitsa* may live near one another and operate as a functioning group. The Rom have large families, however, and most *vitsi* tend to grow. The majority of American *vitsi,* therefore, function as a group on only two occasions: at a Gypsy trial *(kris romani)* and at a death feast *(pomana),* especially where the deceased has been a respected elder.[55]

After a certain point, a *vitsa* may simply become too large, whereupon a split often takes place, usually along sibling or cousin lines. Sutherland cites the Minesti as an example of a large *vitsa* that has recently divided into several smaller *vitsi.*[56] The head of the *vitsa,* incidentally, is generally a respected male elder, although leadership problems do arise—and may be another reason for a *vitsa* to split.

Although some *vitsi* are reputed to be international in scope, these would be exceptions. In fact, as Coker points out, while *vitsa* membership may be found in various parts of the United States, most *vitsi* tend to be concentrated in a given area, such as Philadelphia, New York, Chicago, the Southwest, or the Pacific Coast.[57]

How are the various *vitsi* named? The process of nomenclature sheds some light on the Gypsy thought processes:

> Each *vitsa* has a name which may be derived from a real or mythical ancestor (the descendants of Pupa will be called Pupeshti). A *vitsa* may also be named after an animal, object, or defining characteristic of the people in that *vitsa.* For example, Saporeshti comes from *sap* (snake),

[55]Sutherland, *Hidden Americans,* pp. 82–83.
[56]Ibid., p. 194.
[57]Coker, "Romany Rye," p. 87.

Kashtare from *kash* (wood, tree), and Bokurishti from *bok* (hunger, hence "hungry people").

Some names are supposedly given in jest, such as the Papineshti, who were so named because they were adept at stealing geese (*papin* means goose).[58]

Gypsies identify themselves—and other Rom—by their *vitsa* affiliation and by the liberal use of nicknames. However, they also have one or more names which are used in dealing with the *gadje.* These *"gadje"* names, according to Clark, are often popular American names such as John, George, and Miller.

> The *gadjo* may find a John George, George John, Miller John, John Miller, Miller George, and George Miller. He may even find a Gypsy named Johnny John or Miller Miller. But he probably won't find the John George Miller he is looking for unless the man wants to be found.
>
> The Rom deny that this is done deliberately to confuse the *gadje.* With a broad smile, a Gypsy explained that these were just nice names and everybody liked them.[59]

According to their custom, Gypsies have the right to belong to either their mother's or their father's *vitsa.* In practice, most Rom choose their father's, although later in life they sometimes change their affiliation. Similarly, when a man marries a woman from another *vitsa,* the woman generally identifies with the husband's *vitsa.* Some *vitsi* grow to be large and powerful; others become ineffectual and die out. But the more prestigious a *vitsa* becomes, the greater the number of descendants and affiliates who will seek membership.[60]

The status or prestige of a *vitsa* is determined by both variable and invariable factors. Variable factors would include size, reputation, leadership, wealth, and power. These factors can—and often do—change over time, so that in this sense the prestige of a particular *vitsa* may fluctuate. One *invariable* factor, however, is the *natsia,* or nation, to which the *vitsa* belongs. *Natsiyi* have their own status hierarchy, and this fact is reflected in the status accorded the various *vitsi.*

Although a number of considerations are involved, Sutherland gives the following rank order of the *natsiyi:*

1. Machwaya
2. Lowara

[58]Sutherland, *Hidden Americans,* p. 183.

[59]Marie Wynne Clark, "Vanishing Vagabonds: The American Gypsies," *Texas Quarterly,* 10 (Summer 1967): 208.

[60]Sutherland, *Hidden Americans,* pp. 182–92.

3. Kalderasha
4. Churara

Sutherland goes on to state that in her Barvale, California, study, "even the wealthy Churara families usually have lower status than the poor Kalderash families, and the poor Machwaya families always remind the more powerful Kalderash of their superior status as Machwaya."[61]

Not all *vitsi* are able to provide the same services for their members. Those that are plagued by weak leadership and internal dissension may actually work to the detriment of their affiliated *familia.* A strong *vitsa,* however, is often able to protect its members against police harassment, provide economic and political assistance, aid in travel arrangements, and so on. One other very important *vitsa* function is to provide members with a ready supply of acceptable marriage partners.

Arranged Marriages and the *Daro*

Gypsies may be the only group in America who follow the olden practice of arranged marriages! Indeed, such marriages are apparently a cornerstone of the Rom the world over.[62] Matrimony is important to Gypsies, and they have traditionally been loath to place their young people in Cupid's hands. This is not to say that the young are forced into marriage. Clebert emphasizes that while Romany marriages may be arranged, the parents do not arbitrarily impose their will.[63] Parents do play a major role in the mate selection process, though, and the arrangements for the bride price, or *daro,* are entirely in their hands.

It must be kept in mind that Gypsy culture stresses the importance of group rather than individual activity. And as Gropper observes, "Marriage for the Rom is quite definitely more than a union of husband and wife; it involves a lifetime alliance between two extended families."[64]

Arranged marriages normally include a *daro,* a payment by the groom's family to the bride's family. The actual figure varies from less than $1,000 to as high as $10,000. The more desirable the girl, and the

[61]Ibid., p. 198. See also the discussion pp. 181–90.
[62]Salo and Salo, *Kalderash,* p. 42.
[63]Clebert, *Gypsies,* p. 170.
[64]Gropper, *Gypsies in the City,* p. 86.

higher the status of her *familia,* the higher will be the asking price.

Although a *daro* of several thousand dollars is quite common, part of the money is spent on wedding festivities. The money is also used to pay for the bride's trousseau, to furnish the couple with household equipment, and so on.[65] Additionally, part of the money may be returned to the groom's father "as a sign of good will."[66]

Weddings themselves are private in that they involve neither religious nor civil officiants. They are, in a very real sense, *Gypsy weddings,* and are usually held in a rented hall. The festivities—involving ample food and drink—are fairly elaborate, and while formal invitations are not issued, all Gypsies in the community are welcome to come.[67]

The *daro* has traditionally served as a protection for the young wife. That is, if she should be mistreated by her husband or his *familia,* she can return home—whereupon the money might have to be forfeited.

Whether Gypsy wives are abused more than other wives is doubtful, but it is true that both sexes marry at a relatively young age. Marriages of eleven- and twelve-year-olds are known to occur, although the desired age range is between twelve and sixteen, and "not over 18 for a first marriage."[68] It seems likely, therefore, that many Gypsies are marrying under the legal age, although this fact would cause them no undue worry. The Rom are not overly concerned about things like marriage licenses, birth certificates, and other vital statistics.[69]

While any two Rom can marry, most marriages involve partners from the same *natsia.* Young people are also encouraged to marry within the *vitsa,* provided the relationship is not that of first cousin or closer. The Rom feel that by having their youth marry someone in the same *vitsa*—a second cousin, for example—the prospects for a happy marriage will be increased. *Vitsa* members not only have blood ties, but follow the same customs, have the same *marimé* proscriptions, and so forth.

(Despite the fact that these endogamous unions are becoming more popular, Gypsy marriages seem to have a high rate of failure. While the reasons can be debated, one of my informants felt that the system of arranged marriages was simply not successful, and that too many

[65]Ibid., p. 86.

[66]Sutherland, *Hidden Americans,* p. 232.

[67]Gropper, *Gypsies in the City,* p. 158.

[68]Sutherland, *Hidden Americans,* p. 223.

[69]See the discussion by Tomkins and by Sutherland in Sutherland, *Hidden Americans,* pp. 107–08.

of the Rom were marrying at too early an age. It is interesting to note that in society at large, early marriages also show a relatively high incidence of divorce.)[70]

The *Bori* After the wedding, it is customary for the young wife to live with her husband's *familia.* She is now known as a *bori* and comes under the supervision of her mother-in-law.

> The groom now has a wife who caters to his needs and whom he orders about, so his mother and sisters may devote less time to him. The bride, on the other hand, is now a *bori,* to be ordered around by all. She is expected to be the first one to awake in the morning and the last one to go to bed.
>
> She should do much of the housework as well as work as a fortune-teller, giving her earnings to her husband and mother-in-law. She should eat sparingly and only after everyone else has finished. She must ask neither for clothing nor for an opportunity to go out. She should be grateful if she gets either.[71]

It should be mentioned that unlike in our own culture pattern, Gypsy girls tend to be *older* than the boys they marry. As Sutherland explains, "It is important that the girl be older than the boy, since after marriage she must be able to perform her duties as a *bori* and make money for her husband; however, her husband need not take many responsibilities until he is fully mature."[72]

In spite of the age difference, there is no doubt that many a *bori* has experienced genuine difficulties in adapting to her new role. More than occasionally, she simply gives up and returns to her own *familia.* In many instances, of course, the *bori* is treated well—as it is to everyone's advantage to have a smooth-running household. One *bori* made the following comment:

> They [father and mother-in-law] are like father and mother to me now. I didn't know anything when I married. I was twelve, and all I knew was what my mother-in-law told me: cook, clean, and sweep up. They taught me everything, and they are the main family I know now.[73]

The *bori,* naturally, is expected to bear children—lots of them. Birth control measures apparently are not utilized. On the contrary, childless marriages are looked upon as a great misfortune. Clebert states that according to Gypsy tradition, female sterility was be-

[70]William M. Kephart, *The Family, Society, and the Individual* (Boston: Houghton Mifflin, 1981), pp. 231–32.

[71]Gropper, *Gypsies in the City,* p. 162.

[72]Sutherland, *Hidden Americans,* p. 223.

[73]Ibid., p. 172.

lieved to be caused by having coitus with a vampire.[74] At any rate, "the *bori* does not fully become a wife until a child has been born."[75]

Once in a great while sex roles are reversed, and the boy lives with the girl's *familia.* This situation might occur because the boy was unable to meet the bride price, or because he possessed some undesirable physical or mental trait. Such a person is called a "house Rom," and because he is under the domination of his parents-in-law he loses the respect of the other men in the community.[76]

Changes in the System Although arranged marriages and the *daro* remain integral parts of Gypsy culture, the system may not be so rigid as it once was. Like society at large, the Gypsy world is witnessing increased freedom on the part of its young people. The Salos note, for example, that at one time young Gypsies were not permitted to date without chaperones being present, a custom that is now often disregarded.

Parents are paying more heed to their children's wishes, and romantic love seems to be gaining in popularity. John Marks concludes that "parents still arrange the marriage, but now some young people fall in love whereas they used to marry without ever seeing each other beforehand."[77] Premarital chastity on the part of the girl, however, has always been highly regarded—and it remains so.

Elopements are reported to be increasing, and some of the young men "are willing to defend their wives against their mothers."[78] Some adults are openly critical of the traditional marriage system, although others stoutly defend it. Thus far, the number of families that have actually dispensed with the *daro* is relatively small.

The "Passing" Question In spite of the above changes, there is one Gypsy custom that has remained unaltered: the prohibition against marriages with the *gadje.* The *gadje* are *marimé,* and intermarriage with them is also *marimé.* To repeat, this is the Gypsy definition of the situation, and they show no signs of relenting on the issue.

Despite the prohibition, such marriages do take place—much to the chagrin of the Gypsy community. When they do occur, it is usually a marriage between a Gypsy boy and a *gadji* (non-Gypsy girl). The

[74]Clebert, *Gypsies,* p. 161.
[75]Salo and Salo, *Kalderash,* p. 132.
[76]Sutherland, *Hidden Americans,* p. 175.
[77]Quoted in ibid., p. 219.
[78]Gropper, *Gypsies in the City,* p. 163.

frequency of such marriages is a matter of debate. In her study of Barvale, California, Sutherland found that Rom-*gadje* marriages comprised only 5.5 percent of all Gypsy marriages.[79]

Lauwagie maintains, however, that the Rom-*gadje* intermarriage rate must be fairly high, and that significant numbers of Gypsies are "passing"; that is, becoming part of the larger community. She argues that the Rom have a substantially higher birth rate than non-Gypsies, and that if a significant number of them did not pass every year, the Gypsy population would be much larger than it is at present.[80]

Lauwagie's argument is persuasive, and it may be that more Gypsies are being assimilated than is commonly realized. Passing, however, is probably not a major problem insofar as the Rom are concerned. At least, none of those I talked with felt that it posed any real threat to the Gypsy world. Still and all, in the absence of any reliable demographic data, the entire "passing" question must be held in abeyance.

Economic Organization

Gypsies are not the world's best workers. They have traditionally been involved in marginal and irregular occupations: horse trading, scrap metal, fortune-telling, blacktopping (repairing driveways), auto-body repair, and carnival work. Clebert adds the phrase "musicians and mountebanks,"[81] and Block contends that begging and stealing are among their principal occupations.[82]

Actually, as Hancock notes, the American Rom are to be found in a variety of pursuits, including "real estate, office work, acting, and teaching."[83] Nevertheless, as a group, Gypsies have not been noticeably successful in climbing the socioeconomic ladder, and it is doubtful whether this type of success has much appeal for them.

The Rom are quite willing to use banks, credit cards, charge accounts, and other appurtenances of a competitive economic system, but as a group they are loath to become involved in what they perceive to be the "rat race." Indeed, many Gypsies are quite adept at staying out of the race.

In his Chicago study, Polster found that the Gypsy men did not

[79]Sutherland, *Hidden Americans,* p. 248.

[80]Beverly Nagel Lauwagie, "Ethnic Boundaries in Modern States: *Romano Lavo-Lil* Revisited," *American Journal of Sociology,* 85 (September 1979): 310–37.

[81]Clebert, *Gypsies,* p. 96.

[82]Block, *Gypsies,* p. 142.

[83]Hancock, "Gypsies," p. 442.

have steady jobs but worked only when they felt like it.[84] In their Canadian investigation, the Salos concluded that the Rom saw work as a necessity and not as a goal or way of life.[85] They go on to say that

> although the Gypsy is ingenious in adapting occupationally, the true commitment of each man is to earn the respect of his people. The pursuit of social prestige among his fellow Rom makes up a significant portion of his life. The Rom must be free to visit, gossip, politick, arrange marriages, and to undertake journeys connected with these activities. The earning of a livelihood is a secondary though necessary activity.[86]

In his study of English Gypsies, Sandford found somewhat the same philosophy. The following remarks were made by one of his Gypsy informants:

> The Gypsy philosophy is to live. Nothing else matters. Don't become clots, we say, like the *Gadje,* get up at 8, work till 5, watch television till 10, go to bed, get up at 8, back to work till 5. Their clocks is what they serve, the *Gadje,* they're automatons. Well, our people, we don't behave like that.
>
> We get up when we feel like it, we eat and drink when we're hungry and thirsty, and we do what we want. We work to live rather than live to work. . . . When Gypsies go to work, it's the pleasure of the work. They enjoy what they do. The *gadje* don't.[87]

It should be mentioned that the Rom face a number of economic and occupational handicaps. Many of their traditional pursuits have dried up. Horse trading has long been defunct. Metalwork, a traditional Gypsy standby (Kalderash actually means "coppersmith"), has largely been taken over by factory methods. Carnival work has been reduced.

The Rom are also penalized by their lack of education, since all the professional occupations require college and postcollege training. And finally, a number of jobs—plumber, nurse, certain kinds of hotel and restaurant work—are off limits to the Rom because of the *marimé* proscriptions.

All things considered, the wonder of it all is not that Gypsies have failed to climb the socioeconomic ladder, but that they have adapted as well as they have.

[84]Gary Polster, "The Gypsies of Bunniton (South Chicago)," *Journal of Gypsy Lore Society* (January–April 1970): 142.

[85]Salo and Salo, *Kalderash,* p. 73.

[86]Ibid., p. 93.

[87]Sandford, *Gypsies,* pp. 77–78.

The *Kumpania* It is important to note that the Rom produce none of their own material needs. "These must all be obtained from the *gadje."* And the Salos go on to state that "putting one over on the *gadje* is psychologically as well as economically rewarding."[88]

According to Sutherland, "The *gadje* are the source of all livelihood, and with few exceptions the Rom establish relations with them only because of some economic or political motive."[89] The same author points out that *economic relations among Gypsies* are based on mutual aid, and that they consider it immoral to earn money from other Gypsies. The only legitimate source of income is the *gadje,* and "skill in extracting money from them is highly valued in Rom society."[90]

The economic unit in this "extraction" process is not the *familia* or the *vitsa,* but the *kumpania.* Yoors believes that the *kumpania* was originally a group of wagons—a caravan—that traveled together for economic purposes, staking out a "territory" along the way.

> Whenever another group, or even a single wagon, passed through an area not its own, it was the accepted custom to compensate the present Gypsy "owners." In exchange, the "owners" helped the new arrivals in their dealings with the authorities. . . . The Rom were aware that in rendering these services to other Gypsies they were building up good will and that in return they could hope for repayment in days of need.[91]

Although caravans and wagons have vanished from the American scene, the *kumpania* has persisted, especially in urban areas. Lee writes as follows:

> The Gypsies of each town and city of the U.S.A. and Canada are organized into what we call *kumpaniyi* or "unions." Each *kumpania* is composed of all the male members of the community inhabiting that particular town or city, and they together with their families are under the supreme authority of the *kris romani* (tribunal of Gypsy elders), which is their only authority in matters of Gypsy law and ceremonial behavior *(Romania).*[92]

The *kumpania* is thus an economic territory whose functions include regulating competition, providing police protection, settling competitive problems, and dealing with the *gadje.* Some *kumpaniyi*

[88]Salo and Salo, *Kalderash,* pp. 70–73.
[89]Sutherland, *Hidden Americans,* p. 65.
[90]Ibid.
[91]Yoors, *Gypsies,* p. 122.
[92]Ronald Lee, "Gypsies in Canada," *Journal of Gypsy Lore Society* (January–April 1967): 42.

are small, loosely organized, and relatively ineffective. Others are solidified units, with substantial economic and political power. An effective *kumpania,* for example, would determine the number of blacktopping businesses or fortune-telling establishments to be permitted in the area, whether licensing or political protection was necessary, and so on. Such a *kumpania* would have the power to keep out unaffiliated *familia.* A loose *kumpania* would lack such power. *Familia* could come and go at will, making for an untenable social and economic situation.[93]

The *kumpania* takes on added meaning when seen from the vantage point of Gypsy culture. As part of their effort to maintain a sharp boundary between themselves and the *gadje,* the Rom avoid working with non-Gypsies. If necessary, they will accept employment in a factory or commercial establishment, but this is not their normal practice. Typically, Gypsies operate in terms of *wortacha,* small work units consisting of adult members of the same sex. Thus two or three men might engage in blacktopping or auto-body maintenance. Women might work in small-sized groups doing door-to-door selling or fortune-telling.

This kind of territoriality has both advantages and disadvantages. On the one hand, it minimizes internal wrangling over resources and makes for a relatively smooth economic organization. On the other hand, as Gypsy population pressures mount, the struggle for territories becomes increasingly severe. Some writers feel that, because of this economic framework, Gypsies are having a more and more difficult time making a living. However, given their attitude toward the *gadje*—their definition of the situation—it is not easy for the Rom to come up with a satisfactory alternative.

Welfare Practices A number of Gypsiologists have commented on the ability of the Rom to extract money via the welfare route. In Sutherland's study, for instance, virtually all the Rom in Barvale, California, were receiving some sort of aid from the Welfare Department.[94]

> The Rom believe that acquiring welfare entails the same kinds of skills that other occupations require; that is, the ability to understand, convince, flatter, cajole, pressure, and manipulate the social worker. Welfare is not considered a hand-out; it is money that they convince the *gadje* to give them. . . .
>
> They do not consider themselves a depressed minority having to beg

[93]See Sutherland, *Hidden Americans,* pp. 34–35.
[94]Ibid., p. 83.

for charity from the middle-class majority. On the contrary, welfare is to them an incredible stroke of luck, yet further proof of the gullibility of the *gadje.*[95]

Reporting on the New York City scene, Mitchell gives the following descriptive account:

> The Gypsy women went into relief offices with their children following along behind and broke down and cried and said they were starving to death, and if that didn't impress the officials they screeched and fell on the floor and fainted and used foul language and swept papers off desks and stood in doors and wouldn't let people pass and brought everything to a standstill. They pretty soon got their families on relief.[96]

There is evidently some geographic variation in welfare practices, however, for none of the Gypsies in Coker's Philadelphia study were reported to be on welfare.[97] Similarly, in his article in the *Harvard Encyclopedia of Ethnic Groups,* Hancock makes no mention of Gypsy welfare proclivities.[98]

Fortune-Telling Fortune-telling has always been one of the Rom's principal stocks-in-trade, and this is still true, at least in certain areas. It is an easy occupation to learn, overhead expenses are negligible, and—depending on the location—business may be good. Clark cites the old Gypsy saying: "A fortune cannot be true unless silver changes hands."[99] And there have always been enough *gadje* who believe this to make crystal gazing, palmistry, and card reading profitable ventures. Fees typically range from $2 to $5 per session, with a surprising number of repeat customers.

Gypsies themselves, incidentally, do not really believe in fortune-telling; at least, they do not practice it among themselves. Yoors writes that

> besides being an obvious source of income, fortune-telling is at least as important as a means of surrounding the Gypsies with an uneasy, magic aura. It gives substance to their use of curses against outsiders who brutally mistreat them, and often prevents such treatment. They never practice it among themselves in any form.[100]

[95]Ibid., p. 78.

[96]Joseph Mitchell, "The Beautiful Flower: Daniel J. Campion," *The New Yorker,* June 4, 1955, p. 55.

[97]Coker, "Romany Rye," p. 89.

[98]Hancock, "Gypsies," pp. 440–45.

[99]Clark, "Vanishing Vagabonds," p. 205.

[100]Yoors, *Gypsies,* p. 7.

The specifics of Gypsy fortune-telling vary somewhat, though not a great deal. In a few areas, Romni still travel in pairs, telling fortunes on a catch-as-catch-can basis. The most common practice, however, is to set up a fortune-telling parlor, or *ofisa,* with living quarters in the rear. The actual location of an *ofisa* depends in good part on the availability of large numbers of shoppers or passers-by, which is why resort and vacation areas are considered choice places to set up shop.

I know one Gypsy fortune-teller who has been a fixture on the Atlantic City boardwalk for twenty-five years, although this is a rather exceptional case. In many instances, the life-span of an *ofisa* is relatively short-lived, some lasting for only a summer or winter holiday season. Another common practice is for the *ofisa* to remain at the same location, with the same decorations but with a series of different proprietors.

Although crystal gazing and palmistry are still seen, many Gypsy fortune-tellers prefer tarot cards. Trigg writes that "a tarot pack consists of 78 gaily decorated cards marked with a number of archaic symbols. . . . Each card has its own astrological, alchemical, numerological, and philosophical meaning. . . . There are, of course, many different methods which are used for interpreting the tarot cards."[101]

What do Gypsy fortune-tellers think of their customers? The following statement speaks for itself:

> Gypsies cannot understand why the *gadje* take bogus readings so seriously; they assume that it is because non-Gypsies are stupid. What the Rom fail to take into account is that it is mostly the less intelligent or maladjusted who come to them for readings. Occasionally, the Gypsies are approached by younger people or a courting couple who want their palms read merely for a lark. . . .
>
> In the large cities, fortune-telling stores are often seen in underprivileged neighborhoods; few are seen in affluent sections.[102]

The *Bujo* On occasion, Gypsy fortune-tellers have been accused—and convicted—of flimflam, or *bujo.* The *bujo* is nothing more than a swindle, whereby a gullible customer is cheated out of a goodly portion of his or her savings. One common ruse is called "switch the bag." In this instance, a bag of fake money or cut-up paper is substituted for a bag of real cash—which the customer had brought to the *ofisa* in order to have the evil spirits or curse removed. (In Romany, *bujo* means "bag.")

According to the New York police, *bujo* swindles in excess of

[101]Trigg, *Gypsy Demons,* p. 48.
[102]Gropper, *Gypsies in the City,* p. 43.

$100,000 have occurred. And according to Mitchell, there are some Gypsy fortune-tellers "with a hundred or more arrests on their record."[103] Obviously, these are unusual cases; in fact, many Rom frown on the *bujo* because it causes bad community relations and is likely to bring police action.

At the same time, the *bujo* has occurred often enough to cause many areas to outlaw fortune-telling. Major cities like New York, Philadelphia, and San Francisco—and most Canadian regions—have banned fortune-telling. Indeed, some observers feel that the illegalization of fortune-telling has become the Gypsies' biggest problem.

In practice, the Rom still ply their trade, although on a somewhat restricted scale. They often pose as "readers" and "advisors" rather than as seers. And this, in turn, may necessitate a measure of police protection. But by one method or another, the Gypsies survive. Gypsies always survive.

Life-Style

Although it is difficult to generalize about the life-style of any people, the Rom do have certain cultural traits that set them apart from other groups. At or near the top of the list—and a trait that has been alluded to several times in the present account—is the Gypsies' love of freedom.

The Rom do not like to be tied down—by schools, businesses, material possessions, community affairs, financial obligations, or any other social or economic encumbrance. Their life-style not only reflects this predilection, but they are quite proud of it—as I was told by more than one Gypsy informant. Other writers, both Gypsy and non-Gypsy, have also commented on the matter. Ronald Lee, a Gypsy, says:

> The Gypsy is invisible and he has many weapons. You have a name but he has two: one you will never know and one he is always changing. Today he is Tom Jones, yesterday he was William Stanley, and tomorrow he might be Adam Strong.
>
> He can melt away at a moment's notice, which is his way of dealing with bill collectors. You cannot do this, for you have a name, an identity in the community, and a job which ties you down. You are a prisoner of your society, but he, existing beyond the pale of public morality, has only his wits, his cunning, his skills, and his faith in a just God.[104]

[103]Mitchell, "Beautiful Flower," p. 46.

[104]Lee, "Gypsies in Canada," pp. 38–39.

Gypsies also associate freedom with fresh air and sunshine, a belief that goes back to the days of the caravan. In this earlier period, the Rom linked illness and disease with closed spaces. Fresh air was believed to be a cure-all. Clebert reports that at one time a Gypsy would not die in bed but would be moved outdoors so as not to pollute the home.[105]

Clark cites the following old Gypsy song, which is indicative of their quest for freedom:[106]

> Worldly goods which you collect, own you and destroy you.
> Life must be like the blowing wind, fresh and invigorating.
> Capture the wind within walls and it becomes stale;
> Open tents, open hearts. . . . Let the Gypsy wind blow free!!

Along with their love of freedom is the Gypsy tendency to live in the present rather than to plan for tomorrow. Perhaps the two traits go together; that is, it may be that "freedom" is reduced by the necessity to plan ahead. Webb writes that "the Rom live only for today. Why should a man hurry? Who knows what the morrow may bring? . . . Today is a happy time, and men grow old quickly enough. Why wish away life by looking for tomorrow?"[107]

Travel and Mobility Nowhere is the Gypsy love of freedom more apparent than in their fondness for travel. As Lee points out, the Rom may no longer be nomads, but they remain a highly mobile people.[108] One important reason for their mobility is the economic factor. While many—perhaps most—Rom have a home base, a *kumpania,* job opportunities may arise elsewhere. Roofing, auto-body repair, carnival work, summer harvesting—all may require periodic travel. In at least some cases, overseas journeys are involved. The Salos report that

> the dispersion of the Rom, coupled with an efficient system of communication provided by the *gadje,* allows them to be aware of economic conditions far afield. Some of the Canadian Gypsies have contacts in or first-hand knowledge of conditions in Ireland, Wales, England, Belgium, France, Yugoslavia, Greece, U.S. (including Hawaii), Mexico, Australia, and South Africa.[109]

The Rom also travel for social reasons: to visit friends and family, to find a *bori* (bride), to celebrate Gypsy holidays, to attend weddings

[105]Clebert, *Gypsies,* p. 187.
[106]Clark, "Vanishing Vagabonds," p. 210.
[107]Webb, *Secret People,* p. 123.
[108]Lee, "Gypsies in Canada," p. 37.
[109]Salo and Salo, *Kalderash,* p. 76.

and death feasts. Illness is a special category, and Gypsies will travel long distances to be with a sick relative.

The Rom frequently travel for "tactical" reasons: to avoid the police, social workers, school authorities, landlords, and the like. Also, in the case of feuding within the *kumpania,* those involved may be asked to leave until the dispute is settled.

A final reason for travel—and a very important one—is simply that Gypsies like to move about. It makes them feel better, both physically and mentally. Sutherland notes that the Rom associate traveling with health and good luck, "whereas settling down is associated with sickness and bad luck. . . . Barvale Rom all agreed that when they were traveling all the time they were healthy and never needed doctors, but now that they live in houses they are subjected to many *gadje* diseases."[110]

The Life Cycle Gypsy children arrive in large numbers, and they are welcomed not only by their *familia* but by the entire Gypsy community. Although they are supposed to show respect for their parents, youngsters are pampered. Corporal punishment is used sparingly—and reluctantly. A Romany child is the center of attention, at least until the next one comes along.

In many ways, Gypsy children are treated like miniature adults—with many of the same rights. Their wishes are respected in much the same manner as those of other adults.[111] Subservience and timidity are not highly regarded by the Rom—and children are encouraged to speak up.

Gypsy children also spend much more time in adult company than do their non-Gypsy counterparts. This would almost have to be the case, since the Rom do not have much faith in formal education. While some government-funded Gypsy schools have been set up in various parts of the country, the Gypsy child's real training comes either at home or in what Adams et al. call "participatory education."[112] From the age of eight or nine, boys accompany their fathers on various work assignments, while the girls engage in household activities and start to observe fortune-telling routines.[113]

Although aggressiveness in children may be encouraged, adolescents—boys in particular—often need no encouragement. Like teen-

[110]Sutherland, *Hidden Americans,* pp. 51–52.

[111]Gropper, *Gypsies in the City,* p. 130.

[112]Barbara Adams, Judith Okely, David Morgan, and David Smith, *Gypsies and Government Policy in England* (London: Heinemann, 1975), p. 136.

[113]Gropper, *Gypsies in the City,* p. 138.

agers the world over, Romany youth do cause problems. They misbehave, they are disrespectful, they sometimes mingle with the *gadje.* In fact, Clark believes that a major problem in the Gypsy world right now is their adolescents, "who want to be teen-agers first, and Gypsies second."[114] In most cases, fortunately, maturity seems to serve as a panacea—with no harmful aftereffects.

In Gypsy culture, both sexes tend to achieve higher status as they get older. A young man marries, matures, and has children. And as his children grow, "so does his status."[115] When he is ready and able to marry his youngsters off, his position in the community is generally secure.

As he grows older, he will be expected to solve family problems and settle altercations. He also acts as a repository for Gypsy traditions and culture. He will spend increasing time and energy "on the affairs of the band rather than on those of his own immediate family. He is becoming an Old One and a Big Man."[116]

A parallel sequence is followed in the case of the Gypsy female. As a young girl she is expected to assist in the housework. Later on —when she marries and becomes a *bori*—she is under the domination of her mother-in-law. But as she ages and has children of her own, she achieves a measure of independence and her status rises accordingly.

In many Gypsy communities, it is the woman rather than the man who deals with outsiders—school officials, social workers, and the like. And if she is successful in this regard, her position in the community becomes one of respect. She, too, is looked upon as a repository of wisdom, especially when it comes to dealing with the *gadje.*

Both sexes look forward to becoming parents, and both look forward to having grandchildren. Grandchildren, it is said, signify true independence, for now the Old Ones have both their children and their children's children to look after them.[117] Gypsies do not maintain homes for the aged. The elderly are cared for by their own families, in their own homes.

Sex Roles Gypsies have sharply defined sex roles. Indeed, one Gypsiologist states that "the male-female division is the most fundamental in Rom society."[118] The sex roles, furthermore, are characterized

[114]Clark, "Vanishing Vagabonds," p. 206.
[115]Gropper, *Gypsies in the City,* p. 165.
[116]Ibid.
[117]Sutherland, *Hidden Americans,* p. 154.
[118]Ibid., p. 149.

by separateness. Whether the occasion is a Gypsy social function or simply day-to-day activity within the *familia,* men tend to gather on one side of the room, women on the other. The Rom are great talkers, but unless a special situation arises, the conversation will probably not be a mixed one.[119]

This separateness extends even to the marital sphere. Except for having a sex partner and someone besides his mother to cater to his needs, the groom's life-style changes very little.

> Gypsy marriage is not predicated on romantic love, and the Rom frown on any display of affection between husband and wife. The husband wants the wife to perform services for him, but he continues to spend much of his time with his brothers and cousins. Husband and wife rarely go out together.[120]

Occupationally, also, sex roles tend to be definitive. Women tell fortunes; men are responsible for the physical layout of the *ofisa.* Women cook and take care of the household chores. Men are responsible for the acquisition and maintenance of transportation facilities. In many areas, the women bring in more money than the men. In fact, Mitchell claims that, economically, one Gypsy woman is worth ten men.[121] And while this may be an exaggeration, the women's income seems to be steadier and more reliable than the men's. It is the men, nevertheless, who normally hold the positions of power in the *familia,* the *vitsa,* and the *kumpania.*

Social Control

Romania—not an easy term to define—refers to the Gypsy way of life and their view of the world. It embraces their moral codes, traditions, customs, rituals, and rules of behavior. In brief, as Hancock puts it, *romania* is what the Gypsies consider to be right and acceptable.[122] It is the glue that holds their society together.

Romania is not a set of written rules, however. It is, rather, a built-in aspect of Gypsy culture. And because it is not a written code, the Rom face two problems: (a) Who determines what is and what is not *romania?* and (b) How to handle those who knowingly or unknowingly fail to comply? These questions raise the whole issue of social control.

As used by sociologists, the term *social control* refers to the meth-

[119]Ibid., pp. 149–50.
[120]Gropper, *Gypsies in the City,* p. 88.
[121]Mitchell, "Beautiful Flower," p. 54.
[122]Hancock, "Gypsies," p. 443.

ods employed to "keep people in line." *Informal control* would include the application of gossip, ridicule, reprimand, and scorn. *Formal control* refers simply to the use of law, backed by physical force. Sociologically, informal control is considered more important than formal, and the Gypsies are a good case in point. The Rom have dispensed almost entirely with formal controls and rely largely on the informal variety.

Gossip, ridicule, and wisecracks, for example, are highly effective because the Rom are a closed society. Individual members cannot escape into anonymity—as is often the case in society at large. In any Gypsy community, therefore, reports and rumors of aberrant behavior lose no time in making the rounds.

Leadership: The *Rom Baro* In most groups, leadership serves as an important instrument of social control, but in this respect Gypsies are not so fortunate. The Rom are not known for their leadership qualities. For one thing, Gypsy leadership is a function of age; that is, the older one gets, the greater knowledge one has of *romania*—and knowledge of *romania* is a recognized source of power.[123] Almost by definition, then, the Rom seldom have any young leaders.

Another drawback is the tendency for Gypsy leadership to be fragmented. Theoretically at least, each *familia,* each *vitsa,* and each *kumpania* has its own leader. And while there is some overlap—and some real harmony—there is also much bickering and infighting, especially when different *natsiyi* are involved.

Leadership starts in the *familia,* where the head is known as a *phuro.* As the *phuro* ages and as his *familia* grows in size and strength, his standing in the community—and his power—increase accordingly. Should his judgment prove sound, should he show genuine interest in the various members of his *familia,* and should he prove effective in his dealings with the *gadje,* the *phuro* might become the leader of the *vitsa* or of a *kumpania.* He would then be known as a *Rom Baro* or "Big Man."

The Big Man has a dual function: to provide help and services for his followers, and to serve as a liaison with the non-Gypsy community, especially in a political sense. The following account of Big Mick, a *Rom Baro* from California, was provided by a social worker:

> "Big Mick" now freely admits that he is the regional Gypsy leader and says his territory extends as far north as Santa Rosa and as far south as Oakland. He officiates at weddings and funerals, negotiates with the police on behalf of Gypsies who are in trouble, and takes up collections for funerals and to bail someone out of jail.

[123]Sutherland, *Hidden Americans,* p. 104.

He has unsuccessfully attempted to set up a fortune-telling business in this area by negotiating with the police. Fortune-telling here is illegal. "Big Mick" has close contact with the police, and I suspect that he is an informant on occasions when he wishes to punish someone.[124]

A Big Man rules by persuasion and discussion rather than by coercion, and should his persuasive powers fail he may be replaced. Also, should he be convicted of a crime, his tenure as a *Rom Baro* may be terminated.

While there are any number of Big Men in the Gypsy world, there really is no "King of the Gypsies," even though certain individuals often make the claim in order to ingratiate themselves with local authorities. The most famous (or infamous!) Gypsy leader in modern times was Tene Bimbo, *Rom Baro* of the Bimbulesti *vitsa.* Tene Bimbo pursued power from coast to coast, and in the process he was reportedly arrested 140 times—for everything from petty larceny to murder! "If there are any charges that have not been brought against Tene Bimbo," one newspaper reported, "it is probably just an oversight."[125]

Tene Bimbo died in 1969 at the age of eighty-five, and there has been no *Rom Baro* like him since that time—and there probably never will be. Although his descendants speak fondly of him and liken him to a modern Robin Hood, most Gypsies are glad that he is no longer on the scene. They feel that he brought unwanted notoriety to the Rom and was responsible for a distorted view of the Gypsy world. (Peter Maas' *King of the Gypsies,* mentioned earlier, was based on the struggle for power that erupted after Tene Bimbo's death.)

***Marimé* as Social Control** While Gypsy leadership may or may not be an effective source of social control, *marimé* has traditionally been a powerful instrument. Indeed, it may be the single most important factor in keeping the Rom in line.[126] The reason is not hard to find, for *marimé* is more than a simple declaration that a person or thing is polluted. A Gypsy who has been declared *marimé* is ostracized by his group. Other Rom will have nothing to do with him or her.

It cannot be emphasized strongly enough that within the confines of their own society, Gypsies are gregarious. They are never really alone. Practically all of their waking moments are spent in the com-

[124]Cited in ibid., pp. 106–07.

[125]Cited in Maas, *King of the Gypsies,* p. 4.

[126]See Sutherland, *Hidden Americans,* p. 257, and the discussion by Miller, "American Rom," pp. 41–54.

pany of other Rom. Talking, laughing, working, arguing, gossiping, and—most important, perhaps—eating—all are considered group activities. To be declared *marimé,* therefore, effectively cuts a Gypsy off from the very roots of his existence. He brings shame not only upon himself but upon his family.

Sutherland writes that *marimé* "in the sense of being rejected from social intercourse with other Rom is the ultimate punishment in the Gypsy society, just as death is the ultimate punishment in other societies. For the period it lasts, *marimé* is social death."[127] This statement should not be taken lightly. A permanent *marimé* sentence is not only the most severe form of Gypsy punishment, but if there is no way to win reinstatement, the person involved may prefer to end his life by suicide.[128]

The *Kris Romani* Fortunately for the Rom, *marimé* need not be permanent. Accused Gypsies have the right to a trial in order to determine whether they are guilty as charged. The trial is known as a *kris romani.* As used by the Rom, the term also refers to their system of law and justice, for they do not generally utilize American courts.

The *kris romani* consists of a jury of adult Gypsies, presided over by an impartial judge. Certain judges, or *krisatora,* are known for their wisdom and objectivity and are in great demand. No judge, however, will accept a case unless the litigants agree beforehand to abide by the verdict. In addition to allegations involving *marimé, kris* cases include disputes over the bride price, divorce suits, feuds between *vitsi,* allegations of cheating, and so on.

A *kris* is convened only for serious reasons, since Gypsy trials are time-consuming—and expensive. Personnel may come from other parts of the country, and it may be necessary to use a rented hall. In a lengthy trial, "courtroom" supplies may include food and liquor, payment for which must be made by the guilty party.[129]

Because of the above factors, a *kris romani* is not likely to be held until all other attempts at adjudication have failed. Ordinary disputes, for example, may be settled by the *Rom Baro* or by informal debate. And even if these efforts should fail, a *divano*—a public discussion by concerned adults—can be requested.

Is the *kris romani* an effective instrument of social control? It is hard to say. In most cases, probably yes—but there is a built-in

[127]Sutherland, *Hidden Americans,* p. 98.
[128]Gropper, *Gypsies in the City,* p. 100.
[129]See the discussion in ibid., pp. 81–102.

weakness to the system. Presumably the disputants agree beforehand to abide by the decision. If they do not, theoretically at least they have no recourse but to leave the Gypsy world. In the last analysis, however, what can really be done with Gypsies who refuse to obey their own laws? As Acton observes, "It is difficult today for any Gypsy group larger than the extended family to exert effective sanctions on their members."[130] Yoors puts it as follows:

> The *kris,* or collective will of the Rom, is a structure in flux. . . . The effectiveness of the pronouncements of the judges depends essentially on the *acceptance of their decisions by the majority of the Rom.* There is no direct element of coercion to enforce the rule of law. The Rom have no police force, no jails, no executioners.[131]

Prejudice and Discrimination

Prejudice and discrimination are realities that virtually all Gypsies must learn to face—and live with. The sad fact is that the Rom have been persecuted in practically every country they have ever inhabited. As was mentioned, the Nazis murdered hundreds of thousands during World War II. Entire *vitsi* were wiped out. Furthermore, Kenrick and Puxon note that during the many months of the Nuremberg war crimes trial, not a single Gypsy was ever called as a witness![132] Nor was any monetary restitution ever made to the surviving Romany groups.

Although the wholesale slaughter ceased with the downfall of Hitler, Gypsy problems continued in both Western and Eastern Europe. About three-quarters of the European Gypsy population currently reside in Communist countries. Seeger writes about them:

> In dozens of Budapest restaurants, Gypsy orchestras perform for foreign tourists and local citizens in Eastern Europe's most pleasurable city. These musicians, however, are the fortunate handful among tens of thousands of Gypsies who are an unassimilated, poverty-stricken, despised minority scattered across Central and Western Europe. . . .
>
> Thirty years after the end of World War II, when thousands of Gypsies were exterminated by the Nazis along with the Jews, the Gypsy population is large enough to present Communist governments with major social problems.
>
> At a recent session of the U.N. sub-commission on the Prevention of Discrimination, Grattan Puxon, general secretary of the World Romany

[130]Acton, *Gypsy Politics,* p. 99.
[131]Yoors, *Gypsies,* p. 174. (Italics added.)
[132]Kenrick and Puxon, *Destiny of Europe's Gypsies,* p. 189.

> Congress, said that the five million Gypsies living in Eastern Europe were "at the bottom of the social pile despite 30 years of socialism."
>
> The U.N. body responded to the plea by asking that "those countries that have Gypsies within their borders give them the full rights to which they are entitled."[133]

American Gypsies, too, continue to face prejudice and discrimination. Some large cities—like New York and Chicago—have special police assigned to the Rom. In the smaller towns, sheriffs will often escort Gypsies to the county line, glad to be rid of them. A recent issue of *The Police Chief* contains an article advising the police on how to keep their districts free of Gypsies.[134] Hancock reports that

> various states have also directed laws against Gypsies. As recently as 1976, a family was expelled from the state of Maryland, where the law requires Gypsies to pay a licensing fee of $1,000 before establishing homes or engaging in business, and there is a bounty of $10 on the head of any Gypsy arrested who has not paid this fee.
>
> In New Hampshire in 1977, two families were legally evicted from the state without being charged with any crime, solely for reasons of their ethnic identity.[135]

Why does the persecution continue? Some observers contend that it is a matter of ethnic prejudice, similar to that experienced by blacks, Chicanos, and other minorities. However, it is also possible that the Rom are perceived as a *counterculture.* Sociologists use the term *counterculture* in referring to a more-or-less permanent behavioral grouping that arises in opposition to the prevailing culture. As Stewart and Glynn note, "Other subcultures may very well have values that conflict with the major culture, but they have not arisen mainly as a reaction against it."[136] Whether or not the American Rom actually comprise a counterculture can be debated, but that is beside the point. If people *perceive* of Gypsies as a counterculture, then unfortunately for all concerned, prejudice and discrimination might be looked upon as justifiable retaliation.

Adaptability: The Gypsy Trademark

It is doubtful whether the Rom spend much time thinking about the causes of discrimination. Being realists, they expect it. And being

[133]Murray Seeger, "The Gypsies," *Philadelphia Inquirer,* October 9, 1977.

[134]Hancock, "Gypsies," p. 444.

[135]Ibid.

[136]Elbert Stewart and James Glynn, *Introduction to Sociology* (New York: McGraw-Hill, 1971), p. 54.

Gypsies, they learn to live with it. In fact, being Gypsies, they learn to live with a great many things they do not like or agree with. This, indeed, is the Gypsies' trademark: adaptability.

In addition to coping with discrimination, Gypsies have also had to adapt to a vast panorama of social change. Times change, customs change, governments change—sometimes it seems that nothing is permanent—but whatever the transformation, the Rom seem to make the necessary adjustments. *They adapt without losing their cultural identity.*

Examples of their adaptation are numerous. Gypsies have never had their own religion. In all their wanderings and migrations, they have simply adapted to the religion—or religions—of the host country. The same is largely true of clothing styles, although as Polster observes, Gypsy women often do wear colorful outfits.[137] And aside from a seeming fondness for spicy dishes, the Rom adapt to the foods and cuisine of the country or area they are living in.

During the days of the caravan, Gypsy nomads camped outside the towns and cities—off the beaten track. When changing conditions forced them from the road, they took to the cities, where they have adapted rather well. Today, most of the American Rom are to be found in urban areas.

When horses were replaced by mechanized transportation, the Rom adapted. Instead of being horse traders, they learned auto-body repair and motor maintenance. When metalworking—long a Gypsy specialty—was superseded by factory-type technology, the Rom turned to roofing and blacktopping. When fortune-telling became illegal in various places, Gypsies became "readers" and "advisors." And when these latter efforts were challenged, the Rom resorted to bribery and police protection.

Gypsies make no claim to being quality workers, or even to being industrious. But both in America and elsewhere they are versatile. *They adapt.* As one Gypsy remarked to Adams and her colleagues, "Put me down anywhere in the world, and I'll make a living."[138]

It should also be mentioned that some Gypsies manage to do well even when they are not "making a living." Despite their literacy handicap, and despite their unfamiliarity with (and disdain for) documentary records, they have learned to adapt to the welfare bureaucracy with—in many cases—remarkable results.

[137]Polster, "Gypsies of Bunniton," p. 139.

[138]Adams et al., *Gypsies and Government Policy*, p. 132.

The Future

What does the future hold for the American Rom? Not even a Gypsy with a crystal ball can tell. It is possible, nevertheless, to make some educated guesses.

To begin with, it is likely that Gypsy activism will increase—somewhat. On the international scene, meetings such as the World Romany Congress have had some success in focusing attention on Gypsy problems. In the United States, the American Gypsy Organization and other groups have also been established. Such organizations cannot help but have a positive effect on Gypsy-*gadje* relations.[139]

At the same time, there are inherent limits to Gypsy activism. The American Rom are a low-profile group. It is often difficult to find them, let alone activate them! They have traditionally resorted to travel and avoidance rather than organization and demonstration. Mass protest, for example—often used by other minorities—would hardly strike a responsive chord in most Gypsy communities. (Stranger things have happened, of course. Hoffman reports that in 1978, "British Gypsies threatened to block highways unless they received better treatment from local authorities."[140] Whether American Rom would employ such tactics is problematical.)

Looking ahead, it is likely that the widespread illiteracy that has characterized the Rom will be reduced—somewhat. Schools for Gypsy youngsters have been set up in California, Washington, D.C., Philadelphia, Chicago, Seattle, and Camden, New Jersey, and the trend may continue. As Hancock points out, however, failures have thus far outnumbered successes, and "the majority of Gypsies remain opposed to schooling of any kind."[141]

Assuming that their illiteracy rate is reduced, the position of the Rom in the American job market should also improve—somewhat. Even now, there are Gypsies to be found in white-collar and professional positions. Their number is relatively small, however, for the Rom have scarcely penetrated the realm of college and graduate education.

Still looking ahead, relations between the Rom and the *gadje* may improve—somewhat. As sociologists have known for some time, ethnicity can be both economically and culturally retarding. This is especially true of the American Gypsies, for in many ways they have

[139]See Hancock, "Gypsies," pp. 444–45.

[140]Paul Hoffman, "Here Come the Gypsies: Call Them Citizens," *New York Times,* April 30, 1978, Section E, p. 8.

[141]Hancock, "Gypsies," p. 444.

cut themselves off from the rewards of the larger society. To partake of these rewards they will probably have to change their attitude toward the *gadje,* and the extent to which they will do this can only be conjectured.

The Rom may also soften the rules pertaining to *marimé*—somewhat. In certain Gypsy communities, these rules have already been softened. And if the trend continues, improvement in the relations with the larger society may be one of the by-products. At the same time, most Rom know full well that the concept of *marimé* lies at the heart of the Gypsy world. Without *marimé,* social control would be difficult to maintain. Whether any further erosion of the rules will occur, therefore, remains to be seen.

To sum up, it would appear that any changes in the Gypsy way of life, or in *romania,* will be moderate rather than drastic. The Rom are keenly aware of what they are and who they are—and they are proud of it. And while they may make some changes that will improve their adaptation to the larger society, it is unlikely that they will become a functioning part of that society. They will not assimilate. They will not give up their unique identity. They will not renounce their culture. Thus, in all probability they will continue to feel the twin prongs of discrimination and harassment, albeit on a reduced scale.

Exactly how much change the Rom will allow—or what form these changes will take—is debatable. But one thing seems certain: the Gypsies will survive. Gypsies always survive . . .

SELECTED READINGS

Acton, Thomas. *Gypsy Politics and Social Change.* London and Boston: Routledge & Kegan Paul, 1974.

Adams, Barbara; Okely, Judith; Morgan, David; and Smith, David. *Gypsies and Government Policy in England.* London: Heinemann, 1975.

Clark, Marie Wynne. "Vanishing Vagabonds: The American Gypsies." *Texas Quarterly,* 10 (Summer 1967): 204–10.

Clebert, Jean-Paul. *The Gypsies.* London: Vista, 1963.

Coker, Gulbun. "Romany Rye in Philadelphia: A Sequel." *Southwestern Journal of Anthropology,* 22 (1966): 85–100.

Dodds, Norman. *Gypsies, Didikois, and Other Travelers.* London: Johnson, 1976.

Gropper, Rena C. *Gypsies in the City.* Princeton, N.J.: Darwin, 1975.

Hancock, Ian. "Gypsies." In the *Harvard Encyclopedia of American Ethnic Groups,* ed. by Stephan Thernstrom, pp. 440–45. Cambridge, Mass.: Harvard University Press, 1980.

Kenrick, Donald, and Puxon, Grattan. *The Destiny of Europe's Gypsies.* New York: Basic Books, 1972.

Lauwagie, Beverly Nagel. "Ethnic Boundaries in Modern States: *Romano. Lavo-Lil* Revisited." *American Journal of Sociology,* 85 (September 1979): 310–37.

Lee, Ronald. "Gypsies in Canada." *Journal of Gypsy Lore Society* (January–April 1967): 38–51.

———. *Goddam Gypsy: An Autobiographical Novel.* Montreal: Tundra, 1971.

Maas, Peter. *King of the Gypsies.* New York: Viking, 1975.

Miller, Carol. "American Rom and the Ideology of Defilement." In *Gypsies, Tinkers, and Other Travelers,* ed. by Farnham Rehfisch, pp. 41–53. New York: Academic Press, 1975.

Polster, Gary. "The Gypsies of Bunniton (South Chicago)." *Journal of Gypsy Lore Society* (January–April 1970): 136–51.

Rehfisch, Farnham, ed. *Gypsies, Tinkers, and Other Travelers.* New York: Academic Press, 1975.

Salo, Matt, and Salo, Sheila. *The Kalderash in Eastern Canada.* Ottawa: National Museums of Canada, 1977.

Sandford, Jeremy. *Gypsies.* London: Secker and Warburg, 1973.

Sutherland, Anne. *Gypsies: The Hidden Americans.* New York: Free Press, 1975.

Yoors, Jan. *The Gypsies.* New York: Simon and Schuster, 1967.

TWO

THE OLD ORDER AMISH

The Amish also survive. In fact, incredible as it may seem, the Amish and the Gypsies have a number of traits in common. Both believe in —and wholeheartedly practice—separatism. Neither group will condone marriage to outsiders. Both groups have a remarkably high birth rate, and neither practices birth control. Both have an oral rather than a written culture, and both tend to converse among themselves in a language other than English. Both take a dim view of higher education, believing that it is not pertinent to their way of life. Both believe in male superiority. Both show respect for their aged and reject the idea of old-age homes. Both look askance at many aspects of society at large. And both groups have made remarkable adaptations in spite of harassment and persecution.

Despite these similarities, however, it would be hard to find two more *dissimilar* groups than the Amish and the Gypsies. Indeed, in many ways the two are polar opposites. But let us begin at the beginning.

Background

The Amish are a branch of the Mennonites, and the Mennonites are direct descendants of the Swiss Anabaptists. In a historical sense, three names—corresponding to the three existing Anabaptist groups —stand out above all the rest:

Jacob Hutter (Hutterites)
Menno Simons (Mennonites)
Jacob Amman (Amish)

Jacob Hutter will be discussed in chapter six. Menno Simons was born in 1492 in the Netherlands. He was an ordained priest of the Roman Catholic Church, but like his contemporaries, Luther and Zwingli, he broke with the church and eventually formed his own movement. His teachings were similar to those of other Anabaptist leaders, and included separation of church and state, adult baptism, and refusal to bear arms or take oaths. Menno Simons' followers were originally called "Mennists," a term which, after his death in 1561, was changed to "Mennonites."

Unlike the Hutterites, the Mennonites did not—and do not—advocate collectivism or communal living. Menno Simons did, however, believe in the *Meidung*—the shunning or avoiding of excommunicated members. It was the *Meidung* controversy that eventually led to the formation of the Amish.

The *Meidung* Controversy Jacob Amman was a Mennonite preacher. Little is known of his early life, although he seems to have been born in Switzerland, possibly in 1656. He rose rapidly in the church hierarchy, and by 1693 had become a bishop. From all accounts, he was a stern and righteous man—not unlike an Old Testament prophet—journeying from place to place, admonishing, exhorting, dutifully defending the faith.

What distressed him most was the fact that in some districts, Mennonite bishops were not enforcing the *Meidung*. One thing led to another, factions developed, and by about 1700 it became obvious that the *Meidung* controversy was irreconcilable. Those who believed in the ban joined Amman's group and became known as the Amish. The others—evidently in the majority—stayed within the Mennonite fold.

When the two groups came to America a few years later, the schism persisted, as indeed it does to this day. The *Meidung* itself, moreover, is no small thing, and although the details will be discussed later, a brief description is in order at this point.

As practiced by the Amish, the *Meidung* is an extremely potent measure. When the presiding bishop places an errant member under the ban, that member becomes persona non grata to all other Amishmen. No one—including his own family members—will have anything to do with him. Even his wife is forbidden to have normal marital relations with him. Moreover, any Amishman who does associate with the shunned member is himself placed under the ban. And since an Amishman normally associates only with other Amishmen, the *Meidung* effectively isolates the errant member. It is no exaggeration to say that the *Meidung* is the very heart of the Amish system of social control. So effective is it that it seldom has to be imposed. When it is, the errant member soon recants—or leaves the Amish fold entirely.

What do the present-day Amish think of Jacob Amman? A difficult question, and I am struck by the range of responses. Some Amish contend that Amman was overly harsh in both his views and his implementation, although others defend his actions as necessary—given the temper of the times. Certainly he is not a revered leader. In fact, most of the Amish persons I've talked with show little knowledge of—or interest in—the man.

The reason is not hard to find. Jacob Amman was a strong leader with strong convictions—qualities that the Old Order Amish tend to *deemphasize.* The Amish are devout believers in humility, group discussion, and consensus, and they are suspicious of those with leadership aspirations. Little wonder that their attitude toward Amman is one of ambivalence. Still, one wonders whether the Amish would have survived as a disparate group had it not been for the unbending hand of Jacob Amman.

America Interestingly, no one knows when the first Amish came to America or where they settled. Both sailing lists and land records are inconclusive, although so far as is known there were no Amish in America during the 1600s. In the early 1700s, a number of Amish names make their appearance in various Pennsylvania counties, albeit genealogical corroboration is lacking. In 1737, the ship *Charming Nancy* brought a number of families whose genealogy has been documented as Amish. As the first "Amish ship," it carried enough families to make an Amish congregation possible.[1]

While they faced the usual environmental hazards of the colonists, the Amish found an almost matchless opportunity for agricultural development. Climate, soil, rainfall, and topography were excellent. Best of all, the land was cheap and seemed to be in almost limitless supply. The Amish had come upon a farmer's dream, and they proceeded to make the most of it.

They grew and prospered—from a relatively small number of families in the 1700s to tens of thousands in the 1800s. Indeed, the "almost limitless" supply of land in Pennsylvania turned out to be anything but that, and in order to form new settlements, the Amish were forced to migrate to other states: Ohio, Indiana, Missouri, Iowa, Wisconsin, Michigan, New York, Tennessee, Kansas, Florida . . . Today the Old Order Amish have communities in twenty states as well as in Canada, Central America, and South America. Paradoxically, there are no Amish in Europe, their original homeland.

Although their religious practices, mode of dress, and general life-

[1]John A. Hostetler, *Amish Society* (Baltimore: Johns Hopkins University Press, 1980), p. 56.

style are basically the same wherever they live, there are some regional differences among the various Amish settlements. Districts in the Midwest tend to be more "worldly" in some respects than those in the East. My own experience—including five years in Lancaster County—has been largely with the Pennsylvania Amish. Unless otherwise noted, therefore, the present account deals largely with the Lancaster County group, one of the oldest, largest, richest, and most conservative of all Amish groups.[2]

". . . A Peculiar People"

In his ancient attire and his horse and buggy, the Amishman appears to be someone driving out of yesterday. Actually, however, he is much more than simply old-fashioned. Conservatism is part of his religion, and as such it dominates his entire life.

The Old Order Amish believe in a literal translation of the Bible and rely heavily on the statement, "But ye are a chosen generation, a royal priesthood, an holy nation, a peculiar people" (1 Peter 2:9). Since they have been specifically chosen by God, the Amish take great pains to stay "apart" from the world at large. They do this not only by living apart, but by rejecting virtually all the components of modern civilization: automobiles, television, higher education, political involvement, movies, jewelry, electric lights, pictures, wristwatches, life insurance, musical instruments—the list goes on and on. Pressures come and pressures go—and when they come they may be severe—but the Amish simply will not conform to worldly ways.

Appearance and Apparel Sociologists often use the term *in-group* to depict those who think of themselves as a unit, in contrast to the *out-group,* or nonmembers. An in-group is generally characterized by the loyalty, like-mindedness, and compatibility of the constituents. Members refer to the in-group as "we" and to the out-group as "they." In the case of the Amish, wearing apparel is one of the most distinguishing features of the in-group.

No one could ever mistake an Amish man or woman for anything but—an Amish man or woman. Their attire, mostly black, is distinctively simple and has not changed in any significant way for 250 years!

[2]Readers familiar with Lancaster County will recognize the picturesque names of the towns and villages in Amishland: Intercourse, Fertility, Smoketown, Leola, White Horse, Compass, Bird-in-Hand, Paradise, and others.

Men's hats—probably the most characteristic feature of their attire—are of low crown and wide (four- to six-inch) brim, smaller models being worn by the youngsters. Coats are without collars, lapels, or pockets, and generally include a vest. (An Amishman and his vest are not easily parted.) Trousers are also distinctive in that (a) they never have creases or cuffs, and (b) they are always worn with suspenders. Belts are taboo, as are sweaters, neckties, and gloves.

Following the biblical injunction, Amish women keep their heads covered at all times: indoors, by a small white lawn-cap; outdoors, by the familiar black bonnet. Dresses are of a solid color, with long skirts and aprons. Stockings are black cotton, and shoes are the black, low-heeled variety. In public, women also wear shawls and capes.

For both sexes, jewelry of any kind is taboo, since whatever is worn is presumed to be functional. An ornamental exception might be the Amishman's beard, though this does have recognition value: prior to marriage the young men are clean-shaven, while married males are required to let their beards grow. Mustaches—which in the European period were associated with the military—are completely taboo.

Amish males wear their hair long, unparted, in a Dutch bob, with the necessary trimming done at home. Amish females also have their own special hairdo, both cutting and curling being forbidden. Their braiding is distinctively Amish, and a classroom of twenty Amish girls—all with identical hair styles—is an intriguing sight to behold!

The Old Order Amish are well aware that they look different, and they have no intention of changing. In fact, their "difference" makes them feel close to one another and accentuates the in-group feeling. Some observers believe that, since the Amish are thrifty, they deliberately utilize clothing that never goes out of style. This is not the reason, however. True, the followers of Jacob Amman are thrifty; indeed, they may be the thriftiest group in America. But the reason they will not change clothing styles is because they consider such change to be worldly—and worldliness has negative connotations.

C. G. Bachman has written as follows on this point:

> Through this maintenance of clothing styles that have remained unchanged for more than two centuries, the Amish seek to show that they are not of this world with its changing fashions; that they are concerned, not with the outward which man sees, but with the inward, which is seen only by God.[3]

[3]C. G. Bachman, *The Old Order Amish of Lancaster County* (1942; reprint ed., Lancaster, Pa.: The Pennsylvania German Society, 1961), p. 89.

Actually, there have been some stylistic changes, but they have been minor. Amish women used to wear high-button shoes, but since these are no longer manufactured, permissible shoe styles have been modified. (While the Amish make most of their own clothes, they buy their shoes and hats.) It used to be that buttons were forbidden on men's clothes, "hooks and eyes" being used instead, but today buttons are permitted in virtually all Amish districts. There seems to be no rational explanation for the change.

On the other hand, where reasonable change might have been expected, none has occurred. No matter how cold it gets in winter, for example, an Amishman will never wear gloves. Nor will he (or she) wear a wristwatch, despite its utilitarian value. It might be mentioned that the Amish are not an especially articulate group, and if asked about the reason for such bans, the reply would probably be, "It has always been so."

General Life-Style It was Thorstein Veblen, one of the early giants of sociology, who first used the term *conspicuous consumption,* by which he meant the tendency to gain attention through the overt display of one's wealth.[4] But whereas such display might be expected on the part of many Americans, it has no place in Amishland. On the contrary, the Old Order Amish are the plainest of the "plain people," and they make no bones about it. Homes, for instance, are well kept but rather stark in appearance. Food is more than ample but is cooked and served simply. Clothes, as we have seen, are functional. Women will not use makeup, and neither sex will wear adornments of any kind, including sunglasses and wedding rings.

Among the Amish, pride is considered to be a cardinal sin. As a consequence, actions that are more or less commonplace in society at large are seldom encountered in Amishland. Boasting, for example, is rare. Having one's portrait painted or picture taken is prohibited; in fact, cameras are completely taboo. Such actions would be considered manifestations of self-aggrandizement.

It should also be kept in mind that the Old Order Amish emphasize conformity rather than variability. Bicycles, motorcycles, and automobiles, for instance, are strictly *verboten* in the Lancaster County settlement, and any adult who bought one would soon be subjected to severe group pressures. The automobile is the best-known case in point, and—as will be shown later—the entire Amish life-style is probably dependent on their rejection of this "contraption."

[4]Thorstein Veblen, *The Theory of the Leisure Class* (New York: Modern Library, 1934).

In their business ventures, the Amish also follow a conservative route. They have no interest in stocks, bonds, or other forms of "speculation." They invest in one thing: land. They will take out mortgages, borrow money from banks, and utilize checking accounts. Banks consider them excellent customers and excellent risks.

The Old Order Amish are not interested in politics. In most cases, they apparently neither register nor vote, particularly in national elections. They are staunch believers in private enterprise, however (unlike the Hutterites), and on occasion they have voted against farm subsidies and other forms of collectivization. When they do vote, they tend to vote Republican. They take somewhat more interest in local elections and favor conservative candidates they feel they can trust.[5] The Amish themselves have never held a major office of any kind. It is doubtful whether their religion would permit it.

The Old Order Amish reject most forms of commercial insurance, including life insurance, although they do have mutual-aid programs and voluntary hospitalization plans. They also have self-help organizations, and a neighbor in distress can usually count on generous assistance. A sick farmer, for example, will find his fields tended, and even harvested, by his neighbors. Should an Amish family's barn burn down, up to a hundred neighbors will gather, and in a single day a new barn will be raised. Amish barn raisings have attracted nationwide publicity.

Readers will be interested to learn that the Amish have even rejected all forms of social security! In the mid-1950s, they sent a delegation to Washington bearing a petition signed by some fourteen thousand members. The petition stated that they were quite willing to continue their social security *payments.* What they were asking Congress for was special legislation exempting them from the social security *benefits.* Knowing that "most people come to Washington to get something," congressmen were flabbergasted at the request. The law was changed, however, and today the Amish neither make payments nor receive benefits.

Actually, there was a good deal of logic behind the Amish offer. In Amishland there are no rest homes, convalescent homes, or homes for the aged. Each family takes care of its own aged and infirm members, and no Amish person has ever been on welfare. Amish leaders were afraid that once social security checks started to arrive, the entire self-help program would be undermined, with a corresponding weakening of both family and community.

It is this system of intrafamily support, group solidarity, and mutual

[5]Hostetler, *Amish Society,* p. 253.

aid which prompts the Amish community to reject insurance. When trouble strikes, they know that help is no further away than the nearest Amish farm. At one time, they were even reluctant to patronize doctors and hospitals, and some Amish still refuse to do so. Most members, however, now utilize medical facilities whenever the situation calls for it. Amish women, for instance, used to have their babies at home, but the majority are now born in hospitals.

It should be mentioned, in connection with medicine and health, that the Old Order Amish are conservative in death as well as in life. Their funerals are plain: no flowers, no metal caskets, no music, no decorations, no mourning bands, no crepe. Most districts permit embalming, but some do not. There are no Amish undertakers, however, and even funeral parlors are taboo. The wooden coffin is made by an Amish carpenter, services are held at home, and an Amish bishop presides. The olden custom of holding a wake—sitting up all night around the body of the deceased—still prevails.

Amish cemeteries, like Amish homes, are startlingly plain. There are no flowers, no decorations, no elaborate tombstones, and no mausoleums. Indeed, there is not even a caretaker, so that the graves sometimes have a run-down look. The only man-made signs are small, uniform headstones with the name and dates of the deceased —no scrolls, epitaphs, or other inscriptions. Most Amish cemeteries are off the beaten track. They are—or were—part of an Amish farmer's land, and there is no charge for the use of burial lots.

The entire cost of an Amish funeral and burial is probably in the area of a hundred dollars!

The Amish Farmstead

Amish life—literally as well as figuratively—revolves around the home. Most inhabitants of Amishland are born at or near home, they work at home, and they very probably will die at home. "Home," however, has a special meaning, for the Old Order Amish are predominately a rural people, and their dwelling can best be described as a farmstead. In effect, farm and home are synonymous, and most of the Amish would have it no other way.

Amish farms are acknowledged to be among the best in the world. In addition to fairly extensive crop acreage, their farmsteads often consist of large, well-kept houses and barns, stables, springhouses, silos, tobacco sheds, and storehouses. And, since the Old Order Amish maintain no homes for the aged, a farmstead may include three, four, or even five generations. Additions are made to the farmhouse as the need arises. The presence of so many oldsters on the farm, of course, serves as a self-perpetuating conservative influence. At any rate, it is little wonder that some of the larger Amish farms give the appearance of being miniature villages.

Level of Aspiration While farming is their chief occupation, not all Amish are farmers, although all—or nearly all—would like to be. As will be shown later, there is a "land squeeze" in certain areas, and some of the men have not been able to procure farms. As a consequence, increasing numbers of Amishmen have become carpenters, butchers, plumbers, carriage makers, beekeepers, shoemakers, tool sharpeners, locksmiths, and the like.[6]

In certain instances, Amishmen have even taken factory jobs. Huntington reports that in some settlements "small factories have been built to take advantage of the cheap [nonunion], skilled, reliable labor the Amish supply."[7]

It should be noted that in many of the above instances the jobs are only temporary—to be held until the Amishman can procure a suitable farm of his own. Despite the obstacles, all Amish settlements are agricultural communities. In fact, the question is often raised whether the emphasis on farming has a stultifying effect on those whose talents and aptitudes lie elsewhere.

The answer is yes, but not so often as one might think. The explanation for this hinges on what the sociologist calls *level of aspiration.* That is, in society at large there is often a gap between what a person wants to be (aspiration level) and what he actually is (achievement level). If the gap is substantial, the person may have adjustment problems. These are minimal among the Old Order Amish, however, for they believe that by working the soil they are following the path that God intended. In an occupational sense, therefore, the level of aspiration is the same throughout Amishland.

Occasionally someone does leave the fold, but it is seldom for occupational reasons. One Amish farmer made the following remarks:

> When I was a young feller, I wanted to go to the city and work in one of them big factories. The pay was real good, and I didn't care none for farming. A lot of my friends felt the same way.
>
> But as we got older, we seen the error of our way. God knows best, and He wants us to be farmers. I'm just glad I had the sense to listen to Him. This is where I belong, nowhere else.

[6]Ibid., p. 141.

[7]Gertrude Enders Huntington, "The Amish Family," in Charles Mindel and Robert Habenstein, eds., *Ethnic Families in America* (New York: Elsevier, 1976), p. 319.

The Farming Operation The Amish believe not only that God meant them to till the soil, but that He intended them to till it in a certain way. This way is sometimes confusing to outside observers.

Basic to the Amish agricultural system is the fact that they do not employ tractors in the field. Whereas such a handicap might be almost insurmountable to other farmers, the Amish try to turn it to their advantage. True, by using a team of horses instead of a tractor, the Amish farmer must spend more time in covering less ground. On the other hand, he does not mind hard work. He has ample free labor in the form of his sons. He saves money by not having to buy a tractor. He is not plagued by mechanical breakdown. And his horses supply him with a rich source of natural fertilizer. As one Amish farmer is reported to have said, "When you put gasoline in a tractor, all you get out is smoke!"

Aside from tractors, the Amish use a variety of up-to-date farm machinery: sprayers, cultivators, binders, balers, and haymaking equipment. Gasoline engines are permitted, and often a stationary tractor is used as a source of power.

As for the crops themselves, the Old Order Amish have a regular calendar of events. In December and January, tobacco is stripped, and meat animals are killed. In February, equipment is repaired, and young chickens are brought in from the hatchery. March finds the fields being rolled and clover or alfalfa planted. Potatoes are started early in April. Vegetables are also planted in the garden, and corn is planted in May. In June, young tobacco plants are moved to the field, and corn and potatoes are cultivated. Alfalfa and clover are cut. During July, wheat is cut and threshing begins. In August, threshing continues, and there is a second cutting of alfalfa. September and October are the harvest months for corn, tobacco, and potatoes—the busiest and most rewarding time of the year. In November, the corn stalks are shredded for feed, and tobacco stripping is begun. And in December, the Amish farmer is ready for another year . . .

Crop failure is rare, for the Amish farmer is a master of his trade. He understands his soil and his crops, and he loves his work. His agricultural products are choice, and he is able to sell them for top dollar. And while he sometimes buys food on the open market, much of what he and his family eat is home-grown. In view of present-day food prices, this is a tremendous advantage. Farming also supplies the Amishman with what is probably his chief topic of conversation.

Amish Homes Like the farm, an Amish home is well kept and well run. It is plain, of course, and lacking in modern conveniences, but it is clean, in good repair, and solid as an oak. (It had better be, for untold generations of the same family will live there.)

Most of the houses are fairly large, for several reasons. The Amish have a high birth rate, and at any given time there are likely to be a number of children living at home. Also, Amish farmers tend to retire early in life—often in their fifties—and they usually turn the house over to one of their sons while they themselves continue to "live in." And finally, the Old Order Amish have no church buildings. Their home is their church, and services are held on a rotating basis. Houses, therefore, must be big enough to seat the congregation.

Rooms are large, particularly the kitchen, where enormous quantities of food are cooked and served. (There is no dining room.) Throughout the house, furnishings are functional though not drab. The Amish religion does not forbid the use of color. Walls are often light blue, dishes purple; articles like quilts and towels can be almost any color. Outside the house, there is nearly always a flower garden and a lawn. Fences, walls, posts, and landmarks are also brightly colored.

Though they love colors, the Amish never mix them. A garment, a towel, or a fence may be of only one color. Plaids, stripes, and prints are considered too fancy. For this reason, contrary to popular impression, the Amish never put hex signs on their barns.

Much of their furniture is homemade, and what is bought is usually second-hand. (The Amish habitually patronize auction sales, bazaars, and flea markets.) But whatever the origin of a particular piece of furniture, the odds are that it will be in the same house—perhaps the same spot—for many generations!

Floors are without rugs or carpets, though linoleum is often used. There are no curtains, mirrors, photographs, or paintings in an Amish household. Even wallpaper is taboo. Electrical appliances are also forbidden, although in some districts gasoline-powered washing machines are permitted. Telephones are prohibited, as are electric lights. For illumination, oil lamps are used.

Amish homes contain no furnaces, no running water, and, in some outlying districts, no indoor toilets. Television sets, radios, and electric refrigerators are out of the question. There are no doorbells. Neither houses nor barns have lightning rods. The list of prohibitions seems endless.

By modern standards, the prohibitions may also seem meaningless, but such is not the case. The Amish base their life on resistance to change; hence they are often loath to permit even minor alterations in life-style. Frequently they use biblical injunctions to support their position. The requirement that women wear a head covering, for instance, is based on 1 Corinthians 11:5: "Every woman that prayeth or prophesieth with her head uncovered dishonoreth her head."

The Old Order Amish have another reason for resisting change, particularly in the sphere of technology, and their argument is a powerful one. It is a wise man, they contend, who makes himself as *self-sufficient as possible.* And it is this lack of dependence on the outside world which is one of the hallmarks of Amish society. No matter how serious the fuel shortage or energy crisis, for example, the Amish would be relatively unaffected, since they depend on neither oil nor electricity for their existence.

The average American family, on the other hand, would find themselves in dire straits. Without oil or electricity their food would spoil, they would be immobile, they would live in darkness, and in cold weather they might well freeze to death. This is one reason the Amish will not allow utility companies to run water or electricity lines into their dwellings. By using wells and handpumps for their water supply, and mechanical rather than electrical power for their other needs, their dependency on outside agencies is greatly reduced. And since the Amish have no difficulty in making their own clothes or raising their own food, their goal of self-sufficiency has largely been attained.

Of course, the Amish resistance to change is not based solely on biblical exhortation or the desire for self-sufficiency. Conservatism is a cornerstone of their life, and if some of their customs seem illogical, they make no apologies. When an Amishman is asked, for instance, why he is permitted to wear a vest but not a sweater, or why his children are permitted roller skates but not bicycles, or why all Amish women have identical hair styles, his answer will be the same: "It has always been so."

A Typical Day The Amish are early risers, and the usual day begins at four in the morning. Following prayers—always the first obligation—the animals are cared for. This is a time-consuming job and takes an hour or two. Cows must be milked, horses fed and prepared for the field. The Amish have a special place in their heart for horses, and they give them excellent care. This is only natural, since horses take the place of tractors in the field and also serve as transportation. In any case, the horses are curried with a steel comb, brushed, and harnessed. Meantime, the hogs, chickens, and cows are also being fed—by the boys if they are old enough, or by the hired hand. The latter is usually an Amish boy from a nearby farm. Amish farmers do not like to hire non-Amish helpers, since the latter "dawn't work hard 'nuf."

Around six A.M. breakfast is served—and a huge breakfast it is, for the Amish do not stint on food. Like all meals, it is preceded and followed by a prayer. At seven, the men are in the fields and the women are going about their household duties.

During the busy season, it is not uncommon to see women and men working side by side in the fields. Most of the year, however, the wife and daughters are kept busy with the tasks that have occupied farm women since time immemorial. It must be remembered that the Amish supply much of their own food, so that food preparation—cooking, preserving, canning, curing, baking—takes up a prodigious amount of time. It is not unusual for an Amish housewife to bake a dozen pies a week on a more or less regular basis. Some wives have been known to put up over a thousand quarts of preserved fruits and vegetables in a single season!

At eleven o'clock the bell sounds for the midday meal, and again it is a big one: meat, potatoes, vegetables, bread and butter, milk, salad, and two or three kinds of dessert. It might be thought that the Amish would not eat between meals, but this is not the case. During harvest season, snacks—in the form of sandwiches, cookies, and cold drinks—are often brought to the men in the field.

By half-past twelve the men are back at their jobs, and the women continue theirs. Since the Old Order Amish generally practice rotation of crops, there is usually plenty to do. What with planting, spraying, fertilizing, cultivating, and harvesting, there is no time for idle hands.

Except on special occasions such as harvesting, work in the field normally stops at four. The animals are fed, equipment is put away, and then—and only then—supper is served. The evening meal consists of soup, cold meat, fried potatoes, bread and butter, milk, fruit, and (the Amish favorite) pie. After supper there are some evening chores to be done—milking the cows again, gathering eggs, gardening, cleaning up—and then the day's work is finished. The family may gather in the kitchen (really an all-purpose room) for an hour or so, but by nine or nine-thirty it is bedtime. If the hour seems early, it should be kept in mind that in just seven hours the adults will be getting up for a new day.

Leisure and Recreation

The Amish work hard; in fact, it is difficult to see how any group could work harder. Recreation and leisure are another matter, however, for in these spheres the Amish have rather restricted options. There are a number of reasons for this.

To begin with, the typical Amish farmer and his wife do not have much time for leisure. For the husband, the prohibition on tractors means that field work is laborious and time-consuming. And since the wife is denied the use of any electrical appliances, her routine chores —preparing food, sewing, cleaning—must be done largely by hand.

Also, the Amish do not have a wide range of interests. Except for necessary business trips, they stay away from the cities. They feel strongly that city life epitomizes worldliness, and worldliness is synonymous with wickedness. But this means that the Old Order Amish effectively cut themselves off from the cultural life of America. They do not attend operas, ballets, or concerts. They do not patronize movies or stage shows. They do not go to art exhibits. Generally speaking, they do not dine out—nor do they go to bars or nightclubs. Attendance at sporting events is strictly *verboten.*

At home, the Amish are similarly restricted in their choice of activities. They do not have television, radio, or stereo. They do not dance, play cards, or drink liquor. They have no pianos or other musical instruments. They do not read popular magazines or novels. They are not even permitted that great American invention, the telephone!

The Old Order Amish do not celebrate most of our holidays. Memorial Day, Labor Day, Lincoln's and Washington's birthdays, Mother's Day, the Fourth of July—all are ignored. Christmas and Easter are celebrated, although the emphasis is religious rather than secular. Christmas, for instance, does not involve a Christmas tree, lights, decorations, Christmas cards, or Santa Claus. All work is suspended, however, and the children are given presents.

The Ban on Autos Another restrictive factor—perhaps the most significant one of all in terms of leisure and recreation—is the Amish ban on automobiles. The ban on ownership is unequivocal, although it is permissible to ride in someone else's car. It is also permitted, on occasion, to take a bus or taxicab. But no member of the church may own an automobile. To do so would mean excommunication and the *Meidung.*

Several reasons have been suggested for the ownership ban. It has been pointed out that horses are mentioned in the Bible. It is said that automobiles—and their maintenance—are expensive compared to the horse and buggy. The matter of fertilizer (or lack of it) has already been mentioned. But while all of these factors may be contributory, they do not constitute the real reason. The real reason is that the Old Order Amish feel that automobile ownership would disrupt their entire way of life.

When automobiles first became popular in the 1920s, they were expensive and unreliable. They were, nevertheless, a major invention and represented a sharp break with traditional forms of transportation. Accordingly, they were rejected by the Amish. They were also rejected by most Mennonite and Hutterite groups. But whereas the Mennonites and Hutterites eventually lifted the ban, the Amish refused to budge, a position they have held to this day.

As the Amish see it—and they may be correct—acceptance of the automobile would undermine their conservative ideology. To be an Amishman is to embrace farming, and the automobile would provide too easy a method of leaving the farm. To be an Amishman is to be a hard worker, and the automobile is too convenient a way of finding leisure through travel. The automobile would be followed by the tractor and then by the mechanization of the entire farm, and that would be against God's will. Also, adoption of the automobile would give the young an excuse to go "traipsing off to town," away from the watchful eye of the oldsters.

The Old Order Amish have come under heavy pressure to permit the ownership of automobiles. Modern highways are dangerous, and Amish buggies have been smashed by oncoming cars, especially at night. State laws require lights on moving vehicles, and the Amish have had to install night lights, powered by under-the-seat batteries.

As the followers of Jacob Amman moved to different states, automotive transportation came to be the most practicable way to visit relatives. Indeed, pressures for automobile ownership have become so great that occasionally an Amish family will leave the church and join the Beachy Amish, a more liberal (but much smaller) group which permits its members to own and drive automobiles.

For years, some observers have predicted that it would only be a matter of time before the Amish converted to autos, but the predictions have not come true. The reason is based on the Amish *definition of the situation.* Just as the Gypsies have defined the *gadje* as *marimé,* so the Old Order Amish have defined the automobile as a threat to their social equilibrium—and they are acting accordingly.

Both individually and collectively, the Amish are wedded to the soil, to the farm, and to the horse and buggy. The automobile would represent a major change, and for the followers of Jacob Amman major change is tantamount to group extinction. True, they may be wrong in their judgment. The auto might not bring with it the feared aftereffects. But that is irrelevant. The Amish have already defined the situation, and they can hardly change the definition without also changing their entire perspective.

Relative Deprivation The automobile aside, Amish culture does appear somewhat top-heavy; that is, there seems to be an overabundance of work and a scarcity of leisure. The question is often asked why, with so much work and so little play, the Amish aren't disgruntled. Don't they desire to lead a fuller life?

The answer is no. The large majority of Amish have no desire whatsoever to lead any other kind of life. They do engage in some leisure activities, but even if they did not, it is doubtful whether their outlook would be appreciably dampened. The fact is that they believe wholeheartedly in the simple, uncomplicated way of life, and neither hard work nor the lack of modern conveniences disturbs them.

One of the reasons for their willingness to dispense with modern conveniences can be explained by *relative deprivation,* a concept widely employed by sociologists. According to this concept, a person feels aggrieved not because of what he is deprived of in any absolute sense, but *because of what he is deprived of in terms of his reference group.*

A man who receives a two-thousand-dollar raise would probably be satisfied if he knew that the amount was as high or higher than anyone else in his department received. But if he discovered that most of the others had received larger increments, his morale would suffer accordingly. Similarly, students are generally satisfied with a B grade—until they learn that the majority of the class received A's, with B the lowest grade given.

Applied to the Old Order Amish, relative deprivation explains a great deal. Most Amish arise at four A.M. day in and day out. They work exceptionally hard yet are not permitted such things as television sets, automobiles, and electrical appliances. But the point is, the entire reference group—all of Amishland—is experiencing the same set of restrictions. A feeling of relative deprivation, therefore, is lacking.

The Amish are not disgruntled. They lack modern conveniences, true, but they *all accept this* as the will of God. They work hard, but since they love their work they do not consider this a burden. As a matter of fact, an Amishman and one hired hand have little trouble operating a 150-acre farm. The difficulty is not in running a large farm but in finding a farm large enough to keep the Amish family busy!

The Positive Side Thus far, we have discussed the negative side of Amish recreation—things they do not do. But what do they do in terms of leisure and recreation? Much of their social activity revolves about their religion. Socializing—usually men with men and women with women—takes place both before and after church services. On Sunday evenings, the young people hold "singings," social gatherings which serve as a kind of prelude to dating and courtship. Certain religious holidays afford opportunities for further socializing, and—as will be shown later—weddings are gala occasions.

Just plain visiting is perhaps the Amish people's principal form of entertainment. Church services are held every other week, and on alternate Sundays most families visit (or are visited by) relatives or friends. In spite of the many restrictions, life in Amishland is far from somber.

The Old Order Amish are also fond of outings and picnics, and from the amount of food consumed at these events, eating should probably be classed as a major recreational activity! One of their favorite outings, incidentally, is a visit to the zoo. The Amish have a special place in their hearts for animals of all kinds, and it is quite common to see an Amish family enjoying the various zoological exhibits.

Within their own homes, the Amish do some reading, though they are not a bookish group. They read the Bible, the *Ausbund* (the Amish hymnal), and *Martyrs Mirror,* the story of early Anabaptist persecutions. Farm journals are fairly common, and some families subscribe to local papers. Interestingly enough, there is one Amish newspaper, *The Budget,* put out by a non-Amish publisher.

The Amish occasionally play games, such as chess and checkers, and the youngsters engage in their own brand of athletics. Adult males chew tobacco, and many districts—including those in Lancaster County—now permit smoking. And while drinking is forbidden, individual Amishmen are sometimes known to "take a nip." Generally speaking, the Amish evidence a certain degree of tolerance toward drinking. However, I have never heard of an Amish female who smoked or drank.

Religious Customs

Although outsiders are often unaware of it, the Old Order Amish have neither churches nor any kind of central church organization. They have no paid clergy, no missionaries, and no Sunday schools. Yet they are one of the most devout groups in America, and their decentralized church structure—which is simplicity itself—has been remarkably successful.

The Amish are organized into church districts, each district covering a certain geographical area and including a certain number of families. Membership varies, depending on circumstances, but most districts average around two hundred members. When the figure exceeds this number, the district usually divides—a not infrequent occurrence, since the followers of Jacob Amman have always had a high birth rate.

Amish districts do not have church buildings, services being held in individual homes on a rotating basis. (In fact, the Old Order Amish are sometimes referred to as the House Amish, to distinguish them from the Church or Beachy Amish, a much smaller, more liberal group which does have church buildings.)

The Old Order Amish, as was mentioned earlier, hold church services every *other* Sunday. Each district has a set of benches, which are hauled ahead of time to the designated house. (In order to accommodate the district membership, Amish houses often have sliding partitions on the ground floor.) Services start at eight-thirty in the morning and last about three hours. Men and women sit separately, with the men occupying the first few rows and the women at the rear.

The sermons—almost entirely in German—are quite lengthy, and it is not uncommon to see members start to squirm after the first hour or so, especially since the benches have no backs. Occasionally an adult can be seen dozing, and more than occasionally some of the children do not pay attention. (In certain districts, it is customary to pass a tray of cookies to the youngsters.) Generally, though, church services are taken seriously, for they are high points in the Amish way of life.

Since the Old Order Amish do not permit musical instruments, it is sometimes thought that they prohibit singing, but this is not so. Hymns are an integral part of their Sunday service; in fact, their hymnbook—the *Ausbund*—was first published in 1564 and is the oldest hymnal used by any Protestant group.

The hymns themselves—140 in number and written for the most part by Anabaptist prisoners—tell of great suffering and steadfastness. The amazing thing is that the tunes are handed down orally from one generation to the next, for the *Ausbund* has no written notes, only words! Despite the lack of notation, however, Amish adults know and enjoy the hymns, which are sung at a slow tempo—almost a chant—without musical accompaniment of any kind. It takes time, of course, for the youngsters to learn the tunes. Also, it is reported that, with the passage of time, the tunes have come to vary somewhat in different parts of the country.

The Clergy Each Amish district is normally presided over by four clergymen: a bishop, two preachers, and a deacon. The bishop (*Volle Diener,* minister with full powers) is the spiritual head of the district. One could really say "spiritual and secular head," because in Amishland the two spheres tend to blend. In any case, the *Volle Diener* is the head man. He presides at weddings, funerals, baptisms, communion services, and excommunication. He also preaches, though this is not his main job. His main job is to prescribe and enforce the rules and otherwise hold the community together. And since the rules of the church are never written, they are—in point of fact—what the bishop says they are.

The *Volle Diener* is, of course, bound to a certain degree by the wishes of the group. Before each service, for example, he meets with the other three church officials to discuss congregational matters, rules of conduct, problems with members, and so forth. On important issues, such as the imposition of the *Meidung,* the bishop must first get the approval of the adult membership.

Still and all, the *Volle Diener* is a powerful figure. He sets the tone for the entire district. Should one of his congregation disagree with him—usually because of too strict an interpretation of the rules—the errant member might find it expedient to move to a more lenient district.

The two preachers (*Diener zum Buch,* minister of the Book) assist the bishop at ceremonial affairs such as communion and baptism. But their chief duties are delivering the Sunday sermons, leading the congregation in prayer, and interpreting the Bible. The preachers must be well versed in biblical authority and must be able to stand in front of the congregation and deliver their sermons without notes or books of any kind.

The deacon (*Armen Diener,* minister of the poor) also assists at the Sunday services and at ceremonial affairs. His chief functions, however, have to do with the day-to-day operation of the district. For example, the deacon serves as go-between during marriage arrangements, he obtains information about reported rule infractions, he tries to settle internal difficulties, he looks after families with problems, particularly those involving widows and orphans, and so on. The Old Order Amish have neither a church treasury nor a Sunday collection plate, and while they are quite ready to assist needy members, the assistance is voluntary. It is the *Armen Diener* who takes care of the details; hence his name, "minister of the poor."

It should be kept in mind that the four clergymen are not salaried. They must attend to their farms and their families like any other Amishmen. And since the church has no property, no treasury, and no centralized administration, the four officers have their work cut out for them.

If two or more districts are in "full fellowship" with one another—that is, if they agree on specific rules of conduct, mode of dress, allowable gadgets, and so forth—they may exchange preachers on a given Sunday. If the districts are not in full fellowship, there is little or no contact between them. In some areas, such as Lancaster County, the bishops of the various districts meet twice a year to discuss church matters and iron out differences. But this is as close to a centralized church organization as the Amish ever get.

Chosen by Man and God Old Order Amish clergy are always selected by a "combination of man and God"; that is, they are nominated by a vote of the adult congregation, but the "winner" is chosen by lot. More specifically, if a vacancy should occur in the rank of preacher, the congregation is asked to make nominations. Any member who gets at least three votes has his name entered in the lot. On the day of the selection, a number of Bibles are placed on a table, the number corresponding to the number of candidates. One of the Bibles contains a slip of paper with a biblical quotation. As the candidates walk by, each one selects a Bible, and whoever draws the Bible with the slip is the new preacher. He is thus believed to have been chosen by God.

This is the procedure followed for the selection of preachers and deacons. However, the Amish believe the bishops should have some prior experience, and when a vacancy occurs at this level, the selection is made directly by lot from among the preachers and deacons. Once selected, clergy of all ranks normally hold their position for life. And while in many ways the job is a thankless one, most Amish clergymen apparently consider it an honor to have been chosen.

The system of leadership employed by the Old Order Amish has advantages and disadvantages. Many of the clergy keep their jobs for forty or fifty years, thus denying younger men a chance to serve. Women, by tradition, are excluded altogether. Some men who would like to be preachers never get the chance, while others may be chosen against their wishes. The system also provides no real training for the ranks of deacon and preacher.

On the other hand, the system seems to work well enough in practice. The fact that there is no church maintenance or salaries means a considerable savings to the congregation. Also, since the final selection is by lot, politics and factions are kept to a minimum. And finally, while it is doubtless true that the system works to keep the older men in positions of importance, this is exactly what the Amish want. People tend to become more conservative as they get older, and the followers of Jacob Amman thrive on conservatism.

While all the clergy are important, there is no doubt that the bishop is the central figure, since it is he who regulates the character of the district. Although outsiders may see little difference among the various Amish communities, the differences are indeed there, and the bishop is aware of them down to the last detail. William Schreiber puts it as follows:

> No detail of life on the farm is too slight to escape the watchful eye of the Amish leader. The most insignificant or trivial item—a straight pin, a button, the flap of a pocket, a curl in the hair, a tiny glass window in the rear or side curtain of the buggy, a reflector on the rig, a clasp on the horse's harness, the pocket on a man's shirt, the band on the black hat, the trimming of the ragged beard—all these things become meaningful.
>
> Conformity to the bishop's proscription about such things becomes a behavior essential to salvation. It is easy to see why the leaders exert such tremendous influence in the narrowly confined rural districts when their judgment on conformity or deviation is held to distinguish saint from sinner.[8]

It is also easy to see why some Amish districts do not have full fellowship with their neighbors. In some districts, the buggies have gray tops; in others, black tops; in others, white tops; and in others, yellow tops. Districts vary in the tempo of their hymn singing. In some districts, men wear their hair at shoulder length; in others, the hair does not even cover the ears. The style of women's head coverings and the length of their skirts vary. Permissible items in the way of home furnishings also vary. And so on.

Sanctions The term *sanctions* refers to the rewards and punishments employed by the group to bring about desired behavior on the part of individual members. Sanctions can thus be either positive or negative, and most groups—including the Old Order Amish—utilize both kinds. The Amish have been more successful than other groups, however, because of the nature of their religious and social organization.[9]

Positive sanctions used by the Amish community are quite similar to those used by other groups: membership privileges, group approval, clerical blessings, rites and rituals such as baptism and communion, opportunities for socializing, and, of course, the satisfaction of worshiping God with one's own people.

For negative sanctions, the followers of Jacob Amman employ a

[8]William Schreiber, *Our Amish Neighbors* (Chicago: University of Chicago Press, 1962), pp. 134–35.

[9]Victor Stoltzfus, "Reward and Sanction: The Adaptive Continuity of Amish Life," *The Mennonite Quarterly Review,* 51 (October 1977): 308–18.

series of penalties or punishments ranging from the very mild to the very severe. The first step involves informal sanction: gossip, ridicule, derision, and other manifestations of group disapproval. Such responses are used by groups everywhere, but each Amish community is a small, closely knit unit, and the operation of adverse opinion is especially effective.

The next step is a formal admonition by one of the clergy. If the charge is fairly serious, the offender might be visited and admonished by both preacher and bishop. The errant member might also be asked to appear before the congregation at large—to confess his sin and ask for the group's forgiveness.

The ultimate sanction is imposition of the *Meidung,* or ban, but because of its severity, this form of punishment is used only as a last resort. The Amish community relies heavily on the individual's conscience to tell him what is right and wrong. And since the typical Amishman has a finely developed conscience, actions like gossip or reprimand are usually sufficient to bring about conformity. The *Meidung* would be imposed only if a member were to leave the church, or marry an outsider, or break a major rule (such as buying an auto) without being repentant.

Although the *Meidung* is imposed by the bishop, he will not act without the near-unanimous vote of the congregation. The ban, however, is total. As noted earlier, no one in the district is permitted to talk or associate with the errant party, including members of his own family. Even normal marital relations are forbidden. Should any member of the community ignore the *Meidung,* that person would also be placed under the ban. As a matter of fact, the *Meidung* is honored by *all Amish districts,* including those which are not in full fellowship with the district in question. There is no doubt that the ban is a mighty weapon. Jacob Amman intended it to be.

On the other hand, the ban is not irrevocable. If the member admits the error of his ways—and asks forgiveness of the congregation, in person—the *Meidung* will be lifted and the transgressor readmitted to the fold. No matter how serious the offense, the Amish never look upon someone under the ban as an enemy, but only as one who has erred. And while they are firm in their enforcement of the *Meidung,* the congregation will pray for the errant member to rectify his mistake.

Although imposition of the ban is infrequent, it is far from rare. Males are involved much more often than females, the young more frequently than the old. The *Meidung* would probably be imposed on young males more often were it not for the fact that baptism does not take place before age sixteen, and sometimes not until eighteen. Prior to this time, young males are expected to be—and often are—a little on the wild side, and allowances are made for this fact. The prebaptismal period thus serves as a kind of safety valve.

Baptism changes things, however, for this is the rite whereby the young person officially joins the church and makes the pledge of obedience. Once the pledge is made, the limits of tolerance are substantially reduced. More than one Amish youth has been subjected to the *Meidung* for behavior which, prior to his baptism, had been tolerated.

Theological Beliefs Like most other aspects of their lives, Amish theological beliefs are the essence of simplicity. Basically, members believe that they are only temporary visitors on earth, and that their principal duty is to prepare for the next world. The present world—and all that it connotes—is bad; hence the Amish try to remain aloof from it. This belief explains why they insist on being "peculiar"; that is, dressing differently, acting differently, and living differently.

Since they are on earth for only a short period, the Amish have little interest in improving the world or making it a better place to live in. Their entire orientation is otherworldly. They believe that the Word of God calls for self-denial and are quite content to make the necessary sacrifices. God, furthermore, is a personal, literal God, and the Bible is a literal transcription of His word.

As for personal salvation, the Amish believe in eternal life, which involves a physical resurrection after death. The eternal life, however, may be spent in either heaven or hell, depending on how one lives during one's visit on earth. Members can expect to go to heaven if they follow the rules of the church, for by so doing they put themselves in God's hands.

Although there are no written rules, all the Amish know what is expected of them. Furthermore, there is always the Bible to turn to; in fact, a good many of their customs—including the *Meidung*—are based on specific biblical passages.

Courtship and Marriage

As might be expected, Amish courtship and marriage patterns differ substantially from those of society at large. Dating customs are dissimilar. There is no engagement or engagement ring. There is no fancy wedding. There is no honeymoon, wherein the newlyweds have a chance to be by themselves. And both before and after marriage, woman's place is firmly in the home. There is no such thing as a women's liberation movement in Amishland. While the connubial process does show some similarity to that of the larger society, the Amish usually have their own way of doing things.

Dating Practices Amish boys and girls are much more restricted in their courting activities than are the youth of other groups. For one thing, Amish youth work longer hours; hence they have less time for "running around."[10] Also, Amish youngsters have a limited number of places to meet the opposite sex. They do not attend high school or college, so they are deprived of the chief rendezvous of American youth. They do not normally frequent fast food places, bars, dance halls, movies, and other types of *urban divertissement.* Nor are their families permitted to have automobiles, which places a further limitation on their amorous activities.

Another restrictive factor has to do with the so-called endogamous provision. Anthropologists employ the term *endogamy* to denote marriage within the tribe or other social unit, in contrast to *exogamy,* or marriage outside the group. Sociologists use the terms with reference to broad groupings such as religion, race, nationality, and social class. But in contrast to the trend in society at large—where exogamous practices seem to be on the increase—the Old Order Amish remain strictly endogamous.

Amish parents forbid their young people to date the "English" (non-Amish). As a matter of fact, the only permissible dating is (a) within the district or (b) between districts that have full fellowship with one another. Endogamy among the Amish, therefore, does serve to limit the number of eligible mates. In outlying districts, this limitation may present some real problems.

It should be mentioned, finally, that—unlike the English—Amish youth cannot capitalize to any great degree on physical attraction. The boys all dress alike, and the girls all dress alike, even including identical hair styling. The girls do not wear makeup or adornments of any kind.

In spite of all of the above factors, Amish dating seems at least as successful as that practiced in society at large. Most Amish boys and girls have their share of dates, most of them seem to enjoy themselves, and nearly all of them marry.

Courtship When an Amish boy reaches the age of sixteen, it is customary for his father to buy him his own horse and buggy. The

[10]"Running around" is an Amish expression and seems to be one of the few terms the outside society has borrowed from them.

"courting buggy," as it is aptly called, is smaller than the family buggy and—in contrast to the latter—is always open-topped. Possession of the courting buggy is the signal that the owner has parental approval to begin dating. Since Amish youth marry at about the same age as the English—girls between twenty-one and twenty-three, boys between twenty-two and twenty-four—both sexes have a fair amount of exposure to dating.

Amish courtship activities begin with and revolve around the "singings," held on Sunday night. These usually take place at the same farm where the church services were held. Singings are run entirely by the young people themselves and generally involve participants from several districts. Refreshments are served, songs are sung, and there is always a good deal of banter, joking, and light conversation. If he has a date, the boy may bring her to the singing. If he does not, he tries to get one in the course of the evening, so that he may drive her home. Amish youngsters are inordinately shy, however, and it is not uncommon for a boy to get a friend of his to act as a go-between. If the girl refuses, at least the boy's feelings are spared somewhat.

If the girl permits the boy to take her home, a dating situation may or may not develop, just as in the outside society. Unlike the larger society, however, Amish youth place minimal importance on romantic love and physical attractiveness, favoring instead those traits which will make for a successful farm life: willingness to work, cheerfulness, reliability, and the like.

Amish youth are most secretive about their dating activities. Even after a couple are going steady, they do their best to keep the relationship secret. When the boy hitches up his courting buggy, he is noncommittal about where he is going. When he "sneaks over" to his girl friend's house, he waits until after her folks have gone to bed. If either boy or girl is questioned about their involvement, they stoutly deny any serious intent. The parents, however—knowing the rules of the game—seldom ask questions. The couple themselves, incidentally, never evidence any display of affection in public, and this professed disinterestedness is an accepted part of Amish courtship culture.

When the couple decide to get married, the young man is required to visit the deacon and make his intentions known. The deacon then approaches the girl's father and requests formal permission for the marriage. Needless to say, permission is generally granted. In fact, both sets of parents are probably well aware of developments and may already have started preparations for the wedding.

Bundling Since bundling is usually thought of as an early American custom, and since the Amish life-style today is much the same as it was in the colonial period, bundling and the Amish seem to go hand in hand. Unfortunately, in the case of both the Amish and the non-Amish, it is difficult to separate fact from fiction.

The practice itself simply consists of the courting couple's going to bed together—with their clothes on. And as thus defined, there is little doubt that bundling was practiced in the colonies, although how often it occurred is not known. Presumably, the idea was to conserve firewood and candles, since colonial houses were cold, and there were no sofas.

The rationale for bundling can be seen from the following verse, written in 1786:

Nature's request is, give me rest—
Our bodies seek repose;
Night is the time, and 'tis no crime
To bundle in our clothes.

Since in a bed a man and maid
May bundle and be chaste,
It doth no good to burn up wood;
It is a needless waste.[11]

However, in view of human nature—and because premarital pregnancies were hardly unknown in the colonies—it seems reasonable to suppose that bundling was sometimes undertaken for reasons other than fuel conservation.

As far as the Amish are concerned, scholars are generally agreed that bundling did occur at an earlier period; in fact, it may have been a fairly common custom. In all likelihood, the practice declined over the years, although at a much slower rate than in society at large.

According to the best evidence available, bundling still occurs in some Amish districts.[12] It is not, however, condoned by the church. Indeed, in those districts where it is reported to occur, it is probably the exception rather than the rule. It seems safe to say that bundling is a vestigial culture trait among the Amish which, in the course of time, will pass from the scene, if it has not already done so.

Among the Lancaster County Amish, bundling does not seem to occur, except in isolated cases. The preachers and bishops make no mention of it in their sermons. If they were aware of the practice, they

[11]Henry Reed Stiles, *Bundling: Its Origin, Progress, and Decline in America* (New York: Book Collectors Association, 1934), p. 97.

[12]Hostetler, *Amish Society,* p. 150.

would most assuredly condemn it. But premarital sex is not a major problem among the Amish. It would be most surprising if it were. Things that we associate with premarital sex in society at large—drinking, drugs, automobiles, contraception, motels, coeducational living—are taboo in Amishland. Occasionally an unmarried girl becomes pregnant—much to the distress of all concerned—but the rate of such occurrences is only a small fraction of what it is among the "English."

Marriage Weddings are the most gala occasions in Amishland. Marriage is a crucial institution to the Old Order Amish, and they go out of their way to emphasize this fact. The announcement is first made by publishing the banns at church service, usually two weeks before the wedding. Unless the abode is too small, the wedding is held at the home of the bride. (June is not a popular month, as it comes in the midst of planting season. More than 90 percent of Amish weddings take place in November and December, after harvest.)

The ceremony itself is not elaborate, though it is rather long, certain sections of the Old Testament being quoted verbatim. There are no bouquets or flowers of any kind. The bridal veil, maid of honor, best man, photographs, decorations, wedding march or other music—all are missing. The groom wears his Sunday suit, and the bride wears a white cape and white apron. (The only other time she will ever wear white is after death—when she is laid out in a casket.) At the conclusion of the ceremony, no wedding rings are exchanged, nor do the couple kiss. The bishop says simply, "Now you can go; you are married folk."

While the wedding ceremony is unpretentious, the meal that follows is a giant. Enormous quantities of food are prepared, for the entire district may be invited, plus assorted friends and relatives. It is not uncommon, therefore, to find two hundred or more people in attendance. Add to this the fact that the Amish seem to have the healthiest appetites in the United States, and it is easy to visualize the feast that takes place on a wedding day. One such meal included a dozen each of chickens, ducks, and geese, fifty loaves of bread, several bushels of potatoes, vats of assorted vegetables and sauces, sixty pies, a dozen layer cakes, bowls of mixed fruit, and an endless supply of fresh milk. With such an assortment, it is no wonder that belching at the table is accepted as a sign of approval!

To help in the preparation and serving of the food, women of the district volunteer their services. Kitchens are often large enough to accommodate six or eight cooks at a time, and the guests must be served in shifts. Smith states that "frequently the same dishes are used without benefit of washing between 'shifts,' and one dish is typically used for many different types of food."[13] Such a procedure would repel most readers, yet if some dish-saving system were not adopted, things might soon become unmanageable. While they are large, Amish kitchens are old-fashioned and have few labor-saving devices. Even ordinary meals present a problem, as the following account indicates:

> When you eat in an Amish home, you are often expected to use one plate for almost everything served at the meal. This plate is often a large soup bowl, and if the meal starts with chicken noodle soup, you eat the soup from this plate, and later, when meat and vegetables or salad are put on the table, you use this same bowl for these foods also.
>
> It is assumed that you will eat everything you put on your plate, for any residue is not only a waste of food but a nuisance, because it has to be taken from the plate to make room for the next course. Further, garbage creates more work, for there is no garbage collection, and the Amish periodically bury it or use it for fertilizer. When the main portion of the meal is completed, home-canned fruit, jello, custard, pie, or whatever is served for dessert is frequently placed on the same plate.[14]

Festivities over, the young bride and groom start on their honeymoon. While for most people the honeymoon is a vacation whose chief aim is privacy, among the Amish it is merely an extended series of visits with friends and relatives. Since most Amish have lots of relatives, the visits often last for two or three weeks. As guests on the honeymoon circuit, the newlyweds receive a variety of wedding presents, usually in the form of practical gifts for the home.

After the honeymoon, the couple take their place in the community as man and wife. If all goes well, they will settle down to the business of farming. If it is the youngest son who has married, he and his wife may live in his parents' home, gradually taking over both farming and household duties. Even in the other instances, however, the young couple will try to live close by, in a house purchased (with considerable parental help) because of the proximity.

The Amish Family System

There is a saying in Amishland that the young people should not move further away "than you can see the smoke from their chimney." And it is true that the large majority of Amish brides and grooms

[13]Elmer Smith, *The Amish People* (New York: Exposition, 1958), p. 29.
[14]Ibid., p. 99.

were born in the same county their parents were born in. Rarely will the Amish sell a farm out of the family. Moreover, the only time an Amish breadwinner will move from the area is when there is no more land available or when he has had a deep-seated rift with the bishop. In most cases, therefore, the Amish family system is perpetuated generation after generation, with relatively little change. The church not only forbids major change, but—should young couples get ideas —parents and other relatives are usually close enough to act as restraining influences.

The Amish family system is at once simple and effective. Both husbands and wives are conscientious workers. They take pride in their endeavors and have the reputation of being completely honest and trustworthy. They are known to be such excellent farmers and so thrifty in their spending that outsiders often believe them to be quite wealthy. In a monetary sense, this is not so, although the Amish do possess sizeable holdings of extremely valuable land.

Since the farm is an Amishman's daily concern, he usually has a large number of children to aid in the enterprise. As will be shown later, Amish youngsters are generally exempt from higher education, so that things like compulsory school laws and child labor laws have little meaning. Consequently, unlike children in the larger society, Amish youngsters are considered to be economic assets. Families with ten to fifteen children are not at all uncommon; in fact, the *average number* is around seven or eight!

To the Amish, parenthood is quite in keeping with the nature of things. Birth control—of any kind—is prohibited. So far as I am aware, the subject is not even discussed. The upshot is that, except for the Hutterites, the Old Order Amish probably have the highest birth rate in North America. While national figures are lacking, in some areas the Amish are known to double their population every twenty-three years![15]

Role of Women It is widely understood throughout Amishland that woman's place is in the home. The subject is neither debated nor discussed. Should the question be raised by an outsider, the answer, again, would likely be, "It has always been so," or "It says so in the Bible." ("Man is the image and glory of God; but the woman is the glory of the man" [1 Cor. 11:7]).

Whatever the answer, there is no doubt that "Papa" is boss. It is he who makes most of the major decisions. Amish wives do not lack for kindness and respect—so long as they maintain their subordinate

[15]Huntington, "Amish Family," p. 300.

status. For instance, on the infrequent occasions when the Amish family goes to town, Papa can often be seen walking in front, followed by his wife and children. When a guest is invited into an Amish home, the man of the house will do most of the talking. Should the wife forget her place and commence to chatter, her husband will probably admonish her with a polite but firm "Mama!"

On their part, Amish wives seem "wonderfully well" adjusted to the patriarchal way of life. They realize that their English sisters have achieved a much greater degree of equality, yet there is little indication that Amish women have any real desire to change the status quo. Of course, they are far from automatons. They have a voice both in home management and in rearing the children. And—quite important—they have an official vote in all church matters, including nominations for the clergy.

One final word on the subject of women. In any Amish gathering, it can be seen that men tend to associate with men, women with women. Amish men are never seen to kiss their wives or utter words of endearment. From this, it might be inferred that Amish spouses have only moderate affection for one another, but this is hardly the case. What the Amish object to is not affection but its overt display. After all, the followers of Jacob Amman are a conservative people, and the idea of kissing, fondling, or holding hands *in public* would be unthinkable. In private, they are doubtless as affectionate as any other group.

Amish Kinship Structure The subject of Amish kinship is of special interest to American scholars because (a) followers of Jacob Amman seldom marry outside the group, and (b) outsiders seldom marry into the group. And since the number of Amish families immigrating to America was small, virtually all of the present membership can trace their genealogy back to these original families. Amish surnames today are much the same as they were in the 1700s.

As a matter of record, while there are now close to fifteen thousand Amish in the Lancaster County area, a dozen or so surnames—Stoltzfus, King, Fisher, Beiler, Lapp, Zook, Esh, Smucker, Glick, Riehl, Blank, and Petersheim—would just about cover the entire group. Believe it or not, around half of the Amish in southeastern Pennsylvania have the surnames Stoltzfus, King, or Fisher. Indeed, there is an oft-told story about the one-room Amish schoolhouse in which thirty-nine of the forty-eight pupils were named Stoltzfus!

(In Indiana, the names Miller, Yoder, and Bontrager comprise 50 percent of the Amish population. In Ohio, the Millers, Yoders, and Troyers make up 54 percent. Hostetler also reports that "the post office at Kalona, Iowa, must distinguish between 450 Miller families on the rural mail routes!")[16]

To add to the confusion, the Amish generally use biblical names for first names, and records show that seven male names—John, Amos, David, Jacob, Samuel, Daniel, and Christian—and seven female names—Mary, Annie, Katie, Sarah, Fannie, Lizzie, and Rebecca—comprise around half of all the given names. Anyone who sends a letter to John Beiler or Katie Stoltzfus, with nothing more than a standard rural-delivery address, runs the risk of creating a minor community disruption.

Given the structure and frequency of their names, how do the Amish themselves—in referring to one another—manage to communicate? The answer is that they are ingenious in their use of nicknames and employment of other identifying features. Hostetler has written:

> Name differentiation is achieved by adopting an abbreviation, describing the physical traits of the person, noting individual preferences or habits, relating a humorous happening, or by referring to the person's occupation or place of residence.
>
> Chubby Jonas, Curly John, and Shorty Abner are indicative of physical traits. Applebutter John, Butter Abe, and Toothpick John derive from personal habits. Gravy Dan stuck with one Amishman when he poured gravy instead of cream into his coffee.
>
> Jocky Joe is a horse trader, Chicken Elam operates a chicken farm, and Chickie Dan works for him. Gap Dave, Gap Elam, and Gap Joe live near a village named Gap. When my own family moved from Pennsylvania to Iowa, my father was nicknamed "Pennsylvania Joe."
>
> Among young people, there is a great deal of nicknaming, especially among boys. Examples are Ashpile, Beanbag, Blip, Bull, Dog, Fatz, Fegs, Fuddy, Gomer, Pinky, and Yo-Yo.[17]

Ogburn's Theory of Family Functions A number of years ago, William F. Ogburn, a sociologist interested in the study of cultural change, made an interesting observation apropos of the American family. From the colonial period to the present, he said, the family has been characterized by a progressive *loss of functions.* He went on to list the declining functions as education, religion, protection, recreation, and the economic function. The thrust of his argument was that other institutions had taken over these functions. Thus the function of religion, once centered in the home, had been taken over by the church. Education had become the province of the schools. Recrea-

[16]Hostetler, *Amish Society,* pp. 241–44.

[17]Ibid.

tion had been usurped by commercialized ventures. The economic function had been lost because the family was no longer a producing unit—due largely to the fact that child labor laws and compulsory school laws prohibited children from working. Ogburn's conclusion was that, because of these declining functions, the American family had been weakened.[18]

Some sociologists have accepted Ogburn's thesis, others have questioned it, and the issue is by no means dead. Some feel that, while the family may have lost some functions, it has gained others.[19] The Old Order Amish add another dimension to the debate, for the functions which Ogburn claimed had disappeared from the mainstream of American family life are still being performed by the Amish family.

Economically, the Amish family is an effective producing unit. Education is still largely a family function, as is recreation. Even religious services are held in the home, and, of course, prayers play an integral part in the life of every Amish family.

The upshot is that in a functional sense the Amish family is a remarkably strong unit. This strength, moreover, is manifest in a number of other ways. Indeed, there is considerable evidence that the Old Order Amish maintain one of the most stable family systems in America. Their birth rate is exceptionally high and is unaffected by social or economic conditions. They have a low infant mortality rate. They seldom marry outside the group. Loss of membership is not a serious problem. Husband-wife-children units are wedded to the land and show strong family and group loyalty. Their farm economy has proved both durable and successful.

The Amish have no sex problem to speak of. Illegitimacy and adultery are almost unheard of. Desertion is practically unknown, and no divorces have yet been reported.

Compared to the larger society, the Amish experience fewer problems with the young—and with the old. The youth are seldom in trouble with the law, and the oldsters are cared for by their own families, not public institutions. Orphans, widows, and other dependents are looked after by the community, and no Amish person has ever been on welfare.

In brief, most Amish marry, they have large families that are functionally strong, and they take care of their own dependency cases. Spouses stay married, furthermore, until death intervenes—with the

[18]William F. Ogburn, "The Changing Family," *The Family* (July 1938): 139–43.

[19]See the discussion in William M. Kephart, *The Family, Society, and the Individual* (Boston: Houghton Mifflin, 1981), pp. 3–10.

survivor often living to a ripe old age. For example, on January 27, 1981, Salina Stoltzfus, an Amish widow of Lancaster County, died at the age of 108. At the time of her death, according to available figures, she was the oldest person in the state of Pennsylvania!

Every so often newspapers carry obituary columns like the following:

> Mrs. Katie King, an 89-year-old Amish widow from Bareville, Pa., who died Friday, left 350 direct descendants, including 7 children.
>
> She had 72 grandchildren, 252 great-grandchildren, and 19 great-great-grandchildren. She had had two other children who preceded her in death. The number of direct descendants is believed to be a record for Lancaster County.[20]

So far as I am aware, the record for the largest family is also held by an Amishman—John Miller of Ohio, who died at the age of 95.

> He was survived by 5 of his 7 children, 61 grandchildren, 338 great-grandchildren, and 6 great-great-grandchildren, a total of 410 descendants. At the end of his life, the postman was bringing John Miller word of the birth of a new descendant once every 10 days.[21]

In view of the above figures, it is easy to see why many Amish funerals have five hundred or more persons in attendance!

Education and Socialization

It is commonly believed that the Old Order Amish are against education, but this is not true. What they are against is the kind of education that would tend to alienate their young people and threaten their conservative, agrarian way of life. In Amishland, therefore, schooling is likely to mean reading, arithmetic, penmanship, and sentence construction—plus some elements of geography, history, and hygiene.

Conflict with the Law Each state has its own school laws, which regulate such things as length of the school year, teacher certification, curricula, compulsory school age, and the like. In some states, the Amish have been harassed and arrested for not complying. In others —now a clear majority—sympathetic officials have worked out an accommodation.

Where conflicts have occurred, they have generally been due to the fact that the Amish have either refused to send their children to

[20]Ibid., p. 155.
[21]Ibid.

a non-Amish grade school or refused to send their children to a high school of any kind. Most Amish parents are more than willing to have their youngsters attend school—provided it is an Amish school—for the first eight grades. But beyond that they balk. They feel that the years fourteen to eighteen are crucial, and they object to having their teen-agers exposed to high-school worldliness. The Amish community will not give in on this point, and some parents have either left the state or gone to jail rather than violate their own consciences.

Fortunately for all concerned, some states have now worked out a compromise whereby Amish children may apply for a farm work permit at age fifteen. Other states permit Amish teen-agers to attend a farm vocational school—a kind of on-the-job training program—in lieu of high school.

The other major conflict—refusal of the Amish to send their children to public school for the first eight grades—also seems in the process of being resolved. More and more Amish communities are opening their own schools. Issues like building codes, teacher certification, attendance, and length of school year are being worked out. Court cases and legal harassment seem to be on the decline, and in general the picture looks encouraging.

In 1968, Amish parents in Wisconsin were convicted for refusing to send their children to the local high school. In a case that went all the way to the Supreme Court, *the Amish parents were found to be in the right.* In a 7-0 decision, the Supreme Court ruled as follows:

> A State's interest in universal education, however highly we rank it, is not totally free from a balancing process when it impinges on other fundamental rights and interests, such as those specifically protected by the Free Exercise Clause of the First Amendment, and the traditional interest of parents with respect to the religious upbringing of their children. . . .
>
> The record in this case abundantly supports the claim that the traditional way of life of the Amish is not merely a matter of personal preference, but one of deep religious conviction, shared by an organized group, and intimately related to daily living. . . .
>
> Enforcement of the State's requirement of compulsory formal education after the 8th grade would gravely endanger if not destroy the free exercise of respondents' religious beliefs.[22]

Perhaps the brightest spot on the educational horizon is the fact that public opinion seems to have swung to the side of the Amish. In

[22]Quoted in Gerald Gunther and Noel Dowling, *Constitutional Law and Individual Rights in Constitutional Law* (Mineola, N.Y.: Foundation Press, 1974), pp. 434–435.

a society noted for its religious tolerance, newspaper pictures of Amish parents being led off to jail appear grossly out of place—and the public apparently recognizes this anomaly.

The Amish School Amish schools are an accurate reflection of the Amish people: simple, efficient, economical. There are no frills—no school newspaper, clubs, athletic program, dances, or class officers. The Amish have no nursery, preschool, or kindergarten programs; in fact, the large majority of their schools have but one room and one teacher. Average enrollment per school is about thirty.

Amish communities either build their own schools or purchase them from the state. If they are purchased, certain alterations are made, including the removal of all electrical fixtures. Amish school buildings are heated by wood or coal stoves, and generally do not have indoor toilets. But aside from differences in heating, lighting, and toilet facilities, the Amish school—with its blackboards, bolted desks, and coat racks—looks much the same as any other one-room school.

The Amish teacher, who is generally female, is quite different from her non-Amish counterpart. The typical American teacher is a college graduate who, by virtue of having taken specialized courses in education, has acquired a state-issued teaching certificate. The Amish teacher, by contrast, has not even been to high school, let alone college!

The Old Order Amish are convinced that being a good teacher has no relationship to such things as college degrees and state-issued certificates. They feel, rather, that teaching is a kind of calling, and that the calling is a God-given attribute. The ideal Amish teacher is one who, by her very being, can convey to youngsters the Amish outlook on life. Accordingly, she should be well adjusted, religious, and totally committed to Amish principles. She should be able to relate both to her pupils and to the community she serves.

While there are exceptions, naturally, most Amish teachers are dedicated individuals. Although they do not attend high school, many of them take correspondence courses. They have their own teachers' association, attend yearly conferences, and subscribe to the Amish teachers' *Bulletin.* They are often required to serve without pay as teaching assistants for a year or so before being assigned schools of their own. And when they are given their own classrooms, they are willing to work without job tenure, without a written contract, and at a very low rate of pay. In one county, total school costs to the Amish were reported to be less than one-tenth of what they would have been if their children had been sent to the public school![23]

The Amish teacher, incidentally, is more than "just a teacher." She is also principal, janitor, nurse, custodian, playground supervisor, and disciplinarian. Although Amish children are better behaved than most, disciplinary problems do arise, in which case the teacher applies the usual antidotes: reprimands, lectures, admonitions, keeping children after school, or having them write their "sins" on the blackboard. For serious infractions—such as willful disobedience or leaving the schoolyard without permission—most Amish teachers will not hesitate to use corporal punishment.

Values As used by sociologists, the term *values* refers to ideals and beliefs which people feel strongly about. In fact, values are so basic to those who hold them that they tend to be accepted without question. Most people, furthermore, seem to feel more comfortable when they are in the company of those with a similar value system.

As much as anything else, it is the *totality of values* which sets one group apart from another, a point which is well illustrated in the case of the Amish school. It is not simply curriculum and course content which differentiate the Amish school from the public school—it is values. Accuracy, for example, receives much greater emphasis than speed. Memorization of facts and the learning of (Amish) principles are considered more important than analytical thinking and inquisitiveness.

Amish children receive grades—from A to F—but at the same time they are taught not to compete with one another for top marks. To the Old Order Amish, talent—like most other things in this world—is God-given; hence it is no disgrace to be a slow learner. In their hierarchy of values, it is more important to do good and to treat other people with kindness.[24]

It is also safe to say that Amish schools are as much concerned with the children's moral development as they are with their mental prowess. Values such as right-wrong, better-worse, good-bad are alluded to over and over again. It is this repeated emphasis on morality—not only by the school but by the church, the home, and the community—that serves to mold the individual's conscience. This fact was mentioned earlier and is worth repeating, for while the threat of the *Meidung* undoubtedly keeps potential wrongdoers in

[23]John A. Hostetler, *Children in Amish Society* (New York: Holt, Rinehart and Winston, 1971), pp. 97–98.

[24]See the discussion in ibid., pp. 54–96.

line, it is *conscience* which is the key to Amish conformity. It is *conscience* which is more highly developed among the Amish than among almost any other group in America.

One final word on the subject of schooling. Although the Old Order Amish do not believe in educational "frills," their schools are anything but drab. Colorful pictures, posters, and homemade artistry adorn the walls. Group singing (without accompaniment) is practiced. Games of all kinds are played during recess and lunch hour. Teacher and pupils often go on picnics, take nature trips, or visit places of historic interest. The school day generally runs from nine to three-thirty, and the Amish try to strike a reasonable balance between education and recreation.

The Home While the Amish recognize the importance of the school, there is no doubt in anyone's mind that primary responsibility for the socialization of children falls upon the parents. If a youngster has difficulties in school, it is the parents who are consulted. If a boy has trouble within the Amish community, the bishop will talk with the parents as well as with the boy. And if a young person runs afoul of the law, the congregation will sympathize with the parents.

Generally speaking, Amish child rearing embodies a mixture of permissive and restrictive philosophy. Infants are more or less pampered and are seldom alone. As soon as possible, they are fed at the family table and made to feel a part of the group. Relatives and friends shower them with attention. Children soon come to feel that they are welcome members of the community, which in fact they are.

As soon as infants learn to walk, they are subject to discipline and taught to respect authority. Although the Amish family is not authoritarian in structure, it is true that great stress is placed on obedience. This is not a contradiction. The obedience is presumed to be based on love rather than fear, on the assumption—unquestioned in Amishland—that parents know best. Spanking and other forms of corporal punishment are quite common, yet the youngsters harbor no resentment. They learn early that such actions are for their own good and are simply manifestations of parental love and wisdom.

Training at home tends to supplement that received at school. Acceptance of traditional values is encouraged, and inquisitiveness discouraged. Cooperativeness rather than competitiveness is emphasized. Children are conditioned to the view that they are all creatures of God, and that therefore they should have deep consideration for the feelings of others. And, of course, Amish children are taught that they are different from the English, and that they can never follow a secular life-style. They are reminded—over and over again—of the dangers and evils that lurk in the outside world.

Is the socialization process employed by the Old Order Amish successful? Practically all observers agree that it is. Hostetler, the foremost authority on Amish life, writes:

> Amish children are raised so carefully within the Amish family and community that they never feel secure outside it. The faces of many Amish boys and girls reflect pure intent, a sincere, honest, cordial, and well-bred disposition. The extraordinary love and discipline they get prepares them well for Amish womanhood and manhood.[25]

Social Problems

All groups have social problems of one kind or another, and the Old Order Amish are no exception. At the same time, it is clear that the Amish do have a remarkable record in the "problems" area. Crime, corruption, poverty, alcoholism, drug addiction, and other problems which plague society at large—all have a low incidence in Amishland. In fact, their low problem rate makes the Amish wonder what the school controversy is all about. More than one Amishman has said, in effect, "They want us to follow their system and send our youngsters to the public school and the high school—but they're the ones with the problems, not us . . . "

Human nature being what it is, the fact that the Amish have a relatively low problem rate does not make the problems any easier to solve when they do occur. On the contrary, a given problem—involving delinquency or alcoholism, for instance—may cause more anguish in Amishland than in the larger society. At any rate, the following problems are mentioned not because they represent major disruptions, but because they are recurrent headaches which the Amish community must learn to live with.

1. The Youth Problem One of the more serious problems facing the Old Order Amish is that of their teen-age youth, boys in particular. The latter will sometimes get drunk, become disrespectful, indulge in worldly activities (including buying a car), and otherwise violate Amish mores. Even the girls are sometimes involved. During the spring of 1980, a sixteen-year-old Amish girl, hanging from a car window while joyriding, was killed when she was jolted from the vehicle. Lancaster County residents—both Amish and non-Amish—were stunned at the incident.

A young man's buying a car, while relatively infrequent, is far from rare—and naturally the various Amish districts are dead set against

[25]Hostetler, *Amish Society*, pp. 157–58.

such goings-on. But so long as the offender is not yet baptized (hence is not a member of the church), the *Meidung* cannot be imposed. In most cases, baptism, with its attendant responsibilities, will "straighten the boy out," but if not, the chances are that he will leave the fold.

Very few Amish actually leave, however—possibly around 6 percent.[26] On the other hand, baptism does not take place until the late teens, and a fair number of Amish youth—perhaps as high as 22 percent—leave rather than submit to the baptismal vows.[27] Many of those who leave join one of the more liberal Mennonite groups.

2. Threat of Modernization Every decade brings a variety of new inventions and technological improvements to society at large, and the Old Order Amish must continually fight against the inroads. Automobiles, electric lights, indoor toilets, running water, telephones, electric refrigerators, radio and television—such things have taken their toll of the followers of Jacob Amman. Every Amish community knows of adult members who have left the fold because of what they felt were unnecessarily strict rules.

In several cases, entire congregations have seceded. Thus in 1927, an Amish bishop, Moses M. Beachy, led a movement away from the main body. As mentioned earlier, members of this congregation, known today as the Beachy Amish, are permitted to own automobiles and certain other modern conveniences. In 1966, a group known as the "New Amish" began to form. The New Amish have installed telephones, permit the use of electricity, and utilize tractor-drawn farm machinery.[28]

If history tells the Old Order Amish anything, it is that they will probably experience further schisms and secessions in the decades to come.

3. Annoyance of Tourism The Amish are a folk society whose way of life hinges on remaining apart from the outside world. The influx of tourists into Amish communities, therefore, represents an irritating problem. By bus, train, plane, and private automobile, visitors are now pouring into Amishland by the millions. The Lancaster County group has been especially hard hit since they are only an hour or two from Wilmington, Baltimore, Washington, Philadelphia, and New York. Motels, restaurants, commercial "museums," handicraft outlets, souvenir and novelty shops, and numerous other attractions now

[26]Ibid., p. 293.
[27]Ibid., pp. 276–77.
[28]Ibid.

cover the area. In fact, the guide map now lists 241 tourist-related enterprises![29]

Guided bus tours, run by professional agents, are especially obnoxious to the Amish, for the buses clog the narrow roads, block the horses and buggies, park in front of the schools and farms, and otherwise annoy the residents. It is against the Amish religion to have their picture taken, but camera-wielding tourists routinely ignore the taboo.

A few of the Amish have left the area for quieter pastures, although these have been the exception. Nevertheless, the Amish of Lancaster County are reported to be one of the half-dozen largest tourist attractions in America. Under the circumstances, it is difficult to see how —from the Amish point of view—conditions can improve. However, while tourism affects the Old Order Amish everywhere, the situation in most other areas is not so annoying.

4. Government Intervention As the nation grows, the web of government becomes more complex, laws proliferate, bureaucracy increases, and the Amish, no less than other citizens, are confronted with a maze of regulations. At one time or another, they have had run-ins with the local, state, or federal government over a variety of issues—with mixed results.

Because of some bad traffic accidents, the Amish have had to install battery-operated turn signals on their buggies. They also must have their children vaccinated and inoculated. Amish dairy farmers have been forced to have their milk inspected according to government regulation. Like everyone else, Amish workers must pay income taxes, and Amish homeowners must pay property taxes.

On the other hand, the government did relent on social security, and the Old Order Amish neither make payments nor receive benefits. Also, while they had some difficulties during both world wars, the Amish have generally had their conscientious-objector status respected by the government. The biggest and longest controversy—over compulsory school laws—seems to be in the process of being resolved, at least in most states.

There is no doubt that the Amish find government regulations both obstructive and burdensome. Like their cousins the Hutterites, they have had more than their share of bureaucratic grief. And while they have thus far—miraculously—been able to hold their own, the Amish community never knows when trouble will strike again.

[29]Roy Buck, "Boundary Maintenance Revisited: Tourist Experience in an Old Order Amish Community," *Rural Sociology,* 43 (Summer 1978): 221–34.

5. Vanishing Farmland It may well be that the scarcity of farmland is the biggest problem facing the Amish today. Although there is no real shortage of land in the United States, *good farmland* is in short supply in many Amish communities. The reasons are rather obvious. The Old Order Amish are increasing much faster than the population at large, and since most Amishmen turn to farming, the supply of arable land in a given community tends to become exhausted. Furthermore, the Amish must often bid for land not only against other farm buyers but against industrial and commercial enterprises.

In Lancaster County, the price of land has become astronomical. On October 4, 1980, a sixty-nine-acre farm was sold at auction for $432,500, or $6,200 an acre! A local farmer-businessman bought the property "after a spirited challenge from Jacob King, an Amish bidder."[30] The record price for Lancaster County farmland is $8,200 an acre![31]

To meet the shortage of good farmland, the Old Order Amish have been more or less forced to do three things: (a) relocate to other areas (especially in the West and Southwest) where there is still some reasonably priced land available; (b) reduce the size of their farms in the already established areas, thus providing more agricultural opportunities for their young men; or (c) turn to nonfarming occupations. This last choice is most distasteful to the Amish, but sometimes there is little alternative. Amishmen are now more than occasionally found in nonfarming occupations—including factory work. Huntington writes as follows on the subject:

> Perhaps the greatest problem facing the Amish today is the scarcity of good farming land and the availability of factory work. . . . This may have a profound effect on Amish culture. The Amish family and Amish patterns of child rearing are built on the concept of shared parental responsibility, that both parents are almost always in the home and available to support one another and to guide and teach the children. . . . The authority patterns within the family change when the father is absent during most of the day.
>
> On an Amish farm the boys spend most of their time working with or under the direction of their father. In no other occupation can the father so consistently teach, instruct, admonish, and correct his children.
>
> The social structure of the Amish community is based on the availability of brethren and sisters to gather for work bees, for barn raisings, for day-long weddings and funerals. The Amish share labor within the

[30]Reported in the *Philadelphia Inquirer,* October 5, 1980.

[31]Ibid.

family, between families and among church members whenever there is extra or special work to be done. This combination of mutual aid and social interaction keeps the community strong and of one mind. This interaction can be easily achieved in a church district in which most of the households are farmers; it is almost impossible when most of the men work in factories or on construction crews.[32]

Rebuttal

How significant are the various problems facing the Old Order Amish? Will they continue to function as a folk society, or will high-powered, industrial civilization gobble them up, as it has so many other groups? This is an opinion question, naturally, and opinion is divided. Nevertheless, some observers feel that the Amish are changing, and that they will not survive in their present form.

Many of the problems, however, are deceptive. The youth problem, for instance, is probably not so serious as it sounds. True, more than a few of their young people "misbehave," and a number even defect to other groups—*but this process serves as a safety valve.* The Amish know full well that their rules are strict, and that certain individuals will be unable to conform. By giving their young people a certain amount of leeway prior to baptism, therefore, it is felt that those who do join the church will prove to be loyal and conscientious members. In practice, the safety-valve theory seems to work, since—overall—only about 6 percent of the Old Order Amish actually leave the fold. As a matter of record, the Amish have grown steadily: five thousand in 1900; thirty-three thousand in 1950; nearly one hundred thousand at the present time!

Tourism seems to be more of an annoyance than a serious problem. In the one research study that has been done, Buck found that the tourist business was structured so as "to face tourists away from direct contact with the Old Order Amish." The same investigator goes on to report that while the Amish do not like tourism, there were "few indications of culture erosion or personal distress because of it."[33]

Even the problem of vanishing farmland, while serious, is not critical. As a group, the Old Order Amish remain wedded to the soil—and they will not leave it except as a last resort. While there is a real shortage of land in some Amish communities, this would not be true

[32]Huntington, "Amish Family," pp. 319–20.
[33]Buck, "Boundary Maintenance Revisited," p. 233.

in most areas. What will probably happen in the future is that, in certain settlements, the Amish will be forced to spread to new counties and perhaps new states.

Other problems, such as the threat of modernization and government intervention are being taken in stride. Indeed, all things considered, it would appear that the Amish are more than holding their own. Outlook on life, relation to God and the universe, theology, closeness to the soil, separatism, resistance to change, pacifism, fundamentalism, frugality, humility, industriousness, attitude toward education, self-reliance—in brief, all the basic ingredients of "Amishness"—are much the same today as they always have been.

The Future From most of the signs, the Old Order Amish have a most promising future in America. They have outlasted their critics and in all probability will continue to do so. They have problems, but none seems insurmountable. Indeed, modern society appears to be in the process of bestowing certain blessings on the Amish. For instance, the spiraling price of food has meant that the Amish—whose business is food raising—are in an increasingly favorable economic position. The shortage of gasoline and fuel oil gives the Amish, who use little of either, another competitive advantage.

Actually, we seem to be living in a period of chronic shortages—of both goods and services. Self-sufficiency, therefore, and a willingness and ability to do it yourself, have become mighty virtues. And the Old Order Amish, whose entire way of life is based on self-sufficiency rather than on technological dependency, are able to live largely—though not entirely—outside the economy.

The followers of Jacob Amman are also benefiting from another source: public opinion. Tourism has brought tens of millions of Americans to the various Amish communities. And the Amish themselves—growing twice as fast as society at large—are expanding into more and more regions. As people have come to know the Amish firsthand, they have come to respect their way of life. Consequently, in clashes with the government the Amish can often count on valuable public support.

In the past, the Old Order Amish have had their difficulties. They have been misunderstood, ridiculed, fined, and on occasion jailed. In spite of their woes, they have refused to change. Now, apparently, they are coming upon better times. But whether they are—or whether there will be a return to a "sea of troubles"—it is unlikely that the Amish will ever alter their direction. They have placed themselves in God's hands permanently, and they have absolutely no doubts about their future.

SELECTED READINGS

Berry, Wendell. *The Unsettling of America: Culture and Agriculture.* New York: Avon, 1977.

Bryer, Kathleen. "The Amish Way of Death: A Study of Family Support Systems." *American Psychologist,* 34 (March 1979): 255–61.

Buck, Roy. "Boundary Maintenance Revisited: Tourist Experience in an Old Order Amish Community." *Rural Sociology,* 43 (Summer 1978): 221–34.

———. "Bloodless Theatre: Images of the Old Order Amish in Tourism Literature." *Pennsylvania Mennonite Heritage,* 2 (July 1979): 2–11.

The Budget. Sugarcreek, Ohio. (Newspaper published for Amish readers.)

Cowley, W. K. "Old Order Amish Settlements: Diffusion and Growth." *Annals of the Association of American Geographers,* 68 (June 1978): 249–64.

Hamman, Richard. *Patterns of Mortality in the Old Order Amish.* Ph.D. Dissertation, Johns Hopkins University, 1979.

Hostetler, John A. *Amish Society.* Baltimore: Johns Hopkins University Press, 1980.

———, and Huntington, Gertrude Enders. *Children in Amish Society: Socialization and Community Education.* New York: Holt, Rinehart and Winston, 1971.

Huntington, Gertrude Enders. "The Amish Family." In *Ethnic Families in America,* ed. by Charles Mindel and Robert Habenstein, pp. 295–322. New York: Elsevier, 1976.

Jencks, Christopher. "A Reappraisal of the Most Controversial Educational Document of Our Times." *New York Times Magazine,* August 10, 1969, pp. 12 ff.

Kephart, William M. "The Old Order Amish Family." In Kephart, *The Family, Society, and the Individual,* pp. 141–57. Boston: Houghton Mifflin, 1981.

Kollmorgen, Walter. *Culture of a Contemporary Community: The Old Amish of Lancaster County, Pennsylvania.* Washington, D.C.: U.S. Department of Agriculture, 1942.

Landing, James. "Failure of Amish Settlements in the Southeastern United States." *The Mennonite Quarterly Review* (October 1970): 376–88.

———. "The Amish, the Automobile, and Social Interaction." *The Journal of Geography,* 71 (January 1972): 52–57.

Lewis, Russell E. "Controlled Acculturation Revisited: An Examination of Differential Acculturation and Assimilation Between the Hutterian Brethren and the Old Order Amish." *International Review of Modern Sociology,* 6 (Spring 1976): 75–83.

Meyer, Carolyn. *Amish People.* New York: Atheneum, 1976.

Newswanger, Kiehl, and Newswanger, Christian. *Amishland.* New York: Hastings House, 1954.

Redekop, Calvin. *The Old Colony Mennonites.* Baltimore: Johns Hopkins University Press, 1969.

Schreiber, William. *Our Amish Neighbors.* Chicago: University of Chicago Press, 1962.

Schwieder, Elmer, and Schwieder, Dorothy. "The Paradox of Change in the Life Style of Iowa's Old Order Amish." *International Review of Modern Sociology,* 6 (Spring 1976): 65–74.

Smith, Elmer. *The Amish People.* New York: Exposition, 1958.

———. *Studies in Amish Demography.* Harrisonburg, Va.: Eastern Mennonite College, 1960.

Stoltzfus, Victor. "Reward and Sanction: The Adaptive Continuity of Amish Life." *The Mennonite Quarterly Review,* 51 (October 1977): 308–18.

Wenger, John C. *The Mennonite Church in America.* Scottdale, Pa.: Herald Press, 1967.

Yoder, Joseph. *Rosanna of the Amish.* Huntington, Pa.: Yoder, 1940.

Zielinski, John. *The Amish: A Pioneer Heritage.* Des Moines, Iowa: Wallace-Homestead, 1975.

THREE

THE ONEIDA COMMUNITY

Most students are probably familiar with the term *culture:* the total life-style of a people—their customs, attitudes, and values, the shared understandings that bind them together as a society. Not so familiar, perhaps, is the concept of *subculture.* Yet as the term indicates, a subculture is a "culture within a culture." In a true subculture, the shared beliefs and values may have more influence on members' behavior than does the larger society. In fact, voluntary subcultures are often formed because of dissatisfaction with society at large.

The American communal movement is a good case in point. Most communes, in both the nineteenth and twentieth centuries, arose because of specific or general disillusionment with "the way things were." The Oneida Community was not the first venture in American communal living, nor—obviously—was it the last. But all things considered, it may well have been the most remarkable. And it provides an excellent sociological example of a subculture.

Background

Unlike most of the other leaders discussed in the present volume, John Humphrey Noyes, founder of the Oneida Community, was of upper-class origin. His mother, Polly Hayes, was a relative of Rutherford B. Hayes, nineteenth president of the United States. His father was John Noyes, a United States congressman from Vermont and a successful businessman.

Not much is known about the boyhood of John Humphrey Noyes. One of eight children, he was born in 1811 at Brattleboro, Vermont. In 1821, his family moved to Putney, a small town ten miles to the north. Red-haired, freckled, and somewhat self-conscious about his appearance, he was noticeably shy around girls. With members of his own sex, however, he showed clear evidence of leadership. He entered Dartmouth at fifteen, a typical college age at that time, and was eventually elected to Phi Beta Kappa.

Upon graduation, Noyes worked as an apprentice in a New Hampshire law firm. However, it soon became obvious that he was not cut out to be a barrister, and he returned home to Putney. Up to that time, he certainly had no thoughts of founding a subculture, and it is doubtful whether he had ever heard of a place called Oneida.

The early 1830s found the country caught up in a frenzy of religious rejuvenation, and, as luck would have it, a four-day revival was held in Putney in September 1831. Noyes attended, listened—and succumbed completely. To those who knew him, he suddenly seemed to come alive with ideas, spiritual enlightenment, and visions of eternal truth. Although religion had not heretofore been a major part of his life, it was obvious that he had found his calling. Henceforth he would devote himself to disseminating God's word. A few weeks later he enrolled in theological seminary—first at Andover, then at Yale.

At Yale, John Humphrey Noyes acquired the reputation of being a radical, and although he was granted his license to preach in 1833, he was not a success. At one point, for example, he declared himself to be without sin—for which heresy he was called before the theological faculty. He refused to recant, whereupon his preaching license was revoked.

Putney

Jobless, penniless, and now looked upon as a religious oddity, John Humphrey Noyes did not appear to have much of a future. But there were several things in his favor. He was only twenty-three years old. He had an inner flame that was inextinguishable. He was already making a few converts, and soon he would make more. In an often-quoted statement, he said, "I have taken away their license to sin, and they keep on sinning. So, though they have taken away my license to preach, I shall keep on preaching." Events were to prove the statement more prophetic than Noyes realized.

For the next few years he traveled through New York and New England, living on a shoestring and spreading the doctrine of Perfectionism: man could be without sin. Although the concept did not originate with him, Noyes' brand of Perfectionism was genuinely new. And while, over the years, he added a number of additions and refinements, his basic theological postulate remained unchanged: Christ had already returned to earth—in A.D. 70—so that redemption or liberation from sin was an accomplished fact. Given the proper environment, therefore, man could lead a perfect, or sinless, life.

This was a radical notion, of course, and while he made some headway in spreading the gospel of Perfectionism, the existing churches turned a deaf ear to his teachings. Noyes returned home in 1836, sobered by his experience. He would spend the next dozen years in Putney, incorporating Perfectionism into the most radical social experiment America had ever seen.

Things started off innocently enough. Noyes' first converts in Putney were members of his own family: his sisters, Charlotte and Harriet, his brother George, and his mother. (His father rejected the whole idea.) Other converts trickled in, one here, one there. In 1838, he married Harriet Holton, granddaughter of the lieutenant governor of Vermont. She not only was a convert but remained a loyal Perfectionist all her life. By 1844, however, adult membership was still only about two dozen, although there were other small groups of followers scattered throughout New England.

During the early years, the Putney Perfectionists were not a communal organization. Members lived in individual houses and worked at individual jobs. They had resources; in fact, they were incorporated for $38,000, the money coming largely from the estate of Noyes' father. But even before they adopted the communal style of life, one thing was clear: the Putneyites were not a democracy. John Humphrey was both the leader and the binding force. And while he often gave the impression of operating through discussion and persuasion rather than by proclamation, there was no doubt in anyone's mind—including his own—about who made the rules.

Finally, in 1844, the Putney Perfectionists adopted economic communism as a way of life. They commenced to share their work, their food, their living quarters, and their resources. Their children began to attend a communal school. And once every day, for a protracted period, they met together for Bible reading, theological discussion, and a sharing of religious experiences.

In 1846, the group began to share spouses.

Coitus Reservatus Following his marriage to Harriet Holton in 1838, Noyes fathered five children in six years. Unfortunately, all but one were stillborn.[1] The Perfectionist leader grieved deeply, not only

[1]The best source for the Putney era is George Wallingford Noyes, *John Humphrey Noyes: The Putney Community* (Oneida, N.Y.: 1931), esp. pp. 17 *ff.* See also Robert Thomas, *The Man Who Would Be Perfect: John Humphrey Noyes and the Utopian Impulse* (Philadelphia: University of Pennsylvania Press, 1977).

for the lost children but for their mother. Was this to be woman's lot in life, to bear children year after year, whether or not they were wanted? To suffer, to mourn, to be kept out of the mainstream of human activity—all because of nature's imperious call? He thought not, but what could be done about it?

The Shakers had solved the problem—to their own satisfaction, at least—by practicing celibacy. Noyes rejected this "solution," although he came to recognize that, whatever the answer was, it would have to include some sort of birth control. He finally hit upon the novel idea of *coitus reservatus,* or, as he called it, male continence. It was not necessary, he said, for a man to reach ejaculation during the sex act. With a little practice, he could enjoy sex relations without attaining the climax that might lead to conception.

In the pamphlet *Male Continence,* published later, Noyes has this to say:

> Now we insist that this whole process, up to the very moment of emission, is *voluntary,* entirely under the control of the moral faculty, and *can be stopped at any point.*
>
> In other words, the *motions* can be controlled or stopped at will, and it is only the *final crisis* of emission that is automatic or uncontrollable. . . . If you say that this is impossible, I answer that I *know* it is possible —nay, that it is easy. (pp. 7–8)

As it turned out, Noyes' contention was correct. Throughout the whole of the group's existence, *coitus reservatus* was used successfully.

Exodus As might have been predicted, once the Perfectionists began the practice of spouse sharing, the word soon spread. Actually, there was never any attempt—then or later—to keep the matter a secret. In his numerous sojourns and talks, Noyes often alluded to the fact that his brand of communism involved sexual as well as economic sharing.

Nevertheless, as far as the citizens of Putney were concerned, right was right, and wrong was wrong—and sex outside of marriage was wrong. It was the 1840s (not the 1980s!), and marriage meant one man and one woman, joined in the sight of God and legally recorded in the town hall registry. The Perfectionists, quite obviously, were not only living in sin but were more or less flaunting the practice. The following bizarre episode, for example, is cited by Whitworth:

> In June 1847, Noyes "miraculously" cured Harriet Hall, an associate of the group, who had been an invalid for some years, and had been given up by her doctors as suffering from an incurable, and certainly unusual, combination of dropsy and tuberculosis.

> Subsequently, the sectarians cited this case as the most convincing proof of Noyes' spiritual powers. However, the gratitude of Mr. Hall, who had always been ambivalent about the sect, was insufficiently deep to withstand Noyes' admission that sexual intercourse had been part of the treatment. Accordingly, he lodged a complaint with the State Attorney at Brattleboro.[2]

One thing led to another. Finally, irate citizens met in protest and demanded action. In October 1847—amidst rumors of mob violence—John Humphrey Noyes was indicted by a grand jury on grounds of adultery. He was released, pending trial, on $2,000 bail.

Had the trial been held, the Perfectionist leader would almost surely have been found guilty. However, after much soul-searching and discussion—and upon the advice of his lawyer—Noyes fled to New York. As he explained it later, the reason for his flight from Vermont was not to escape justice, but to save his followers and others from the mob violence which was clearly imminent. Oddly enough, though he probably caused more shock and outrage than any other religious leader of his time (with the probable exception of Joseph Smith, founder of the Mormons), John Humphrey Noyes was never to stand trial for his unorthodox—and illegal—practices.

Oneida

All during his stay at Putney, Noyes had made periodic forays into the hinterland to gain converts. His various publications had helped to spread the word. By 1847, when the Perfectionists' sexual system became operative, the popular press was also giving John Humphrey Noyes and his followers a good deal of publicity. When Noyes left Putney, therefore, other Perfectionist centers—rather loosely organized—were available to him. One such spot was a fairly large tract of land along Oneida Creek in New York State.

Formerly a reservation belonging to the Oneida Indians and now the site of a sawmill, the property was owned by Jonathan Burt, an ardent follower of Noyes. Burt had come upon hard times and was quite willing to turn over his land to the Perfectionist cause. Noyes was attracted to the site and wasted no time in reassembling the little flock of Putneyites. Burt and his associates stayed on. Other small groups of followers joined them. They cleared land, made their own implements and furniture, and held discussions. Working as farmers, they were able to buy up adjoining properties. Before long, their

[2]John Whitworth, *God's Blueprints: A Sociological Study of Three Utopian Sects* (London and Boston: Routledge & Kegan Paul, 1975), p. 116.

Oneida holdings totaled nearly six hundred acres. And in spite of adverse conditions, membership grew. By the end of the first year, 1848, there were eighty-seven persons living in the Community. A year later, the number had more than doubled!

From the very beginning, the mission of the group was made crystal clear. With the help of Almighty God, as expressed through the person of John Humphrey Noyes, they were going to create a heaven on earth. There was never any doubt about their utopian goal. Nor was there any doubt about how they were going to attain it.

The Mansion House During their first winter at Oneida, the little group of Perfectionists lived in the existing dwellings: Jonathan Burt's homestead plus some abandoned Indian cabins. Top priority, however, was given to the construction of a communal home. John Humphrey Noyes believed that, in actual day-to-day living, true communism could best be achieved by having all members live under one roof. This was the way the Perfectionists lived throughout the rest of their existence.

In the summer of 1849, the first communal home was built. No one knows how it got the name Mansion House, but it was a wooden affair and was constructed by the entire Community. Membership grew so rapidly, though, that in 1862 the structure was replaced by a brick building. In subsequent years wings were added as needed, and the building still stands in its entirety. Noyes helped in the planning of both the original and the present building, and both were exceptionally well thought out.

Although most adults had small rooms of their own, the building as a whole was designed to encourage a feeling of togetherness rather than separateness. To this end *group facilities* predominated: a communal dining room, library, concert hall, recreation area, picnic grounds, and the like. It was in the Big Hall of the Mansion House that the regular evening meetings were held, and it was here that Noyes gave most of his widely quoted home talks.

Over the years, the Perfectionists developed a lively interest in the performing arts, and—though most of the talent was homegrown—they were able to organize such activities as symphony concerts, choral recitals, and Shakespearian plays. Occasionally, outside artists were invited to perform, but on a day-to-day basis the Community was more or less a closed group, with members seldom straying far from home base.

Sociologically speaking, the Perfectionists' reference behavior related entirely to the group. The larger community, figuratively and literally, was considered to be "outside" and was always referred to as "the World." It was this system of *integral closure,* sustained over several decades, which served as a primary solidifying force. And, of course, it was the Mansion House which made the system operable.

During my firsthand study of the Oneidans, many of those interviewed were unable to separate the old Community from the Mansion House itself. In their minds the two had become one, a fusion of the social and the structural, which again underscores the pervasiveness of the physical setting. Even today the building serves as a kind of community center. A good many of the direct descendants live either in the Mansion House or close by. Somehow, they hate to leave the area. As one of the interviewees put it:

> We all love the old place. Many of our folks lived there, and most of us played there as kids. We know the building down to the last brick and board. It's odd, but so many of the people who moved away come back to the Mansion House as they get older. It's because they had such good times and such happy memories.

Primary-Group Association

Sociologists differentiate sharply between *primary groups* and *secondary groups.* A primary group is a small, face-to-face group characterized by intimate relationships and shared feelings, such as the family, the clique, the friendship circle. A secondary group, on the other hand—such as the large corporation, the business firm, or the government bureau—is characterized by an impersonality of association. Members do not relate to one another in a really meaningful way. It is self-evident, therefore, that human needs such as talking, confiding, sympathizing, and the like are best satisfied in a primary rather than a secondary group. The catch is that as society becomes larger and more complex, secondary groups tend to predominate.

With several hundred people living under one roof, the Oneidans had an interesting problem in human relations: how to enjoy the benefits of primary-group association in an organization that had grown to secondary-group size. They had the advantage, naturally, of believing both in John Humphrey Noyes and in the tenets of Perfectionism, but these beliefs alone would hardly account for the operational smoothness which prevailed.

Their success is explained by the fact that they worked out an amazingly effective system of interpersonal relationships. If it weren't that the discipline of sociology had not yet been envisioned, one would have thought that the Oneidans had somehow gained access to a text in introductory sociology.

Practically everything the Perfectionists did was designed to play down the "I" in favor of the "we." Members ate together at common dining tables, worked together at common tasks, and played together in a variety of recreational pursuits. They shared their property. They shared their sexual partners. And they shared their children.

In their day-to-day activities, they were ever on guard against things that might become "antigroup." Thus tea, coffee, alcoholic beverages, smoking all were taboo. At the dining table, pork products, including bacon and sausage, were never served; in fact, meat of any kind appeared infrequently. The Perfectionists reasoned that activities such as coffee drinking and meat eating might become habitual and hence distractive. By the same token, dancing was encouraged since it was a group activity, while smoking was prohibited because it was too individualistic.

One of the Oneida descendants made the following comments during an interview:

> I imagine the prohibitions were pretty well thought out. They didn't just spring up, but developed gradually. Remember, they were trying to create a spiritual and social brotherhood, and they spent much more time in the art of developing relationships than we do. They had to. After all, hundreds of them were living together as a family, and they worked at it day after day. They were successful, too, for they held together for almost two generations without a major quarrel.

While theoretically the various prohibitions could have worked a hardship on the members, *relative deprivation* prevailed. As in the case of the Amish, the restrictions applied to *all* the Perfectionists; hence no one felt resentful. On the contrary, sacrifice was actually another measure used to emphasize the primary-group relationship.

From an outsider's view, some of the prohibitions seem excessive. I was told, for example, of an episode involving all the girl children. There were several large dolls which, like other material things in the Community, were shared. Around 1850, some kind soul thought it would be better if each of the little girls had a doll of her own, and this plan was put into effect. Unfortunately, it developed that the youngsters spent too much time with their dolls and not enough on household chores. Accordingly, on a specified date, all the girls joined hands in a circle around the stove, and one by one were persuaded to throw their dolls into the fire. From that time on, dolls were never allowed in the nursery.

Often overlooked is the fact that the religious practices of the

Oneidans also served to accentuate primary-group association. It is true that the Perfectionists dispensed with most of the formal aspects of religion. They maintained no church or chapel, held no prayer services, had no paid clergy. Neither baptismal nor communion services were utilized. Since there was no marriage, there were no weddings. Death was played down, and there were no formal funeral arrangements. Christmas was not celebrated as a religious holiday, although in deference to outsiders no work was performed on that day.

At the same time, religion was a central part of the Oneidans' daily lives. This was the whole point. Rather than have special religious celebrations or special days set aside for worship, the Perfectionists believed that every day should involve religious awareness. They were avid readers of the Bible and loved to discuss the various parables. They believed in Perfectionism. And they believed that by listening to John Humphrey Noyes—and following his teachings—they were listening to the voice of God.

The Big Hall Every night of their lives, the Oneidans met in the Big Hall to combine the sacred and the secular. Women brought their sewing and knitting, and both sexes sat in groups around small tables. The program was conducted from in front of the stage by one of the senior members. A hymn was sung, passages from the Bible were read, and if he were present, Noyes would give one of his home talks. The talks themselves, involving as they did the secular application of Perfectionist theology, were one of the highlights of the evening—so much so that if Noyes were traveling, the talk would be read by someone else. Also included in the nightly program were news and announcements, lectures, dancing, comments and suggestions by members of the audience, business reports, and so forth. The evening meetings can thus be seen as another means of promoting group solidarity. According to the *Oneida Circular* of July 17, 1863, the meetings "were the most cherished part of our daily lives."

Noyes, incidentally, was no prude. He enjoyed entertainment and activities of all kinds, and encouraged his followers to do the same. Even on this point, however, he insisted on *group* involvement: a glee club rather than a soloist, a band or orchestra rather than a recital, a play or an operetta rather than a monologue, and so on.

The following account appears in the *Oneida Community Daily* of January 6, 1868:

> At the supper table last night, it was announced that there would be a gathering in the Big Hall, of the family, at half past six—in which there

> would be some games, or plays, and perhaps dancing. Accordingly, the family assembled at the time appointed, and for an hour or more we had lively times.
>
> The chairs were arranged in circles, and each circle had a play distinct from its neighbor. Next, the chairs were re-arranged, and a large circle formed in the middle of the Hall. The popular play "Spat them out" was entered into with considerable enthusiasm.
>
> Dancing followed, at the close of which the family was requested to be seated, and crackers and cheese, apples, dates, and nuts were passed around. The exercises closed with two songs.

Although by modern standards such entertainment might seem rather tame, there is no doubt that the system worked. The Oneidans were clearly successful in their efforts to establish a primary- rather than a secondary-group atmosphere. They were also successful at preventing the development of a *culte du moi* in favor of an integrated and sustained we-feeling. Both in their conversation and their publications, it was "the family" this and "the family" that.

One of the often-told stories of the Community pertains to the time a visitor was shown through the Mansion House. "What is the fragrance I smell here in this house?" the stranger asked. And the guide replied, "It must be the odor of crushed selfishness."

Decision Making

All organizations have a power structure and a decision-making process, and the Oneida Community was no exception. However, the Perfectionists had a special problem since (a) they were all housed under one roof, and (b) they were attempting to combine the social and the economic. They solved the problem by employing a combination of the democratic and the autocratic.

Committee Work In keeping with their emphasis on group solidarity, the followers of John Humphrey Noyes might have been expected to arrive at decisions on a democratic basis. And in one sense, there was ample opportunity for discussion. The Community *Handbook,* for example, states:

> In determining any course of action or policy, *unanimity* is always sought by committees, by the Business Board, and by the Community. All consider themselves as one party, and intend to act together or not at all. . . . If there are serious objections to any proposed measure, action is delayed until the objections are removed. The majority never go ahead leaving a grumbling minority behind. (p. 17)

True enough, but what these lines refer to were the day-to-day, operational decisions. Major decisions, as well as Perfectionist doctrine and Community policy, were made by Noyes.

On operational matters, members were indeed encouraged to speak out at the evening meetings. Moreover, there were a sufficient number of committees and departments to enable everyone to have a real voice in the day-to-day management of the Community. In this respect, the trouble was not that the members had insufficient authority, but that they had too much. Charles Nordhoff reports that there were no less than twenty-one standing committees and forty-eight different departments. Such things as heating, clothing, patent rights, photographs, haircutting, fruit preserving, furniture, music, dentistry, bedding, and painting all involved a committee or a department.[3] There was even a department for "incidentals"!

The committees and committee heads met; departments and department heads met; the business board met. The Community itself met nightly. In a given thirty-day period, there were probably more managerial discussions in the Oneida Community than in any organization of comparable size in the United States.

The upshot was that the Perfectionists wasted too much time thrashing out details and inaugurating meaningless change. In fact, change was almost a fetish with them. They changed the work schedule, the meal schedule, and the number of meals per day, discussing endlessly which foods to serve and which to prohibit. (The debate over whether to serve tea, for example, took several years. They finally decided to permit only a brew made from strawberry leaves.) The prohibition against smoking was also years in the making. The Perfectionists liked to change their jobs and their way of doing things. For some reason, they even had a habit of changing their rooms.

A revealing statement on the matter of change appears in the *Circular* of April 25, 1864.

> It is a point of belief with us that when one keeps constantly in a rut, he is especially exposed to attacks of evil. The devil knows just where to find him! But inspiration will continually lead us into new channels by which we shall dodge the adversary.[4]

The Central Members Noyes was the acknowledged leader of the Community, ruling benevolently but firmly and basing his authority

[3]Charles Nordhoff, *The Communistic Societies of the United States* (New York: Dover, 1966), p. 279.

[4]Quoted in Constance Noyes Robertson, ed., *Oneida Community: An Autobiography, 1851–1876* (Syracuse, N.Y.: Syracuse University Press, 1970); pp. 47, 75.

on divine inspiration. As his son Pierrepont put it, "The Community believed that his inspiration came down what he called the 'link and chain': from God to Christ; from Christ to Paul; from Paul to John Humphrey Noyes; and by him made available to the Community."[5]

On their part, the Perfectionists were quite content with the arrangement. They acknowledged that Noyes was God's representative on earth. As a matter of fact, such acknowledgment was one of the preconditions for membership.

Nevertheless, Noyes was away a good part of the time, and in his absence important decisions had to be made—on some basis other than the twenty-one committees and forty-eight departments. The system employed was the utilization of "central members." These were a dozen or so men and women who more or less served as Noyes' deputies. They were all older, dedicated individuals, many of whom had been with John Humphrey Noyes at Putney.

As Maren Carden points out:

> Noyes and the central members brought issues before the Community at the daily meetings. Although they encouraged all members to contribute their ideas, these powerful figures generally dominated the discussion. The majority merely ratified their conclusions. Yet the central members followed Noyes' directives faithfully: all decisions stemmed from Perfectionist ideals. . . . Without their devotion to Noyes and their willingness to follow his interpretation of Perfectionist ideals, the central members might have exercised their power ruthlessly. Instead they were strict, but for the most part fair.[6]

This, then, was the leadership process. Noyes made the major decisions, aided and abetted by the central members. These decisions encompassed economic policy, sexual matters, relations with the outside, admission of new members, childbearing and child rearing, and Perfectionist doctrine. Day-to-day operational details were handled by committees and departments, in consultation with the general membership.

The Oneida Community was hardly a model of functional efficiency. The Shakers and the Hutterites, both communistic in form, were much better organized. Yet the Perfectionists' system worked. Up to the very end, the Community functioned with scarcely a major quarrel. What they lost in operational efficiency, they gained in their feelings of closeness to one another.

[5]Pierrepont Noyes, *My Father's House: An Oneida Boyhood* (Gloucester, Mass.: Peter Smith, 1966), pp. 132–33.

[6]Maren Lockwood Carden, *Oneida: Utopian Community to Modern Corporation* (Baltimore: Johns Hopkins Press, 1969), pp. 85–86.

Role of Women

Although it was never acknowledged in so many words, the role of women presented something of a problem for the Perfectionists. It is true that they believed in equality. Concepts of rank and privilege were foreign to them. They were communists, and they were proud of it. At the same time, in society at large, women held a clearly inferior position. They were generally excluded from higher education, from the professions, and from public office. All but the most routine jobs were closed to them. When the Oneida Community was founded in the spring of 1848, a wife had no legal control over her own personal property, and the right to vote was more than seventy years away. Indeed, the first Women's Rights Convention—at Seneca Falls, New York—had not yet been held.

The Perfectionists solved their problem by way of a compromise. They refused to acknowledge that, inherently, women were the equal of men. But as far as the allocation of jobs was concerned, the Community was far ahead of the World. The *Oneida Handbook* makes the following statement:

> Communism emancipates a woman from the slavery and corroding cares of a mere wife and mother; stimulates her to seek the improvement of mind and heart that will make her worthy of a higher place than ordinary society can give her. . . .
>
> Gradually, the Community women have risen to a position where, in mind and in heart, they have all and more than all that is claimed by the women who are so loudly asserting their rights. And through it all, they have not ceased to love and honor the truth that "the man is the head of the woman," and that woman's God-given right is to be "the glory of man." (p. 26)

In practice, the Oneida women did women's work, but they also handled jobs that were normally reserved for men. They did the cooking, washing, sewing, mending, and nursing, and were responsible for child care. But they also worked in various business and industrial departments. They held jobs in the library and on the Community newspaper. In a number of other areas, they worked side by side with the men. And they were well represented on the various committees, including that of the central members. As one of the female interviewees remarked:

> Most people have overlooked the fact that Father Noyes delegated a lot more responsibility to the women here than they ever would have received on the outside. Every committee had women on it. It made a difference, too. All the old folks will tell you it made both men and women respect each other.

There were a number of so-called adult educational programs within the Community, and women as well as men were encouraged to take part. Subject matter included mathematics, science, music, and foreign language. At one time, the Perfectionists even discussed plans for the establishment of a university. And while the plans never materialized, there was no doubt that women would have been admitted to the same courses as men. The point is worth mentioning because at the time, in 1866, only Oberlin College in all the United States admitted women.

The New Attire Male members of the Oneida Community dressed much like anybody else, but visitors were caught off guard when they first saw the ladies' attire. It was John Humphrey Noyes, never the one to accept a conventional practice if he could find an "improvement," who first pointed to the impracticality of the standard female attire. "Woman's dress is a standing lie," he wrote in the first annual report of the Community in 1848. "It proclaims that she is not a two-legged animal, but something like a churn, standing on castors!"

He went on to suggest a change: "The dress of children—frock and pantalettes—is in good taste, not perverted by the dictates of shame, and well adapted to free motion." Accordingly, three of the women embarked upon a daring stylistic venture. Following Noyes' suggestion, they proceeded to cut their skirts down to knee length and to use the cut-off material to fashion pantalettes, which reached to the ankle. After a demonstration and discussion at one of the evening meetings, the new garb was adopted forthwith. Thereafter, it was the only attire worn by the ladies.

In addition to short skirts and pantalettes, the Oneida ladies bobbed their hair. Their reasoning was that long hair took too long to fix and was not functional. The new style was quite satisfactory, although some outsiders thought the coiffure too "brazen." Oddly enough, although the Oneida women first bobbed their hair in 1848, the custom was not introduced into the World until 1922 (by dancer Irene Castle).

According to comments made in interviews, the distinctive appearance of the Oneida women was another factor which served to strengthen their we-feeling.

> Your asking of sociological questions about what held the Community together reminds me of something my aunt used to tell me. The Oneidans kept pretty much to themselves, but during the summer months they permitted visitors. Some Sunday afternoons, whole trainloads

of visitors would come. They were served, picnic-style, on the lawn of the Mansion House. I think they were charged a dollar for the whole thing.

Of course, the visitors couldn't get over the way the Oneida women dressed, and they kept staring. My aunt always felt that the way outsiders looked at them and talked about them had a lot to do with their feeling of closeness.

Membership and Secession

All groups face the problem of numbers. Some, like the Amish and Mormons, show fantastic rates of growth. Others, like the Shakers and the Father Divine Movement, lose members so rapidly that survival becomes a problem. The Oneida Community fell between these two extremes. Once they were fully established, their numbers remained fairly constant. Dissolution—in 1881—had nothing to do with loss of membership. In fact, the Perfectionists had much more trouble keeping people out than keeping them in!

What was the total membership of the Community? It depends on what is meant by "total." Available records indicate that at any given time, there were around three hundred members. When deaths and secessions are taken into consideration, total all-time membership was probably in the area of five hundred. There were roughly equal numbers of males and females, although there were somewhat more females at the older age levels.

At one time or another, there were seven branches, all under the leadership of John Humphrey Noyes. In addition to the main group at Oneida, there were smaller branches at Willow Place, New York; Cambridge, Vermont; Newark, New Jersey; Wallingford, Connecticut; New York City; and Putney, Vermont (reopened four years after Noyes departed). The branch at Wallingford, Connecticut—with about forty-five members—survived until the very end.

Except during the early Putney period, the Perfectionists did little or no active proselytizing. Yet they had no difficulty in attracting members. In some years, they received as many as two hundred applications. Over and over again, the *Oneida Daily Journal* reported requests for membership (evidently more male than female), but in most cases the applications were turned down. The following rejection, for instance, appears in the August 8, 1866, issue:

> We certainly feel for you, but we don't feel it probable that you will be called upon to join us at present. . . . There is a general rush toward us right now, and petitions for membership multiply, so that unless

> we know the mind of the Lord, our "life boat" will certainly get swamped. . . .
>
> Yours in truth and sincerity,
> E. Y. J.

The reason for the steady stream of membership applications is not hard to find. The Oneidans were a successful group—and word of their success traveled fast. Their own publications, as well as the popular press, afforded them wide coverage. Noyes himself journeyed and lectured extensively. And, of course, visitors to the Community could not help but be impressed by what they saw. (The total number of visitors must have been staggering. The *Oneida Circular* reports that on one day—July 4, 1863—between fifteen hundred and two thousand persons visited the Community.)[7]

Applicants who were admitted were carefully screened, and once accepted they went through a probationary period for a year or so. The idea was to determine not only whether the newcomers could adjust to Community life, but whether they possessed the necessary devoutness. Over the years, most new members adjusted very well. Educational and recreational programs abounded, work was not excessive, and relations both within the Community and between the Community and the outside world were generally pleasant.

It should be pointed out that, unlike the Shakers or the Father Divine Movement, the Oneida Community was not primarily of lower- or working-class origin. They had more than their share of skilled craftsmen and (especially in later years) professional men. Carden points out that when the Community was first starting, Noyes carefully selected—from among the ranks of enthusiastic Perfectionists—

> those who were deeply committed to his teachings and also were responsible, talented craftsmen and farmers. They could provide for almost all of life's material necessities. . . . They also brought their savings. Few arrived emptyhanded. One suspects that Noyes shrewdly selected at least some of them for their wealth.
>
> By 1857, the members had invested almost $108,000 in the Community and its branches. Without this large capital investment, Oneida would almost certainly have perished, as did such little-known New York experiments as the Bloomfield Association, the Ontario Union, the Moorhouse Union, and the Jefferson County Phalanx.[8]

After the Perfectionists were on a firm footing, their ranks came to include many lawyers, dentists, doctors, teachers, engineers, accountants, ministers, and business managers. Also, many of the chil-

[7]Robertson, *Oneida Community,* p. 71.
[8]Carden, *Oneida: Utopian Community,* pp. 37–39.

dren born in the Community eventually went on to college and professional school.

Secession While most of those who joined Oneida were happy with their decision, some were not. Each year certain individuals left—for a variety of reasons. Some were unable to adjust to the sharing of sex. Others became discontented with the economic philosophy. Still others found themselves disturbed by Noyes' brand of Perfectionism.

A few individuals joined for the wrong reasons and soon became disillusioned. For example, from time to time Noyes would renounce orthodox medical treatment in favor of faith cures. (He himself was alleged to have cured a woman who was both crippled and blind.) Those whose hopes for a miracle cure were not fulfilled were natural candidates for secession.

In general, those who left the group were likely to be from among the more recent additions. Veteran members seldom withdrew. The actual number of seceders is not known, but the figure was probably not excessive. Those who left were permitted to take with them whatever property they had brought, and those who had nothing were given a hundred dollars.

Unlike the Shakers, the Oneidans were not plagued with legal suits based on property rights. And unlike the Mormons, the Perfectionists seldom had to contend with apostates who spread untrue stories. In all the many decades of their existence, there were only two embarrassing experiences. One member, William Mills—for reasons which will be explained later—was asked to leave, refused, and had to be forcibly evicted. Another member, the highly unstable Charles Guiteau, left the Community in 1867 after a short stay. Fourteen years later, Oneidans were dismayed to learn that the same Charles Guiteau had assassinated President Garfield. (Guiteau himself was subsequently hanged.)

By and large, however, those who left did so with good will. A number of them actually came back and rejoined the Community. For the fact was that, on a day-to-day basis, the Oneidans were a happy group—more so, perhaps, than almost any of the other groups discussed in this book.

Corinna Noyes, who was born in the Community, writes:

> The Oneidans led happy, fulfilled lives, in many cases richer lives than would have been the case in what they called the World. . . . Women like my grandmother, who would probably have lived the toilsome and restricted life of a farmer's wife and drudge, were admitted to a larger society, a more varied and interesting experience.

> Those among them who came from more comfortable backgrounds had the privilege of sharing their greater learning with their friends. And above all, as I remember the men and women who nurtured me, all had learned a spiritual lesson of immense value. They had learned to live with one another in concord and contentment.[9]

Even those who eventually voted to disband the Community had kind words and pleasant memories. The following remarks occurred during a personal interview:

> I was too young to remember much. But as I grew older and asked my relatives about the Community days, their faces would light up. My own folks were "come outers"; that is, they thought the thing had gone on long enough and weren't too sorry when the group broke up. But even they loved to talk about the "old days" and how much they missed them. They were wonderful people and they had wonderful times.

Social Control

One indication of the Perfectionists' level of adjustment is the fact that they had virtually none of the social problems associated with the outside world. Crime and delinquency, poverty, alcoholism, drug addiction, suicide—such things were unknown in the Community. One reason, of course, was that the malcontents who might have caused trouble usually left. They were replaced by people eager to follow Noyes' teachings. At any given time, therefore, the Oneidans constituted a high-morale group dedicated to the advancement of Perfectionist philosophy.

Another factor making for group cohesion was the Community's system of social control. As is true of the Gypsies (chapter one), the Perfectionists dispensed almost entirely with formal control. Their informal controls, however, were masterful, three in particular meriting special consideration.

The first was the evening meeting, mentioned earlier. These meetings, held every night, were convened not only for social and business purposes but to thrash out disputes. Begun at Putney, when the little group of a dozen or so would meet in the parlor of Noyes' home, the custom was continued at Oneida. Indeed, for the first few years at Oneida the gathering was small enough to permit an alphabetical roll call. Any person who had a complaint was encouraged

[9]Corinna Ackley Noyes, *Days of My Youth* (Oneida, N.Y.: Oneida Ltd., 1960), pp. 105–06.

to voice it when his name was called. Later on, when the membership grew to several hundred, roll call was abolished, but the custom of airing grievances in public, rather than in private, was continued. Backbiting, gossip, dissension, and the like were thus materially reduced.

The second component of social control lay in the authority and the person of John Humphrey Noyes. Noyes was not a dictator by any means. He was kindly, deeply religious, and preferred to exercise his leadership through discussion and persuasion rather than by fiat. In this, he received valuable assistance from the central members. But when the occasion called for it, his word was law, and the Community accepted this fact. Because they were Perfectionists, they acknowledged the divine authority of John Humphrey Noyes. They could not challenge this authority without repudiating their entire way of life. In the case of unresolved arguments, therefore—which sometimes did occur at the evening meetings—Noyes was the final arbiter. When there were lagging departments or recalcitrant individuals, it was the Perfectionist leader who administered the necessary reprimand. And when it became obvious that a member was deliberately flouting the rules of the Community, his expulsion was handled—quietly but firmly—by John Humphrey Noyes.

Mutual Criticism The third measure of social control—one that was used by no other group—was the Perfectionist system of mutual criticism. Back in his seminary days, Noyes had been impressed by a group of students who met regularly for the purpose of assessing one another's faults. The criticisms were carried on in a friendly but forthright manner, and all the participants—including Noyes—were pleased with the results. Response was so gratifying that Noyes instituted the practice at Putney. It was continued at Oneida and remained in effect throughout the whole of the Community's existence.

The system of mutual criticism changed over the years. Sometimes the person involved simply stood up at the evening meeting and was criticized by each member of the group. As membership grew, however, the system proved unwieldy, and committees were appointed to conduct the criticism. Frequently Noyes added his own comments. But irrespective of the method, the goal remained the same: to bring about self-improvement through the testimony of impartial witnesses.

For certain members, criticism was traumatic. It is not easy for a sensitive person to listen to his own faults examined in public. Some Perfectionists, in fact, left the Community rather than submit to what they felt was unwarranted censure. Most members, however, apparently looked upon the criticism not as a personal attack but as an impersonal expression of group opinion, an expression aimed at maximizing interactive cohesion.

There is no doubt that mutual criticism served as a measure of social control. The Oneidans never contended otherwise. Members who were failing in the spiritual realm, or whose individuality was too pronounced, were requested to undergo criticism, after which they were expected to show some improvement. As Estlake, one of the Perfectionists, put it: "Mutual Criticism is to the Community what ballast is to a ship."[10]

It might be mentioned that all the Perfectionists were subject to mutual criticism, including the central members. The only exception was John Humphrey Noyes, who was never criticized by the Community. On occasion, however, he did undergo self-criticism.

The following brief account appeared July 18, 1866, in the *Oneida Circular,* the Community's weekly newspaper:

> During the evening meeting, Meroa K. was criticized. Much dissatisfaction was expressed with her present unimproving and disobedient state. It was thought that if there was not a thorough change in her spirit she would have to be invited to leave the Community.
>
> She is inefficient in business, is gross in her alimentiveness, and spends a great deal of time in reading novels and newspaper stories. A committee was appointed to talk with her and find out what her real character and purpose are, and determine what course shall be taken with her.

The system of mutual criticism was not used only for purposes of social control. It was also employed whenever a member genuinely desired self-improvement. In this instance, the person would volunteer to be criticized. Although no records were kept, mutual criticism evidently grew in popularity to the point where most sessions were the voluntary type. But voluntary or otherwise, the technique was effective, and most Oneidans benefited. These remarks appeared during 1871–1872 in the *Circular:*

> I feel as though I had been washed; felt clean through the advice and criticism given. I would call the truth the soap; the critics the scrubbers; Christ's spirit the water.

[10]Allan Estlake, *The Oneida Community: A Record of an Attempt to Carry out the Principles of Christian Unselfishness and Scientific Race-Improvement* (London: George Redway, 1900), p. 58.

> Criticism is administered in faithfulness and love without regard to persons. I look upon the criticisms I have received since I came here as the greatest blessings that have been conferred upon me.[11]

Excesses The Oneidans had a habit of going to extremes, and their application of mutual criticism was a case in point. So enamored were they of the technique that sometimes whole departments were criticized. Thus on October 29, 1866, the Community's newspaper, the *Oneida Community Daily,* reports that "in the evening meeting we had a faithful and sincere criticism of the *Journal,* which we hope will result in its improvement." On March 23, 1867, the same publication informs us that

> the criticism of the Machine Shop was in order last night. It was thought that there had been a good degree of enthusiasm in work during the past winter, and a good state of feeling and harmony. Some thought that there was a lack of order in the shop, and a lack of carefulness in some cases regarding thoroughly finishing the products before they were shipped out.

Even children were occasionally involved in mutual criticism. The *Circular* of May 13, 1872, cites the case of a nine-year-old boy

> whose spirit and manners had given offense for some time, and he was advised to offer himself for Criticism. He was old enough to know that it would do him good, and he had grace enough to want to improve, so he offered himself. The children were very sincere. Every one of them had something to say about the boy's selfish, inharmonious ways. Even youngsters of six or seven had been outraged in their sense of what is right and wrong. There was no malice in what the children said. They are too ingenuous to hold a grudge.

The Perfectionists also employed criticism as a cure for various aches and illnesses. Called "krinopathy," the criticism cure was widely used in both children and adults. The *Circular* of December 4, 1863, reports:

> It is a common custom here for every one who may be attacked with any disorder to send for a committee of six or eight persons, in whose faith and spiritual judgment he has confidence, to come and criticize him. The result, when administered sincerely, is almost universally to throw the patient into a sweat, or to bring on a reaction of his life against disease, breaking it up and restoring him soon to usual health.

[11]Quoted in Harriet Worden, *Old Mansion House Memories* (Kenwood, Oneida, N.Y.: privately printed, 1950), pp. 15–16.

Another statement in the *Circular* (June 4, 1853) simply informs readers that "S. P., having a bad cold and symptoms of a run of fever, tried the criticism cure and was immediately relieved." Krinopathy was also used for more serious illnesses.

Perhaps the most bizarre feature of mutual criticism was the fact that death did not necessarily put a stop to the process! Deceased members whose diaries or letters were found to be incriminating might find themselves being subjected *in absentia* to a "rousing criticism."

Aside from excesses such as the above—and these were the exception rather than the rule—there is no doubt that mutual criticism was beneficial. It was acknowledged to be the most effective type of social control employed by the Community. By its very nature, of course, most criticism was negative: it was aimed at revealing a person's faults. Noyes recognized this fact, and sporadic attempts were made at introducing "commendatory criticism," but the idea never took hold.

In view of the Community's success with mutual criticism, why was the technique never adopted by other groups, or by segments of society at large? The answer seems to be that effective mutual criticism entails certain prerequisites, which may or may not be present in a given subculture. Levine and Bunker write as follows on the subject:

> Mutual criticism, to be effective, requires that the individual being criticized respect the opinions of those who are criticizing. To respect another's opinion, one needs to believe that the criticism comes from a disinterested party, in the sense that the critic is free from personal malice or does not represent some other competing position.
>
> Moreover, the individual receiving criticism should feel safe enough to be receptive to the comments of others, even if hearing them is painful. To feel safe must mean that one believes that the group will continue to regard him as a member and meet his needs, even if the momentary treatment feels harsh.[12]

Economic Communism

One of the distinguishing features of the Oneida Community was their total adherence to economic communism. From beginning to end, they rejected all forms of personal wealth and private property. This was their "definition of the situation," and they never once had second thoughts about it.

[12]Murray Levine and Barbara Benedict Bunker, *Mutual Criticism* (Syracuse, N.Y.: Syracuse University Press, 1975), pp. xxi–xxii.

Everything was jointly owned, including such things as clothes and children's toys. Pierrepont Noyes, a son of the Perfectionist leader, writes:

> Throughout my childhood, the private ownership of anything seemed to me a crude artificiality to which an unenlightened Outside still clung. . . . For instance, we were keen for our favorite sleds, but it never occurred to me that I could possess a sled to the exclusion of the other boys. So it was with all Children's House property.[13]

On the subject of clothes, the same author states, "Going-away clothes for grown folks, as for children, were common property. Any man or woman preparing for a trip was fitted out with one of the suits kept in stock for that purpose."[14]

How did the Oneidans make out financially, in view of the fact that they were operating a communistic economy in a capitalistic society? The answer is, very well. Very well indeed, as we shall see. There are, however, some qualifications.

For the first ten years or so, the Community had more than their share of economic woes. Almost everything they tried seemed to fail. They started in agriculture, but although they had a number of experienced farmers in their midst, they somehow could not compete successfully in the open market. They next tried light manufacturing, turning out such products as outdoor furniture, baskets, slippers, and bags, to no avail. Then came commercialism, and the Perfectionists set about "peddling" such wares as silk thread, pins and needles, and preserved fruits and vegetables. Again they lost money.

A few of the lines showed a small profit, but overall, expenditures outstripped profits year after year. At one time, members agreed to sell their watches in order to reduce losses. In fact, if it had not been for the $108,000 brought in by those who joined the Community, the Oneidans would have gone bankrupt. They were losing an average of $4,000 a year.

They failed for several reasons. In some of their endeavors they lacked experience. In others, they had some unfortunate setbacks, such as a fire which destroyed supplies of goods. But the chief reason for their failure was that they were spread too thin: seven different branches in four different states. Accordingly, Noyes decided to retrench. All the branches were phased out except Oneida and Wallingford—with the bulk of the economic operation remaining at Oneida. As it turned out, this was a wise move. But there was a wiser one just around the corner.

[13]Pierrepont Noyes, *My Father's House,* pp. 126–27.
[14]Ibid.

Traps In 1848, shortly after their founding, the Community admitted to membership one Sewell Newhouse. A north woods hunter and trapper, Newhouse was a legendary figure even before he joined the Perfectionists. More or less a loner, he knew every foot of the wilderness surrounding Oneida Lake. And he knew hunting and trapping. Around Oneida, his fame equaled that of Davy Crockett.

Aided by his prodigious strength, Newhouse made his own traps by using a blacksmith's forge, anvil, and hand punch. He made an excellent product and had no trouble selling his traps to local woodsmen. However, he had no real desire to make money or establish a business, and in between sessions of trap making, he would invariably disappear into the north woods for a prolonged period.

Pierrepont Noyes says about Sewell Newhouse:

> Why he joined, even more why the Community let him join, is a mystery to me. Behind his gnarled face was a gnarled character. Perhaps his wife, whom I remember as a very religious woman, persuaded him and persuaded the community.
>
> When, as a boy, I knew him, he was in his sixties. His face was grim, his whiskers gray, and he moved with a shuffling gait that I associated with the Indians who stole through the forests.
>
> He still seemed a woodsman, something of a hero to a boy. For years he had been allowed to make trapping expeditions to the north woods each winter, and his book, *The Trapper's Guide,* was read and reread to help boys trapping and excite their imagination for Indian scouting in the local woods.[15]

Why Newhouse joined may have been a mystery, but his effect on the Community was indelible. At first, no one thought of using the traps as a basic Community product. Among other things, their manufacture involved a secret process of spring tempering which Newhouse was reluctant to reveal. Under Noyes' patient prodding, however, Sewell Newhouse finally relented, and by the late 1850s, the Oneida Community was turning out traps by the hundreds.

Demand for the product grew rapidly. To meet the orders that were pouring in, the Oneidans were forced to use assembly-line methods. In fact, whenever there was a deadline on a large order, the entire Community—including the children—would pitch in! And even this was not enough. By 1860, the Newhouse trap not only had become standard in the United States and Canada but was being used all over the world. Many professional trappers would use no other brand.

By this time, of course, the Perfectionists could not possibly handle all the orders themselves. They began to hire outside workers, the

[15]Pierrepont Noyes, *A Goodly Heritage* (New York: Rinehart, 1958), pp. 120–21.

number eventually reaching several hundred. The trap factory, located near the Mansion House, developed into a typical industrial plant of the period. By the late 1860s, the Community was turning out close to 300,000 traps a year. During one record-breaking period, they actually manufactured over 22,000 traps in a single week![16]

Interestingly enough, once they had "turned the corner" with the trap business, their other products—canned vegetables and preserved fruit, bags, silk thread—proved to be valuable sidelines. So, too, did their tourist business. As the fame of the Perfectionists grew, the number of visitors—with their admission fees—also grew.

Later on, in 1877, the Community began the manufacture of silverware. Although there were some ups and downs, this business also proved successful. In 1881, when the Community disbanded, the industrial component was perpetuated under the name of Oneida Ltd. These silversmiths have grown and prospered, and their products are in wide use today.

It is often said that John Humphrey Noyes was the indispensable man insofar as the Perfectionists were concerned, an assertion which is doubtless true. Without him, there would have been no Community, and after he was gone the Community fell apart. But one question remains. How successful would Noyes have been if it hadn't been for a crusty old woodsman named Sewell Newhouse?

Self-sufficiency and Ethnocentrism Once trap making had made their economic base secure, the Perfectionist brand of communism worked rather well. The Oneidans built their own home; made all their own clothes, including shoes; did their own laundry; raised their own food; and provided their own services. They did all these things, furthermore, at a remarkably low cost. The *Community's Annual Reports* indicate that the yearly expenditure for food was $24.00 per person, while the corresponding figure for clothing was $10.50![17]

Like the Old Order Amish, the Oneida "family" performed functions that were disappearing from society at large. They provided their own recreation and their own religious services. They ran their own school, and—even though they practiced faith healing and krinopathy occasionally—they had their own doctors and dentists. The Perfectionists also had their own social security benefits,

[16]According to the *Oneida Community Daily Journal* of November 5, 1866, if it hadn't been for a mechanical defect, they would have been able to turn out 80,000 traps that week!

[17]*Bible Communism: A Compilation from the Annual Reports of the Oneida Association* (Brooklyn, N.Y.: Oneida Circular, 1853), p. 16.

which included child care, full employment, old-age assistance, and the like.

Functionally, economically, and socially, the Oneida Perfectionists were close to being a self-sufficient community. This self-sufficiency not only enhanced their in-group solidarity but gave rise to ethnocentric feelings. Sociologically, *ethnocentrism* is the belief that one's own group—with its values, beliefs, and ways of doing things—is superior to other groups. The Oneidans were building the best traps. They were making money. Visitors were flocking to their doors, and there was a steady stream of new applications. Little wonder that John Humphrey Noyes and his followers felt that their way of life was superior to that found on the outside. As one of the members put it, "It was never, in our minds, an experiment. We believed we were living under a system which the whole world would sooner or later adopt."[18]

Working Arrangements On a typical work day, Community members would rise between five and seven-thirty and proceed to the dining hall. Following breakfast, there was a short period of Bible reading, after which members would go to their assigned jobs in the trap factory, the mill, the farm, or elsewhere. A square board with pegs—each peg containing a member's name—was located near the library, and at a glance it was possible to tell each person's whereabouts. Dining hours changed over the years, but the Oneidans came to prefer a two-meal-a-day schedule, with dinner being served from three to four. After dinner there were adult classes in French, algebra, science, and other subjects, followed by the evening meeting. By nine or ten o'clock, most of the Community had retired.

It is difficult to describe the work involvement of the Perfectionists. On the one hand, they were not hard workers as compared, say, to the Amish or the Shakers. The followers of John Humphrey Noyes spent much time on educational matters and business discussions. Also, they tended to jump from one thing to another and were extremely receptive to new ideas.[19]

The Perfectionists also liked to combine the social and the economic. Men and women worked side by side, and there was incessant talking and laughing. During an interview, one former member made the following comments:

[18]The statement was made by Pierrepont Noyes' mother-in-law and is quoted in *My Father's House,* pp. 17–18.

[19]Well ahead of his time, Noyes advocated a six-hour work day! (Robertson, *Oneida Community,* p. 124.)

> As children, we loved to visit the various departments they used to have: the laundry, the kitchen, the fruit cellar, the bakery, the dairy, the tailor shop. The thing is that small groups of people worked side by side in most of these places, and they were able to talk with each other as they worked. It was this sort of thing, year after year, that gave rise to a kindred spirit.

It may well be that the execution of economic tasks through primary-group involvement helped build esprit de corps. But from a realistic business view, this was hardly an efficient method of operation. The fact of the matter is that the Oneidans were not *primarily* interested in the most efficient productive methods. Their primary interest was in the creation of a we-feeling by living as they thought God intended. To this end, they were quite willing to accept a certain efficiency loss.

On the other hand, it should not be thought that the Perfectionists were idlers whose chief preoccupation was socializing. On the contrary, they were good workers. Their methods simply did not include such things as regimentation, time clocks, quotas, and the like. As Constance Noyes Robertson points out, "From the beginning, the Community believed in work; not legally—that is, work forced upon the worker as a duty—but work freely chosen, as they said, 'under inspiration.' "[20]

When there was work to be done, the Oneidans did it—without coercion. For the smaller projects, one of their most effective innovations was a cooperative enterprise known as the bee.

> The bee was an ordinance exactly suited to Community life. One would be announced at dinner or perhaps on the bulletin board: "A bee in the kitchen to pare apples"; or "A bee to pick strawberries at five o'clock tomorrow morning"; or "A bee in the Upper Sitting Room to sew bags."[21]

For the larger tasks—a building project, an influx of visitors, an important industrial order—a much larger proportion of the membership would turn out. All of the above, of course, was in addition to the daily work assignments. Generally speaking, while the Perfectionists never claimed to be a model of economic efficiency, their system worked.

The economic aspects of the Community have been discussed in some detail since most of the other sixty-odd communistic experiments then under way in America failed because of economic difficulties. The followers of John Humphrey Noyes succeeded. In spite of

[20]Ibid., p. 47.
[21]Ibid., p. 103.

the fact that the accumulation of material wealth was not their primary concern, the Oneida Community—at the time it disbanded—was worth some $600,000. In 1881, this was no small amount.

Level of Living On a day-to-day basis, the Perfectionists did not bask in luxury, but neither did they lead a Spartan existence. They ate well, in spite of their dietary prohibitions. They were amply clothed, although, like the Amish, there was no conspicuous consumption. If a man needed a suit, he would go to the Community tailor and—in accordance with a budgetary allotment—get measured for a new one. The same procedure was followed for other needs.

Members could, if they wished, travel or visit on the outside, but few availed themselves of the opportunity. There were too many attractions at home: recreation and entertainment, adult education, a well-stocked library, social and sexual privileges, opportunities for self-expression in the musical and performing arts, physical comforts (the Mansion House even included a Turkish bath)—all this in addition to the spiritual enlightenment provided by John Humphrey Noyes.

Even in the matter of work assignments, the Oneidans were given every consideration. There was no such thing as demeaning labor. A person was respected for the spirit with which he did his work rather than for the work itself. Menial tasks, such as cleaning and mending, were generally rotated. Special skills and abilities, on the other hand, were amply rewarded. Those with writing aptitude were assigned to the Community newspaper, those with a love for children worked in the children's department, and so on.

Pierrepont Noyes cites the following case involving a specialist:

> With one or two assistants, Mr. Van Velzer made all the shoes for the Community. He was a North Vermonter who joined in the early days of the Oneida settlement, and being a specialist in an important department, was one of the few men who never changed jobs.[22]

Robertson cites another case where a member had a hobby of making rustic furniture out of cedar wood.

> Immediately the art of making rustic seats, tables, and chairs for garden use was made a Community project. The product sold so readily that a two-carload lot was sent to Syracuse and sold, and another lot was sent to the State Fair in Utica, where it won a silver medal.[23]

[22]Pierrepont Noyes, *My Father's House,* pp. 119–20.
[23]Robertson, *Oneida Community,* p. 47.

The Oneida Perfectionists were vibrant, moving people, and so was their leader. From the first day at Putney to the last day at Oneida, there was never a dull moment. Wasted activity and too much change of direction, yes—but dullness, no.

Complex Marriage

The world remembers the followers of John Humphrey Noyes not for their social or economic system, but for their practice of complex marriage. Rightly or wrongly, just as the term "Mormon" brings to mind polygamy, so the term "Oneida" conjures up thoughts of the "advanced" sex practices of the Community. It was Noyes himself who coined the phrase "free love," although because of adverse implications the phraseology was discarded in favor of complex marriage.

According to Noyes, it was natural for all men to love all women, and for all women to love all men. He felt that any social institution which flouted this truism was harmful to the human spirit. Romantic love—or "special love," as the Oneidans called it—was harmful because it was a selfish act. Monogamous marriage was harmful because it excluded others from sharing in connubial affection. The answer, obviously, was group marriage, and throughout the whole of their existence, this was what the Oneidans practiced.

Noyes' views on matrimony were also based on biblical interpretation. In the *Bible Argument,* published by the Oneida Community, the following statement appears:

> In the kingdom of heaven, the institution of marriage—which assigns the exclusive possession of one woman to one man—does not exist (Matt. 22:23–30).
>
> In the kingdom of heaven, the intimate union, which in the world is limited to pairs, extends through the whole body of believers. . . . (John 17:21). The new commandment is that we love one another, not by pairs, as in the World, but en masse.[24]

Over and over again, on both secular and religious grounds, John Humphrey Noyes criticized monogamy and extolled the virtues of group marriage.

> The human heart is capable of loving any number of times and any number of persons. This is the law of nature. There is no occasion to find fault with it. Variety is in the nature of things, as beautiful and as useful

[24]Quoted in ibid., p. 267.

in love as in eating and drinking. . . . We need love as much as we need food and clothing, and God knows it; and if we trust Him for those things, why not for love?[25]

Although he did not say it in so many words, Noyes hoped that the sharing of partners would serve as yet another element in the establishment of group solidarity. That he was able to succeed in this realm—despite the fact that the bulk of his followers had Puritan backgrounds—attests to his leadership capacity.

The system of complex marriage was relatively uncomplicated. Sexual relations were easy to arrange inasmuch as all the men and women lived in the Mansion House. If a man desired sexual intercourse with a particular woman, he simply asked her. If she consented, he would go to her room at bedtime and stay overnight. Once in a while, because of a shortage of single rooms, the above arrangements were not practicable, in which case the couple could use one of the "social" rooms set aside for that purpose.

Sexual Regulations Sex is never a simple matter (among humans, at least), and from the very beginning, complex marriage was ringed with prohibitions and restrictions. Other modifications arose over the years. By the early 1860s, a fairly elaborate set of regulations was in force, so that throughout most of the Community's existence, sexual relations were not nearly so "free" and all-encompassing as outsiders believed.

As early as Putney, Noyes taught that sex was not to be considered a "wifely duty"; that is, something accepted by the female to satisfy the male. Later on, the notion was stated in more positive terms, as in the following excerpt from the *Handbook:*

> The liberty of monogamous marriage, as commonly understood, is the liberty of a man to sleep habitually with a woman, liberty to please himself alone in his dealings with her, liberty to expose her to childbearing without care or consultation.
>
> The term Free Love, as understood by the Oneida Community, does *not* mean any such freedom of sexual proceedings. The theory of sexual interchange which governs all the general measures of the Community is that which in ordinary society governs the proceedings in *courtship.*
>
> It is the theory that love *after* marriage should be what it is *before* marriage—a glowing attraction on both sides, and not the odious obligation of one party, and the sensual recklessness of the other. (p. 42)

[25]Quoted in Robert Parker, *A Yankee Saint* (New York: Putnam, 1935), pp. 182–83.

Noyes went to great pains in his discourses to separate the "amative" from the "propagative" functions of sex. It was only when the two were separated, he said, that the true goals of Perfectionism could be attained. In practice, this meant that males could have sexual intercourse up to, but not including, ejaculation. (Females, of course, could achieve sexual climax at any time.)

There were two exceptions to the nonejaculatory rule: (a) when the male was having intercourse with a female who was past menopause, and (b) when a child was desired. Authorization for childbearing involved a special procedure and will be discussed in the following section. However, by permitting males to achieve ejaculation only with postmenopausal females, the Perfectionists not only were employing a novel method of birth control—effective, as it turned out—but were using an ingenious method of providing the older, less attractive women with sex partners.

The *Handbook* also points up the desirability of courtship, and there is no doubt that in the Oneida Community sustained courtship was the order of the day. Men were eager to win the ladies' favor, so they acted accordingly. And the ladies evidently found it refreshing to be wooed by the men. Pierrepont Noyes catches the full flavor of the relationship in the following passage:

> There has survived in my memory an impression, a dim recognition, that the relation between our grown folks had a quality intimate and personal, a quality that made life romantic. Unquestionably, the sexual relations of the members under the Community system inspired a lively interest in each other, but I believe that the opportunity for romantic friendships also played a part in rendering life more colorful than elsewhere.
>
> Even elderly people, whose physical passions had burned low, preserved the fine essence of earlier associations; child as I was, I sensed a spirit of high romance surrounding them, a vivid, youthful interest in life that looked from their eyes and spoke in their voices and manners.[26]

As in society at large, the men were apparently more enthusiastic than the women, at least in a strictly sexual connotation. The practice of having the man ask the woman for sex relations, therefore, was soon replaced by a new system.

Use of a Go-between Under the new system, the man would make his request known to a central member—usually an older woman—who in turn would pass on the request. In practice, the use of a go-between served a number of purposes. It spared the women—it

[26]Pierrepont Noyes, *My Father's House,* p. 131.

was they who suggested the system—the embarrassment of having to voice a direct refusal or conjure up an excuse. As one of the interviewees told me: "Sex relations in the community were always voluntary. There was never any hint at coercion. But after they started using a go-between, it made things easier for everybody."

Employment of a go-between also gave the Community a measure of control over the sexual system. For example, the Perfectionists were ever on guard against two of their members falling in love—special love, as they called it. So if a particular couple were having too-frequent relations, the go-between would simply disallow further meetings between them. In the matter of procreation, too, it was important that the Community be able to establish paternity. And while this was not always possible, the go-between greatly facilitated the identification process.

It should be mentioned that the Oneidans considered sex to be a private matter. Aside from the particular go-between involved, "who was having relations with whom" never became common knowledge. Indeed, the subject itself was taboo. Public displays of affection, vulgarity of any kind, sexual discussions or innuendoes, immodest behavior—all were forbidden. During the many decades of their existence, the Perfectionists had but one unpleasant experience along these lines.

William Mills was accepted into the Community during the early 1860s. A rather vulgar person, it soon became obvious that he was a misfit. The women would have nothing to do with him. As a consequence, he started to cultivate the friendship of teen-age girls. Breaking the Perfectionist taboo, Mills would discuss sexual matters openly with them, asking them about their amours and boasting of his own. The situation soon became intolerable, and he was asked to leave. He refused. The central members were in a quandary: from time to time others had been requested to leave, but none had ever refused. After several discussions, it was decided—in an almost literal sense—to take the bull by the horns. According to Robert Parker:

> Mills found himself, one winter night, suddenly, unceremoniously, and horizontally propelled through an open window, and shot—harmlessly but ignominiously—into the depths of a snowdrift. It was the first and only forcible expulsion in the history of the community.[27]

Taken collectively, the regulations concerning sex were designed to permit maximum freedom for the individual without jeopardizing the harmony of the group as a whole. This involved a delicate balance

[27]Parker, *Yankee Saint,* p. 223.

of rights and responsibilities, and Noyes was well aware of this fact. He strove mightily to keep sex "within bounds," and whenever there were excesses he moved to correct them.

To take one example, the original procedure had been for the man to go to the woman's room and remain all night. Some of the women evidently complained that the practice was too "tiring," and Noyes saw to it that a change was made. Henceforth, the man would stay for an hour or so and then return to his own room. This was the procedure followed throughout most of the Community's existence.

Along these same lines, the Perfectionist leader constantly inveighed against the so-called fatiguing aspects of sexual intercourse. Instead of advocating *coitus reservatus,* for instance, he could have endorsed *coitus interruptus*—both being equally effective as birth-control techniques. But Noyes was convinced that ejaculation had a debilitating effect on the male; hence he preached against its danger.

He was also against *coitus interruptus* on theological grounds, since the practice is condemned in the Bible. That is, when Onan had intercourse with his deceased brother's wife, he refused to ejaculate in natural fashion. Instead, he "spilled it on the ground, lest that he should give seed to his brother. And the thing which he did displeased the Lord" (Gen. 38:9–10).

Additionally, Noyes totally rejected all forms of contraception. For reasons best known to himself, he looked upon them as "machinations of the French" and refused even to consider them. To be acceptable, birth control had to include a strong element of (male) self-control.

Interestingly enough—and in spite of some rather questionable logic—John Humphrey Noyes' ideas about sex and birth control proved workable. His goal was to provide complex marriage with a spiritual base, and he apparently succeeded. Throughout the whole of the Community's existence, there were no elopements, no orgies, no exhibitionism. Nor was there any instance of homosexuality, sadism, masochism, or any other sexual activity that would have been considered reprehensible by the standards then current.

Ascending Fellowship Complex marriage did pose one problem that Noyes went to great pains to solve: how to keep the older, less attractive members of the community from being bypassed in favor of the younger members. True, it was only with postmenopausal women that men were allowed to achieve ejaculation, but this restriction provided an inadequate answer to the problem. The real answer was to be found in the principle of ascending fellowship.

According to this principle, members were ranked from least to most perfect. Any follower who wished to improve himself, therefore, was advised to associate with someone higher on the spiritual scale. (Noyes taught that a high-ranking person would not in any way be downgraded by associating with a person of lower rank.) Since it took time and experience to achieve high spiritual rank, those at the upper end of the scale were nearly always the older, more mature members. It was these older Perfectionists rather than the younger members who were thus held up as the desirable partners.

The Oneida *Handbook* contains the following explanation:

> According to the Principle of Ascending Fellowship, it is regarded as better—in the early stages of passional experience—for the young of both sexes to associate in love with persons older than themselves, and if possible with those who are spiritual and have been some time in the school of self-control—and who are thus able to make love safe and edifying.
>
> This is only another form of the popular principle of contrasts. It is well understood by physiologists that it is undesirable for persons of similar character and temperament to mate together. Communists have discovered that it is undesirable for two inexperienced and unspiritual persons to rush into fellowship with each other; that it is better for both to associate with persons of mature character and sound sense. (p. 39)

There is no doubt that age was shown great respect in the Community. This is the way Noyes wanted it, and this is the way it was. In addition, the fact that younger men were encouraged to have sexual relations with older women served to strengthen the birth-control measures that were used.

Unanswered Questions About Complex Marriage

The foregoing pages give the broad outlines of the sexual system employed by the Oneidans. But many questions remain unanswered. To what extent did the women refuse sexual requests? Was a go-between really used, or was this a formality which was easily bypassed? Did women as well as men initiate sexual requests? Was not the factor of male jealousy a problem? Did the Community women have difficulty adjusting sexually to a large number of different partners? I have attempted to find answers to these questions, but with limited success. One of those interviewed made the following points:

> I grant the questions are of sociological interest, but look at it from our view. If somebody came to you and asked questions concerning the sex

> life of your parents and grandparents, you'd have a tough time answering. The same with us. When the old Community broke up, there was a natural reluctance to discuss sex. Former members didn't discuss their own sex lives, and naturally their children and grandchildren didn't pry.
>
> I often wish the old people had had a regular system of marriage. Then we wouldn't have had such bad publicity—most of it incorrect or misleading. If it weren't for the sex part, the Oneida Community might have been forgotten long ago.

One of the officers of Oneida Ltd. supplied some interesting information. During the decades of the Community's existence, many of the Oneidans were in the habit of keeping diaries. (Diary keeping was evidently much more common in the nineteenth century than it is today.) Some of the Perfectionists also accumulated bundles of personal letters. After the Community broke up, and as the members died over the years, the question arose as to what to do with all these documents. Since so much of the material was of a personal and sexual nature, since names were named, and inasmuch as the people's children and grandchildren were still living, it was decided to store all the old diaries, letters, and other personal documents in the vaults of Oneida Ltd. Several years ago, this officer received permission to examine the material in order to see what should be done with it.

> I went through some of the stuff—old diaries and things—and a lot of it was awfully personal. Names and specific happenings were mentioned—that kind of thing. Anyway, I reported these facts to the company, and it was decided that in view of the nature of the material, it should all be destroyed.
>
> So, one morning we got a truck—and believe me, there was so much stuff we needed a truck—loaded all the material on, and took it out to the dump and burned it. We felt that divulging the contents wouldn't have done ourselves or anybody else any good.

While there is no doubt that the burned material would have shed much light on the sexual behavior of the Perfectionists, the action taken by the company is understandable. Oneida Ltd. is not in business to further the cause of sociological research, and regardless of how much the material might have benefited social scientists, there was always the possibility that the contents would have proved embarrassing to the company or to some of the direct descendants.

The diary-burning episode has been mentioned in some detail in order to show how difficult it is to answer sexual questions of the kind posed above. The interview information presented here should be thought of as a series of clues rather than as a set of definitive answers.

To what extent did the Oneida women refuse sexual requests? The company official who had examined some of the material to be burned reported that there was nothing therein to suggest a high refusal rate. Another male respondent stated that he had been informed by an old Community member that the man "had never been refused." One female interviewee felt that refusal was a problem "in some instances." Most of those interviewed, however, had no specific information to offer. My impression is that female refusal was not a major problem, although the issue probably arose from time to time.

Was a go-between really used, or was this a formality which was easily bypassed? None of those interviewed had any direct evidence to offer. All that can be said is that there were no *reported* instances where the rule was broken. Since the matter was never raised by the Oneidans themselves, it is doubtful whether a real issue was involved. Given the religious orientation and esprit de corps of the members, there is every reason to suppose that the stipulated procedure was followed.

Did the Oneida women, as well as the men, initiate sexual requests? This question drew a generally negative answer from all the respondents. Several said they knew of some coquetry on the part of certain women, but they had never heard of anything more direct. Two of the older female respondents stated that there was one known case where a woman went to a man and asked to have a child by him. In this instance, however, the implication is not clear, since the Perfectionists differentiated sharply between amative and procreative aspects of sex. All reports considered, it appears that the Oneida females were no more disposed to assume the role of active partner than were females in society at large.

Was male jealousy a problem? Apparently not; at least, none of the interviewees knew of any major flareups. One respondent said:

> I don't think it was much of a problem. Certainly the old folks, when they talked about the Community, never made any issue of it. Their religious teachings emphasized spiritual equality, and their whole way of life was aimed at stamping out feelings of jealousy.
>
> Also, with so many women to choose from, why would a man experience feelings of jealousy? Once in a while a man and woman would be suspected of falling in love—"special love" they called it—but it happened infrequently. When it did, the couple were separated. One would be sent to Wallingford, Connecticut—we had a small branch there.

Noyes himself constantly preached against the dangers of male jealousy. On one occasion, he remarked, "No matter what his other qualifications may be, if a man cannot love a woman and be happy seeing her loved by others, he is a selfish man, and his place is with the potsherds of the earth."[28] On another occasion—referring to a man who was becoming romantically involved with a particular woman—he said, "You do not love her, you love happiness."[29]

It is likely that male jealousy was at most a minor problem, though it did receive a certain amount of attention. Female jealousy was evidently no problem at all. It was not mentioned by any of those interviewed, nor, so far as I could ascertain, was the matter ever raised during the Community's existence.

Did the women of the Community have difficulty in adjusting sexually to a large number of different partners? Respondents had little or nothing to report on this matter—which is unfortunate, since the question is an intriguing one. The Oneida women were encouraged to have sex with a variety of men but were not supposed to become emotionally involved with any of them.

The average American woman tends to emotionalize and romanticize her sexual experience, and the Perfectionist system—in which monogamous love played no part in the sex act—might well seem incongruous to her. In the case of the Oneida women, one can but conjecture. If they were indeed gratified by sexual variety, all human experience would be in for a contradiction. And yet, given the prevailing system—and their willingness to follow Noyes' teachings—who is to say what feminine feelings really were?

The Eugenics Program

Since John Humphrey Noyes had so many other "advanced" ideas about life on earth, it was predictable that he would not overlook the subject of children. His views on the matter, however, shocked even those who were used to his radicalism, and little wonder! Not since Plato's *Republic* had such utopian ideas been expounded. Noyes' plans, moreover—unlike those of the Greek philosopher—were more than just words on paper. He both preached them and put them into practice.

It will be remembered that Noyes introduced *coitus reservatus,* or male continence, to spare the Oneida women from being plagued with unwanted children—as they were in the world at large. He also felt that the Oneidans needed time to prove themselves—in both a financial and social sense—before children were permitted.

[28] W. T. Hedden, "Communism in New York, 1848–1879," *The American Scholar,* 14 (Summer 1945): 287.

[29] Quoted in Raymond L. Muncy, *Sex and Marriage in Utopian Communities* (Bloomington: Indiana University Press, 1973), p. 176.

Accordingly, when the Community was founded, the Perfectionist leader announced that there would be no children until further notice. As it turned out, "further notice" stretched for a period of twenty years (1848–1868), during which time the prohibition remained in effect.

From the beginning, Noyes' critics scoffed at his ideas about male continence. No man could practice such restraint for very long, they argued. The system was bound to fail; as proof they pointed to the large number of infants and children in the Community during the period the ban was in effect. In fact, by the Oneidans' own count there were then 135 children living in the community.

But the critics were wrong. *Coitus reservatus* did work, and the ban on children was effective—not 100 percent, to be sure, but effective nevertheless. The reason for so many children in the Community was that most of the couples who joined had children. Also, in those cases where women were nearing menopause, and hence would be unable to wait for the ban on children to be lifted, Noyes would sometimes give special maternity authorization. And, understandably, there were a few accidents of birth. But from 1848 to 1868—the period of the ban—there was an average of only one or two children born a year.

By the late 1860s, it was evident to both John Humphrey Noyes and the general membership that the ban should be lifted. There was much discussion within the Community, and the Perfectionists wondered when the announcement would be made and what form it would take. On his part, Noyes had given the matter a great deal of thought. He was ready to lift the ban on children, but he was not ready to endorse a system of uncontrolled births such as that found in the World.

Some inkling of what the Perfectionist leader had in mind was evident from his earlier works. In his *Bible Communism,* written during 1848, he stated:

> We are opposed to excessive, and of course oppressive procreation, which is unavoidable in the marriage system. But we are in favor of intelligent, well-ordered procreation. The physiologists say that the race cannot be raised from ruin until propagation is made a matter of science; but they point out no way of making it so.
>
> Procreation is controlled and reduced to a science in the case of valuable domestic brutes; but marriage and fashion forbid any such system among human beings. We believe the time will come when involuntary and random propagation will be applied to human generation as freely and as successfully as it is to that of other animals.[30]

[30]Quoted in Parker, *Yankee Saint,* pp. 253–54.

During the next twenty years, John Humphrey Noyes read widely on the subject. He studied Francis Galton's works on hereditary improvement. He read Charles Darwin's *On the Origin of Species.* And the more he thought about it, the more he became convinced that a scientific breeding program could be adapted to the needs of the Oneida Community. Although the word "eugenics" was unknown—it was coined by Galton in 1883—eugenics was precisely what Noyes had in mind. In 1869, the Perfectionists embarked on their program, the first systematic attempt at eugenics in man's history.

Stirpiculture Noyes called his program "stirpiculture" (from the Latin *stirps,* meaning root, stock, or lineage), and from its inception there was no doubt about the goals, methods, or enthusiasm involved. The goal was crystal clear: biological improvement of the Oneida Community. In the words of the *Circular:*

> Why should not beauty and noble grace of person and every other desirable quality of men and women, internal and external, be propagated and intensified beyond all former precedent by the application of the same scientific principles of breeding that produce such desirable results in the case of sheep, cattle, and horses?[31]

The methods were also made explicit: only certain persons would be permitted to become parents. The selection would be made by a stirpiculture committee, headed by Noyes, and the committee's decision would be final. There would be no appeal. And even though this meant that the majority of Oneidans might never become parents, there was no objection from the membership. On the contrary, the Perfectionists endorsed every facet of the program.

Oneida women signed the following resolution:

> That we do not belong to ourselves in any respect, but first to God, and second to Mr. Noyes as God's true representative.
>
> That we have no rights or personal feelings in regard to child-bearing . . . that we will cheerfully renounce all desire to become mothers if, for any reason, Mr. Noyes deems us unfit material for propagation.[32]

A parallel statement was signed by the men:

> We most heartily sympathize with your purpose in regard to scientific propagation, and offer ourselves to be used in forming any combinations that seem desirable to you. We claim no rights. We ask no privileges. . . . We are your true soldiers.[33]

[31]Quoted in Robertson, *Oneida Community,* p. 341.
[32]Quoted in Parker, *Yankee Saint,* p. 257.
[33]Ibid.

At the start of the eugenics program, fifty-three women and thirty-eight men were chosen to be parents. Over the years others were added, so that eventually about one hundred members took part in the experiment. Approximately 80 percent of those who took part actually achieved parenthood. During the decade or so the program was in effect, sixty-two children were born, including four stillbirths.

Interestingly enough, there were also a dozen or so accidental conceptions, a rather high figure in view of the supposed effectiveness of *coitus reservatus.* Despite their pledge, a few of the "unchosen" women evidently did their best to achieve parenthood, with some success. I was informed, for instance, of a passage in one of the burned diaries in which a man—referring to his sexual encounter with a particular woman—said, "She tried to make me lose control." In general, though, both the men and women who were bypassed seem to have accepted their lot willingly enough.

The precise method of selection used by the stirpiculture committee was never revealed. Throughout most of its existence the committee was composed of central members, and presumably they judged applicants on the basis of physical and mental qualities. Most of the candidates applied as couples, although on occasion the committee suggested certain combinations.

While it was never explicitly stated, John Humphrey Noyes was undoubtedly the chief figure in the stirpiculture process. The concept was his, the committee was his, and it was he who served as chief judge and policy maker. The records show, for example, that the fathers were much older than the mothers, a fact which reflects the principle of ascending fellowship. Noyes felt strongly that the qualities necessary for fatherhood could only be acquired through age and experience. And while this was an erroneous, Lamarckian view, it was adhered to. In fact, a number of men in their sixties were chosen as stirpicults. Noyes himself fathered at least ten of the children, so that evidently he was not averse to self-selection. The principle of ascending fellowship was less applicable to women, naturally, because of the menopause factor.

What were the results of the stirpiculture program? Was it successful? Were the offspring really superior? Most observers thought so. During the entire program, no defective children were ever born, no mothers ever lost. As compared to children on the outside, the Oneida youngsters had a markedly lower death rate. A number of them went on to achieve eminence in the business and professional worlds. Several wrote books. And nearly all of them, in turn, had children who were a credit to the Community. How much of the program's success was due to the eugenic factor will never be known, of course, since the children presumably had a favorable environment *as well as* sound heredity.

Perhaps the only disappointing feature of the stirpiculture program was the fact that so few children were born. The program ran for a little over ten years, and some one hundred men and women took part. In view of the high birth rate which prevailed during the 1870s, the fact that the stirpicults produced only fifty-eight live children is difficult to understand. *Coitus reservatus,* practiced by the Oneida males for so many years, may have had an unaccountable effect on their fertility, though this may be a far-fetched explanation.

The evidence suggests simply that Noyes was fearful of the effects of multiple childbirth on the health of women. His own wife, in the pre-Oneida period, had had four stillbirths, and his entire philosophy of life had been shaped by her experience. Nearly all the female stirpicults, for example, were authorized to have but one child. A handful had two children, and only two women had three. If there were other reasons for the Perfectionists' low birth rate, they have not come to light.

Child Rearing

According to Noyes' teachings, all adults were supposed to love all children and vice versa, and the entire program of Community child rearing was based on this philosophy. Excessive love between children and their own parents was called "stickiness" and was strongly discouraged. In fact, the love between men and women (the amative) apparently took precedence over that between parents and children (the philoprogenitive), as the following account indicates:

> At one time, after "discussion and investigation of the parental relation," the Community drew up a list of General Principles. The first of these principles may shock the modern child-centered parent. "The love and care of children in parents should not supplant nor interfere with their love as man and woman. Amativeness takes precedence over philoprogenitiveness, and parental feeling becomes a usurpation when it crowds out a passion which is relatively its superior."[34]

In practice, Oneida children were anything but neglected. For the first fifteen months they were under the care of their own mothers. After that, the youngsters were moved to the Children's House, where

[34]Constance Noyes Robertson, *Oneida Community Profiles* (Syracuse, N.Y.: Syracuse University Press, 1977), p. 144.

they were raised communally. There they were taught to treat all Community adults as they would their own parents, and there they received their formal education. There too they were introduced to John Humphrey Noyes' brand of Perfectionism.

A fair amount of published material exists on the Community child-rearing program. I uncovered some additional data during my interview-study. Evidence from both sources indicates that the program was patently successful. The following question-and-answer session —although totally imaginary—is based on factual information. The answers are those which a Community spokesman might have given, say, in the 1870s.

Q. Where do the Oneida children live?
A. In the Children's House. Originally this was a separate building. However, in 1870 a south wing was added to the Mansion House, and the children have been there ever since.
Q. Do the youngsters have their own facilities?
A. Yes. The south wing was designed with this in mind. The children have their own nursery, sleeping quarters, schoolrooms, playrooms, and so forth.
Q. Who is in charge of the children?
A. I suppose you could say the whole Community. But if you mean who is in charge of the Children's House, there are a dozen or more adults whose full-time job is looking after the youngsters.
Q. Are all these adults women?
A. No. Most of them are, but we do believe in having a show of male authority.
Q. What about the children's education?
A. They are taught the same subjects as other children. But they also receive an equal amount of on-the-job training, in the various departments. And when we have a bee, they often join in like everybody else.
Q. Do you use outside teachers?
A. No, we have our own.
Q. Do the children like school?
A. Do children anywhere?
Q. How is their religious instruction handled?
A. They meet for an hour a day—in prayer, Bible reading, discussions of Perfectionism, confession of faults, and so forth.
Q. How do the children like this type of training? Is it effective?
A. The only thing they like about it is when the hour is over! At the same time, whether they like it or not, we think it is effective.
Q. Do they have their own dining facilities?
A. No. We believe in bringing them into the life of the Community as early as possible. After the age of two, they eat in the regular dining room. And after the age of ten, they are permitted to sit at the same tables as adults.

Q. Do the children have their own toys and playthings?
A. No. Everything is shared. Since we believe in communism, we feel that the sooner they get the idea the better.
Q. But doesn't this lead to fights?
A. Certainly, at least on the part of the boys. It's surprising, though, how quickly they learn to renounce all forms of private property.
Q. Do the youngsters know who their real parents are?
A. Of course.
Q. Whose name do they take?
A. Their fathers'.
Q. Are they permitted to associate with their parents?
A. Oh, yes. They spend a certain amount of time with their parents every week. However, we try to get the children to think of all Oneida adults as their parents.
Q. Doesn't this work a hardship on the children? Isn't there a natural desire to establish a bond of personal affection?
A. Perhaps so. It depends on how a child is conditioned. We think that under our system, a young person gets more love and understanding than on the outside.
Q. It's hard to believe the Oneida youngsters don't yearn for their own parents.
A. Well, one little girl did. She would stand outside her mother's window and call to her, even though her mother wasn't supposed to answer. That was an exceptional case, however.
Q. And you contend that under the Perfectionist system, the children are happy?
A. We do. But why not ask them?
Q. Do you not have problems of discipline?
A. Of course, and both the adults and the children spend a good deal of time discussing the matter. On the whole—since we're a tightly knit group—we probably have fewer disciplinary problems than they do on the outside.
Q. There are reports that Oneida children are afraid of visitors . . .
A. As a matter of fact, some of the younger children are. They usually grow out of it, but we're not entirely satisfied with that end of it.
Q. Are the adult members of the Community happy at being separated from their children?
A. Well, they knew the rules when they joined. However, they are not really separated. They have the love of their children and the pleasure of their company, without the day-to-day burden that plagues most parents.
Q. Is there any likelihood that the Perfectionists will ever change their system of child rearing?
A. None whatsoever. As far as we're concerned, the system has proved itself. It's here to stay.

The End of the Road

All good things must come to an end—or at least, so it must have seemed to the Oneidans by the late 1870s. John Humphrey Noyes had been expounding his Perfectionist views for almost fifty years. Communal living—at both Putney and Oneida—had been successfully practiced for more than forty years. There was no doubt that, sociologically, the Perfectionists had established a genuine subculture. But now the currents were going against them. There was no single reason. The causes ran together like foam on the ocean. Nevertheless, the tide was inexorable.

Outside Pressures By and large, outsiders who lived in the vicinity of Oneida were favorably disposed toward the Community. The Perfectionists were known to be honest, industrious, and law-abiding. Moreover, as time went on, Oneida was recognized as a growing source of employment. Unfortunately, as their fame grew, so did their "notoriety." Free love, complex marriage, scientific breeding—such things were more than nineteenth-century America could accept. And so the pressure grew—from isolated editorials and sermons in the 1860s to a concentrated barrage in the 1870s. Two of the attackers, in particular, are worthy of mention.

Anthony Comstock, self-appointed watchdog of American morals, was in a special position to hurt the Oneidans. Congressman from New York, he sponsored the omnibus state law forbidding immoral works. He also organized the New York Society for the Suppression of Vice. Most important, in 1873 he persuaded Congress to enact a federal obscenity bill which, among other things, forbade the dissemination of all literature dealing with birth control. As fanatical a reformer as the country had ever seen, Comstock succeeded in tarring the Perfectionists with the brush of vice and obscenity. His followers found the Community an easy—and rather defenseless—target.

Less well known than Comstock, but even more effective, was Professor John Mears of Hamilton College. Whereas Comstock was against "obscenity" in any form, Mears' sole obsession was the Oneida Community. Week after week he wrote to the newspapers, gave public talks, and preached Sunday sermons—all against the "debaucheries" being practiced by John Humphrey Noyes and his followers. Typical of his newspaper pieces was the following:

> Here in the heart of the Empire State is an institution avowedly at war with the foundation principles of our domestic and civil order, a set of men banded together for the purpose of practicing shameful immorali-

> ties, and leading the young of both sexes who unfortunately happen to come under their care into impure and shocking practices. . . .
>
> The people of Illinois could not endure the immorality of the Mormons, but drove them from Nauvoo in 1846, and compelled them to take refuge a thousand miles from the outskirts of civilization. Thus was polygamy treated; while the far more corrupt concubinage of the Oneida Community luxuriates in the heart of New York State, is visited by throngs of the curious, by picnic parties organized for this purpose, and even by Sunday School excursions.[35]

Methodists, Presbyterians, Baptists, Congregationialists—all took up the cry. Committees were appointed, conferences held, legal action demanded. Anthony Comstock's help was solicited. And while some editorials were fair, others joined in the diatribe against the Oneidans. Meanwhile, back at the Community . . .

Internal Pressures All was not well. Dissent was not only in the air; it was stalking the corridors and invading the rooms. Behind closed doors, small groups of Perfectionists voiced their complaints. And while there is no doubt that outside pressures were a contributing factor, it was the internal dissension which really destroyed the Community.

To begin with, the nature of Perfectionism was changing. The deeply religious orientation gave way to an emphasis on social science, then in its infancy. Bible reading and sermons were superseded by talks on self-improvement and social engineering. Noyes himself seems to have initiated the trend, announcing in the *Circular* that that publication would no longer be a "strictly religious" paper.[36] While there were some in the Community who went along with the change, others—particularly those in the older age groups—felt that the whole basis of their life was being violated.

Problems, too, were arising with the young people. They resented the principle of ascending fellowship. Young men, in particular, objected to being paired off sexually with the older women. Those of both sexes who failed to qualify for parenthood took umbrage at the fact. Acceptance of John Humphrey Noyes as the ultimate authority came to be resented by the young men, especially those who went to college and returned to live in the Community. Not unnaturally, they demanded a larger role in the decision-making process.

The Townerites At the evening meeting of April 21, 1874, Noyes made an important announcement. (How important, even he did not

[35]Quoted in Parker, *Yankee Saint,* p. 268.

[36]Ibid., p. 274.

realize.) Twelve new members—remnants of the defunct Free Love Society of Cleveland—were being admitted into the Community. Their leader was a minister-turned-lawyer, James W. Towner.

A man of some talent, Towner became a divisive force almost immediately. Those with complaints—a growing number, it seems—found him a ready listener. And although a majority of the Perfectionists remained loyal to John Humphrey Noyes, Towner succeeded in winning over a fair minority of the membership. In retrospect, he seems to have been a "shrewd operator" who was out to gain control of the Community for his own ends. While he failed in the attempt, he succeeded in dividing the Oneidans into two factions, Noyesites and Townerites.

The Townerites complained that Noyes was too autocratic, and they wanted an equal voice. While the entire story is much too long to relate here, an important part centered on a strictly sexual matter.[37]

According to the principle of ascending fellowship, young people were required to have their first sexual encounter with the older, more spiritual members of the Community. Noyes evidently reserved for himself the right to initiate the young girls, although as he grew older he sometimes delegated the authority to one of the central members. However, the Townerites questioned his authority to make the decision, and the controversy became bitter.

Although Noyes exercised the rights of "first husband" for many years, he did so only with girls who had reached menarche (first menstruation). The catch was that some of the girls reached menarche at a very early age—as low as ten in some instances, with a range of ten to eighteen, and an average age of thirteen.[38] The Perfectionist leader's exercise of first husband rights, therefore, provided the Townerites with a powerful weapon. If legal charges were brought, Noyes could be accused of statutory rape; in fact, Towner was rumored to be gathering evidence against the Perfectionist leader. Towner denied the allegation, but the argument continued.

Lack of Leadership Where was John Humphrey Noyes all this time? As Comstock and Mears mounted their attacks, as internal dissension mounted, as Towner succeeded in tearing the Community apart —what was the Perfectionist leader doing? Unbelievable as it may

[37]For an excellent analysis of the controversy, see Constance Noyes Robertson, *Oneida Community: The Breakup, 1876–1881* (Syracuse, N.Y.: Syracuse University Press, 1972).

[38]Ely Van de Warker, "A Gynecological Study of the Oneida Community," *American Journal of Obstetrics and Diseases of Women and Children,* 17 (August 1884):795.

seem, the answer is: nothing. After battling all his life for what he believed in, John Humphrey Noyes—for no known reason—seemed to give up. He left the Community for extended periods of time, and even when he was there he seemed to withdraw more and more from a position of active leadership. Little by little, the central members were permitted to make both operational and policy decisions. Unfortunately, they were not qualified to do so.

The Perfectionist leader not only withdrew from Community life, but the decisions he did make were disastrous. He permitted Towner to join, probably the worst decision of his entire career. He changed the Community's focus from the sacred to the secular—another misjudgment. And he made no provision for succession of leadership, other than to recommend his son Theodore for the job—still another bad decision. It was not only Noyes' spirit that waned, but his judgment as well.

The Breakup In 1877, Noyes resigned. One of his last acts was to appoint a committee to succeed him, headed by Theodore, who actually directed the Community for the next few years. But the group was too far gone to be saved by anyone—least of all by Theodore.

On June 22, 1879, John Humphrey Noyes left the Oneida Community, never to return. He left secretly in the middle of the night, aided by a few close friends. And he left for the same reason that he had fled Putney thirty-two years earlier: to escape the law.

Noyes felt that Mears or the Townerites were about to bring charges against him on grounds of statutory rape, and in view of his vulnerability he decided to leave New York State. Actually, he may have been overcautious. The Townerites could hardly have brought charges inasmuch as they were guilty of the same offense. And since Mears was exceedingly unpopular in the Community, he could hardly have gathered the necessary evidence. Nevertheless, Noyes left for Canada where—through emissaries—he kept in touch with Oneida.

In August, he sent word to the Community recommending that they abandon the practice of complex marriage. The recommendation satisfied both the Noyesites and the Townerites and passed without a dissenting voice. Shortly thereafter, a large number of monogamous marriages took place within the Community. Where it was possible, mothers married the fathers of their children. In the case of some of the younger women, Noyes more or less arranged the marriages.

For a while, the Oneidans continued to live communally, but it was clear to both insiders and outsiders that the end was imminent. Dissension prevailed. The aging Noyes remained more or less isolated in Canada. No new leader appeared. During 1880, plans for dissolution were discussed and approved, and on January 1, 1881, the Oneida Community officially ceased to exist.

The Aftermath

Although the group dissolved itself, it did not—in a literal sense—go out of business. For in spite of the wrangling and dissension mentioned above, the economic side of the Community held up surprisingly well—its net worth was $600,000. At the time of dissolution, a joint-stock company was formed—Oneida Ltd.—and the stock was apportioned among the members.

Like most business organizations, Oneida Ltd. has had its ups and downs. On the whole, however, the company has grown and prospered. For the first fifty years or so, the enterprise was managed—in whole or in part—by Pierrepont Noyes, a son of John Humphrey and an extremely able businessman. It was under his direction that the company phased out the traps and concentrated on silverware.

In 1960, P. T. Noyes—son of Pierrepont and grandson of John Humphrey—took over the presidency. And in 1967, the company was accepted for listing on the New York Stock Exchange—with the simple designation "Oneida." During the late 1970s, under the direction of John Marcellus, the company diversified: copper wire and cooking utensils were added to the silverware lines. Today Oneida Ltd. is a worldwide organization with thousands of employees and net sales of over $300 million a year. Its future looks promising.[39]

What about the other phases of Community life following the breakup? A few members left the area entirely, never to return. A handful of the older members went to Canada, where they could be near their former leader. Towner's influence declined sharply, and a year after the breakup he and some twenty-five of his followers left for California. Many of them prospered, although they made no attempt to live communally. Towner eventually became a county court judge.

John Humphrey Noyes stayed in Canada with a few of the faithful. Most of his time was spent in Bible reading and—most likely—reminiscing. He died in 1886, at the age of seventy-four. He was buried at Oneida in the Community cemetery, his simple headstone identical to all the others.

Most of the ex-Perfectionists remained in the Oneida area. Some

[39] *Financial World,* June 15, 1980, pp. 27–28. See also the *Oneida Daily Dispatch,* May 28, 1981, pp. 1, 14.

stayed on in the Mansion House, in private apartments. Others moved to nearby houses. The majority of the men retained their positions with Oneida Ltd., many becoming officers, a pattern which has persisted down to the present. The Mansion House, over the years, served as a kind of social headquarters for the Oneidans and their descendants. While the social function today is minimal—an occasional wedding, a funeral, an anniversary celebration—the building is still in excellent condition. It contains apartments, a dining hall, a library, a museum, and—if one knows where to look—some fascinating memories.

The Oneida Community: A Contemporary Assessment

Was Oneida a success or a failure, a rewarding venture or a waste of time? Was John Humphrey Noyes a genius, an egomaniac, or simply a religious eccentric? Writers collided over these questions a hundred years ago—when the Community was still in existence—and there is still disagreement. Perhaps there always will be.

In a sociological sense, the Perfectionists were anything but failures. They not only lived together, communally, for many decades, but developed an economic base that was strong enough to spawn a multimillion-dollar corporation. Furthermore, they were able to provide society at large with a genuinely new perspective.

According to Melvin Tumin, *cultural relativism* is the sociological doctrine "which holds that no judgments of comparative value or worth can be made about different culture patterns, because each has its own integrity and rationale for its own members. The doctrine also applies to differing moral standards within a culture, or to subcultures within the larger culture."[40] As a distinct subculture, the Oneida Community provides a good example of the significance of cultural relativism. That is, when the Community was flourishing, most Americans did not agree with the Perfectionist value system. Noyes' brand of communism, after all, had limited appeal. At the same time, it drove home to many Americans—firsthand—*the realization that there were viable life-styles other than their own.*

This lesson is not lost even today. Students who read about the Oneida Perfectionists surely have a keener awareness of a completely different way of life. Most of us show little willingness to relinquish personal property, renounce conjugal love, or reject par-

[40]Melvin Tumin, *Patterns of Society* (Boston: Little, Brown, 1973), p. 417.

enthood. Yet if one gives some serious thought to the Oneidans, their life-style becomes—if not attractive—at least understandable. Through understanding comes tolerance, the great lesson of cultural relativism.

John Humphrey Noyes

Interest in John Humphrey Noyes continues, year after year, decade after decade, for he remains one of the most controversial figures in the history of American religious thought. Robert Thomas writes that

> the tempo of this interest has increased in the past decade or so, and no wonder, since Noyes would undoubtedly have found a niche in the welter of reform and communal movements that emerged out of the tumultuous decade of the 1960's. The debates over sex roles and family life, the proliferation of urban and rural utopian visions and experiments, and the emergence of a secularized Perfectionism would have seemed familiar to him.
>
> Some writers have treated Noyes leniently, praising him for his prescience, idolizing him as a "Yankee Saint." Others have been less charitable, branding him as a Vermont Casanova. . . . These categorical versions of Noyes' life and work, however, do not encompass the complexity of the man, and because he is both interesting and important, his life and work are worthy of further consideration.[41]

Noyes is controversial not only because of his social and theological radicalism, but because of the difficulty in characterizing him as a person. On the one hand, he was capricious, unpredictable, and given to making errors in judgment. On the other hand, he was an original thinker, a sound judge of human nature, and an exceedingly wise man. Little wonder that social historians have been hard pressed to depict the "real" John Humphrey Noyes.

It was often difficult to tell just what the Perfectionist leader was going to do next. Plans and projects were begun, and then—with no warning—were abandoned for something new. At one time, Noyes laid plans for a Community-sponsored university, and the Perfectionists were fascinated by the idea. The plans were dropped abruptly, with no reason given. After spending virtually his entire life in the service of the Lord, Noyes suddenly turned his efforts to something called social science, then in its infancy. A short time later he was attracted to spiritualism—communication with the dead—and for a while seances and mediums became part of the Mansion House repertoire.

[41]Thomas, *The Man Who Would Be Perfect,* p. ix.

When his career is viewed as a whole, however, his attributes seem to have dwarfed his failings. His changeableness was not a serious defect. And while he made some serious judgmental errors, they occurred mainly in his declining years—when he was not really himself. The real John Humphrey Noyes—the Noyes of 1833 to 1873—was a most remarkable person. He was, in fact, the indispensable man. No one in the group could come close to taking his place. Oneida was formed in his image, and as the image faded, the Community faded right along with it.

Like so many magnetic leaders, John Humphrey Noyes had a well of energy which ran far deeper than in other men. He helped design and build the Mansion House, he performed physical labor in the trap shop, he traveled constantly, he read voluminously, and, of course, he served as both legislative and judicial head of the Community. He was also a prodigious writer, a fact which is often overlooked.

Sexualism None of the above activities had any appreciable effect on the Perfectionist leader's sexual proclivities. On the contrary, the record indicates that, in both a mental and physical sense, John Humphrey Noyes was one of the great sexual figures of the nineteenth century. His ideas about sex were genuinely original and a century ahead of their time. Nineteenth-century America, after all, was laboring in the backwash of Puritanism. False shame, Victorian prohibitions, and downright prudery were the order of the day. It was against this backdrop that John Humphrey Noyes spoke—and his message was shockingly clear.

There was no shame inherent in the sex act or the sex organs. "To be ashamed of the sex organs," he contended, "is to be ashamed of God's workmanship . . . of the agencies that give us existence."[42] It was futile, furthermore, to try to ignore man's sexual urges since "nature is constantly thrusting sexual objects upon the mind."[43]

Noyes' sexualism, of course, was not restricted to the world of ideas. He fathered five offspring prior to founding the Oneida Community and at least ten more during the stirpiculture program.

How many different women did John Humphrey Noyes have sexual relations with? While any figure must be viewed largely as a guess, there are a few facts to go on. As leader of the Perfectionists, Noyes exercised "first husband" rights over a fair number of young girls who reached puberty while in the Community. Nor is there any reason to believe that he systematically neglected the middle-aged and older women. Since all-time membership in the Community probably ex-

[42]*Bible Communism*, p. 54.

[43]Quoted in Muncy, *Sex and Marriage*, p. 169.

ceeded five hundred, of whom half or more were female, Noyes presumably had sex relations with not less than one hundred—and perhaps as many as two hundred—different women in the course of his life.

There is no doubt that Noyes' sexual proclivities were an important part of his total makeup. He had tremendous vigor, a vigor that manifested itself in the spiritual, the mental—and the physical. It is no coincidence, certainly, that his utopian Community included a sharing of sex.

In spite of his libidinal powers, however, to believe that Noyes' life was dominated by sex is to misunderstand both his nature and that of the Oneida Community. Throughout most of his career, he was dominated by nothing other than religious zeal. This, together with his wide range of talents, his devastating energy, and his creativity of thought, leads one to the conclusion that he was "a most compleat man." In parallel fashion, the Community he founded aimed at being a spiritual and social organization complete in itself—a subculture, a society within a society. And while the term subculture had not yet been coined, this is exactly what Noyes succeeded in establishing.

Leadership Qualities How was Noyes able to do the things he did? With no real authority other than the force of his own personality, how did he manage to dominate so many people for such a long time? His powers were all the more remarkable when one considers the sexual rigidity that prevailed in the larger society.

To begin with, John Humphrey Noyes was an astute judge of character. He could "read" his followers with uncanny accuracy, knowing when to praise and when to blame. He knew when—and to whom—to delegate authority. His ear was finely attuned to the moods of the Community, and one suspects that he had his own methods of gathering "intelligence." Time and again his home talks anticipated the temper of the group.

At the same time, the Perfectionist leader was forthright and honest in dealing with his followers. He understood their problems and was a sympathetic listener. Yet he made no attempt to mingle with them as a friend. He was their leader, and he acted like one. Here is Carden's description:

> Noyes showed a strength of character, an intellectual scope, an optimism, and an intrepidity that fascinated his followers and convinced them that he was Christ's representative. Noyes was highly intelligent, energetic, and attractive. His features were strong and well formed. He carried himself with a dignified aloofness.[44]

[44]Carden, *Oneida,* pp. 34–35.

There was a saying on the part of the townspeople, "If Mr. Noyes takes a pinch of snuff, the whole Community sneezes." The aphorism was somewhat misleading. The Perfectionists were not puppets. They were not only permitted but encouraged to join in the group discussions. That Noyes' views usually prevailed was not because he forced them on the group but because—spontaneously and without effort—he could convince them of the soundness of his position. As a result, both the central members and the Community at large came to have implicit faith in his judgment. So great was this faith that up to the time of his death—seven years after he had fled to Canada—Noyes was still selecting the board of directors for Oneida Ltd.

Charisma Judgment alone does not a leader make. Many men have sound judgment, but few lead.[45] The leader is a person with a distinctive combination of personality traits, and—as the term is used by sociologists—a *charismatic leader* is one who also emits a kind of emotional spark. And there was never the slightest doubt about the charismatic qualities of John Humphrey Noyes. Over and over in the literature, reference is made to his infectious optimism, his glow, his ability to affect others by his very presence.

Pierrepont Noyes, who guided the destinies of Oneida Ltd. for so many years, has this to say about his father:

> Noyes was the outstanding reality in all of our lives. Just how his presence impinged on boys is beyond me; but it did add an imponderable something which gave to both work and play a peculiar zest.
>
> Old members of the Community have said to me that those who got within the effective area of his personality were reluctant to lose him; that life seemed brighter and more worthwhile when he was about.[46]

In my own study, similar statements were made whenever the subject of John Humphrey Noyes came up. The most illuminating—spoken by a woman whose mother had known the Perfectionist leader quite well—was the following:

> I've often wondered about the traits that made him what he was. I just don't know. You might have got an answer a hundred years ago. Now maybe it's too late. I remember asking my mother the same question when I was a young girl: "Why did you live that way? What was there about him?" And I remember her answering, "Don't ask me to explain it. I can't. All I know is that when you were in his presence, you knew you were with someone who was not an ordinary man."

[45]See Thomas, *The Man Who Would Be Perfect,* pp. 146–66.

[46]Pierrepont Noyes, *My Father's House,* p. 297. See also Whitworth, *God's Blueprints,* pp. 89–166.

SELECTED READINGS

Bernstein, Leonard. "The Ideas of John Humphrey Noyes, Perfectionist." *American Quarterly,* 5 (March 1953): 157–65.

Carden, Maren Lockwood. *Oneida: Utopian Community to Modern Corporation.* Baltimore: Johns Hopkins Press, 1969.

Edmonds, Walter. *The First Hundred Years.* Sherrill, N.Y.: Oneida Ltd., 1948.

Estlake, Allan. *The Oneida Community: A Record of an Attempt to Carry out the Principles of Christian Unselfishness and Scientific Race-Improvement.* London: George Redway, 1900.

Foster, Lawrence. *Religion and Sexuality: Three American Communal Experiments of the Nineteenth Century.* New York: Oxford University Press, 1981.

Handbook of the Oneida Community. Oneida, N.Y.: Office of the Oneida Circular, 1875.

Kephart, William M. "Experimental Family Organization: An Historico-Cultural Report on the Oneida Community." *Marriage and Family Living,* 25 (August 1963): 261–71.

———. "The Oneida Community." In Kephart, *The Family, Society, and the Individual,* pp. 121–40. Boston: Houghton Mifflin, 1981.

Levine, Murray, and Bunker, Barbara Benedict. *Mutual Criticism.* Syracuse, N.Y.: Syracuse University Press, 1975.

Muncy, Raymond Lee. *Sex and Marriage in Utopian Communities.* Bloomington: Indiana University Press, 1973.

Nordhoff, Charles. *The Communistic Societies of the United States.* New York: Dover, 1966.

Noyes, Corinna Ackley. *Days of My Youth.* Oneida, N.Y.: Oneida Ltd., 1960.

Noyes, George Wallingford. *Religious Experience of John Humphrey Noyes, Founder of the Oneida Community.* New York: Macmillan, 1923.

———. *John Humphrey Noyes: The Putney Community.* Oneida, N.Y., 1931.

Noyes, Hilda H., and Noyes, George W. "The Oneida Community Experiment in Stirpiculture." *Eugenics, Genetics, and the Family,* 1 (1923): 374–86.

Noyes, John Humphrey. *The Berean: A Manual for the Help of Those Who Seek the Faith of the Primitive Church.* Putney, Vt.: Office of the Spiritual Magazine, 1847.

———. *History of American Socialisms.* Philadelphia: Lippincott, 1870.

———. *Male Continence.* Oneida, N.Y.: Office of the Oneida Circular, 1872.

———. *Essay on Scientific Propagation.* Oneida, N.Y.: Oneida Community, 1873.

Noyes, Pierrepont B. *A Goodly Heritage.* New York: Rinehart, 1958.

———. *My Father's House: An Oneida Boyhood.* Gloucester, Mass.: Peter Smith, 1966.

Parker, Robert. *A Yankee Saint: John Humphrey Noyes and the Oneida Community.* New York: Putnam, 1935.

Robertson, Constance Noyes. *Oneida Community: The Breakup, 1876–1881.* Syracuse, N.Y.: Syracuse University Press, 1972.

———, ed. *Oneida Community: An Autobiography, 1851–1876.* Syracuse, N.Y.: Syracuse University Press, 1970.

———. *Oneida Community Profiles.* Syracuse, N.Y.: Syracuse University Press, 1977.

Seldes, Gilbert. *Mainland.* New York: Scribners, 1936.

Thomas, Robert. *The Man Who Would Be Perfect: John Humphrey Noyes and the Utopian Impulse.* Philadelphia: University of Pennsylvania Press, 1977.

Whitworth, John. *God's Blueprints: A Sociological Study of Three Utopian Sects.* London and Boston: Routledge & Kegan Paul, 1975.

FOUR

THE FATHER DIVINE MOVEMENT

In the late fall of 1978, Americans were astounded and horrified to learn that more than nine hundred of their countrymen had killed themselves in a small South American country called Guyana (formerly British Guiana). It was one of the worst mass suicides in history. The locale was Jonestown, named after the Reverend Jim Jones, leader of the so-called People's Temple. Jones was a seriously disturbed individual, with accelerating delusions of grandeur. No one, however, could have predicted that his hold on his followers would eventuate in a calamity.

This account is well known by now. Indeed, it was one of the most vividly reported news stories of the decade. Not so well known is the fact that several years prior to his demise, the Reverend Jones had tried to take over the Father Divine movement. Jones had actually managed to lure a few of the Divinites to California and had openly announced that he intended to take Father Divine's place. Fortunately, the Reverend Jones became persona non grata to the organization, and was ordered not to set foot on any of the Father Divine premises or locations.[1]

In the latter part of the 1970s, the Divinites were "threatened" by one Jesus Allah Emanuel, a sixty-one-year-old black who claimed that he was Father Divine's son. Jesus Allah, whose real name is Robert Gibson, contended that Father Divine had five children by his first wife. According to the rule of primogeniture, therefore, he, Jesus Allah Emanuel, was the rightful heir to, and leader of, the Father Divine movement. Time, he said, would prove him right.

Not so, as it turned out. Time was not on his side. In fact, by the 1980s—as I was told by one of the Divinites—Jesus Allah was "gone with the wind."

As will be shown, Jim Jones and Jesus Allah Emanuel were not the

[1]Reported in the *Philadelphia Inquirer,* December 7, 1978.

first to make claims on or against the Father Divine movement. And in all likelihood they will not be the last. But who, exactly, was Father Divine? And what, exactly, is the movement which bears his name? Perhaps the best place to start would be a description of a Divinite communion banquet as it might have looked twenty-five years ago.

The Communion Banquet

The U-shaped banquet table is decked in spotless linen, shining silverware, and fresh flowers. Each place setting includes a goblet with a cone-shaped napkin, in the center of which stands a small, bristling American flag. Just above the head table is a neon sign, "Father Divine's Holy Communion Table," and underneath the sign there are three large American flags. On the left wall is a felt banner with "PEACE" embroidered in large, even letters. On the right wall is a printed sign with the unsurpassable message "FATHER DIVINE IS GOD ALMIGHTY." All in all, it is a striking scene, and the 250 assembled guests—a mixture of blacks and whites—seem well aware of the fact.

The room itself vibrates with excitement and anticipation. Suddenly the tempo increases. There are several screams and shouts. From somewhere, a female voice rings out, "He's here! Father's here!" There is mass movement toward the doorway, where the curtains are parting. Then Father Divine—accompanied by Mother Divine on his right—breaks into the room with no uncertain step.

He is a short, squat black man with smooth skin. His head is shiny bald, and while at the moment his face is impassive, his eyes are quick and penetrating. He wears jewelry: a diamond ring, an expensive-looking wristwatch, a gold chain across his vest, and two emblematic lapel buttons. Yet the overall effect is not one of pomp or flash. Father Divine's suit is dark and well cut, his tie is a conservative stripe, and his shoes are black.

Perhaps the most observable thing about the man is his height, or lack of it. He seems to be no more than four feet ten inches. (In photographs and real life, Father Divine is invariably seen as the shortest person in the group.) But despite his diminutive size, it is apparent—to most of those present, at least—that he is a commanding personality. Every step of his buoyant walk, every gesture, every nod of his head brings gasps of delight from the onlookers. Several of the women jump high into the air.

Although Father Divine appears to be of indeterminate middle age, Mother Divine is clearly much younger. (She is his second wife, his first wife having died several years earlier.) A striking white woman, Mother Divine is immaculately dressed. Almost a head taller than her husband, she gazes at him from time to time with genuine adoration. In addition to being his wife, it is obvious that she is also one of his most devoted followers.

Together they make their way to the head table. Although the throng presses in closely, no one so much as touches Father. On his part, Father Divine seems to take the adulation for granted. Neither condescending nor overbearing, he acts with good-natured dignity and restraint. It is apparent that he is in command of the situation at all times.

Father and Mother Divine are seated, and since Father's feet do not reach the floor, a cushioned stool is placed under them. His followers return to their tables, and the noise subsides. The communion banquet is about to begin.

And what a banquet it is! A dozen different vegetables, roast beef, fried chicken, baked ham, roast turkey and duck, meat loaf, steak, cold cuts, spareribs, liver and bacon, four different kinds of bread, mixed salad with a choice of dressing, celery and olives, coffee, tea, and milk, and a variety of desserts, including layer cake, pie, pudding, fresh fruit, and great mounds of ice cream.

A corps of waitresses—immaculately clad in white—stand by, ready to help with the food. Each dish is first placed in front of Father Divine, who blesses it by touching the dish or adding a serving fork or spoon. The dishes are then passed on to the guests. The waitresses enthusiastically pour coffee, refill empty plates, help circulate the dishes, and otherwise encourage the diners to enjoy what Father Divine calls "the abundance of the fullness." (As we shall see, food has always played an important part in the Father Divine movement.)

With so many courses, so much food, and so many people, the serving and eating process takes a good deal of time—two and a half hours, to be exact. However, there is never a dull moment; in fact, there is so much happening that it is difficult to follow it all.

A thickset black woman suddenly jumps to her feet and thrusts both arms upward. "I was paralyzed!" she shouts in a throbbing voice. "No movement in the legs—none at all. And then I met you, Father, and you cured me. I am yours forever, Father, with true devotion!" She sits down and buries her head in her arms.

A middle-aged white woman stands up. "I had tuberculosis real bad. It was consumption. I coughed all day, and I coughed all night, and they told me I was a goner. Then you came into my life, Father, and made me well again overnight. I love you, Father, truly love you."

A thin black man with gray-white hair gets up slowly. "Before I was twenty, I was put in jail twice for stealing. Each time, I told the judge I didn't do it, but in my heart I knew I did. I was a bad boy, and I grew up to be a bad man. I set my neighbor's car on fire and never told nobody—till now. It was only when God came to me in the form of Father Divine that I was able to resolve myself. Thank you, Father."

The Rosebuds, the young girls' choir, break into song at this point. They range in age from about ten to thirty-five, and all are dressed in red jackets and navy blue skirts. On the left side of their jackets is a white V—for virtue.

> Just as a Rosebud with its fragrance so sweet,
> A perfect Rosebud, FATHER, we want to be,
> Devoting, directing, dedicating our whole lives
> All to YOU, all to YOU, all to YOU . . .

There are approximately forty Rosebuds in the choir, and they sing their hearts out on every song. Their spirit is indomitable, inexhaustible. Although they are accompanied by a pianist, they have no sheet music to read. All their songs—dozens of them—are memorized. The words are original, though some of the music is from well-known melodies like "White Christmas" and "Anchors Aweigh."

During many of the songs the chorus is repeated, at which point the girls clap their hands and stamp their feet. When this happens, the audience joins in—and the chorus is likely to be repeated several more times. Unmistakably, the room is filled with happy singers. The only person not visibly affected is Father Divine himself, who acts as though the festivities were a routine part of his life. (Which indeed they are!)

Following the Rosebuds' songs, there are more confessions of sin and some additional tributes to Father Divine. One woman stands on a chair and shouts, "I love you, Father! Truly!" There is a chorus of agreement, after which individual testimonials are heard from all parts of the room.

"Blessed is the Lord!"

"I owe you everything, Father! Thank you, Father!"

"Bless his heavenly body!"

"Father Divine is *God Almighty!*"

At this point, the Lilybuds stand up and render a song. Dressed in attractive green jackets with white trim, the Lilybuds are an older version of the Rosebuds. There are perhaps fifty of them, and their ages seem to range from thirty-five up. Although they are not as vivacious as the Rosebuds, they do not lack enthusiasm. And their devotion to Father Divine is obviously unsurpassed. Their song has the ring of utmost sincerity.

We want to be a real true Lilybud,
Basking in our FATHER'S LOVE every day.
We want to be a real true Lilybud,
Obeying and doing what our precious FATHER says.
Isn't HE sweet? Oh, oh, oh!
Such a Darling; my, my, my!
We want to be a real true Lilybud,
Living this Holy Life in every way.

Now, for the first time, people are beginning to dance in the aisles. The dancing is unrehearsed, spontaneous, and individualistic. No two steps are alike, and no two people touch one another. Subdued at first, the movements and gesticulations accelerate as the evening wears on.

Following the Lilybuds' rendition, there is much shouting and applause, and then—as if led by an invisible cheerleader—the entire audience stands up and chants:

Two, four, six, eight. Who do we appreciate?
FATHER DIVINE! MOTHER DIVINE! Yea!

One, two, three, four. Who are we for?
Five, six, seven, eight. Who do we appreciate?
FATHER DIVINE! MOTHER DIVINE! Yea!

Throughout the proceedings, Father Divine remains impassive. Much of his time has been spent in blessing the food plates and starting them on their way. Now he himself eats—slowly and sparingly. If he is impressed by the goings-on, he does not show it. He seems to look at no one in particular, and, with the exception of an occasional comment to Mother Divine, he is silent.

Mother Divine, on the other hand, is anything but oblivious to the situation. She smiles, gesticulates, and often joins in the singing and the clapping. (She is a former Rosebud and on occasion still wears the red jacket with the white V.) When Father Divine speaks to her, she looks at him with unabashed admiration. It is also apparent, on the basis of her movements and facial expressions, that she possesses great natural dignity. She is able—without effort—to combine enthusiasm and graciousness. She seems the ideal person to fulfill the role of heavenly wife.

It is time now for a song from the Crusaders—the men's group. Although they include men of all ages, the Crusaders are a much smaller group than the Rosebuds or the Lilybuds. In fact, a large majority of those present, both uniformed and nonuniformed, are female. There are about fifteen Crusaders, and they are dressed in powder blue coats, white shirts, and dark trousers. They sing lustily and—like their predecessors—with obvious devotion.

I want to love YOU, FATHER,
A little bit more each day,
I want to love YOU, FATHER,
In all I do and say.
I want to love YOU, FATHER,
For the wondrous works YOU do,
For I know YOU'RE GOD ALMIGHTY,
And I've given this heart to YOU!

At the end of the song, the audience erupts with an outburst of clapping and shouting. There are more testimonials, more dancing, and more of the women leap into the air. One oldster lies down across three chairs, sobbing uncontrollably. But all such behavior appears to be taken for granted by the group itself. There seems to be a tacit sequence of events, and if the activity is becoming more feverish, it is because the sequence dictates that the program is coming to a climax. And sure enough, there is a stirring at the head table. Father Divine is getting up to speak.

As he looks into the eyes of his followers, there are shouts of "God! God! God!" "Peace, Father!" "Thank you, dear one!" "Hallelujah!" "I love you, Father!" "God Almighty!" Once he commences to speak, however, all noise stops. For the duration of his talk, the audience gives him their full attention.

Father Divine begins his sermon with the same salutation he uses at many communion banquets:

PEACE, EVERYONE! GOOD HEALTH, GOOD WILL, A GOOD APPETITE, GOOD MANNERS, GOOD BEHAVIOR, ALL SUCCESS AND ALL PROSPERITY, LIFE, LIBERTY, AND THE REALITY OF HAPPINESS!

As he speaks, twenty-five young secretaries take up their notebooks and write down Father's words in shorthand. As a matter of fact, everything Father Divine says—sermons, speeches, discourses, interviews, extemporaneous remarks—is recorded by the ever-ready secretaries. Their shorthand is then transcribed and appears in *New Day,* the movement's biweekly newspaper, thus preserving Father Divine's words for posterity. His speeches and sermons are printed and reprinted over and over again. Indeed, directly under the *New Day* title on the front page is the statement "National & International —Featuring the Works of Father Divine."

(The secretaries have always held a rather exalted position in the organization, since the nature of their work—when the movement was at its peak, at least—required them to stay close to Father Divine day in and day out. Like the Rosebuds and Lilybuds, the secretaries include both black and white members, most of whom are ex-Rosebuds.)

Father Divine speaks in a strong, resonant voice, with a distinctive tone quality. Though he starts slowly—almost methodically—his audience is spellbound from the very first word. The sermon itself is a combination of the practical and the profound, the esoteric and the absurd, yet his phrasing is such that it is often difficult to tell which is which.

> Though we have Blessings unlimited economically, and though we have physical comfort and convenience for ourselves and for millions of others, yet back of all of it is IT, which said, "Let there be light, and there was light."
>
> Back of all of it was, as it is, the same, that while on the water, as so to speak, invisible, and spoke into visibility the earth upon which we are living, the beginning of the material and economic things of life![2]

Several times in the course of his sermon, Father Divine punctuates an affirmation with "Aren't you glad!" And each time the audience answers with a resounding "Yes, so glad!" or "So glad, Lord!"

When the sermon is finished, there is a tumultuous burst of applause, and shouts of "So true, Father!" "Thank you, Father!" "Lord God Almighty!" People jump and whirl, and a number have tears in their eyes. Almost all are visibly moved. One woman clutches herself and screams, "I love you, sweetheart!" Another lies on the floor motionless, scarcely noticed by the others. An elderly man takes his cane and whacks it against the table as hard as he can, the vibrating silverware adding to the din.

In the midst of all the exuberance, the Rosebuds rise and sing one of their inimitable songs, and there is more stamping and clapping. Additional testimonials and confessions follow—and further expressions of adulation for Father. Then the Lilybuds rise and sing. Then the Crusaders. Genuine ecstasy. Genuine rapture. No doubt about it. Only Father Divine manages to take it all in stride. In a few minutes, he and Mother Divine—with their entourage of secretaries and others—will leave and, quite possibly, visit another of their "heavens," where a similar spectacle will unfold.

"God in a Body" Although it may read like fiction, this description of a Father Divine communion banquet is based on fact. Between the 1940s and the 1960s, I attended the banquets many times, and the foregoing scene is a composite picture of the actual happenings. Father Divine died in 1965, and while the movement

[2]Full texts of sermons such as the above are reprinted periodically in the *New Day,* 1600 W. Oxford Street, Philadelphia, Pa.

continues, the "enthusiasm" has been necessarily dampened. Nevertheless, while he was alive he was a phenomenally successful leader. It is quite possible that at the height of his career Father Divine was more ardently acclaimed and revered by his followers than any religious leader in United States history. To those who believed, he was more than just an exalted person. He was, quite simply, God.

Who was this man, this superman, this "God in a body"? When and where was he born? What was his youth like? When did he first aspire to be God? Whence cometh his financial support? How did his movement get to be worldwide in scope? Can it survive, now that "God" is no longer on earth?

Some of these questions are answerable; some—at the moment, at least—are not. From World War I to the present, the Father Divine story is traceable. It is far from complete, but the broad outlines are known. The period prior to World War I is the stickler. Here the picture is murky and tantalizing, and this is unfortunate. For if we knew the real origin and background of Father Divine the man, we would have a much better understanding of Father Divine in his role as God.

The George Baker Story

Very few books have been written about Father Divine, and most of those that have been written are of World War II vintage.[3] With one exception, furthermore, all the books were written by journalists, and there are some gross differences in their reporting.

The only full-length book by a trained social scientist is the recent work by Kenneth Burnham, based on his doctoral dissertation.[4] Burnham's is a contemporary study, much of the data being gathered through painstaking interviews and participant observation. The au-

[3]See Robert Allerton Parker, *The Incredible Messiah* (Boston: Little, Brown, 1937); John Hoshor, *God in a Rolls Royce: The Rise of Father Divine* (1936; reprint ed., Freeport, N.Y.: Books for Libraries Press, 1971); Sarah Harris, *Father Divine: Holy Husband* (1953; reprint ed., New York: Macmillan, 1971, with a preface, introduction, and afterword added). See also the series by St. Clair McKelway and A. J. Liebling, "Who Is This King of Glory?" *The New Yorker,* June 13, 1936, pp. 21 ff; June 20, pp. 22 ff; and June 27, pp. 22 ff. There have been hundreds of articles about Father Divine in publications such as *Time, Newsweek,* and the *New York Times.* The principal historical sources, however, seem to be those just cited.

[4]Kenneth E. Burnham, *God Comes to America: Father Divine and the Mission Peace Movement* (Boston: Lambeth, 1979).

thor did not attempt to unearth primary historical sources. The upshot is that our knowledge of Father Divine's early period is decidedly spotty and stems from journalistic accounts. On the basis of these accounts, such as they are, it is said that there was once a man named George Baker . . .

His date of birth is reported as anywhere between 1860 and 1880, depending upon who is doing the reporting. Since no official birth certificate has ever been uncovered, the specific date is largely guesswork. His place of birth is said to be around Savannah, Georgia, though there is no proof of this, either. Some observers believe George Baker's parents were slaves, which might account for his obscure background. Others believe they were sharecroppers, of Baptist persuasion.

Between the time of his birth and the turn of the century, George Baker's whereabouts and activities remain unknown. There are isolated reports of his refusing to attend Jim Crow schools, of being jailed for riding in the "whites only" section of a trolley car, of being a Sunday school superintendent, and of spending six months on a chain gang. None of the accounts has been proved—or disproved. It is not until around 1900 that the various biographical reports tend to converge.

By that year, George Baker had apparently settled in Baltimore, working as a gardener during the day and as an assistant preacher at night and on Sundays. He was neither more nor less successful than other black ministers of the period who were forced to take outside jobs. Until fate intervened in the form of one Samuel Morris . . .

Although reports differ on how the two men met, the meeting itself had a profound and lasting influence on George Baker. Samuel Morris rejected the usual hellfire-and-damnation approach to salvation and instead taught that God dwells within every man. One report has it that Morris proclaimed himself to be God—and, upon being evicted from the church where he was preaching, was befriended by George Baker. Another report makes no mention of this episode but states simply that Baker was drawn to the religious philosophy of Samuel Morris, returning "again and again" to hear him preach.[5]

In any case, it may have been at this time that George Baker caught the idea of becoming God. Prior to his association with Morris, his sermons had given no inkling of heavenly aspiration, but by 1907 he seems to have become intertwined—apparently forever—with the Deity.

[5]See works in footnote 3 for historical details—and variations—of the pre–World War I period under discussion.

Although the details at this point are not clear, Samuel Morris and George Baker evidently worked out an arrangement whereby they shared the Godship. Also, at this time, both men apparently changed their names (or were "reborn"). Samuel Morris was henceforth known as Father Jehovia, and George Baker became known as the Messenger.

In 1908 they were joined by a third man, John Hickerson, a tall, black minister with an imposing voice. Not to be outdone by his companions, Reverend Hickerson also adopted a more spiritual name, St. John the Vine. Although Father Jehovia (Samuel Morris) seems to have been number one, the three men were somehow able to share their divinity, and for the next several years they were as flamboyant a preaching team as the area had ever seen.

The Messenger In 1912 the triumvirate broke up. Presumably they were no longer willing to share their divine authority, and in any case they went their separate ways. St. John the Vine Hickerson traveled to New York City, where he founded his own church. Father Jehovia passed from the picture and for all intents and purposes was never heard from again. The Messenger (George Baker) turned southward, gained some converts, and—if we can believe his biographers—ran into a pack of trouble.

At Valdosta, Georgia, in 1913, the Messenger was preaching the gospel in his inimitable style. The townspeople were entranced and turned out in large numbers to hear the man who called himself God. While the reports vary, there were apparently some in the audience who were unimpressed. Among the skeptics were certain local pastors, who had the Messenger arrested and taken to court. The charge: any person who believes himself to be God must be of unsound mind.

For reasons best known to themselves, the jury upheld the charge, and the Messenger was declared insane. Instead of committing him to a mental institution, however, the court ordered him to leave the state of Georgia forthwith. He did so, and as far as we know he never returned.

There are other references in the literature to the Messenger's incarceration in a state institution, but this episode is not reported in the standard biographical accounts.[6] However, in spite of the resistance and harassment he met in the South, the Messenger did succeed in gaining converts. They were few in number, to be sure—probably not more than a dozen—but they were dedicated believers, and they

[6]Reported by J. R. Moseley in *Manifest Victory* (New York: Harper, 1941), pp. 106–09, and cited in Charles Braden, *These Also Believe* (New York: Macmillan, 1960), pp. 7–8.

would form the nucleus of his forthcoming religious organization. One person is worthy of particular mention: a stout, black woman called Peninah, or Sister Penny. Before the group left the South, Sister Penny was reportedly the Messenger's chief angel.

The New York Maelstrom

In 1915, the Messenger and his disciples arrived in New York City, undaunted by their troubles and apparently none the worse for wear. After a brief stay in Manhattan, the little group settled in Brooklyn. Starting in a rooming house—under the leadership of the Messenger—they began to develop the format for what would one day be a worldwide religious organization.

As the little group struggled to survive in the big city, the Messenger himself was in close touch with his old friend and fellow deity, St. John the Vine Hickerson. Hickerson had his own church—the Church of the Living God—and had been fairly successful. The Messenger attended Hickerson's services, checked his methods, asked questions, and otherwise borrowed from St. John the Vine's repertoire.

Along with modest success, however, Hickerson was also having some difficulty. Like his mentor, Samuel Morris (Father Jehovia), St. John the Vine taught that God was not in heaven but within every person. This meant that although Hickerson could be God, there could be any number of auxiliary Gods—and this is exactly what was happening. Wearing "gold" and "silver" crowns and royal purple robes, these deities clogged the path to Hickerson's church. There were Father Obey, Joe World, Elijah of the Fiery Chariot, Saint Peter, Father Paul, Steamboat Bill, Father Joshua, and many others. Later on there would be cult leaders and other exotic personalities, like Barnaby Bill, Sufi Abdul Hamid, and Daddy Grace. New York was fast becoming a religious maelstrom!

Before long, St. John the Vine's church fell under the weight of its own gods. Although he did not pass into oblivion like Samuel Morris, John Hickerson became a relatively obscure figure. Following World War I, he is heard from less and less. What it amounts to is that almost from the moment the Messenger appeared on the New York scene, St. John the Vine Hickerson's crown began to slip. Hickerson himself, at least in retrospect, was well aware of the connection. Biographers agree that he harbored bitter feelings toward the Messenger and blamed him for many of his difficulties.

The Messenger himself severed all connection with John Hickerson and never referred to him publicly again. The little group in Brooklyn, meanwhile, was holding its own—perhaps even growing a bit. A few of the original members had left, but new ones kept joining. The Messenger was a persuasive speaker, and his followers genuinely revered him. He ran a tight ship, however, and unlike St. John the Vine, permitted only one God—himself. He made all the rules and brooked no interference, and he followed that practice all his life.

As to its living arrangements, the group operated communally. The Messenger himself did no outside work—nor would he, ever again. Instead, he ran an employment service, supplying domestics and menial workers to those who were looking for honest, reliable help. Whether or not they got their jobs through his employment service, however, the Messenger's followers presumably turned their wages over to him. He then paid the rent, bought the food, and took care of the necessary bills.

Peninah was in charge of the actual household management—including shopping and food preparation—and from all accounts she was an indefatigable worker. In fact, some observers believe that the Messenger married her during this period, though others set the date much earlier. But whatever the date, the marriage was spiritual in nature. It may also have been legal—though no marriage license has been uncovered—but it was not sexual. Quite early in the movement, the Messenger decreed that sex was unclean, a mark of depravity, and hence was forbidden. Neither he nor his followers have been known to violate the decree.

Name Changes During the New York period, another interesting phenomenon occurred: the Messenger underwent further name changes. The reason is not entirely clear, but presumably he felt the need for a more appropriate title. In any case, just as George Baker evolved into the Messenger, so the Messenger evolved into Major Jealous Devine. (More than one biographer has suggested that the Messenger borrowed not only St. John the Vine's ministerial techniques but his surname as well!)

To complete the cognominal sequence, Major Jealous Devine was eventually shortened to M. J. Devine, and finally—over a period of years—M. J. *Devine* became Father *Divine.* These latter changes, though gradual, are a matter of record and are not really in dispute. The dispute arises over the earlier sequence: the transition from George Baker to the Messenger, and from the Messenger to Major Jealous Devine.[7] Before continuing with the rest of the story, therefore, let us pause and examine a genuine mystery.

[7]For an interesting account, see Burnham, *God Comes to America,* chapter one, pp. 1–9.

Man, Myth, or Both?

The George Baker–Messenger–Father Divine story told in the preceding pages is based largely on the handful of available biographies. It is most certainly *not* the account told by Father Divine's followers, or for that matter by Father himself. Whenever he was asked when he was born, he would be likely to reply, "I wasn't born. I was combusted one day." He also answered queries about his birth with a scriptural "Before Abraham was, I am."

In a more serious vein, Father Divine downgraded the physical manifestation of the human body. Over and over again, he told his followers that it was not necessary for him to be physically present in order for them to establish spiritual contact. True believers could establish such contact at any time. His followers not only believed this but actually practiced it. Thousands of them never saw him—those in foreign countries, for example—yet many of them reportedly maintained a spiritual closeness with Father Divine all their adult lives.

With a faith as strong as this, it might be expected that his followers would reject the George Baker story. And reject it they do. To them, George Baker is nothing more than a myth, invented by Father Divine's many enemies. Burnham, an authority on the subject, writes:

> All attempts to describe Father Divine's history have been rejected by his followers on the ground that his life can be understood only from his own words in the publications of the Movement. They believe that the only true statements about him have come from his own lips.[8]

What does the best evidence really indicate?

The early biographers—who presumably researched their subject—all believed that Father Divine was indeed George Baker, and that his divinity had its inception around the turn of the century in Baltimore. Moreover, all but one of the biographies were written in the mid-1930s, when those close to the movement would have been expected to know something about Father Divine's early background. By implication, at least, the biographers actually talked to informants of this type.

On the other hand, the biographies were only three or four in number, and—as was mentioned earlier—none was written by a trained social scientist. References, research sources, and general documentation are largely lacking. The methodology is not rigorous,

[8]Ibid., p. 6.

and there are time gaps in the narratives. It is hardly surprising that there are some sharp discrepancies among the various accounts. In brief, they are popular books—no more, no less.

Certain logical questions present themselves. Is there any independent documentation which would link Samuel Morris, George Baker, and John Hickerson in place (Baltimore) and time (early 1900s)? Are there no local or state records available to establish that George Baker was in fact convicted by a court and served time in jail or on a chain gang? Are there no documents to shed light on his movements during the developmental (1908–1914) period?

The one key witness in this historical entanglement is St. John the Vine. It is he, really, who identifies Father Divine as George Baker. Writing in the early 1950s, for example, Harris—the latest biographer—notes that St. John the Vine Hickerson was *the only person alive today who knew Father Divine before he became God.* According to Hickerson:

> Sure, he was just plain little George Baker in 1899. He lived in Baltimore. You know what he did? Gardening. Working around the white neighborhoods for fifty cents a day. He used to live for Sundays because he used to teach Sunday school and be an assistant preacher.[9]

But how much credence are we to put in this story—knowing of Hickerson's bitterness? After all, St. John the Vine was a failure, and Father Divine a success, and since Hickerson blamed much of his own failure on Father Divine, the George Baker allegation should be weighed carefully. Hickerson's story may certainly be true, but what is needed is some independent corroboration.

Why, for example, was Samuel Morris never interviewed regarding the authenticity of the George Baker story? Morris had no ax to grind, and he was certainly in a position to know the facts of the case. Yet he apparently made no statement on the subject. Indeed, there is no indication that he was ever asked, although he did turn up as a caretaker in New Jersey during the 1930s.

Both John Hickerson and Samuel Morris are now dead—as are most of the earlier biographers. If further evidence on George Baker is forthcoming, therefore, it will probably be from new sources.[10] Here is a ready-made research project for someone!

I have heard Father Divine speak on any number of occasions, over a period of many years—and nothing he ever said during this time

[9]Harris, *Father Divine,* p. 6.

[10]Leo Everett and La Vere Belstrom, long-time followers of Father Divine, are currently working on a book to be titled *Father Divine and the Peace Mission Movement.* Their findings may shed some much-needed light on the early period.

related in any way to George Baker. Father Divine did not have a southern accent, though his intonation did suggest that he probably spent part of his youth in the South. His own sermons—as well as songs sung by his followers—contain references to his southern persecutions, and one story has it that he escaped from lynch mobs thirty-two times. During an interview in 1951, Father Divine stated that he had "been in the hands of all sorts of mobs and came out unharmed."

The fact that Father Divine probably spent some years in the South does not mean that he did so under the name of George Baker. Yet the tantalizing question remains: If he was not George Baker, who was he?

Sayville—The Turning Point

Starting in 1919, the chronicle of Father Divine and his followers becomes increasingly clear. During that year, he and his little group, numbering not more than two dozen, moved from Brooklyn to Sayville, Long Island. The house they moved to—an attractive, twelve-room dwelling at 72 Macon Street—still stands. It is used by the followers as a kind of shrine, for it was here that the movement first gained national and international recognition.

Things started off peacefully enough. The deed to the house was in the name of Major J. Devine and his wife, Peninah. And if the white community was less than enthusiastic at the prospect of blacks setting up in their midst, no overt reaction was apparent. In fact, for several years Sayville and its environs made good use of Father Divine's services. Operating an employment office—as he did in Brooklyn—Father Divine was able to supply reliable domestics for the many nearby estates.

From all accounts, Father Divine was also a good neighbor. He kept 72 Macon Street spic and span. He worked in the garden. He was polite and friendly, with a ready smile. His followers did not inundate the neighborhood, as some had feared. The group did manage to grow in number—but slowly. They were not loud or unruly. There was no drinking. And there were never any sex problems.

Things went on this way for ten happy years.

Father Divine appeared to be consolidating his position. He was, in effect, learning how to combine the role of businessman with that of deity. On both counts he was successful. As a businessman he had the confidence and respect of the community—in spite of the general racial situation. And in his role as deity he was superb.

The Negro of the 1920s was likely to be a downtrodden individual.

Faced with both social and economic discrimination, he often had a low level of aspiration and—more than occasionally—a feeling of hopelessness. Father Divine succeeded in imbuing his followers with a sense of hope and purpose.

He gave them economic security in the form of lodging, food, and employment. He encouraged self-respect by insisting that they give their employers an honest day's work for a day's pay. He forbade them to accept tips. He gave them a sense of self-discipline by prohibiting smoking, drinking, swearing, and "immodest behavior." And—above all else—he gave them spiritual security. For if he, Father Divine, was God Almighty, then his followers were assured of everlasting salvation.

To be sure, his followers had to make certain sacrifices. They had to renounce sex and marriage. They had to abide by Father Divine's rules and regulations, for he did not tolerate backsliders. And again, they presumably turned all their wages over to him. But these were small sacrifices compared to the economic and spiritual benefits involved.

Slowly but surely the fame of M. J. Devine—"better known as Father Divine"—spread. As the 1920s wore on, membership increased steadily. On Sundays, busloads of visitors would arrive at 72 Macon Street to see and hear God and partake of the mighty meals. Thirty to forty courses every week, and all for free! No collection plate was ever passed, no request for donations was ever made. When—invariably—the question was asked, "But where does the money come from to pay for it all?" the answer was always the same: "It comes from God."

In 1930, the Sunday bus excursions were joined by private automobiles. First dozens, then hundreds. To local residents, it seemed like an endless caravan. The banquets also grew in size and vigor. There were testimonials and increasing reports of miraculous cures. (Father was clearly omnipotent.) Then came the songs and the clapping. And the sermon. And the hallelujahs. And so on. To the good citizens of Sayville, at least, things seemed to be getting out of hand. It was time that something was done.

At first there was police harassment—tickets for traffic and parking violations in wholesale lots. When this tactic failed, the district attorney planted a female undercover agent at 72 Macon Street. Dressed as a poor black working girl, the agent tried to verify rumors of sexual relations between Father Divine and his female followers. When this also failed, she tried to seduce Father Divine, but—by her own account—he ignored her. The only thing she could report was that everyone treated her with sympathy and kindness.

Next there were town meetings, with groups of angry residents demanding Father Divine's ouster. A committee of leading citizens was selected to visit 72 Macon Street and make their demands known. Father Divine received the group and listened patiently while they explained their point of view. Then he explained his. He and his followers were good citizens. They had broken no laws. He himself had helped Sayville economically by providing an employment service and by buying large quantities of food and supplies from local merchants. Furthermore, Father Divine pointed out, the Constitution guaranteed freedom of religion. So he was not going to leave Sayville. On the contrary, he was quite likely to expand his activities.

Father was polite, speaking in an even tone. But something in his manner told the committee that further discussion was futile, and they left. A short time later—during one of the Sunday services—police broke into 72 Macon Street and arrested Father Divine and eighty of his followers for disturbing the peace. The Sunday in question was November 15, 1931, a date that quite possibly marks the real beginning of the Father Divine movement. While the arrest itself was peaceful enough, the entire episode was a shot heard round the Negro world.

Judge Lewis J. Smith Despite the flimsiness of the case, Father Divine was indicted by the grand jury and held (on $1,500 bail) for trial. The black press—and a goodly segment of the white press as well—took up the cry of racial discrimination, and the fight was on. News stories made the front pages, and publicity grew by leaps and bounds. Within a few weeks, Father Divine had become a cause célèbre. He himself, though not visibly perturbed, vowed to fight the case—and if necessary to "rot in jail" rather than succumb to the forces of intolerance and bigotry.

John C. Thomas, a black lawyer who had been an assistant United States district attorney, offered his services to Father Divine, who accepted. The presiding judge in the case was Lewis J. Smith, who—the record would show—was clearly antagonistic in his attitude toward the defendant. One of the judge's first acts was to cancel Father Divine's bail and remand him to prison for the duration of the trial. This action, based on a legal technicality, set the tone for the entire trial.

The actual proceedings were fairly clear-cut. The prosecution contended that Father Divine and his followers had annoyed the neighbors, disturbed the peace, obstructed traffic, and were a public nuisance. The defense naturally denied the allegations. Most of the witnesses were either neighbors (prosecution) or Father Divine's followers (defense). The only thing really noteworthy during the trial was the antagonism shown by Judge Smith toward several of the defense witnesses. It was easy to see where his sympathies lay.

Even in his charge to the jury, the judge showed partiality. He stated that Father Divine was a bad influence in the community, that his real name was not Father Divine but George Baker, that Mother Divine was not his legal wife, that he was not an ordained minister, and that he was able to induce others to turn their wages over to him.

After deliberating a short while, the jury—not unexpectedly—returned a verdict of guilty. They did, however, recommend leniency. Judge Smith adjourned the court for several days while he contemplated the sentence. The defendant, meanwhile, stayed in jail.

Public reaction was mixed. There were those who felt that Father Divine was guilty as charged. Many fair-minded people, however, had come to the conclusion that he was innocent, a victim of unadulterated prejudice.

What of Father Divine's followers? What were their reactions? We can only conjecture. Very probably, they were distressed to see their leader in jail. To some, perhaps, it was an embarrassment. But race bias or no race bias, God had no business being behind bars! Perhaps the feelings of many could be summed up in the words of one follower who said, "If the judge tried to sentence him to jail, Father Divine would sentence the judge to death."[11]

Undaunted, Judge Smith reconvened the court and imposed the stiffest sentence the law allowed: one year in jail and a fine of five hundred dollars. Also undaunted, Father Divine went to jail, a benign expression on his face.

Three days later, Judge Lewis J. Smith was dead!

Only fifty years of age and in apparent good health, he reportedly had died of a heart attack.

When asked—in his cell—whether he had any comments about Judge Smith's demise, Father Divine replied, somewhat mournfully, "I hated to do it."

Afterwards, the appellate court quickly reversed Father Divine's conviction, basing its decision on the "prejudicial comments" voiced by (the late) trial judge.

[11]Hoshor, *God in a Rolls Royce,* p. 69.

Why They Joined

The death of Judge Smith had an overwhelming effect on large segments of the black community. Although most white newspapers carried the story in routine fashion, the black press used banner headlines. In some neighborhoods, blacks held parades and rallies. On June 26, 1932, for example—the day after Father Divine's release from prison—a "Monster Glory to Our Lord" rally was held at the Rockland Palace in Harlem. Lines started to form at five A.M., even though Father Divine wasn't scheduled to appear until noon. Over seven thousand persons jammed the auditorium, and thousands more were turned away.

Father Divine did not let his followers down. Shunning his usual enigmas, he delivered one of the clearest talks of his career. Among other things, he said:

> You may not have seen my flesh for a few weeks, but I was with you just the same. I am just as operative in the mind as in the body. There were many who thought I had gone someplace, but I'm glad to say I did not go anywhere.
>
> I held the key to that jail all the time I was in it, and was with you every time you met. They can prosecute me or persecute me, or even send me to the electric chair, but they can never keep me from you or stop me from doing good![12]

When Father Divine finished his talk, the human explosion almost tore the roof off Rockland Palace. Eruptions of "Hallelujah!" "Sweet Savior!" "Father Divine is God Almighty!" rocked the auditorium. People jumped, screamed, shouted, shook, and whirled. Most were ecstatic, but some were overcome and wept. Harlem had never seen anything like it before.

After the waves of acclaim had passed, testimonials were heard. One woman had been cured of cancer through Father's intervention, another of arthritis. A cripple had been healed and had thrown away his crutches. On and on they went, a spontaneous cascade of miracles.

Then the tone of the audience changed, and people began to complain not of their physical afflictions, but of their social oppression. They were poor and hungry. They lived in squalor and could not get jobs. They had no hope. No future. They needed help, and they needed it now—from God! Little by little, louder and louder, the chant was taken up: "Need you, Father! Need you! Need you! Need you!"[13]

[12]Harris, *Father Divine,* pp. 42–44.

What were the sociological factors which accounted for this mass attraction? To answer the question in generalized terms is easy: the right man was in the right place at the right time—with the right people. A more specific answer would involve a number of points.

To begin with, the nation was in the grip of a wicked depression, and as low man on the economic totem pole, the black was the hardest hit. In many black neighborhoods the housing was dreadful: run-down buildings, congestion, rats and roaches, three and four families sharing one toilet, no hot water, inadequate heat in the winter. Year after year after year. Sickness, ill-health, inadequate medical facilities, poor sanitary conditions, a high death rate. Year after year. Unemployment, desertion, drug addiction, hopelessness. Year after year. The black American—particularly the lower-class member—did indeed need someone. And in the absence of a more appropriate candidate, it looked as though that someone might be Father Divine.

Of particular relevance here is the food factor. Social security, unemployment compensation, Aid to Families with Dependent Children (AFDC), United Fund, old-age assistance—such programs were still many years away. One of the first problems facing an unemployed person, therefore, was hunger. It is easy to see why Father Divine—whose daily services included huge quantities of free food—had such ready appeal. And whenever the question was asked, "But where does all the food come from—who pays for it?" the answer was the same. "It comes from God, and God don't need money."

The Racial Stereotype The Depression was not the only cause of the blacks' economic difficulties. Prejudice and discrimination were so widespread that even when jobs were available, blacks were likely to be excluded. The younger generation of Americans may not realize it, but in the 1930s even clerical and semiskilled occupations were generally closed to black applicants. One did not see black salesclerks in stores or black secretaries in offices. One did not see black bus drivers, or mechanics, or tradesmen.

The fact of the matter is that in the 1930s racial stereotyping was the order of the day. Originally defined as "pictures in the head," the term *stereotype* can best be described as a kind of conceptual shortcut, often of an erroneous nature. Thus the belief that blacks are lazy or inferior is a typical racial stereotype. And while sociologists are well aware that stereotyping still occurs, it is probably not so preva-

[13]Ibid.

lent as it was a generation or two ago. In the 1930s, certainly, it was commonly believed that blacks were listless, unreliable, happy-go-lucky, and largely incapable of holding a job.

Since so much of Father Divine's program was aimed at the elimination of racial stereotyping and job discrimination, it is easy to see why he had such an impact on the black community. It is no accident that his appeal was greatest in those areas where congestion, unemployment, and discrimination were rampant: Brooklyn, Manhattan, Newark, Jersey City, Philadelphia.

Alienation Things were so bad for black Americans in the 1930s that a feeling of alienation often prevailed. As used by sociologists, the term *alienation* refers to a sense of futility and insignificance. An alienated person feels that those in power have neglected him, and that there is nothing he can do about it. He believes that he has little or no control over his own destiny, and that—in effect—he has become dispensable.

More than any other leader of his time, it was Father Divine who fought against the spread of alienation, and he was a superb practitioner. He understood the masses. He could talk to them. He could engender feelings of self-respect, and he could play the role of God. Most important, he never lost sight of the two basics: food and jobs. These were the bedrock. As long as he was helmsman, his followers would have ample food at little or no cost. And—through his employment service or within his own economic establishment—they would have jobs.

Overview Food, jobs, and a joyous war against racism and alienation. No wonder large numbers of blacks flocked to Father Divine's banner. Add to these his personal magnetism, his heavenly claims and obvious knowledge of the Bible, his penetrating voice and allegorical speech, his presumed healing powers, his spontaneous and vibrant manner, his intense concentration on goodness and fairness —for his followers, the result spelled God.

The Economic Structure

Over the years, there has been much misunderstanding and confusion regarding Father Divine's economic operations. His followers commonly believed that since he was God, he could "materialize" all the money he wanted, a notion that Father took no steps to dispel. The Internal Revenue Service, which had some doubts about his deification, wondered why he never paid any income tax. After all, they reasoned, a man who wore expensive suits and diamond rings, who rode in Cadillac limousines and ate lavishly—such a man must also have a lavish income. Father Divine denied the imputation, and in a series of showdowns between "church and state," the state lost.

During his long career, Father Divine never paid a penny in income taxes. His critics contended that, under the mantle of the Lord, he used his workers' salaries to line his own heaven with gold. His supporters countered with the argument that Father Divine had never asked anyone for money in his life, and that even in his own churches there was no such thing as a collection plate.

Actually, Father Divine's economic operations were not so complicated—or so secretive—as his critics claimed. While much of the day-to-day procedure never became public knowledge, enough is known to permit a reasonable description. The basic economic principle was remarkably simple: to feed and house ten people communally did not cost ten times as much as it would to feed and house a single individual, especially if the ten were willing to let the Lord handle the fiscal details. This was the principle Father Divine (as the Messenger) had followed in Brooklyn during the World War I period, and he adhered to it throughout his entire career.

Perhaps the clearest way to explain Father Divine's economic operation is to contrast it with a regular capitalistic venture. If a man wants to open, say, a motel and restaurant, he must first raise the necessary capital. This usually entails borrowing a sum of money, which must be paid off from future earnings. When the motel-restaurant becomes operative, the owner must hire chefs, waitresses, desk clerks, chambermaids, maintenance men, and so forth. He must buy food and supplies, contract for laundry services, purchase insurance. If all goes well—if the business is effectively managed—the owner will make a profit. The catch is, of course, that the risk is great; that is, the debt is usually substantial, labor and equipment costs are high, and the profit margin may be small. And considering the vagaries of the marketplace, one or two bad years might bring on bankruptcy.

Under the system devised by Father Divine, virtually all the risks were minimized. If he thought that a hotel at a given location was needed, he would so inform his followers, and a group of them would voluntarily put up the money. No loan or mortgage was ever involved because all transactions were made with cash. (Many were the stories of Father Divine's followers lugging suitcases full of money—sometimes hundreds of thousands of dollars—to pay for their purchases.) In a legal sense, the hotel would be run on a cooperative basis by "joint tenants with right of survivorship."

When it came to labor, problems were also minimal. Instead of being staffed by employees demanding union wages, the hotel would employ Father Divine's followers, who would work for no wages whatsoever. Instead, they received room and board and the eternal care of a loving God, whom they were privileged to serve on a regular basis.

Even in the matter of food, supplies, and maintenance, the hotel had a built-in advantage over competitors. Much of the food was raised on Father Divine's cooperative farms. Canned goods could be obtained from one of the cooperative groceries. Maintenance work—a big factor in any hotel—was done by the followers. And so it went. Because of low overhead, the hotel could charge rock-bottom rates: a few dollars a week for a room, twenty-five to fifty cents for a full-course meal.

Under such a system, were not profit margins thin? Indeed they were. Some enterprises showed no profit at all. They were set up as charitable, nonprofit organizations, aimed at helping the needy and strengthening the movement. In any case, the Father Divine organization was not a single economic unit but a series of independent cooperatives, owned and operated by the followers. Father Divine invested no money in any of the ventures, and he received no income from them. Those who contended that he siphoned money "off the top" were wrong.

Following the Sayville episode and the reception at Rockland Palace, the movement grew rapidly. Membership increased; the number of churches, or missions, increased; and the various business enterprises grew by leaps and bounds. Hotels, apartments, rooming houses, restaurants, groceries, fish markets, shoemakers, tailors, jewelers, dry cleaners, clothing stores, auto-repair shops, and so on. Soon there were hundreds of businesses, and while most of them were in the Northeast, some were as far away as California.

Some of the businesses, of course, were better run than others. While the profit motive was not primary, those enterprises which did not carry their own weight were presumably dropped by the movement. In the smaller establishments, business failures were not uncommon. In the larger enterprises, the record was remarkably good.

The Hotel Business Of all the economic enterprises under the aegis of Father Divine, none was more successful than the hotel business, the structural network around which the movement revolved. For example, although the organization had a number of churches, or missions, many of the meetings and rallies were held in the hotels. Communion banquet services, like the one described earlier, were held in the hotels. A large proportion of the followers lived in the hotels. Father and Mother Divine had suites of rooms in all the hotels. And, of course—because they served outsiders—the hotels were profitable. This in turn enabled the movement to feed thousands upon thousands of needy people virtually free of charge.

Reasons for the profit have been discussed above, but one further point should be mentioned. Father Divine and his followers did not build their hotels; they bought them. Often in run-down condition, the buildings were refurbished—with the help of the faithful—and then opened for business. Father Divine had a remarkable eye for real estate values, and much of his success stemmed from his uncanny ability to ferret out bargains. Once he made his intentions known, it was not difficult to find the necessary backers. Large urban hotels such as the Divine Tracy (Philadelphia), the Divine Hotel Riviera (Newark), the Divine Fairmount (Jersey City), and the Divine Lorraine (Philadelphia) were all acquired in this manner, and all were operated successfully. As a matter of fact, all are still in operation today.

Father Divine was a strong believer in racial integration, and his hotels gave him the opportunity to practice what he preached. Blacks and whites not only worked together side by side but—as a matter of policy—were assigned to the same room. Father Divine said the hotels were his "demonstrators of democracy in action."

Employment Service Father Divine first started his employment service during the New York period (1915–1919). He had an obvious knack for handling menial workers, and throughout his career the employment service remained his most successful operation, with the possible exception of the hotels.

The reason for his success is that Father Divine insisted on an honest day's work for a day's pay. Over the years, his workers' reputation—for honesty, reliability, and devoutness—grew. Indeed, as many housewives in the New York–New Jersey–Philadelphia area can attest, the demand for domestics was greater than the supply. Father Divine forbade his workers to accept tips or gifts. The following announcement has been printed and reprinted in *New Day,* the movement's newspaper, hundreds of times:

To Whom It May Concern

> A true follower of Mine does not want or desire a gift, or present, or anything of that type for Christmas or any holiday, and considers it to be unevangelical, unconstitutional, and not according to scripture. . . . MY true followers, as long as they receive just compensation for their labor, will not accept tips, gifts, or presents. . . .

This leaves ME Well, Healthy, Joyful, Peaceful, Lively, Loving, Successful, Prosperous and Happy in Spirit, Body and Mind, and in every organ, muscle, sinew, joint, limb, vein, and bone, and even in every ATOM, fiber and cell of MY BODILY FORM.

Respectfully and Sincere, I AM
REV. M. J. DIVINE
(Better known as FATHER DIVINE)

The ending is one that Father Divine used in his written communiqués. The message in the body of the letter is self-explanatory and is another example of how he could be crystal clear—when he wanted to be.

It should also be mentioned that Father Divine's followers could work inside or outside the movement. If they worked inside—in a hotel, restaurant, or larger business establishment—they toiled in the service of the Lord, without wages. If they worked outside—as domestics, for example—what they did with their wages was up to them. Presumably, many of them did turn their wages over to the movement, but they were not forced to do so.

Social Organization and Group Cohesion

All the groups discussed in the present volume are outside the mainstream of American life. To adapt successfully in the face of "encroaching society," each of the groups has used a series of sociological techniques aimed at enhancing internal solidarity. The Father Divine movement has employed a combination of the sacred and the secular. Their churches, for instance, not only serve as places of worship but are designed to house and feed people.

Formerly known as "heavens," the churches and their branches are officially designated as "kingdoms, extensions, and connections," and many of the followers live in these buildings. Not all of them, to be sure: it is permissible to live at home. But the dedicated followers —sometimes called the "inner circle," "children," or "holy family" of Father Divine—do live within the walls of the "kingdoms." (It is from this group that the Rosebuds, Lilybuds, Crusaders, and secretaries have generally been drawn.)

Actually, the kingdoms, extensions, and connections are no more —and no less—than hotels, apartments, rooming houses, and other buildings used for all-purpose quarters by the faithful. Outsiders may also live in the kingdoms, but while they are on the premises they are subject to the same strict rules of living as the followers. When the movement was at its peak—which is the historical present we are now discussing—there were over 175 kingdoms, extensions, and connections.

Followers who live in one of the kingdoms are closely knit and—like the Oneida Community discussed in the previous chapter—would comprise a genuine primary group. Describing an assembly of followers who were waiting for the appearance of Father and Mother Divine, Burnham writes as follows:

> It was here that it was possible to experience the primary-group nature of the rank and file of the Movement. They have known each other from five to forty years. They have worked together, traveled together in the church cars, lived together in buildings they own jointly, and eaten together at Communions served by fellow believers, and in restaurants owned and staffed by "brothers" and "sisters."[14]

Dedicated followers are united in ways other than by living and working together. *They also believe together.* They are convinced that Father Divine is God and that all his statements are literally true. They believe in the Bible, but for spiritual guidance they frequently turn to the movement's newspaper, *New Day,* which carries the sermons of Father Divine over and over again. True followers help the movement in every way they can. They even change their names for Father!

Nomenclature It is quite likely that followers of Father Divine have the most picturesque names of any religious group in the world. Although the press has sometimes derided their nomenclature, the names themselves—when one thinks about it—do capture both the essence of the movement and the benevolent nature of Father Divine. The following are some names picked at random from *New Day:*

Miss Great B. Love
Miss Merriness Truth
Mr. Enoch Mental
Miss Glad Tidings
Miss Sunshine Bright
Mr. David Guilelessness
Miss Happy Word
Mr. Brilliant Victory
Miss Magnetic Love
Miss Melchizedec Peace
Mr. Joseph Pilgrim
Miss Meekness Branch
Miss Evangeline Faithful
Miss True Sincerity

When asked about the reason for a change of name, Mother Divine replied as follows:

[14]Burnham, *God Comes to America,* pp. 81–82.

> If you are familiar with the Scripture, you know where Nicodemus came to JESUS and JESUS told him that he must be born again if he was to enter into the kingdom of Heaven. . . .
>
> So many people, in order to lose their identity, have prayed to God, and the Spirit has given them a New Name, as it is written in the Scripture that we should be called by a New Name. And you also know that Paul, when he was converted, his name was changed from Saul to Paul. . . .
>
> The followers are all striving to have a new nature, the nature of CHRIST, and lose their mortal or Adamic nature and characteristics.

While not all of Father Divine's supporters change their names, practically all of the inner circle, the true followers, do. And, of course, this name bond serves as another building block in the group-solidification process.

No Sex—No Marriage—No Family

The term *cultural theme* refers to broad, axiomatic principles that serve as guides to behavior. In the Father Divine movement, the theme "It is better to be celibate than to marry" pervades the entire organization. True followers do not believe in sex, marriage, or family. Married couples can join, but if they live in one of the kingdoms they must separate. (The usual procedure is for males to live on one floor, females on another.) If there are children, the children must be reared separately.

With regard to family life, dedicated followers see themselves as children and Father and Mother Divine as parents, and they believe that this type of relationship is more gratifying—and more exalted—than normal family arrangements. Point seven of the Crusaders' "Declaration Concerning God" shows the intensity of their feelings:

> I believe that FATHER DIVINE is my Real FATHER, and that MOTHER DIVINE is my Real MOTHER, and that I never had another.

True followers also abstain from all sexual relationships. In fact, men and women have very little to do with one another. Before and after communion banquets, it is quite common to see the men talking among themselves and the women among themselves. There is no hostility or antagonism, merely a gentle avoidance.

The "International Modest Code," formulated by Father Divine, is the behavioral guide used by all dedicated followers. The code—in whole or in part—is prominently displayed in the various kingdoms, extensions, and connections. It is also reprinted in issue after issue of *New Day,* as follows:

International Modest Code
Established by Father Divine

NO SMOKING * NO DRINKING * NO OBSCENITY
NO VULGARITY * NO PROFANITY
NO UNDUE MIXING OF THE SEXES
NO RECEIVING OF GIFTS, PRESENTS,
TIPS OR BRIBES

True followers adhere to the code, word for word, almost by second nature. But they seem to give special credence and attention to the section "no undue mixing of the sexes." Celibacy, virginity, purity, chastity, virtue—by whatever term, the followers seem almost to flaunt the idea of sexual abstinence.

The Rosebuds wear a white V (for virtue) on their jackets, and of their "Ten Commandments," number six reads, "We will endeavor to let our every deed and action express virginity." The Lilybuds' "Endeavor" says they will "live pure, holy, virtuous, and clean." And the Crusaders pledge to "live a righteous, useful, consecrated Life which is devoted to holiness, purity, . . . self-denial."

A further indication of the importance the movement attaches to sexual abstinence is the vast array of songs dealing with the subject. These songs are sung by the various choirs at communion banquets, special meetings, holiday celebrations, and the like. The following list of titles was taken from selected issues of *New Day:*

Virtue Marches On
Merry is the Virtuous Heart
The Virtue and Holiness Express
International Virginity
Virginity Personified
Virtue
Holiness and Virtue Are Our God
Chimes of Virtue
Behold Virtue
Virtue on the March

One final word on the sexual theme. Several observers have contended that the followers are able to achieve a measure of sexual gratification through their intense physical/spiritual reactions. Thus Hoshor states that "apparently, intensified religious mob hysteria is an effective substitute for sex. Reacting on each other like cantharides, the emotions of the devotees mount and intensify until a sublime climax of spiritual, and with some, also physical, orgasm takes place."[15]

Harris, in describing the "vibrations" of Miss Holy Light, writes as follows:

> Tears come to her eyes. . . . She screams, falls on the floor. . . . She rises and stands rigid. . . . Then she closes her eyes and dances away. She jerks her hips again, and her breasts. "Hallelujah!" she screams out. "I love you—love, love, love you!"
>
> She stops moving and sits down with a happy look on her face. Her vibration has finished. It is apparent that, in her testimony to Father Divine, she has reached a sublime climax of fulfillment. This is apparent in the way she holds her fists clenched and her eyes tight shut as though she cannot bear to open them, and in the harsh breathing she could not stop if she wanted to.[16]

I have never seen any physical reaction of the type mentioned above. Nor has Dr. Burnham, who has observed the Divinites over a period of several decades. On occasion, the communal banquets have been spirited affairs, certainly, and the love expressed for Father Divine is something to behold. But it stops far short of any physical-sexual manifestation. As far as I could determine, the followers do not consider sexual deprivation a major problem. They look upon it, rather, as a willing and loving sacrifice, made in accordance with the word of God.

The Rewards

It should not be thought that the followers of Father Divine lead a completely sacrificial life. Far from it. They must renounce normal marital and familial relationships and abjure the profit motive, but the rewards—from their point of view—are far greater than the sacrifices.

Dedicated followers will never get rich, obviously, but then they have no need for riches. Their expenses are near zero. They have no family to support, no parents to look after. They pay no rent, have no mortgage or other expenses connected with a house. Their recreational and travel costs are minimal. They have no food bill. What need have these followers for wealth? The movement will care for their material needs as long as they live. And they in turn will provide the movement with a lifetime of dedicated service.

In the intangible sphere, dedicated followers' rewards are even

[15]Hoshor, *God in a Rolls Royce,* pp. 108–09.
[16]Harris, *Father Divine,* p. 118.

greater. They have the day-to-day satisfaction of serving and being close to their God. They have the comfort of living and working with like-minded people. They are spared the normal worries of family living. They have no financial woes. They have peace of mind and a sense of spiritual well-being which outsiders often envy.

This latter point is perhaps the most important, for no one can be around the group very long without being intrigued by their spiritual outlook. They give the impression of inner security because they *understand.* Their love of God—Father Divine—is so great that it has given them an understanding, both of themselves and of the outside world.

Love of God Understanding, inner security, love of God: these are the distinguishing characteristics of the dedicated follower. Note that it is not the worship of God, not the fear of God that is the key—it is the *love* of God. It is this feeling which permeates the entire movement.

Manifestations of love seem to be everywhere: the expressions they use ("We love you, Father dear! We love your sweet face!"); the ads they run in *New Day* ("Eternal Love and Devotion to our Beloved Father and Mother on this Eternal Holiday Season"); the songs they sing ("No Greater Love," "Father, I Will Love You Always"); even their names (Miss True Love, Mr. Cyril Lovemore).

The Here and Now The followers' love is closely related to the "here and now" philosophy of the movement. Nowhere in Father Divine's teachings is any provision made for the hereafter, for the dedicated follower has everlasting life. Father Divine spoke literally, not symbolically, on this point. Over and over again, he promised his followers that if they adhered to his teachings faithfully, they would have perfect health and eternal life. On the basis of these pronouncements, followers refuse to buy insurance of any kind.

Good will toward men, racial integration, righteous government, international modesty—all these things *are desired now,* in this world, not the next. It is on this premise that the plans, policies, and actions of the movement are based. And it is this "here and now" philosophy which gives the true follower a sense of abiding satisfaction. He feels that if he can unashamedly express his love for Father, put his teachings into practice, and show that the system works, then man's salvation will be at hand.

But is it really true that Father Divine's followers do not get sick or die? Of course not. Their morbidity and mortality rates are much the same as for the population at large. However, when someone in the movement does die, it is attributed to the fact that he went astray, that he somehow failed to live up to the principles set forth by Father Divine. Had he abided by those principles, he would not have died.

Enemies and Defectors

Despite his phenomenal success as a religious leader, both Father Divine and the movement he founded have experienced considerable opposition. Segments of the black community have been scornful of the fact that one of their members had the audacity to play God. The popular press has often ridiculed the movement, while serious scholars—with few exceptions—have remained almost completely aloof.

In the early period, much of the opposition came in the form of outside clergymen. There was St. John the Vine Hickerson, who contended that "God" was none other than little George Baker, from Baltimore. Daddy Grace was a more formidable opponent. Wearing colorful costumes and denouncing Father Divine as a false god, he set up "houses of prayer" along the East Coast and—at a dollar a head—performed special baptismal rites on thousands of enthusiasts. However, he was evidently more adept at baptism than he was at filing his income tax returns, and after running afoul of the Internal Revenue Service, he fled to Cuba.

The next opponent was Bishop Lawson. Unlike so many of the others, Lawson was not an exotic or a cult leader but a legitimate—and fairly well known—black minister. He blasted Father Divine in the press and on the radio, calling him an unscrupulous faker. On and on he railed, week after week, month after month. But in the end, the result was the same. He was forgotten, and Father Divine's followers increased by the thousands.

And so it was with all his competitors. Decade after decade they sallied forth, only to be whirled back like pursuers before the Pillar of Fire. In retrospect, none of Father Divine's outside antagonists gave him much cause for concern. His real grief came from those who were within the gates and from two young women in particular, both true followers.

Faithful Mary The first woman was Viola Wilson, by her own account a no-good. Alcoholic, tubercular, selling her body for what little it would bring, she was destitute and near death when she came to Father Divine's attention. Although only in her forties, she had been in the Newark jails on several occasions and was well known to the police of that city. One night in 1933 she was taken, not to jail, but to one of Father Divine's religious services. He talked with her at some length, and before the night was over she had become converted. From then on she was a devoted follower—with all the privileges and benefits thereof—and her new name would be Faithful Mary.

The name was a misnomer, if ever there was one. She should have been called Faithless Mary.

There was never any doubt among the followers that Father Divine cured her of her many physical and spiritual afflictions. She went from a mere hundred pounds to well over two hundred. Her lung condition cleared up. She stopped drinking and stealing and gave up her commercial amours. Throughout her rehabilitation, Faithful Mary gave full credit to Father Divine. She joyfully acknowledged that he had fed her, clothed her, housed her, and imbued her with feelings of self-respect. It seemed as though she couldn't praise him enough.

On his part, Father Divine discovered that Faithful had business acumen, and he put her in charge of several cooperative restaurants and rooming houses. She, in turn, was able to feed thousands of destitute souls in and around Newark. Within a year, she had proved such an efficient businesswoman that Father Divine brought her to New York. Shortly thereafter, she could be seen sitting on his right during the banquet services. This was the seat supposedly reserved for Father Divine's wife, Sister Penny, but the latter was reported ailing. At any rate, Faithful Mary was soon performing the unofficial role of chief lieutenant.

Success, however, apparently went to Faithful's head, for she began to treat Father Divine as an equal rather than as a superior. Followers noticed a coolness developing between them, and Father withdrew some of his patronage. As if in retaliation, Faithful took some $10,000 from a prospective follower for "investment" in one of her enterprises. Father Divine found out and—incensed—demanded that she give back the money. Reluctantly she did, whereupon Father punished her by assigning her to kitchen duty. She refused, left the movement, and denounced Father Divine to the world.

He was, she claimed, more devil than god. He acquired his money through blackmail. He subjected his wife, Sister Penny, to cruel and inhumane treatment. He had a vicious temper. He had nightly sex relations with various female followers. On and on. And, naturally, the press played up the lurid stories in great detail.

After she left the movement, however, things began to go wrong for Faithful. She started the rival Universal Light movement but could find no converts. She failed in various business ventures. She was involved in a serious automobile accident. Finally she started drinking again, but even alcohol was ineffectual.

Bracing herself and swallowing her pride, she went to Father and begged him to take her back. Eventually he did, whereupon she recanted and admitted that she had lied. In front of thousands of followers—and the press—she confessed that everything she had said about Father was false.

Although she was readmitted to the fold, Faithful Mary never regained her former position. For a while she ran one of the cooperative rooming houses in Newark, but after a short period she left the movement for good. Few were sorry to see her go. Between 1933 and 1939, she had given Father Divine some unpleasant moments. She died in California in 1949.

Verinda Brown Faithful Mary was an embarrassment to Father Divine. She violated his trust and brought him bad publicity. But she was as nothing compared to Verinda Brown, who probably caused Father more trouble than all his other "problem children" combined.

Unlike Faithful Mary, Verinda Brown had a respectable background. She had no vices, no jail record, no physical debilities. In fact, when she first met Father she was a happily married woman. She and her husband, Thomas, worked as domestics for a wealthy New York family. They made good money—considering the Depression—and one would not have expected them to join the celibate world of Father Divine. But join they did.

Somehow—they could never explain why—they were drawn to Father, and after attending several communion banquets they were ready to accept him as God. To put aside temptations of lust, Thomas Brown relinquished his job and went to work in one of the kingdoms. Verinda Brown kept her outside job as domestic.

A short while later they adopted new names: Thomas Brown became Onward Universe, and Verinda became Rebecca Grace. To show their allegiance to the movement, they began to convert their insurance, their building-and-loan holdings, and their real estate to cash. Some of the cash they gave to Father Divine outright. With the rest they bought him gifts. At least, that is what they said they did.

Then Father Divine began to treat them rather coolly. Apparently, he was not convinced that they had kept lustful thoughts out of their minds. At first Verinda Brown felt hurt, then resentful, and finally bitter. After thinking things over, she decided to leave the movement, and a short while later her husband followed suit.

But Verinda Brown was not finished. She had, in effect, given Father Divine nearly $5,000—and she wanted it back. She hired a lawyer and took the case to court. Father denied the claim, and produced a host of followers who swore that he never took money in any way, shape, or form. The judge ruled in favor of Verinda Brown, and Father Divine was ordered to pay the full amount plus court costs. Father refused and promptly appealed the case but to no avail. The appeals court upheld the original verdict, and the decision stands to this day.

The decision stands legally, that is. Not morally. For Father Divine refused to pay. Not a dollar, not a dime, not a penny. Instead, he simply left New York and moved his headquarters to Philadelphia, where it has been ever since. The only time he returned to New York was on Sundays, when, according to state law, process papers cannot be served.

Father Divine's refusal to obey the court order was strictly a matter of principle. Over and over, he proclaimed, "The charge was false. The decision was unjust. I would rather rot in jail before paying one cent." Even his lawyers were never able to get him to change his mind. It was their view that the $5,000 was little more than a nuisance claim, and that paying it was preferable to the onus of moving. But Father never budged from his position.

(I am inclined to believe that the 1942 court decision was a poor one. Verinda Brown's story sounded contrived. Witnesses for the defense were largely ignored. And one of the chief witnesses for the prosecution was none other than Faithful Mary, who later acknowledged that she had lied under oath.)

There is no doubt, however, that Father Divine was hurt, both by the court decision and by the adverse publicity. He was also hurt in the sense that the movement was never able to reach its full potential in the New York area because of his forced exodus. Some of the kingdoms, extensions, and connections continued (a few are still operative today), but many of the key personnel moved with their leader to Philadelphia. It was for these very practical reasons that his attorneys advised him to pay the claim.

And yet there is a kind of oblique aftermath to the story, for if Father Divine was hurt, was not New York hurt even more? After all, because of their honesty and reliability, true followers were in demand as workers. In addition, Father Divine was feeding tens of thousands of unemployed New Yorkers every year, virtually free of charge. And, of course, none of his followers were permitted to go on welfare or relief of any kind. In brief, he was saving New York taxpayers a goodly sum of money on a more or less regular basis. So it looks as though New York's loss was Philadelphia's gain.

Membership and Leadership

It is a tribute to Father Divine's leadership that there were so few Faithful Marys and Verinda Browns. Most of his followers worshiped Father, and it seems that the closer they were to him the greater was their feeling of reverence. But exactly what was the system of leadership? Was Father Divine the sole executive and administrator? Or did he have first- and second-line assistants? How large was the movement in terms of numbers? How did the organization operate?

Some of these questions are answerable, some are not. The most difficult ones are those pertaining to numbers, for membership lists were never kept, and neither Father nor Mother Divine has ever given any exact figures, even though they have been asked hundreds of times. The ban on published statistics extends to financial transactions, bank statements, tax returns, and other fiscal records.

The actual procedure for joining Father Divine's organization must have been extremely informal. Several years ago, when the movement was closer to its peak, I asked a follower how one went about joining. "Well," the man said,

> you come to the meetings and services, and show them you're really interested. You keep meeting people and, like, you give them a chance to size you up. Then if you want, you can stay on and try it for a while. It all works out. The wrong kind don't last long.

Somewhat later, during an interview with Mother Divine, I asked the same question, "How does one join your movement?" And she replied simply, "By living the life of Christ."

More recently—in the spring of 1981—I had dinner at the Divine Tracy Hotel (graciously served by Miss Veri Sweete). The question of applying for membership again came up, and Leo Everett, a long-time follower, told me:

> Nobody "joins" in the strict sense of the word. Nor do we attempt proselytizing of any kind. If a person wants to mingle with us, and if that person can live up to the principles set forth by Father—as exemplified in the life of Christ—then he or she would be recognized as having a kindred spirit.

Actually, there are two classes of members: the true or dedicated followers, who live and work within the movement, and the adherents, who live at home. The latter group has always had varying degrees of affiliation and loyalty, and it is this group that has made it difficult to estimate numbers.

It seems likely that the magnitude of the Father Divine movement has been somewhat exaggerated. True, in its heyday, substantial numbers were involved. Standing-room-only crowds were in evidence practically every place Father Divine spoke, and on more than one occasion there was danger that fire laws were being broken. The demands on Father Divine's time and energy were such that he could scarcely keep up with his schedule. *New Day* carried reams of ads. Coverage in the popular press was enormous, with *The New York Times* alone carrying hundreds of articles. *Time, Life, Newsweek, Ebony, Reader's Digest, The New Yorker*—all ran feature stories.

By World War II, the movement had spread to some twenty-five states; in fact, at one time there were regularly scheduled buses from California to New York, so the faithful could see their leader in person. The movement also had branches in several foreign countries, and for many years there was a German edition of *New Day.* Father Divine himself stressed the international flavor of the organization and claimed that he had "millions of members," a claim that was picked up and inflated by the daily press.

But there was another side to the vociferation. Many of the standing-room-only crowds included quasi-members, or simply spectators who were curious to see what "God" looked like. On some occasions, busloads of Father Divine's followers accompanied him from one place to another, adding to the impression that there were followers everywhere. To the press, also, God and his angels were good copy, and reporters played up the circuslike aspects. When Father Divine bought an airplane, one would have thought—according to the press—that he was taking off for heaven. Many of the newspaper stories, furthermore, were clearly inaccurate. Press reports that the movement numbered fifteen to twenty million members represented a figure which was higher than the total black population of the United States at that time.

There were traces of the movement in a number of states, true, but many of the organizations were short-lived. In most of these states, there were never more than one or two branches. The hub of the movement was always New York, New Jersey, and Pennsylvania, and it is doubtful—after Sayville—whether Father Divine ever traveled beyond the Eastern seaboard. Membership abroad apparently never amounted to very much, numerically. A limited number of countries have been involved—Australia, the British West Indies, Canada, Switzerland, England, Germany, Panama—and little is known about the extent of the involvement. Tapes of Father Divine's talks, copies of *New Day,* and letters of correspondence are mailed to the branch churches in the various states and foreign countries.

The peak period for the Father Divine movement came in the 1930s and 1940s. It was during these years that membership reached a maximum, that the movement became national and international in scope, and that Father Divine became a renowned religious leader. The organization remained fairly strong during the 1950s and early 1960s, although some observers felt that the vigor was waning. After 1965, however—the year of Father's death—the movement seemed to go downhill rather sharply. Today the organization survives, reduced in both numbers and energy.

How large was the membership during the peak period? No one can say for sure. The number never approached the twenty-two million claimed by Father Divine or the "millions" regularly headlined in the popular press. If the hangers-on and the spectators are excluded, it is doubtful whether the figure even ran to the hundreds of thousands. Membership probably could be counted in the tens of thousands, but only at the height of the movement. Today the number of followers appears to be quite small, perhaps a few hundred dedicated believers, perhaps less.

There have always been more blacks than whites in the movement. During the peak period, the black-white ratio was about 90:10 or 80:20. Also, females have always outnumbered males, by perhaps three or four to one. And—predictably—the movement has had more appeal to the middle and older age groups than to the young.

Leadership There isn't much to say about the subject of leadership. Arthur H. Fauset writes, "In the Father Divine Movement, Father Divine is the organization. There are no assistant leaders, nor directors, vice-presidents, vice-chairmen, or elders. Whatever directive is carried out is assumed to have been issued by Father Divine."[17] The statement is largely true. It was Father Divine—and no one else—who formulated policy, gave talks, bought property and established businesses (although not in his own name), counseled the followers, dealt with the public, made the decisions, and otherwise controlled the destiny of the movement. None of the other religious leaders discussed in the present volume had anything like the authority vested in Father Divine.

The movement encompasses six mother churches, all rendering allegiance to Father Divine.[18] Some of the churches have branches, although each church and each branch—in a legal sense—is independent. And since the church buildings are designed to house and feed people, there are day-to-day management problems, paper work, ser-

[17]Arthur H. Fauset, *Black Gods of the Metropolis* (Philadelphia: University of Pennsylvania Press, 1944), p. 56.

[18]Circle Mission, Inc.; Peace Center, Inc.; Unity Mission, Inc.; Nazareth Mission, Inc.; Palace Mission, Inc.; all of New York; Palace Mission, Inc., of New Jersey.

vice details, and so forth, responsibility for which resides in duly elected officers and trustees.

Nominally, each church holds yearly meetings, at which time the officers are elected. Actually, it was an open secret that Father Divine made the selections, with the congregation joyously approving them. (*New Day* invariably carries the proceedings, and the same officers tend to be reelected year after year.) When he was alive, Father Divine could count on a group of faithful lieutenants who assisted in local operations. In the years since his death, these officials have often continued their local functions.

The Rosebuds, Lilybuds, Crusaders, and secretaries have generally been drawn from the inner circle of the movement, and—in terms of helping Father and Mother Divine—they can be counted on to do whatever has to be done. The secretaries (whose numbers have dwindled from a high of around twenty-five to a mere handful at the present time) have always had high status in the movement. Their jobs include handling appointments, greeting visiting dignitaries, taking care of correspondence and other paper work, and, of course, recording and transcribing the various talks given by Father and Mother Divine.

This, then, is the leadership structure of the movement. On the one hand, there is no doubt that Father Divine had substantial help; after all, he was running an organization of thousands. On the other hand, when the movement was at its peak, there was scarcely a person in the organization who could make a significant move without prior approval from Father. This was the way he wanted it and the way his followers wanted it.

The current leader of the movement is Mother Divine, who has proved to be a remarkable woman. Since she has always occupied a special place in the leadership structure, let us examine both her socio-historical and her present role.

Mother Divine

In spite of tribulations involving Daddy Grace, Bishop Lawson, Faithful Mary, and Verinda Brown, the movement continued to grow and prosper all during the 1930s. Father Divine was emerging as a man to be reckoned with, and political figures—including the mayor of New York—courted his favor. But what about Sister Penny, Father Divine's first wife? She was seen at his side less and less often. Finally, her appearances ceased altogether, and she was not heard from after 1940.

It was not until August 1946, however, that Father Divine broke the sad news to his followers. Peninah had died six years earlier. She had had a protracted illness, had grown old and weary in body, so—acceding to her wishes—Father Divine had permitted her to "pass." He had been reluctant to do so. He had also been reluctant to tell his followers the sad news and had waited until the right time to do so. But the right time had come, and on April 29 he had taken a new bride: Sweet Angel, one of his young (white) secretaries. The wedding had been performed in Washington, D.C., by the Reverend Albert Shadd.

As might be expected, the announcement of Father Divine's second marriage came as something of a shock, both to the public at large and to those within the movement. Most Americans in the 1940s were intolerant of interracial marriages. In sociological terminology, such marriages were against the *mores,* that is, those customs or beliefs about which the majority of people have strong emotional feelings. Someone can violate the *folkways*—routine customs such as table etiquette or matters of dress—and get away with it. But when a person violates one of the *mores,* he must be prepared to pay the price, which often means social ostracism.

As a matter of fact, at the time, interracial marriages were illegal in no fewer than thirty states. (It was not until 1967 that the Supreme Court declared such laws unconstitutional.) At any rate, the public was shocked and angered at Father Divine's action. Even for some of the followers, the announcement of Peninah's death plus the second marriage was too much. They simply left the movement.

After the first shock waves had passed, however, the new marriage proceeded to work out remarkably well. The public grew accustomed to seeing the couple together, true followers soon took Sweet Angel to their hearts, and Sweet Angel herself proved to be more of a help than even Father had foreseen.

So successful was the marriage that at the end of the first year a giant wedding anniversary banquet was held. From all accounts, it was something to behold. Indeed, it just may have been the most lavish ever given in the United States: 60 different kinds of meat, 54 vegetables, 20 relishes, 42 hors d'oeuvres, 21 different kinds of bread, 18 beverages, 23 salads, 38 different desserts. On and on. All told, there were some 350 different kinds of food served, with the marathon meal lasting a full seven hours.

Since then, the wedding anniversary celebrations have become one of the movement's most important yearly events, with followers attending from across the nation. A typical invitation, printed in *New Day,* looks something like this:

PEACE
You are cordially invited to
attend the Anniversary Celebration
of the
Holy Marriage
of
Father Divine
to
His Spotless Virgin Bride
Holy Communion Services
Reception
Devotional Services
NO Wedding Anniversary Presents
NO Smoking or Drinking NO Obscenity
NO Donations or Collections, but ALL are requested to donate for
sleeping accommodations, the use of church cars, banquets, and
other
refreshments.

At the wedding anniversary banquets, it was customary for Father Divine—and later Mother Divine—to expatiate on the spiritual nature of their marriage. Over and over again, listeners were reminded that Mother Divine had remained as spotless and pure as the day she married. Not that the followers ever had any doubts about the matter. In fact, neither inside nor outside the movement was the sexual issue seriously raised. But just the same, Father seemed to take pleasure in reminding his followers.

For the record, Mother Divine was born Edna Rose Ritchings, in Vancouver, Canada. Her father was a well-established florist, who would have been able to send Edna Rose to college. But her interest lay more in religion, particularly in Father Divine's brand. She became acquainted with the movement in Canada, and when she was twenty-one she came to Father's headquarters in Philadelphia. A few weeks later, she was made one of the secretaries. (She was a trained stenographer.) Together with the other secretaries, she accompanied Father everywhere he went, performing her duties flawlessly. At the time of her marriage, Sweet Angel had not yet reached her twenty-second birthday. She would eventually carry heavy responsibilities.

According to the pronouncement made by Father Divine, Mother Divine was the reincarnation of Sister Penny, his first wife—and this is the view of all true followers today. But reincarnated or not, Mother Divine, formerly Sweet Angel, formerly Edna Rose Ritchings, has worked out very well indeed. When Father Divine was alive and in good health, she was at his side during virtually all the communion banquets, meetings, and interviews. During his declining years—

roughly 1961 to 1965—she and the secretaries took over more and more of the movement's managerial duties. Referring to this period, Mother Divine told me, "Father Divine was preparing us to take over more and more of the duties. He never said so, but—looking back—we know that is what he was doing."

After Father's death, Mother Divine became head of the movement. She now presides at the communion banquets and other meetings, handles correspondence, grants interviews, visits the various branches, gives talks, and makes the major decisions necessary in day-to-day operations.

Many of Mother Divine's interviews are published in *New Day*, and over the years she has talked with politicians, students, clergymen, college professors, and others. She is quite knowledgeable about the movement and answers questions—many of them pointed—with facility. She has a wide grasp of the Bible and is able to relate many of the movement's policies to biblical precedents.

Perhaps Mother Divine's outstanding trait is her devotion to Father and the causes he espoused. At the communion banquets, for example, several pictures of Father Divine stand propped in front of her, and as songs are sung she looks at the pictures with genuine love and adoration. Though his body is gone, Father's presence is very much felt by dedicated followers. During the banquets his chair is always kept vacant, and his place—next to Mother Divine—is always set. Before the food is passed around, Mother Divine offers every plate to him.

There is no doubt that the movement has been going downhill, a trend which at the moment appears irreversible. However, if it were not for the efforts of Mother Divine and a small group of followers who work closely with her, the entire organization might already have dissolved.

Father Divine: The Man and the God

What manner of man was this Father Divine? How was he able to convince tens of thousands of followers that he was God Almighty? What was there about him . . . ?

Although *charisma* was discussed in the previous chapter—in connection with John Humphrey Noyes—the concept can also be applied to Father Divine, particularly in the sense that Max Weber used the term. According to Weber, who gave it its modern meaning, charisma refers to the "quality of an individual personality by virtue of which he is set apart from ordinary men and treated as endowed with supernatural, superhuman, or at least specifically exceptional powers or qualities."[19]

Weber is not too explicit about the sources of charisma; that is, whether they derive primarily from within the individual or whether they arise because of certain cultural configurations. Perhaps both sets of factors are involved. In the case of Father Divine, circumstantial phenomena have already been mentioned: the economic plight of blacks during the Depression; the abysmal state of race relations in the United States; the fortuitous death of Judge Lewis Smith; the need for a dynamic black leader; and so on. But what of Father Divine himself? Circumstances aside, what was there in the way of personal characteristics that would help explain his charisma?

Physical and Mental Traits Father Divine's height, paradoxically, might have worked to his advantage. Just as a tall person stands out in a crowd, so does a short one—at least, if he is the center of attention, which Father certainly was. Actually, Father Divine had many of the traits we associate with a tall person. He had a resounding—some would say strident—voice that could fill an assembly hall without benefit of microphone. His voice had an inimitable, attention-commanding quality, a quality that comes through even today when we listen to recordings of his talks made several decades ago.

In everything he said and did, Father Divine exuded enthusiasm, zeal, and self-confidence. His walk, his motions and gesticulations, his facial expressions, all attested to the fact that he was on earth to help humanity—and that all the forces of evil combined would not stop him.

His energy was prodigious. Sermons, talks, interviews, conferences, business meetings, consultations, trips to the various branches —day after day, year after year—all on four hours of sleep a night! As he himself might have put it, his energy was embedded in every organ, muscle, sinew, joint, limb, vein, and bone, and even in every ATOM, fiber, and cell of HIS BODILY FORM.

His health, also, was a little short of phenomenal. If he had any physical ailments, they did not manifest themselves while he was still active. As Mother Divine says, "He never complained." This is all the more remarkable considering his age. If—as those close to him contend—he married Peninah in 1882, he would have been over 100 years old when he died (1965). This in turn would mean that when he was

[19]For an excellent discussion of Weber, see Burnham, *God Comes to America,* pp. 2 ff.

actually guiding the movement (1930–1960), Father Divine was between 65 and 95 years old.

Some biographers feel he was closer to 85 when he died, although there is no proof of this. His death certificate lists him as being 101. But even if we accept the lower estimate, Father Divine was well up in years during the time he actively engineered the movement. In either case, the overall picture is close to incredible. This undersized, old, black man was as improbable a figure of God as one could imagine.

But, say his followers, so was Christ. And that is the point. For if, when God periodically returns to earth, He does so in the form of an unlikely human figure, then Father Divine's age, race, and physical stature were all positive attributes. This is the position of the true followers.

Father Divine's mental traits, on the other hand, were in sharp contrast to his physical appearance. He was intelligent, witty, quick, with a sharp memory. He abounded with original ideas. He had an excellent understanding of human nature and was a remarkably good businessman. He knew his Bible and could quote long passages verbatim. Despite the fact that he gave hundreds of sermons, talks, and addresses over the years, *he never prepared for any of them.* So far as is known, they were all extemporaneous.

The Father Divine Idiom In the case of any orator, two essential ingredients are voice power and word power. And to anyone who ever heard him, there was no doubt that Father Divine had both of these attributes. He had a mighty voice, which seemed even more compelling than it was because of the small body which housed it. And when it came to words and sentences, he was a veritable magician.

Unheard-of expressions rolled off Father Divine's tongue like counterfeit bills off a private press. Words like invisibilate, unfoldment, contagionized, convincement, transnipotent, physicalate, convictable, omnilucent, tangibilated—all these and countless others enlivened both his writing and his oratory. And when he was not tangibilating new expressions, he was, as Hoshor puts it, tossing out words that never before had been used in the same sentence.[20] For example, from one of his sermons:

> Someone tries to measure GOD with the measure of the mortal versionated concept of man, but THEY CAN'T DO A THING! "WHERE DID

[20]Hoshor, *God in a Rolls Royce,* p. 50.

GOD START AND WHERE DID HE BEGIN?" EVEN IF SO, WHY, YOU COULD GO BACK THERE AND THEN, AND FROM THENCE ON FROM THERE, AND THEN WHERE WOULD YOU FIND HIM STARTED AT? AREN'T YOU GLAD."

("We're so glad, ALMIGHTY GOD!" came the eager response.)

It was not only in his public addresses that Father Divine employed his unfoldment. The following two excerpts are taken from personal interviews:

QUESTIONER: You did not say you were God, did you?

FATHER: I don't need to say it. Did you not hear ME say "the personification of the Fundamental made real, and the universalization of the Personification of God"?

QUESTIONER: I notice that YOUR followers claim that YOU are GOD.

FATHER: *(softly but firmly)* I do not deny it.

QUESTIONER: YOU do not deny it, but YOU do not actually claim it—is that right?

FATHER: I need not claim anything for MYSELF. I do what I AM and express it in the Actuated Words of Expression.

QUESTIONER: I see.

In spite of his omnilucence and verbal agility, Father Divine could be as clear as the blue sky when he wanted to be. On those occasions when he resorted to obfuscation, there was probably a reason for it.

Personality and Character It is difficult to characterize Father Divine because he was not a simple man. He refused to discuss his past. He did not keep statistical records pertaining to the movement. And his statements were frequently unclear. He also had both a conservative and a flamboyant side, and this duality resulted in different writers having different impressions of the man.

On the conservative side, Father Divine was never known to smoke, drink, or gamble. He did not use profanity. He ate sparingly and evidently renounced all forms of sex quite early in life. Throughout his career he dressed moderately and never wore ceremonial garb of any kind. At a time when other cult leaders in Harlem arrayed themselves in garish costumes, Father Divine wore plain business suits. He worked hard, was intensely patriotic, and preached a more or less standard sermon: honesty, modesty, a day's work for a day's pay, peace on earth . . .

But did he not also have a flamboyant side? After all, how many men have Cadillacs and Rolls Royces, an airplane, and twenty-five secretaries? How many men coin new words, write to the heads of foreign governments, and date their letters A.D.F.D. (*anno Domini*

Father Divine)? How many serve hundred-course meals to their guests? And how many claim to be omniscient, omnipotent, and omnilucent?

All things considered, it would seem that Father Divine's so-called flamboyance was not an inherent part of his personality. In both his personal habits and official pronouncements, he revealed himself to be a basically conservative individual. All the rest—the secretaries and the Cadillacs—were probably features that he felt added to the effectiveness of his role. And even in these instances—which were overblown in the popular press—there was often a logical reason involved.

The secretaries, for instance, were not simply stenographic frills. They actually served as the nucleus—a center of loyalty—around which the movement revolved, and as such they comprised a stratum of subleadership. To transport the secretaries and other members of his staff from one meeting to another, it was necessary to have several large cars, and Cadillacs served this purpose as well as adding a touch of elegance to the entire movement.

Father Divine did not throw money away on status symbols, however. His much-publicized airplane—which he scarcely used—was bought secondhand for $700. And his Rolls Royce, bought as a used car in 1933, cost only $150. The other things—the sumptuous communion banquets, the linguistic idiom, the omnilucence—were not so much acts of flamboyance as necessary components of the movement as he was shaping it.

To the popular press, Father Divine was always good copy, and they tended to look upon him as a showman. But while the movement doubtless had its ostentatious aspects, reporters conveniently overlooked the fact that Father Divine was a man of character and principle. A *principle,* according to the dictionary, is a guiding sense of right conduct, a proposed rule of action or conduct; and this definition aptly characterizes Father Divine's deportment. He believed strongly in certain maxims or canons, and both his life and his movement were based on them. In his thousands of deeds and words—most of the latter being preserved for posterity—he never once altered his position or changed his principles.

In his secular operations, Father Divine was clearly a man of rectitude. At Sayville he went to jail rather than give in to racial prejudice. In the case of Verinda Brown, he left New York—and took his staff with him—rather than pay what he felt was an unjust claim. In fact, when one considers the size of his organization, the number of branches involved, and the unique economic system, it is remarkable that so few charges were ever brought against Father Divine.

Unknown Factors It must be admitted that many—perhaps most—of Father Divine's personality traits remain unknown to the world at large. Even today, his dedicated followers will talk at great length regarding his attributes as God—but not of his traits as a man. Next to nothing has been released with respect to his personal likes and dislikes, his habits, his leisure, his temperament, his moods and idiosyncracies.

Most of what we know stems from his overt actions, his published talks, and his sermons. In both talks and sermons, he spoke sometimes as God, sometimes as a preacher. But he seldom conversed as an ordinary mortal, and hence his "human" side remains sketchy at best.

The Movement: Weaknesses and Strengths

Weaknesses The basic weakness of the movement was that it developed as a one-man operation. Like the Oneida Community—but unlike the Hutterites and the Mormons—the movement made virtually no provision for succession. It was assumed that Father Divine would go on forever. Although present followers may deny it, his illness and death apparently decimated the movement. Father himself taught that true followers would never experience illness or death—and when he died, large-scale disaffection followed.

Granted, Father Divine's death would have created problems even if provisions for succession had been made. But the problems could have been solved. Other groups have faced and overcome similar obstacles. Oddly enough, however, the movement seems to be compounding the error in the case of Mother Divine: death is not contemplated, and no successor has been designated. When I raised the question of succession with one of the followers, the answer was unmistakably clear: "But Mother Divine will always be with us, just as Father has always been with us . . ."

There seems little likelihood, furthermore, that the movement will change its position on the subject. The following exchange took place during one of Mother Divine's interviews:

> QUESTIONER: Sometimes it's heard that FATHER DIVINE's followers will live forever. Would you comment on the statement that if you believe in FATHER, you can't die?
>
> MOTHER DIVINE: Absolutely! A true follower of FATHER DIVINE will live and not die! But this is nothing strange or different than what JESUS said 1900 years ago. . . . Sin is the cause of not only sickness, but of death! . . . And in this advanced age, it's really a shame that

> people are so ignorant of the fact that they can live and have the Victory over sickness and death; and that's the whole sum and substance of FATHER's WORK and MISSION—to bring this SALVATION.

The movement's position on celibacy is related to their belief in immortality; that is, if dedicated followers live forever, there is no need for procreation. Of course, the fact that they do die means that the movement has no effective means of growth.

Exactly why Father Divine invoked the celibacy rule is not clear. Some writers feel that since the movement was interracial and since—at that time—attitudes toward miscegenation were decidedly negative, Father solved the problem neatly by prohibiting both sex and marriage. This explanation seems a little far-fetched. If he thought he was in the right, Father Divine would never have been deterred by public opinion. A more likely explanation is simply that he desired his followers to live the life of Christ, a position that was—and is—expressive of the very heart of the movement.

Irrespective of the reason, celibacy must be listed as one of the weaknesses of the organization. All groups grow in one of two ways: by natural increase and/or by proselytizing. The Mormons utilized both methods, and they have grown rapidly. The Hutterites and the Amish have rejected all forms of birth control, and they have also shown rapid growth. The Shakers embraced celibacy and, in later years, made few attempts to proselytize—and they are now close to extinction. Is the same fate in store for the Father Divine movement?

Strengths The movement has already made some positive contributions. During the Depression, the various branches fed thousands of destitute people at little or no charge. The homeless were provided with a clean room at a dollar or two a week. Alcoholics, prostitutes, beggars, thieves—all were welcomed into the movement and given respectable jobs.

Once they joined, followers were taught the value of honesty and hard work and the importance of building self-respect. They were forbidden to accept tips or gratuities, and they were admonished to dress moderately, eschew vulgarity, and act kindly toward their fellow man.

In the field of race relations, Father Divine was clearly a generation ahead of his time. The movement of the 1930s and 1940s was pressing for reforms that would not be enacted until the 1960s and 1970s: laws prohibiting segregation in schools and public places, laws establishing fair employment practices, removing "race or color" designation on personnel forms and official records, outlawing restrictive covenants in housing, and so on.

In the political field, also, Father Divine proved to be a seer, for many of the planks in his Righteous Government platform came into being following World War II: minimum wage laws, changes in welfare policy, changes in tariff schedules, expansion of civil service coverage, and the like.

It may be true that the various reforms would have come about with or without the assistance of Father Divine. But it is equally true that he spoke out in no uncertain terms when others were silent. Without the impetus of the Father Divine movement, these reforms might have been slower in arriving.

There is one other feature of the movement that should be mentioned: the great emphasis on peace. Father Divine probably desired peace as fervently as any man who ever lived. Peace between nations. Peace between races. Peace between ethnic groups. Peace among people, and peace with oneself. This is what he stood for, and this is what he preached. He called his organization the Peace Mission movement, a name it is known by even today.

Current readers may be quite familiar with demonstrations and editorials calling for an end to war, but it was not always so. In the 1930s and 1940s, such protests were few and far between. It must have seemed to Father Divine that he and his followers were virtually alone in carrying on the peace crusade. But carry on they did—and still do—in their own inimitable fashion.

When followers greet one another, or greet an outsider, they say not "Hello" but "Peace." When one of them rises to speak at a public gathering, the opening words are "Peace Father, Peace Mother." When Mother Divine gives a talk or a sermon, her standard opening is, "Peace FATHER Dear! Peace Everyone!" And should you receive a letter from the movement, you will find the back of the envelope solidly covered with the organization's "peace stamps."

The Present Scene

The Peace Mission movement provided large numbers of blacks with an escape from the dismal reality of a white man's world. It gave them a sense of physical and spiritual well-being. And it tried to develop self-pride. On a societal level, the movement served as the tip of a spear, penetrating into the murky areas of civil rights and international peace. It also served as a reminder that Righteous Government principles could be adopted by persons other than politicians.

Yet today the Peace Mission movement is in trouble. Times change, and the 1930s are a far cry from the 1980s. The societal context has shifted, and a new set of social problems has emerged. But the movement has not changed. Its goals, organization, and method of operation are much the same today as they were fifty years ago.

In the 1930s, the urban masses—both black and white—needed food, and Father Divine gave it to them. But for some time now, starvation has not been a problem in the United States. Fifty years ago, blacks were excluded from hotels, restaurants, movies, organized sports—even from routine clerical jobs—and Father Divine railed against such blatant discrimination. Today, discriminatory levels have changed, and young blacks are increasingly concerned with getting a college education and making their mark in the business and professional worlds.

Fifty years ago, blacks, particularly those in the lower classes, needed an inspirational leader who could stand up to the white man and show some results. And Father Divine filled that role. Today, leadership in the Peace Mission movement is white, and one suspects —given the temper of the times—that this fact may have a negative effect on black recruitment.

Sayville, Judge Lewis Smith, and the days of retribution are far behind. Father himself is no longer physically present to spark the membership and expand the organization. As a group, the followers are aging. Many have already died, and others have left the movement. The social climate which spawned the Peace Mission program has changed drastically. In brief, aside from self-perpetuation and the continuation of traditional rituals—such as publication of *New Day,* convocation of communion banquets, and the observance of holidays —there doesn't seem to be a great deal for the organization to do.

In some ways, the movement is still a going concern. Thanks to Father Divine's perspicacity, the organization is well endowed financially and owns a number of valuable properties. True followers can still put on a spirited performance at their get-togethers. They are absolutely devoted to Mother and Father Divine, and to the movement itself. Inexorably, however, celibacy continues to block the main arteries of growth. New converts are hard to come by, and—numerically—the membership is at an all-time low.

Although the movement can still boast of members who live in California, Panama, Australia, and Europe, there is no real attempt at expansion. Nor is there any proselytizing. During a lengthy interview with one of the true followers, I was told that "conversion must originate from within the human spirit rather than on the basis of outside pressures." The interviewee continued as follows:

> You can't really go by numbers. It's like trying to gauge the infinite by a finite resource. During the Depression of the 1930s, there appeared to be greater numbers. But due to the obvious need, many came primarily for the material benefits. An example would be that of Jesus feeding the five thousand. Today we think of quality of membership rather than quantity.
>
> Father Divine said it best when he said that our problems are man-made—crime, poverty, sickness, death. To avoid them, we must reach a higher level of consciousness—a higher spiritual reality. We recognize that Father Divine is God, and through Him we can attain that higher level. The potential is within all of us, but only those of us who give ourselves to God wholeheartedly—totally—can transcend the material. These are the members we accept today.

This, then, is the present status of the movement. It is rapidly reaching the point—if it has not already—where the entire membership will consist of a small, spiritually elite group. One follower compared the present state of the movement with an earlier quiescent period of Christianity, the implication being that sooner or later there would be an inextinguishable resurgence for the Divinites.

All of which may be true. To an objective observer, however, there is nothing on the secular or spiritual horizon to suggest a rejuvenation. But whether there is or not, Father Divine will remain one of the indelible figures in the history of twentieth-century religious thought. He was—with the possible exception of Brigham Young—the most remarkable of all the leaders discussed in this book. He was also a man of infinite goodness.

SELECTED READINGS

Alam, Sterling E. "Middle Class Commune: A Contemporary Model." *International Review of Modern Sociology,* 6 (Spring 1976): 181–88.

Allen, Walter R. "Black Family Research in the United States: A Review, Assessment, and Extension." *Journal of Comparative Family Studies* (Summer 1978): 167–89.

Burnham, Kenneth E. *God Comes to America: Father Divine and the Peace Mission Movement.* Boston: Lambeth, 1979.

Cavan, Ruth. "Communes: Historical and Contemporary." *International Review of Modern Sociology,* 6 (Spring 1976): 1–11.

Crumb, C. B. "Father Divine's Use of Colloquial and Original English." *American Speech,* 15 (1940): 327–37.

Fauset, Arthur H. *Black Gods of the Metropolis.* Philadelphia: University of Pennsylvania Press, 1944.

Harris, Sarah. *Father Divine: Holy Husband.* 1953. Reprint. New York: Macmillan, 1971.

Higginbotham, A. Leon. *In the Matter of Color.* New York: Oxford University Press, 1980.

Hoshor, John. *God in a Rolls Royce: The Rise of Father Divine.* 1936. Reprint. Freeport, N.Y.: Books for Libraries Press, 1971.

Hostetler, John. *Communitarian Societies.* New York: Holt, Rinehart and Winston, 1974.

Kephart, William M. *The Family, Society, and the Individual.* Boston: Houghton Mifflin, 1981. See chapter seven, "The Black Family," pp. 175–201, and chapter 20, "Communes," pp. 529–534.

McKelway, St. Clair, and Liebling, A. J. "Who Is This King of Glory?" *The New Yorker,* June 13, 1936, pp. 21 ff.; June 20, pp. 22 ff.; June 27, pp. 22 ff.

Moseley, J. R. *Manifest Victory.* New York: Harper, 1941.

New Day. Published biweekly by the New Day Publishing Company, Philadelphia, Pa.

Parker, Robert Allerton. *The Incredible Messiah.* Boston: Little, Brown, 1937.

Shey, Thomas. "Why Communes Fail: A Comparative Analysis of the Viability of Danish and American Communes." *Journal of Marriage and the Family,* 39 (August 1977): 605–13.

Staples, Robert, ed. *The Black Family: Essays and Studies.* Belmont, Calif.: Wadsworth, 1978.

Stinnett, Nick, and Birdsong, C. W. *The Family and Alternative Life Styles.* Chicago: Nelson-Hall, 1978.

FIVE

THE SHAKERS

Under the "Notes" section of a recent issue of the *Gypsy Lore Society Journal,* the following curious item appeared:

A QUAKER GYPSY IN NORTH AMERICA

Ann Lee, born February 29, 1736, in Toad Lane, Manchester, England, was one of eight children of John Lee, A Gypsy blacksmith.[1]

A Quaker Gypsy? No such thing! Gypsies in North America during the 1700s? Problematical, at best. Ann Lee, founder of the Shakers, a Gypsy? Hard to believe. In fact, based on her appearance, her religious convictions, and her secular life-style, it is difficult to conceive of a more un-Gypsylike person than Ann Lee.

True, there were Gypsies in England during the 1700s. It is also true that Lee is a common Gypsy name and that blacksmithing was a traditional Gypsy occupation. But so far as I know, none of Ann Lee's numerous biographers mentions anything about a Gypsy background. Nor do the various Shakers I've talked with put any credence in the story. (Gypsies themselves claim to have no knowledge of Ann Lee.)

The difficulty is that no record of Ann Lee's birth exists. Shaker tradition has it that she was indeed born on February 29, 1736, in Manchester—though not of Gypsy parents. She did, however, come from a poor family, and while much of her background remains obscure, there is no doubt that Ann was one of the "common folk." She herself had no education of any kind and at an early age was forced to work at menial jobs. From all indications, her working-class origins and bleak childhood were instrumental in shaping both the Shaker economy and the Shaker philosophy.

When she was twenty-two, the turning point came in Ann Lee's life, although neither she nor anyone else realized it at the time. She became acquainted with Jane and James Wardley, leaders of a radical religious sect. Originally Quakers, the Wardleys had "seen the light" and broken away from the Society of Friends.

[1]*Gypsy Lore Society Journal* (1972–1973): 118.

It is difficult to describe a religious meeting of the Wardley group, but it must have been a sight to behold. Starting with a silent meditation so typical of the Quakers, the Wardleyites would suddenly erupt into a paroxysm of shouting, singing, shaking, and talking with the Lord. Because of these "agitations of the body," the group became known as the "Shaking Quakers," or "Shakers."

These early Shakers retained some of their Quaker practices—such as simplicity of dress and pacifism—but they had no definitive theology or philosophy. And while Ann Lee was welcomed, she had no immediate impact on the group. In 1762, however, an event took place which was to have a lasting effect on both Ann Lee and the Shakers. She married one Abraham Stanley. (Being illiterate, both signed the marriage registry with an X.)

Concupiscence Exactly why the marriage took place is not known, for the couple were obviously not suited to one another. In addition, Ann had grave difficulties during childbirth. She had four children, all of whom died in early infancy. For the last child, forceps were employed, and Ann Lee's life was in real danger. Although she survived, she was convinced that children signified trouble.

Ann Lee interpreted the childbirth catastrophe as a sign of God's displeasure. In her view, she had given way to temptations of the flesh—not once, but several times. And on each occasion she had been punished severely. Thus it was "concupiscence," or sexual desire, which was the root of all evil, and unless a person could repress this desire, he or she would have to answer for the consequences. Since sex and marriage were strongly intertwined, *marriage per se must be wrong.*

Soon Ann started to avoid her husband. By her own confession, she began to regard her bed "as if it had been made of embers." She also took a more active interest in the Wardley group, speaking out against sins of the flesh. And while not all her colleagues agreed with her, she eventually won them over. Before long, the Shakers were not only condemning all carnal practices but were criticizing the established church for permitting such activities.

The townspeople were quick to react. Allegations of sorcery, heresy, and blasphemy were made, and on several occasions angry mobs attacked Ann Lee. Once she was imprisoned for "disturbing the congregation" of Christ Church, Manchester. Shaker tradition has it that she was treated cruelly, locked in a small cell for two weeks, and left without food. She would have died except for one of her ardent disciples who, during the night, managed to insert a small pipe into the keyhole of her cell, through which he fed her milk and wine.

Although the story is probably an exaggeration, it does show the reverence with which Ann Lee had come to be regarded.

Christ's Second Appearing Almost without warning, Ann Lee found herself the Shaker leader, saint, and martyr all in one. The Wardleys had felt for some time that the second coming of Christ was imminent, and that it would be in the form of a woman. After Ann Lee's prison experience, they were sure she was that woman. From that day on, she was known as Mother Ann Lee and invested with a female messiahship, a belief that the Shakers hold to this day. In fact, while the term "Shakers" is accepted by them, the official name of the organization is the United Society of Believers in Christ's Second Appearing, or Believers for short.

What kind of person was Ann Lee that she could command such devotion and reverence on the part of her followers? Physically, she was a short, thickset woman with brown hair, blue eyes, and a fair complexion. According to her followers, she had a dignified beauty that inspired trust. By all accounts, she was a dedicated, unselfish, thoughtful, and totally fearless individual.

As with so many other leaders discussed in the present volume, however, verbal descriptions are grossly inadequate. Ann Lee had a genuinely charismatic bearing, a compelling inner force which made itself felt whenever she was among her followers. In some indefinable way, she was able to make them feel that they were in the presence of a heavenly person.

Beginnings in America

A few months after her release from prison, Mother Ann Lee had a divine revelation in which she was not only directed to go to America but was assured that in the New World the Believers would prosper and grow. Revelation aside, it was becoming apparent that the Shakers had little future in England or on the Continent. Their physical gyrations and their renunciation of sex had brought them little except physical abuse and legal prosecution. Accordingly, they made plans for their overseas voyage, and in May 1774 Ann Lee and eight of her followers set sail for New York. Oddly enough, the Wardleys did not accompany her. Odder still—and for reasons best known to himself—her husband did!

Arriving in August, the little band of Believers soon established themselves at Niskayuna, an Indian-named tract of land just outside Albany. They put up buildings, cleared land, planted crops, and brought in money through blacksmithing, shoemaking, and weaving. But in a spiritual sense, progress was discouragingly slow. Records indicate that by 1779 they had gained but a single convert. Abraham Stanley, moreover, seems to have vanished from the scene. Apparently he had become tired of being one of history's most frustrated husbands!

Some of the group became disconsolate over the failure of Shakerism to make much headway, but Mother Ann preached patience. When the time was right, she would say, new converts would "come like doves." Sure enough, before many months had passed, converts did indeed come streaming in. The most important convert was Joseph Meachem, a Baptist minister and one of the most influential clergymen in the area. Meachem not only became one of Mother Ann's most eloquent supporters but ultimately proved to be one of the two or three most influential figures in the history of Shakerdom.

Sex-Role Behavior In spite of her success, Ann Lee faced two difficulties sometimes overlooked by historians. The first of these pertains to what sociologists call *sex-role behavior.* Role, according to Babbie, refers to what people do and are expected to do because of the positions they occupy.[2] Thus an army officer has a set of behavioral responses which accord with his military position, a nurse has her own set, and so on. Role responses constitute learned behavior, and it is on the basis of this behavior that the participant and society are able to interact with reasonable smoothness.

In the 1700s, role behavior was sharply defined by gender. Men and women had quite different roles, particularly in the occupational sphere, and there was little overlapping. The professions, for example —doctors, dentists, lawyers, professors, clergymen—were male provinces, and any female who sought admittance was suspect. For all intents and purposes, the clergy was entirely male, and the fact that Ann Lee was not only the head of her church but the female reincarnation of Christ was a handicap of major proportion.

The second difficulty faced by Mother Ann was the fact that her position on sex and marriage was not popular. True, she was preaching in a period close to Puritanism, yet the Shaker doctrine was an extreme one even for that day and age. The fact that Ann Lee was able to win adherents in spite of the celibacy rule is a further tribute to her spiritual and charismatic nature.

[2]Earl Babbie, *Society by Agreement: An Introduction to Sociology* (Belmont, Calif.: Wadsworth, 1977), p. 14.

Persecution and Prosecution

It should be kept in mind that the decade 1774–1784 virtually coincided with the Revolutionary War. And the Shakers—recently arrived from England—were naturally suspected of being British sympathizers. It was almost inevitable that the followers of Ann Lee would run afoul of the law, and in 1780 the inevitable happened. Among those jailed were Mother Ann Lee, Joseph Meachem, William Lee, Mary Partington, John Hocknell, and James Whittaker.

Joseph Meachem has already been mentioned. William Lee was Ann Lee's brother. The Hocknells and Partingtons were the only members of the original group to come from the moneyed class; in fact, John Hocknell had supplied most of the capital for the Shakers' passage to America and for the land at Niskayuna. And it was James Whittaker who had reportedly kept Ann Lee from starving to death in an English jail by feeding her through the keyhole. Thus, virtually the entire Shaker leadership was in jail because of alleged British sympathies.

Even after they were released from prison, unruly mobs showered the Believers with indignities and abuse. Fines, expulsions, jail sentences, beatings, clubbings—at times it must have seemed as though God had deserted them. James Whittaker was beaten and left for dead. William Lee had his skull badly fractured by a rock. Mother Ann was stoned and severely mauled on several occasions. And while all three managed to survive, the fact that they died at a relatively young age is attributed to their recurrent exposure to hostile mobs.

The Death of Mother Ann In September 1783, Ann Lee and her lieutenants returned to Niskayuna, after having been on the road for more than two years. In most respects, their trip had been successful. They had spread the Shaker faith to those who had never heard it before. They had gained a great many converts. They had laid the specific groundwork for at least a half-dozen Shaker societies. By their devotion to principle and refusal to yield to pressure, they earned the sympathy and respect of many Americans who otherwise disagreed with their position.

On the negative side, however, it was obvious that the sojourn had taken its toll. The first to succumb was William Lee, who died only ten months after the return to Niskayuna. He was a strapping young man who had served as a kind of bodyguard to his sister, but the ravages of mob action had taken their toll. His death visibly affected

Mother Ann, also in declining health. Two months later, on September 8, 1784, Ann Lee died, although she was only forty-eight years old. Apparently she had had premonitions, because a few days before her death she was heard to remark, "I see Brother William coming, in a golden chariot, to take me home."

Thus ended the short but very remarkable career of a very remarkable person. Through the quiet force of her own personality, she was able to transform a tiny band of ineffectual ecstatics into a respected and rapidly growing religious body. And while the United Society of Believers in Christ's Second Appearing was not to become one of the major religious organizations, it was to have a prolonged and interesting history. Indeed, with the exception of the Hutterites, the Shakers were to become the largest, longest-lasting, and probably the most successful of all the communistic groups in America.

The Attractions of Shaker Life

For the next seventy-five years or so, the Believers grew and prospered, eventually expanding into nineteen different societies in eight states—with a reported all-time membership of some seventeen thousand. This figure is especially noteworthy when one considers that most other experimental groups of the period—New Harmony, Brook Farm, the Fourierists, and others—fell by the wayside after a few short years.

Shaker societies imposed strict rules on their members: confession of sins, rejection of marriage, celibacy, manual labor, separation from the world, and total renunciation of private property in favor of a communistic economy. Taken collectively, these factors would seem to weigh against a growth in membership. Yet in practice, there was a very pronounced growth. Why?

Although a combination of factors was involved, one sociological concept should be mentioned at this point in the Shaker story. This concept is *manifest vs. latent function,* first proposed by Robert Merton. According to Merton, many social processes and institutions have a dual function: a conscious, deliberate, or "manifest" function, and an unconscious, unrealized, or "latent" function.

College fraternities and sororities, for example, have the manifest function of providing food, housing, and camaraderie for interested students. But there is also a latent function: the conferring of social status upon those invited to membership. And so it was with the Shakers. Men and women joined manifestly because they believed in the religious orientation of the group, but in a latent sense, the Shaker community provided them with certain rewards not otherwise attainable.

To begin with, there is no denying the fact that some people joined because of an unhappy married life. Today couples who are dissatisfied have easy recourse to the divorce courts, but it was not always so. In many of the colonies, there was simply no provision for divorce. Even where it was permitted, divorce was a rare occurrence because it was socially unacceptable. For unhappy spouses, therefore, the United Society offered a legitimate way out. A couple could join one of the many Shaker communities, and by following the rules—one of which was that the sexes be segregated—they could start a whole new way of life.

But was not sexual abstinence an excessively high price to pay? This is a difficult question, and about all that can be said is that most of the converts were in the middle and older age groups, whose sexual ardor had perhaps been dimmed. For women, particularly, the sex factor was probably not of major importance. In the eighteenth and nineteenth centuries, sexual gratification was considered to be largely a male prerogative, and it is doubtful whether many women of the period thought of marriage in sexual terms.

It may be, additionally, that those with high sex drives—male as well as female—did not join the Shakers in any great number. At any rate, the membership has always shown a preponderance of females over males, the ratio being about two to one. Whitworth makes the following observations:

> In the case of the Shakers, it seems likely that celibacy would have had an especial appeal for those whose sexuality was undeveloped, or whose experiences had been unsatisfactory.
>
> The emphasis on obedience and humility probably appealed to submissive rather than aggressive personalities. Several observers concluded that the sect appealed to timorous and socially inadequate individuals whose domestic and financial situation was precarious.[3]

It should also be mentioned that Shakerdom provided a haven for those women whose husbands had died and who had no real means of support. This was especially true for women with small children. Life insurance was virtually unknown in this period, and jobs for women were severely limited, both in number and kind. Widows,

[3]John Whitworth, *God's Blueprints: A Sociological Study of Three Utopian Sects* (London and Boston: Routledge & Kegan Paul, 1975), p. 40.

therefore, often had a hard time of it—another reason why converts to Shakerdom were so often women.

A widow who joined, incidentally, retained her married name. But a married woman, writes Raymond L. Muncy, "relinquished her husband's name and resumed her maiden name in order to eradicate, as much as possible, all traces of the marriage."[4]

It was not only widows, of course, who were attracted to the economic security provided by the Believers. Some Americans were simply not suited to the demands of capitalism. By virtue of such factors as temperament, ability, or outlook on life, they simply had no desire to engage in the day-to-day tumult of a competitive system. Such individuals found a more relaxed atmosphere and a more secure way of life within the confines of a communistic organization.

Anomie First used by Emile Durkheim and now a part of the sociological vocabulary, *anomie* refers to a sense of powerlessness or worthlessness, leading eventually to a feeling of alienation. Anomic persons feel left out of the mainstream of society, and because of this state of normlessness, they may feel that their very their very survival is at stake. At least, this was Durkheim's belief.

As applied to the Shakers, it seems likely that in some cases, *anomie* was a reason for joining. As a matter of fact, the social aspects of Shaker life probably drew as many adherents as did the economic. Group living, emotional security, camaraderie, the constant presence of like-minded people, the sociality of everyday life—such things had an understandable appeal. This appeal was apparently strong enough to overcome the very real hardships that Shaker life also entailed.

Emotionality and Mysticism Another reason for the Shaker success with converts was that some Americans genuinely embraced the mysticism and emotionality that were the hallmarks of the United Society's worship. Throughout most of their existence, the Believers engaged in some rather frenzied activities. And while their day-to-day routine was marked by order, steadfastness, and laborious attention to the details of community living, their religious services were something else. The stamping, whirling, mystic utterances, and rampant emotionalism that characterized these services might have struck most observers as extreme, but for some people such activity represented the epitome of religious devotion.

[4]Raymond L. Muncy, *Sex and Marriage in Utopian Communities* (Bloomington: Indiana University Press, 1973), p. 20.

Mother Ann A fair number of Americans also concluded that Mother Ann was indeed the feminine incarnation of Christ. She was a remarkable woman and—in her own way—an inspirational leader. Shaker literature has attributed a number of miracles to her, and as time went on it was natural that the legends would grow. Her gift of healing included mending broken bones and crippled joints, curing infections and sores, obliterating cancer, healing lameness, and so on. For those who believed in these miracles, it is easy to see why the United Society came to be accepted as the one true faith.

The above points comprise the Believers' "definition of the situation" and have been mentioned in some detail since the *only way* the Society could grow was by conversion. Being a celibate group, their birth rate was zero. Conversions were their life blood, and for many decades the blood flowed with amazing vitality.

The Period of Growth

James Whittaker succeeded Ann Lee as head of the Shakers, and upon his death in 1786, Joseph Meachem assumed the leadership. Again it was a matter of the right man in the right place at the right time. For by now, what the Believers needed above all else was someone to systematize, organize, and set the stage for expansion. Joseph Meachem was the man.

Father Joseph was a brilliant organizer, and one of his first acts was to appoint Lucy Wright to the headship "in the female line." Lucy was an exceptionally intelligent woman and a sound leader in her own right. These two guided the Society for ten years, and following Joseph Meachem's death in 1796, Mother Lucy continued in the top position for another twenty-five years. Joseph Meachem and Lucy Wright were the first of the American-born Shaker leaders. They were also probably the greatest.

After the head community was established at New Lebanon, New York, the United Society of Believers grew—both numerically and geographically—for many decades. Some of the settlements were founded with no undue difficulty. Others, however, were begun under the most deplorable conditions: persecutions and mob violence, topographical handicaps, attacks by Indians, inadequate medical facilities, and other perils associated with a frontier environment. Considering the poor roads of the period, and the fact that travel was generally by foot or on horseback, Shaker expansion seems even more impressive. Most of their communities were hundreds of miles apart.

The following, in chronological order, are the dates, locations, and membership estimates of the various Shaker societies:[5]

Date	Location	Total Membership
1787	New Lebanon, N.Y.	3,202
1787	Niskayuna (Watervliet), N.Y.	2,668
1790	Hancock, Mass.	548
1792	Canterbury, N.H.	746
1792	Enfield, Conn.	739
1792	Tyringham, Mass.	241
1793	Alfred, Maine	241
1793	Enfield, N.H.	511
1793	Harvard, Mass.	500
1793	Shirley, Mass.	369
1794	Sabbathday Lake, Maine	202
1806	Union Village, Ohio	3,873
1806	Watervliet (Dayton), Ohio	127
1809	Pleasant Hill, Ky.	800
1810	South Union, Ky.	676
1811	West Union (Burso), Ind.	350
1822	North Union, Ohio	407
1825	Whitewater, Ohio	491
1826	Groveland, N.Y.	793

Like the Divinites discussed in the previous chapter, the Believers were reluctant to reveal their numbers. And as Whitworth points out, "they justified this reluctance by biblical reference."[6] Nevertheless, in addition to the locations listed above, there were at least a dozen other branches and short-lived communities in states as far south as Georgia and Florida. It is certain, therefore, that the membership figure of seventeen thousand, given in standard reference works, is a gross underestimation. In fact, on the basis of his own documentary research, Theodore Johnson, director of the Shaker Museum and Library at Sabbathday Lake, Maine, estimates that total membership ran to about sixty-four thousand![7]

[5]See Charles Nordhoff, *The Communistic Societies of the United States* (New York: Dover, 1966); Marguerite Fellows Melcher, *The Shaker Adventure* (Cleveland: Western Reserve Press, 1968); Edward Andrews, *The People Called Shakers* (New York: Oxford University Press, 1953). Membership figures are very rough approximations and are based on records of the Western Reserve Historical Society, cited by Andrews, pp. 290–91. See also Whitworth, *God's Blueprints,* pp. 37–47.

[6]Whitworth, *God's Blueprints,* p. 37.

[7]Written communication to the author.

The Believers were active proselytizers, in spite of the fact that their own societies were strictly separatist. According to Whitworth: "The Shakers sought converts enthusiastically and ardently. Each accession of new members vindicated the utopianism of the sect, and the establishment of each new society was seen as a distinct step towards the conversion of the earth into the Kingdom of God."[8]

Economic Organization

For the United Society of Believers in Christ's Second Appearing, economic communism was a natural outgrowth of their religious philosophy. Their reasoning was that in order to practice celibacy, they had to live apart from the world. And to live apart successfully, it was necessary to abolish private property.

Some Shaker leaders also felt that Christian virtues like humility and charity were best exemplified through common ownership. Throughout Shakerdom, at least, there would be no rich, no poor; no masters, no slaves; no bosses, no underlings. Such a system, admittedly, constituted what sociologists call an *ideal type;* that is, a hypothetical situation where all the preconceived criteria are met or where everything goes according to plan. The ideal type has value in that it enables the sociologist to compare the actual situation with the conceptualized ideal. In this sense, the Believers came reasonably close to attaining their ideal.

Manual Labor In both theory and practice, manual labor held an exalted position in the Shaker scheme of things. Exalted. No other word will do. "Put your hands to work and your hearts to God," Ann Lee had been fond of saying, and the Shakers used these words as the cornerstone of their economy.

With the exception of the aged and the infirm, every adult was expected to work at some manual task. This applied to the leaders as well as to the group at large. Ann Lee had worked as a mill hand, James Whittaker was a skilled weaver, Joseph Meachem was a farmer, and so on. Shakers held that this was the natural order of things and pointed out that Jesus had been a carpenter, Paul a sailmaker, and Peter a fisherman.

Believers felt strongly that manual labor was not something imposed on individuals. It was, rather, a feeling that came from within, and took the form of a moral commitment. Thus, while there were

[8]Whitworth, *God's Blueprints,* p. 37.

men and women in charge of the various trades and departments—orchard deacon, cabinet deacon, herb deaconess, and so forth—their job was not to boss or supervise but rather to handle paper work, allocate supplies, and otherwise handle administrative matters.

Work: A Cultural Theme Non-Shakers often had difficulty in understanding just what made the Believers such busy bees, since there were no apparent work pressures of any kind. Similarly, some of those who joined the United Society expecting their duties would be easy—the so-called Winter Shakers—could not adjust to the energetic work pattern and soon resigned from the organization. Work was indeed one of the *cultural themes* of the Believers, as the following expressions—all by Mother Ann Lee—indicate:

> You must not lose one minute of time, for you have none to spare.
> The devil tempts others, but an idle person tempts the devil.
> The people of God do not sell their farms to pay their debts, but they put their hands to work and keep their farms.

As Henri Desroche puts it, Ann Lee looked upon idle conversation

> as time lost from work. Laziness, play, and self-indulgence were taboo. The Shakers lived standing up. Their furniture will long testify to this inspiration. From the tone of these moral warnings, one concludes that Shaker economic efficiency was closely tied to their idea of salvation: there are no idlers in heaven.[9]

The same inner commitment that prompted the Believers to work hard was also responsible for the exceptional quality of their labor. Whether the product was a chair, a table, or a broom, the buyer could be assured of top workmanship. Shaker-made furniture was of top-grain wood, properly cured, functionally designed, joined and fitted to perfection, and constructed for long, tough usage. It was not simply work but *quality work* that constituted the Shaker trademark. Even in selling fruits and vegetables, choice quality was maintained. If a buyer bought a basket of apples, he knew that each layer would be uniform, with no "plugs" hidden underneath!

Which particular occupation a person followed was left pretty much a matter of individual choice. A number of Believers were skilled at more than one trade and divided their efforts as needed. The total list of Shaker skills approximated that of society at large: carpenter, cabinetmaker, farmer, blacksmith, weaver, metalworker, mechanic, and so forth.

[9]Henri Desroche, *The American Shakers: From Neo-Christianity to Presocialism* (Amherst: University of Massachusetts Press, 1971), p. 228.

Women and children were integral parts of the occupational structure. In fact, all youths were required to learn a trade. As in the outside world, women did most of the domestic chores: cooking, sewing, mending, housekeeping. The reason for this was not only tradition but also that the Believers' moral code forbade men and women to be in close proximity to one another. Thus, in each of the Shaker communities, the female work order paralleled that of the male, with each sex having separate workshops.

Within their order, women worked at box making, spinning and weaving, herb preparation, canning, butter making, cheese pressing, and so forth. They were also active in teaching, nursing, and administration. During a good portion of its existence, the United Society of Believers had women as leaders.

Of course, not all Shaker craftsmen were of equal skill. As in the world at large, some were better than others. The same applied to the various Shaker societies—some were more efficient than others. Throughout the whole of Shakerdom, however, the basic motif was functionalism. Frills, scrolls, refinements, ornaments, elaborations—such things had no place in the United Society. To be right, a chair had to be light, strong, durable, easy to clean, and comfortable. Building such a chair along straight, simple lines was the mark of Shaker genius. As a former member put it, "Bureaus, chests, and tables were all made with simple, straight lines, but with fine workmanship. There was nothing slipshod about the Shakers. You could depend on it—everything about them, from their religion to the things they produced, was genuine."[10]

Shaker furniture has an esthetic quality all its own: the lines invariably are right, and the viewer perceives them as such. It is interesting that whereas Shaker religion has left no real mark on the world, Shaker furniture has become appreciated as a distinctive art form.

Shaker Inventions The Believers are also credited with a number of significant inventions, such as the circular saw, brimstone match, screw propeller, cut nail, clothespin, flat broom, pea sheller, threshing machine, revolving oven, and a variety of machines for turning broom handles, cutting leather, and printing labels. Oddly enough—with few exceptions—the Shakers did not patent their inventions, believing that such a practice was monopolistic.

No Shaker ever received money for his or her work. This rule extended to church officials as well as to regular members. On the

[10]Sylvia Minott Spencer, "My Memories of the Shakers," *The Shaker Quarterly,* 10 (Winter 1970): 126–33. See also June Sprigg, *By Shaker Hands* (New York: Knopf, 1975).

other hand, no Believer was ever in need. When someone wanted a pair of shoes or a new shirt or dress, he or she simply went to the common store and signed for them. At mealtime, members went to the common dining room, where they could eat their fill.

There is no doubt that a fair degree of ethnocentrism pervaded the various Shaker communities. Members were convinced that Mother Ann had pointed the way, and that their life-style was superior to any other. As a group, they showed little inclination to mingle with the outside world. The trustees, however, carried on a fairly extensive economic interrelationship.

An Assessment of the Shaker Economy

In the last analysis, of course, the question that must be asked of any economic experiment is, does it work? Applied to the Believers, this was a doubly important question, for they were attempting to operate a collectivist economy in the midst of a capitalist system.

Simple questions, alas, do not necessarily have simple answers—and this was certainly true in the issue at hand. As we shall see in the next section, the United Society worked out a rather effective social system. Their day-to-day activities went smoothly, there was a minimum of internal discord, and—considering the size of the various Shaker communities—social cohesion was consistently strong. In assessing their economic efficiency, however, a number of complicating factors arise.

For one thing, it is difficult to tell whether the success of the Shaker economy was due to the socialistic factor or to plain hard work. With their zeal and dedication, would not the Believers have been equally successful as a corporate enterprise?

How much of their economic success was due to their religious zeal, and to the fact that their economy and their religion were intertwined? And how much was due to the succession of forceful leaders: Ann Lee, James Whittaker, Joseph Meachem, Lucy Wright, Richard McNemar, and Frederick Evans?

The extent to which these factors were interrelated will probably never be known. However, there is no denying that the collectivist factor, per se, did contribute to their economic viability. Their ready supply of labor, their self-sufficiency, and their ability to deal profitably with the outside world—these were all positive features. And finally, of course, the fact that they paid no salaries and had no stockholders meant that all profit could be reinvested in the society.

It seems likely, therefore, that up to the Civil War, at least, the success of the Shaker economy was due in fair measure to the socialistic aspects. This was the opinion of most writers of the period.

The Seceders The early days of Shakerdom were marked by hostility and persecution. As time went on, however, and the United Society acquired a reputation for honesty, hard work, and devoutness, much of the ill will abated. In place of the persecutions, unfortunately, a new threat arose: the lawsuit, usually brought in the guise of economic recoverance.

When a person joined the Shakers, he signed a covenant relinquishing all his property and permitting the Society to make use of it as they saw fit. Any time a member wished to withdraw, he was not only permitted to do so but would have his original property returned. If he had joined empty-handed, he would be given a liberal monetary allowance.

Upon withdrawing, however, some individuals insisted that they be remunerated for their services during the period of their membership. This the Believers refused to do, and in consequence a number of bitter lawsuits were fought. Some of the suits were simply brought by profiteers; others were brought by those who felt they had a just and moral claim. In general, though, the suits were unsuccessful, and the courts sided with the United Society.

Nevertheless, the cases did provoke bitterness, and the allegations often made front-page headlines. Furthermore, the suits were so numerous that handling them became one of the trustees' recognized duties. Eventually, the wording of the covenant was tightened and made into a binding contract. The remarkable thing was that although the trustees were not lawyers, few of the legal challenges to the Society were successful.

Social Organization

Unlike most of the other communistic experiments in the United States, the Shaker venture involved large numbers of men and women spread over many states. At its peak, the United Society of Believers in Christ's Second Appearing owned more than a hundred thousand acres of land and hundreds of buildings. Caring for these vast holdings was no easy task, but the Shakers managed their affairs with a minimum of bureaucratic involvement. Mistakes were made —some of them serious—yet the Believers must be given a high rating for overall efficiency.

Each of the nineteen Shaker societies was divided into "families" of approximately a hundred members. The families—a rather ironic term—lived separately, worked separately, and were administered separately. Thus, at Niskayuna there were four families; at Hancock and Union Village, six; at New Lebanon and Pleasant Hill, eight; and so on. Although the various families and societies were socially and economically independent of one another, it was commonplace for one group to help another, particularly in time of trouble.

(Not all Shakers lived in families. Some were permitted to follow the gospel in their own homes and were known as First Order, or Novitiate, Shakers. Exactly how many First Order Shakers there were is unknown, since membership lists contained only those who had been "gathered" into one of the families.)

Each family was ordinarily governed by two elders and two eldresses, and their rule was absolute—subject only to the approval of church headquarters at New Lebanon. The elders were responsible for both the spiritual and temporal order of things within their family. They heard confessions, conducted meetings, enforced rules of conduct, served as preachers, acted as missionaries, and admitted (or rejected) new applicants.

The elders were also responsible for economic policy, work assignments, and financial transactions with the outside world. On such matters, however, they customarily appointed assistants in the form of deacons and trustees. The deacons were in charge of the various workshops and food-production centers, while the trustees carried on the business activities with the outside world. That the trustees occupied a special place in Shakerdom can be seen from the following account:

> Since the trustees had complete control of all buying, selling, stocking, and loaning, their economic powers set them above the deacons, who were responsible for managing all work within the Family.
>
> The trustees' freedom of action, however, was severely controlled. . . . Their accounts were examined once a year by the ministry in the presence of witnesses. In sum, there was a continuous, careful, and sometimes bothersome check brought to bear on the lives of these businessmen-believers, exposed as they were to all the dangers attending contact with the outside world.
>
> Trustees traveled by twos and threes. They were not permitted to go on trips lasting more than four weeks. They were forbidden to participate in unnecessary conversations with people of the world. And when conversations did become necessary, the trustees were expected to give an accurate account of them to the ministry.
>
> In the last analysis, being a trustee was a delicate job. If a trustee committed the serious sin of incurring debts for the community, or if he

> committed the no-less-serious sin of becoming too important on his job, he was recalled and replaced. Among the Shakers, a job like this was not an enviable one. . . . It was also the only post in the Shaker hierarchy which women did not hold along with the men.[11]

The elders themselves were appointed, or approved, by the church headquarters at New Lebanon, although it was customary for a family to accept an appointed elder by acclamation. Acclamation or no acclamation, however, the United Society of Believers was anything but a democracy. There was no vote. There were no elections. There was no appeal. The family elders, or ministry, were housed in separate quarters, and their decisions were final—albeit on policy matters they normally consulted with New Lebanon.

The central ministry at New Lebanon was also composed of two elders and two elderesses, with the head elder (or elderess) being the official head of the church. This group was self-perpetuating: they not only appointed their own successors, but the head of the church could claim a mantle of divine authority straight back to Mother Ann Lee. The central ministry determined overall church guidelines, printed and distributed rules of conduct, kept its hand on the pulse of the various societies and families, and otherwise molded the disparate Shaker elements into a unified body.

One might think that, with their near-absolute powers, the various ministries would use their position to become oppressively dictatorial. But while there may have been some despotic characters, they seem to have been few and far between. The nature of the Shaker faith—with its stress on humility, confession of sins, and service to God—was such as to preempt the unjust use of authority.

The elders, deacons, and trustees were devout, responsive individuals who nearly always inspired the trust of their followers. And since they had to work at a manual trade in addition to their ministerial duties, their record becomes all the more impressive.

The general membership included persons from all walks of life: doctors, lawyers, farmers, unskilled workers, merchants, artisans. For the most part, though, converts were drawn from the working class rather than from the upper socioeconomic levels. Most of the major religious bodies were represented—Baptists, Methodists, Adventists, Presbyterians, Jews, although there is no record of any Roman Catholic having joined. Blacks could—and did—belong, and the same was true of the foreign-born. All ages were represented, from the very young to the very old, although in later years the bulk of the membership was composed of middle-aged and older people.

[11]Desroche, *American Shakers,* pp. 215–16.

At all times, membership in the United Society was voluntary. Shakers believed firmly that any member who wanted to should be permitted to resign. And while some individuals did not find the austerity to their liking, the number of apostates was not excessive. One reason for this was the fact that all applicants were carefully screened and instructed by the elders and, upon acceptance, underwent a period of probation.

Separation of the Sexes

It must be kept in mind that another of the Society's *cultural themes* was their total renouncement of sex and marriage. Indeed, Believers were quite fond of proclaiming the "joys of celibacy." They looked upon such joys as a mandate from heaven and acted accordingly. As Muncy puts it, "The theme of celibacy filled the Shaker hymnals."[12]

All this fervor notwithstanding, segregation of the sexes was not left to the members' discretion. Printed rules emanated from the ministry at New Lebanon and were carefully enforced by the elders of the various families. It would not be much of an exaggeration to say that never in history were men and women so systematically precluded from physical contact with one another. It was not simply sex that was prohibited, but *physical contact of any kind.*

Men and women ("brothers and sisters") slept in different rooms on different sides of the house. They ate at different tables in the common dining room. They were not permitted to pass one another on the stairs, and—as if this were not enough—many of the dwellings included separate doorways. Even the halls were made purposely wide so that the sexes would not brush by one another. Needless to say, all physical contact was prohibited, including shaking hands, touching, and "sisters mending or setting buttons on the brethren's clothes while they have them on."

Men and women were not permitted to be alone together without a third adult present, a rule which applied both to business and social occasions. Wherever possible, all association of the sexes was done in groups. Moreover, brothers and sisters were not even allowed to work together *in groups* without special permission of the elders.

The children's order was also run along sexually segregated lines. Boys and girls lived in separate quarters and were permitted no physical contact with one another. Boys were generally under the supervision of the brothers, girls under the sisters. It was thus possi-

[12]Muncy, *Sex and Marriage,* p. 36.

ble for a young child raised in a Shaker family to live virtually his or her entire life without once touching a member of the opposite sex!

While all families were strict with regard to segregation of the sexes, some apparently went to extremes; for example, the elders would spy through shuttered windows or make surprise visits to the dwelling quarters. One of the largest Shaker societies, at Pleasant Hill, Kentucky, went so far as to have watchtowers on the roof!

In general, though, relations between the sexes were not marred by incidents. There was no tenseness, no unpleasantness, no antagonism. On the contrary, men and women lived together in genuine harmony, with a security that comes from inner peace. For example, each brother was assigned a sister, who looked after his clothes, took care of his laundry and mending, and otherwise kept a "general sisterly oversight over his habits and temporal needs." In return, the brother performed menial tasks for the sister, particularly those involving heavy manual labor.

Special mention should also be made of the "union meetings" between men and women. The meetings were held three or four times a week in one of the brethren's rooms, a half-dozen or so of the sisters sitting in a row facing an equal number of brothers. The two rows were a few feet apart, permitting each sister to converse with her counterpart.

The pairs were presumably matched (by the elders) on the basis of age and interests. The ensuing conversation might relate to aspects of Shaker economy, theology, or similar topics. Although the talks were required to be on an impersonal basis, the participants employed levity, humor, and other techniques used by people everywhere. Occasionally the get-together developed into a songfest. The principle of the union meeting, however, was to encourage a positive relationship between the sexes rather than the strictly negative one that might arise from forced segregation.

A Typical Shaker Day

Days began early in the United Society—four-thirty A.M. in the summer and around five during the winter. There were six Believers to a "retiring room," and at the sound of the morning bell each would arise and kneel in silent prayer. Then the beds were stripped, the bedding placed neatly on the chairs, and the chairs hung on the ever-present pegs which bordered the walls. The allotted time for this activity was fifteen minutes, after which the designated sisters would clean the room, make the beds, and replace the chairs.

While other sisters prepared breakfast and set the dining room tables, the brothers performed the morning chores: they brought in the wood, started the fire, fed the livestock, milked the cows, and arranged the day's work.

Breakfast was served at six-thirty, and as with all meals, the brothers and sisters gathered beforehand in separate rooms for a period of quiet prayer. Then, led by the elders and elderesses, they entered the dining room through separate doors—brothers on the left, sisters on the right. After taking their places at separate tables, the entire congregation knelt for a moment of grace. The food was then served.

Each table seated from four to eight adults—children were served separately—and the bill of fare was ample if not fancy. Dietary matters varied from one society to the next, but in general the Believers preferred dairy products and vegetables to meat. In some societies, meat was not served at all, and pork was forbidden throughout Shakerdom.

More important than dietary rules, however—which were fairly liberal—were the rules of conduct which governed dining behavior. Good posture was required at all meals; elders and elderesses were to be served first; members were permitted as many helpings as they wanted, but all food taken was to be eaten, nothing was to be wasted; knives and forks were to be placed in a specified position when the meal was finished; food was not to be taken from the table; meat cut from the platter was to be cut square and of equal part "lean, fat, and bones."

Perhaps the most unusual measure was the rule which forbade all conversation at mealtime. The prohibition was in force throughout all Shaker societies, and if the idea of silent meals seems rather dismal to most of us, all that can be said is that, in the religious atmosphere which prevailed, the Believers apparently took the practice in stride. As a matter of fact, one suspects that the followers of Mother Ann were not the world's most adept conversationalists, and that the idea of silent meals was not overly punitive.

After breakfast, each Shaker, including the elders, proceeded to his or her specific work task. Household duties were shared by the sisters, each one spending a month at cooking, washing, and cleaning. Jobs involving heavy equipment were generally handled by the men, but most of the other positions were open to either sex.

The bell for the midday meal sounded a little before noon, and the earlier ritual was repeated. Afternoons were devoted to regular work activity, followed by supper at six. Most evenings were taken up by planned activity of some sort: general meetings, religious services, singing and dancing sessions, the aforementioned union meetings, and so on. Bedtime was usually between nine and nine-thirty.

Although the Shakers did not all wear similar apparel—as do the Amish—their clothing styles were more or less prescribed. Despite some changes over the years, typical attire for men included broad-brimmed hats, plain shirts buttoned at the throat and worn without neckties, vests and long coats, and dark trousers.

Women wore loose bodices with ankle-length skirts. Aprons were required, as were capes and Shaker bonnets. More than one observer commented on the fact that female attire was deliberately formless, so as not to arouse feelings of lust on the part of the men. By the same token, while both sexes were permitted the use of color, only the subdued shades were authorized.

"Entertainment" for the Believers was rather limited because of their lack of contact with the outside world. Except in a real emergency, members of the Society would not even call in an outside doctor, preferring instead to treat their sick brothers or sisters with herbs, extracts, and whatever Shaker assistance was available. For most members, the only prolonged sights of the outside world came during their journeys to other Shaker communities. Visiting of this type was one of the high points of their year.

By worldly standards, the United Society of Believers in Christ's Second Appearing was anything but a joyous organization. Day-to-day living was a serious undertaking. The Believers had a regimented existence and a restricted range of opportunities. Their list of prohibitions was a formidable one. No sex, no marriage, no money, no private property. No conversation at mealtime. No outside contacts, and a minimum of entertainment. Few visits and fewer visitors. Even household pets were prohibited, because it was feared they would somehow arouse maternal feelings on the part of the young girls. The only pets permitted were cats, used to control rodents.

Order Rosabeth Kanter, an authority on the subject, believes that *order* is a common characteristic of utopian communities. She states that "in contradistinction to the larger society, which is seen as chaotic and uncoordinated, utopian communities are characterized by conscious planning and coordination. . . . Events follow a pattern. . . . A utopian often desires meaning and control, order and purpose, and he seeks these ends explicitly through his community."[13]

The Shakers were a good case in point, for in their societies order

[13]Rosabeth Moss Kanter, *Commitment and Community: Communes and Utopias in Sociological Perspective* (Cambridge, Mass.: Harvard University Press, 1973), p. 39.

and purpose were combined to produce a definitive life-style. Their buildings, for example, were severely furnished: no rugs, no pictures, no photographs, no ornamentation. Such things were considered dirt catchers, and as the Believers were fond of saying, there was "no dirt in heaven." (It was hardly an accident that one of the very first Shaker industries involved broom making!) Furniture was sparse, since most cabinets and drawers were built into the walls. Here is Marguerite Melcher's perceptive account:

> Cleanliness and order were bywords in any region where Shakers lived. Their houses were so constructed and so furnished that whatever dirt might collect was plainly visible. There were no elaborate moldings in the rooms, no pictures on the walls, no ornamentation on the furniture. The handmade rugs on the floors were removable and washable, the windows were uncurtained.
>
> Around the walls of every room were flat narrow boards in which were set rows of wooden pegs to hold chairs when the floors were cleared for sweeping. Each outside door had its footscraper. Each stove had its dustpan and brush beside it.
>
> The word *orderliness* was coupled with that of cleanliness. Shaker buildings were planned for orderly communal living. Most of the rooms had built-in cabinets and drawers, designed to hold the necessary tools or supplies. There were drawers of all sizes and shapes: drawers for seeds and seed bags in the seed sorting room; drawers for herbs in the herb shop; drawers in the retiring rooms.
>
> The cobblers' shops had racks on the walls to hold lasts of shoes, for each Shaker brother or sister had his or her own last. Although the Believers never tried to make life easy for themselves on the spiritual plane, they spared no pains to provide the best facilities for shop and household.[14]

The Sabbath Sunday was a special day throughout the United Society. Although it was a holy day, with no work being performed, it was not—as in so many Christian groups—a solemn day. On the contrary, for Shakers of all ages it was a time of spiritual uplift, rejoicing, singing, and dancing. It was as though the quiet, the reserve, the temporal subjugation—traits in evidence six days a week—were released on the seventh day in an outpouring of spiritual ecstasy.

The dances themselves—or "marches," as they were called—ranged from mildly exuberant to highly explosive. On the mild side were rhythmic exercises in which the participants would march "with their hands held out in front of the body, and with elbows bent, moving the hands up and down with a sort of swinging mo-

[14]Melcher, *Shaker Adventure,* pp. 156–57.

tion, as though gathering up something in the arms. This motion signified 'gathering in the good.' They also believed in 'shaking out the evil.' "[15]

The following account by an ex-Shaker gives some idea of what the more volatile dances were like:

> In the height of their ecstasy, Shakers were constrained to worship God in the dance. . . .
>
> The *rolling exercise* consisted in being cast down in a violent manner, doubled with the head and feet together, and rolled over and over, like a wheel—or stretched, in a prostrate manner, turning like a log. . . .
>
> Still more mortifying were the *jerks.* The exercise began in the head, which would fly backward and forward and from side to side, with a quick jolt, . . . limbs and trunk twitching in every direction. And how such could escape injury was no small wonder to spectators.
>
> The last grade of mortification was the *barks.* These frequently accompanied the jerks . . . and one would take the position of a canine, move about on all fours, growl, snap the teeth, and bark.[16]

All things considered, however—in spite of the ecstatic dancing—the Shakers lived a serious life. It was also a contented life, and this puzzled outsiders. But the fact was that the followers of Ann Lee had an inner serenity that was hard to disturb, one they would not have found in society at large.

Understandably, outsiders had mixed feelings about the United Society. On the one hand, the Shakers were resented because they led an "unnatural" life and because they would not vote, participate in public life, or bear arms for their country. On the other hand, they were genuinely admired for their honesty, their spiritual devoutness, and their capacity for hard work. As the nineteenth century wore on, the Believers came to be treated as respected members of the larger community.

Children

From all reports, it seems that children were one of the less successful Shaker ventures. While no children were ever born into the United Society, youngsters of every age were accepted, either as orphans or as children whose parents had converted. When they reached twenty-one, however, they were given the choice of staying in the Society or leaving. And a large majority chose to leave. Results were

[15]Spencer, "My Memories of the Shakers," pp. 126–33.

[16]Desroche, *American Shakers,* pp. 118–19.

so poor that after the Civil War more and more Shaker societies stopped accepting children altogether.

The following abstract, taken from the journal entry of a Kentucky Shaker Society in 1867, contains an all-too-familiar story:

> Gone at last! Achille L'Hotte left clandestinely today, being the last one of eighteen boys brought from the orphan asylum at New Orleans in 1843. One very good youth and two others untried died here. All the rest chose the world. Achille, the last to go, is 34 years old.
>
> The oldest of the lot was only 12 years of age, the youngest 8. They are all gone and out of sight in 24 years. It becomes a question whether . . . we should be taking in destitute children. Certainly there cannot be much gain if not one in 20 remains true to the good cause. We now have between 30 and 40. Shall not one be saved?[17]

Eventually the Shakers came to accept only adults. But why did they fail with the children? The reasons are not fully understood. The youngsters were given the best of care and were treated with kindness. Corporal punishment was frowned upon. In the 1800s, the idea of public education took hold in the United States, and the Believers followed suit with schools of their own. Their youngsters were taught the three Rs in sexually segregated classrooms; there was typically a winter term for boys and a summer term for girls.

In day-to-day living, Shaker children followed much the same routine as the adults. Each youngster was taught one or more manual skills. Pride in workmanship was instilled at an early age. Cleanliness was stressed. The sexes were kept strictly apart. Dietary rules and regular dining procedures were observed. Even the clothing was identical with that of the adults, visitors often commenting on the fact that the children looked like miniature Shakers. And, of course, permeating virtually every aspect of their lives was the inculcation of the religious values laid down by Mother Ann Lee.

Since the children were more than adequately cared for, why did so many of them renounce Shakerism as soon as they came of age? While the answers are perhaps conjecture, the fact seems to be that the Believers were a special kind of people. It was not everybody who could renounce normal marital and familial relationships. For an adult to *choose* this way of life was one thing, and most who made the choice apparently led a contented life. But for the average person—especially the average young person—a regimented life without love, sex, or children must have seemed a grim prospect.

[17]Julia Neal, *The Kentucky Shakers* (Lexington: Kentucky University Press, 1977), p. 81.

Educational Policy Another factor which must have discouraged young people from remaining in the Shaker fold was the negative attitude of the Believers toward education. Although the Shakers themselves tended to gloss over the matter, they were distrustful of most intellectual and artistic pursuits.

Ann Lee said, "Put your hands to work and your hearts to God," a principle that the Believers have followed to the present. But she had made no mention of the mind, and the omission also became part of Shaker policy. Education, as carried out in the Society's schools, did not go much beyond the basics of English, arithmetic, and geography. Subjects such as science, literature, foreign language, history, and the fine arts had little place in the Shaker scheme of things.

It is true that young people in the United Society were given training that many outside youth never received. In addition to learning a manual or domestic skill, Shaker boys and girls were given extensive instruction in religion and the Bible. They were taught humility, honesty, kindness, punctuality, and sincerity. They were cautioned against the evils of the flesh. They were encouraged to promote the happiness of other people and to avoid contention. In brief, as the elders saw it, they were given training in the development of character and moral responsibility.

But for the young boy or girl with real intellectual curiosity—with some feeling for the world of the mind—the United Society must have been a bleak environment. Books, magazines and journals, philosophical debates, abstract ideas, political discussions—all were discouraged. Of higher education there was none. No Shaker youth ever went to college. None ever became a doctor or lawyer.[18] None ever held a significant public office. None ever achieved fame in the natural or physical sciences.

In the arts, the situation was much the same. Poetry, drama, literature, sculpture, painting, symphonic and operatic music—all were missing in Shaker culture. For a youngster with talent along these lines, the path cleared by Mother Ann was painfully narrow.

Reference-Group Behavior Sociologically speaking, a *reference group* is one which people look to for standards of behavior and appropriate conduct, one which can bestow or withhold approval. It is the group against which a person measures himself. For adult

[18]As stated earlier, the Believers did have some doctors, lawyers, and clergymen in their midst. However, these were men who converted to Shakerism after they had achieved professional status.

Shakers, their own Society was their reference group, and they behaved accordingly.

But for the youth who were taken into the Society, it was a different story. These youngsters did not choose Shakerism. They did not *voluntarily* look upon the Shaker community as a reference group, and hence they were not overly influenced by reference-group acceptability. While they were largely kept apart from the outside world, they were certainly not immune to its influence.

A young man or woman with normal sexual desires, or with more than a modicum of intellectual or artistic ability, must have found it difficult to remain within the Shaker fold. One would predict that when they were given the choice at age twenty-one of staying or leaving, they would leave. And in practice, this is exactly what seems to have happened.

Shaker Theology

The theological doctrine of the United Society of Believers in Christ's Second Appearing was neither complex nor extensive. But it was radical, particularly by nineteenth-century standards. The Shakers rejected such concepts as original sin, the Trinity, damnation, the immaculate conception, resurrection of the body, and atonement. For the most part, they believed in a literal interpretation of the Bible—but they also believed in revelations later than the Bible.

In rejecting the Trinity, they held that God is made up of dual elements, male and female, and that this bisexuality is reflected throughout nature. Even angels were believed to have a male and female counterpart, and the same was true of Adam. Christ was considered to be a spirit, appearing first in the person of Jesus and —much later—in the person of Mother Ann. This male-female duality constituted another definition of the situation, and, in both a secular and a religious sense, the concept permeated the entire Shaker organization.

The Believers were convinced that the primitive, or pentecostal, church—with emphasis on common property, pacifism, separatism, and celibacy—was based on right principles, but that later denominations and sects had strayed from the proper path. Violation of celibacy was a good case in point.

The Shakers' position, one from which they would never swerve, was that sin came into the world because of the action of Adam and Eve in the Garden of Eden. This "action," of course, was the sex act and was in direct disobedience of God. Henceforth, it was only by overcoming physical nature and conquering the desires of the flesh that men and women could achieve salvation. And since the Shakers had succeeded in this struggle, they felt that they alone, among the world's peoples, were carrying out God's will.

With regard to the elimination of the human race—a phenomenon which would surely occur if Shaker dogma prevailed—no serious problem was involved. The Believers thought the millennium was at hand, and consequently there was no real reason for the continuance of mankind. In the new order of things, spirituality would take the place of sensuality.

Interestingly, and perhaps contradictorily, the Shakers did not feel that man's nature was basically sinful. They believed in Adam's sin via the Garden of Eden, but they also felt that the Lord was too just to penalize all men because of the mistakes of one. In like fashion, they refused to categorize marriage on the part of the world's peoples as sinful. They did feel, however, that non-Shakers were of a lower spiritual order.

Spiritualism The Shakers were among the forerunners of modern spiritualism, the belief that the living could communicate with the dead. Members of the United Society were quite explicit on this point. They contended that they were able to talk—face to face—with their recently departed brethren, as well as with others "born before the Flood."

Communication with the spirit world varied from one Shaker community to the next and also seems to have varied over time, with the 1830s and 1840s being a particularly "vibrant" period. For a while, the religious services were so animated that the elders closed them to visitors. It is easy to see why . . .

Since the Believers had little entertainment, their religious services tended to take up the slack. After a greeting and some prayers by the elders and elderesses, the sisters and brothers would form two large circles, one within the other. Although the sexes never touched each other at any time, the participants would group and regroup themselves in a variety of intricate patterns—all the while singing, chanting, and clapping hands.

At a certain point in the proceedings, a marked change would sweep over the dancers. A mood of expectancy would prevail. Suddenly there would be a loud "whoosh!" from the group, signifying that the devil was making his appearance. Then, in unison, those present would stamp their feet, shouting and chanting, "Stomp the devil!"

Next, two or three of the sisters would whirl round and round to cries of "Shake! Shake! Shake! Christ is with you!" When the whirlers sank to the floor from dizziness or exhaustion, their places would be taken by others. Midway in the sequence of shaking, jumping, shouting, clapping, and stamping, someone would hold up his hand and announce that Mother Ann was present—with gifts of fruit for everybody. One by one, each member would come forward and receive his basket, then go through the motions of peeling and eating the contents.

Then one of the elders would proclaim that Mother Ann had a message: some nearby Indian chiefs were on their way to join the meeting. Whereupon the group would start to chant in a strange tongue and point to the door, waiting for the appearance of the Indians.

Hardly was this ritual finished when the brothers and sisters would form parallel rows and begin another sequence of dances and gyrations. This time the Indians were reported appearing at the windows, and there was an outpouring of joyous clapping. Then another "whoosh!" and some more stomping. The devil was loose again.

On and on and on the dances went, sometimes long past the curfew. While there was some variation from one service to the next, spiritual manifestations were more or less taken for granted. Mother Ann Lee was the most frequent visitor, although American Indians—for whom the Shakers seemed to have a spiritual affinity—were a close second. Other frequent guests included Alexander the Great, Napoleon, George Washington, and Benjamin Franklin.

The visions, hallucinations, messages, apparitions, and communications seemed endless. It was as though the followers of Mother Ann, by ecstatically embracing the spirit world, were able to work off all their worldly inhibitions.

After 1850, spiritualism in the United Society apparently died down or at least there is less of it reported. More than a trace remained for many decades, however, and the Believers never formally renounced the practice. As for the dances, they remained the vibratory signature of the Society for as long as the brothers and sisters had the vitality to stomp the devil.

Decline of the Order

The Shakers reached their peak around the time of the Civil War. Thereafter, membership declined, slowly at first, then faster and faster. By the mid-1870s, the Society was forced to advertise in the newspapers for new members. The following ad, for instance, appeared in several New York newspapers during 1874: "Men, women, and children can find a comfortable home for life, where want never comes, with the Shakers, by embracing the true faith and living pure lives. Particulars can be learned by writing to the Shakers, Mount Lebanon, New York."[19]

By the end of the century, whole Shaker communities were folding. By 1925, most of the remaining groups had dissolved. And by 1950, the end seemed clearly in sight, with only a scattering of hardy souls remaining.

What had happened to this once strong and spirited group? What was it that had brought about the so-called decline of the order? The answers are not hard to find.

To begin with, it was obvious that even before the Civil War, the American economy was changing. The old handicraft system, which was perfect for the Shakers, was being supplanted by the factory system. In spite of their emphasis on quality—or perhaps because of it—the Shakers could not compete with modern assembly-line methods. Ann Lee had said, "Put your hands to work and your hearts to God," but she had not mentioned the modern factory.

Transportation and communication were also affecting the life-style of the Society. With the advent of the railroad—and later the automobile—it was harder for the Believers to maintain their separatism. The younger members, in particular, found it difficult to resist the various attractions of the outside world. By 1900, it was apparent to both Shaker and non-Shaker that the era of isolation had run its course.

Leadership in the Society was likewise undergoing change. The original heads—Ann Lee, James Whittaker, Joseph Meachem, and Lucy Wright—were men and women of courage, wisdom, and foresight. Later on, able leadership was provided by men like Richard McNemar and Frederick Evans. But over the years it seemed that too often the ministry was unable to cope with the problems of a changing society. This was true in both the sacred and secular spheres.

In the sacred sphere, church leadership was unable (a) to provide the spiritual guidance necessary to keep Shaker youth within the fold, or (b) to gain enough adult converts to make up for the loss of the children.

In the secular sphere, there were too many examples of economic mismanagement. Some of the trustees were clearly unsuited to their jobs. The Shaker group at Enfield, New Hampshire, lost $20,000 be-

[19]Quoted in Whitworth, *God's Blueprints,* p. 75.

cause of poor business practices. At Union Village, Ohio, the Society lost $40,000 when one of the trustees absconded with the money. The Shaker branch at South Union, Kentucky, lost over $100,000 because of difficulties stemming from the Civil War. And so it went. A number of the Societies also lost money because of costly lawsuits. These sums, of course, represent nineteenth-century dollars, not the modern inflated variety.

Another factor that led to the decline of the order was the changing attitude toward sex in society at large. It was one thing to preach against evils of the flesh in the 1700s and early 1800s, when America was still living in the backwash of Puritanism. But by the 1900s, it was evident that fewer and fewer people thought of sex as sin. And with the emergence of more wholesome attitudes toward sex, the Shakers' position became correspondingly weaker.

Social welfare practices were also changing. Increasingly, various government agencies began to provide assistance for the sick, the widowed, the aged, and the orphaned. And as the whole concept of welfare came to be looked upon as a government obligation, the role of the United Society—as a haven for the needy—declined.

In a way, Shakerism has always contained the seeds of its own destruction. After all, in the interest of growth—or even survival—celibacy is a self-defeating doctrine. It may represent man's subjugation of the flesh, but the end product, biologically speaking, is stagnation. True, the celibate orders of the Roman Catholic Church may continue to flourish, but they represent only a small percentage of the membership. With the Believers, the *entire organization* was involved. And when the rate of conversions declined, the end was just a matter of time.

One final reason for the demise of the Society should be mentioned: the loss of a certain vitality or spirit. The early Shakers were reasonably young men and women who believed in their cause with a zeal bordering on fanaticism. Their dedication, spirit, and pride were unmistakable. But over the decades, something seemed to happen. Desroche gets to the heart of the matter in the following passage:

> The characteristic Shaker dance rituals were slowly modified and eventually abandoned. Instrumental music and more conservative songs displaced the early chants and folk spirituals. The forces of religious ardor, holding compact the life of the sect, were wearing themselves out.[20]

[20]Desroche, *American Shakers,* pp. 116–17.

The Shaker Heritage

What exactly is the Shaker heritage? In their two hundred years of existence, what have they done to make us remember them? There is no right-or-wrong answer to these questions. In some ways, the Shaker venture was an obvious failure; in others, it was a marked success. Where the balance lies depends in part on the personality of the assessor.

On the negative side, the Believers certainly failed in their primary objective—the establishment of a utopia, a heaven on earth. As a matter of record, they failed in both the secular and spiritual spheres. In a secular sense, Shakerdom simply did not flourish, and nothing can change this fact. Starting around the time of the Civil War, the movement has declined inexorably.

Spiritually, the Believers' mark on the world is so faint as to be indiscernible. Their theology is virtually unknown today, their spiritualism is an embarrassment which is best forgotten, and their dancing or marching belongs, perhaps, in a similar category. In brief, for all their efforts and their sincerity, the Shakers have had virtually no impact on modern religious thought.

On the other hand, there is no doubt that the Believers made some significant cultural contributions to Americana. Their inventions—circular saw, screw propeller, flat broom, clothespin, brimstone match—have already been mentioned. Of equal importance was their stylistic contribution to American furniture. Tables, chairs, cabinets—all bear the functional workmanlike imprint of the United Society. And in the musical sphere, as Patterson reminds us, the Shakers contributed a substantial number of folk songs and spirituals.[21]

Perhaps more than any other group, the Shakers were able to link their name with *quality.* Their fruits and vegetables were top-grade. Their seeds and herbs were the best. Their furniture was fantastically sturdy. Even their buildings were seemingly indestructible. Many are still in use today, having been purchased by outside organizations following the demise of the various Shaker settlements. The buildings are used for schools, museums, state institutions, Catholic orders, and private residences, and most of them are in remarkably good condition, despite their age.

In terms of nonmaterial culture, the followers of Mother Ann also made significant contributions. Their hoped-for utopia failed to materialize, yet they were able to eliminate many of the social problems

[21]Daniel W. Patterson, *The Shaker Spiritual* (Princeton: Princeton University Press, 1979).

that plagued society at large. Poverty and unemployment, crime and delinquency, alcoholism and drug addiction were all absent in the United Society. This is no small accomplishment, surely, since our own culture is still beset by these same problems. The point is that the Shakers were able to demonstrate to the world that communal living and separatism could be made to work.

Another contribution of current significance was their insistence on equal treatment for all members. Old, young, rich, poor, male, female, black, white, native-born, foreign-born—nobody felt left out in Shakerdom. All were treated as equals. And if this practice was not followed in the larger society, the latter at least had the benefit of a working example.

The Believers were also able to demonstrate the combined traits of courage and devotion, an amalgam that must have perplexed many of those on the outside. For despite long and harsh treatment, the followers of Ann Lee never once faltered in their beliefs. In the end, it was the outsiders who gave up and stopped the persecution.

Finally, of course, the United Society demonstrated to the world at large the magnitude of their self-restraint. As the contents of the present volume amply attest, America has seen any number of groups with unusual marital and sexual practices. But for an entire organization to abstain from sex on a permanent basis was all but incomprehensible to outsiders. Yet the Shakers not only abstained but gloried in the abstention. As they were fond of proclaiming, "He who conquereth himself is greater than he who conquereth a city."

All things considered, the United Society of Believers in Christ's Second Appearing added a new and interesting dimension to American culture. There has never been another group like them. If a society is enriched by its cultural diversity, then we must give the Shakers a strong plus for their contribution. Whether they can continue as a viable group will be discussed in the following section. But if they do not—a very real possibility—it is probable that we shall never see their likes again.

The Present Scene

What is the present status of the United Society of Believers in Christ's Second Appearing? Are new members still being accepted? Or is it too late for a secular and spiritual resurgence?

In a physical sense, there is no doubt that the Society survives today. Several settlements remain, with dozens of buildings. Both buildings and furnishings are in excellent condition. Interestingly enough, one "family" still exists, with both male and female members. Furthermore, their membership door remains open: new applicants having been accepted in both the 1970s and 1980s.

On the other hand, most of the Shaker settlements (Hancock, Massachusetts; Pleasant Hill, Kentucky; Mount Lebanon, New York; Canterbury, New Hampshire) are neither run nor maintained by Believers. They are actually *former* settlements that are maintained by historical societies.

It is true that there is still one family of Shakers—at Sabbathday Lake, Maine. But while their buildings and grounds are in splendid condition, membership—numerically speaking—is precarious. There are only ten living members, most of them quite elderly. Since the mid-1950s, a mere handful of applicants have been accepted, and most of these have not remained. Publication of the *Shaker Quarterly* has been suspended.

If the Believers are doing well in an economic sense, it is due to tourism rather than to any traditional Shaker pursuits. In brief, with an aging population and only a trickle of new members, prospects for a revival do not seem bright.

What the future holds, of course, no one can say. Only time will tell whether the United Society of Believers in Christ's Second Appearing will indeed die out—after more than two hundred remarkable years. When I raised the question at Sabbathday Lake, one of the interviewees replied: "It all depends on God, of course. Whatever He says. . . . Our destiny has always been in His hands, and it still is. But we have things to offer. People are interested in us. *Thousands* of visitors take our guided tours through here every year. There's no reason why we can't continue. . . ."

SELECTED READINGS

Andrews, Edward. *The People Called Shakers.* New York: Oxford University Press, 1953.

Desroche, Henri. *The American Shakers: From Neo-Christianity to Presocialism.* Amherst: University of Massachusetts Press, 1971.

Foster, Lawernce. *Religion and Sexuality: Three American Communal Experiments of the Nineteenth Century.* New York: Oxford University Press, 1981.

Holloway, Mark. "Shaker Societies." In *Strange Cults and Utopias of 19th Century America,* pp. 64–79. New York: Dover, 1966.

Johnson, Theodore E. "The Diary of a Maine Shaker Boy: Delmer Wilson." *The Shaker Quarterly,* 8 (Spring 1968): 3–22.

Kanter, Rosabeth Moss. *Commitment and Community: Communes and Utopias in Sociological Perspective.* Cambridge, Mass.: Harvard University Press, 1973.

Melcher, Marguerite Fellows. *The Shaker Adventure.* Cleveland: Western Reserve Press, 1968.

Melton, J. Gordon. *The Encyclopedia of American Religions.* 2 vols. Wilmington, N.C.: Consortium Books, 1979.

Muncy, Raymond. *Sex and Marriage in Utopian Communities.* Bloomington: Indiana University Press, 1973.

Neal, Julia. *The Kentucky Shakers.* Lexington: Kentucky University Press, 1977.

Nordhoff, Charles. *The Communistic Societies of the United States.* New York: Dover, 1966.

Patterson, Daniel W. *The Shaker Spiritual.* Princeton: Princeton University Press, 1979.

Spencer, Sylvia Minott. "My Memories of the Shakers." *The Shaker Quarterly,* 10 (Winter 1970): 126–33.

Sprigg, June. *By Shaker Hands.* New York: Knopf, 1975.

Weis, Virginia. "With Hands to Work and Hearts to God." *The Shaker Quarterly,* 9 (Summer 1969): 35–46.

Whitworth, John. *God's Blueprints: A Sociological Study of Three Utopian Sects.* London and Boston: Routledge & Kegan Paul, 1975.

SIX

THE MORMONS

According to Melton's authoritative *Encyclopedia,* there are some twelve hundred distinct religions in the United States.[1] It seems safe to say that none has had a more tumultuous and controversial history than the Mormons. As a matter of fact, it would not be much exaggeration to claim that—in this respect—the Mormons are in a class by themselves. Born in controversy and vilified during most of the nineteenth century, they have nevertheless succeeded in establishing a social and religious organization of astonishing vitality.

The Golden Plates

It all started in the 1820s in western New York State—an area known as the "burned-over district" because of the innumerable religious revivals held there. Never in our history has so much religious fervor been packed into one geographical area. Bibles, revelations, preachers, and prophets came (and went) with startling rapidity.

The Millerites proclaimed that the world was coming to an end. Emanuel Swedenborg announced that he had communicated directly with God. Ann Lee's Shakers renounced sex and marriage and formed a nearby settlement. Jemima Wilkinson, ruling by revelation, built her colony of Jerusalem. John Humphrey Noyes started the Oneida Community. The Fox sisters, through an ingenious system of rappings, founded the modern spiritualist movement. All of this occurred in western New York between, roughly, 1825 and 1850. Even the older denominations—Methodists, Baptists, Presbyterians—were torn by schism and dissent.

Into this religious maelstrom came Joseph Smith. Taken to Manchester, New York, as a teen-ager, young Joseph soon became disturbed by "this war of words and tumult of opinions." Which group

[1] J. Gordon, *The Encyclopedia of American Religions*. 2 vols. (Wilmington, N.C.: Consortum Books, 1979).

was right? Which was wrong? In genuine perplexity, according to his own account, he turned to the Bible and was struck by a passage in the Epistle of St. James: "If any of you lack wisdom, let him ask of God . . . and it shall be given him" (James 1:5).

Accordingly, Joseph Smith "retired to the woods" to ask God the all-important question. It was here that he had his first religious experience, for he was visited by both God the Father and His Son, Jesus Christ. Among other things, he was told that he was to join none of the existing sects, "for they were all wrong."[2] Joseph was only fifteen years old at the time, and the visitation remained engraved on him forever.

He made no attempt to hide the fact of his heavenly visitation. With the natural exuberance of a teen-ager, he divulged what had happened, but his story fell on deaf ears. "I soon found," he said, "that my telling the story had excited a great deal of prejudice . . . and though I was an obscure boy of only fifteen, yet men of high standing would take notice sufficient to excite the public mind against me, and create a bitter persecution."[3]

Although he could not know it at the time, Joseph Smith's persecutions would continue as long as he lived. In fact, they would accelerate. Nevertheless, he never once recanted or wavered in his spiritual beliefs. His revelations and heavenly visitations continued right up to the day of his death.

The next visitation came three years later (1823), when Joseph Smith was eighteen. This was the most noteworthy of all his religious experiences, since it involved the angel Moroni and the discovery of the golden plates. These plates, or tablets, form the very foundation of Mormonism, so let us listen to Joseph Smith's own account:

> After I had retired to my bed for the night, a personage appeared at my bedside, standing in the air, for his feet did not touch the floor. He had on a loose robe of most exquisite whiteness. . . .
>
> He called me by name, and said that he was a messenger sent from the presence of God, and that his name was Moroni; that God had work for me to do. . . .
>
> He said that there was a book deposited, written upon gold plates. He said that the fullness of the everlasting Gospel was contained in it. Also, that there were two stones in silver bows—and these stones, fastened to a breastplate, constituted what is called the Urim and Thummin, and that God had prepared them for the purpose of translating the book.[4]

[2]Joseph Smith, *Pearl of Great Price* (Salt Lake City: The Church of Jesus Christ of Latter-day Saints, 1974), pp. 48 ff.

[3]Ibid., p. 49.

[4]Ibid., pp. 50–51.

After several more visits—in which Moroni repeated his instructions—Joseph Smith was ready to unearth the plates. On the west side of the highest hill in the county, he came across a large stone. "Having removed the earth, I obtained a lever which I fixed under the edge of the stone, and with a little exertion raised it up. I looked in, and there indeed did I behold the plates, and the Urim and Thummin, as stated by the messenger."[5]

Eventually, Joseph Smith removed the plates from the hill (now known as Cumorah) and took them home. Each of the plates measured eight inches square, and as there were a number of them—the stack was six inches thick—the total weight must have been considerable. Yet young Joseph experienced no difficulty in transporting them, or at least made no mention of the fact. He did, however, have trouble keeping them out of evil hands. "For no sooner was it known that I had them, than the most strenuous exertions were used to get them from me. But by the wisdom of God, they remained safe in my hands, until I had accomplished what was required."[6]

Although the golden plates were written in an ancient tongue, Joseph Smith—aided by the Urim and Thummin—translated them with ease. When he had finished, the angel Moroni came and took back both the original set of plates and the Urim and Thummin. The translation, of course, remained on earth and became known as the Book of Mormon.

Considering the theme of the book and the circumstances surrounding the writing, it is little wonder that the Book of Mormon has become a source of contention. Indeed, it is one of the most controversial books ever written, and its author—twenty-three years old at the time—remains one of the most perplexing figures in American social history.

Mormons regard Joseph Smith as a true prophet of God, in much the same way that they regard other prophets of the Old and New Testaments. And they believe that the Book of Mormon reveals the true word of God, just as surely as does the Bible. Many non-Mormons believe that Joseph Smith was little more than a charlatan and a faker, and that the Book of Mormon is nothing but the product of a young man's ingenious imagination. However, we are getting somewhat ahead of our story. It was necessary to describe the episode of the golden plates in some detail because they form the backbone of the Mormon faith. But in a purely factual sense, what manner of man

[5]Ibid., p. 53.
[6]Ibid., p. 54.

was this Joseph Smith—and how did he fashion an organization that was to attract so many millions of followers?

Joseph Smith—Man of Controversy

Joseph Smith was born in 1805 at Sharon, Vermont, of old New England stock. Whether any of his early activities foreshadowed future events is a matter of opinion. His grandfather claimed to have had heavenly visions and actually had his experiences published in book form. Joseph himself was fond of using a "peep-stone," a kind of native quartz or crystal, to locate hidden treasure. And while the digging never unearthed anything of value, the boy did show evidence of lively imagination and—quite important—the ability to lead men older than himself. Use of the peep-stone, incidentally, was a rather common practice of the period.

In a strictly religious vein, Joseph Smith was not precocious. He seemed neither more—nor less—attracted to the Lord than other boys his age. Nor was he bookish or intellectual in any known sense. He could read and write, but his education, like that of most of his peers, was severely limited. He seems to have been a pleasant, likable young man, not significantly different from others of his age group—except, perhaps, for his preoccupation with treasure hunting.

Although the Smiths were never destitute, Joseph's father had some difficulty earning a living. When they moved to New York, their fortunes did not improve—and neither did young Joseph's luck with treasure hunting. How he would have fared in a competitive economy will never be known, for at an age when most young men were serving their apprenticeships, Joseph Smith was discovering and translating the golden plates. And at an age when most of his boyhood acquaintances were starting up in business or agriculture, Joseph was founding a church.

The Book of Mormon As transcribed by Joseph Smith, the Book of Mormon is a mammoth and fairly intricate work. The present edition runs to 568 double-column pages, divided into fifteen books—Nephi, Jacob, Enos, Jarom, Omni, and so forth. Each book is subdivided into chapter and verse, so that in style it is not unlike the Bible; indeed, a number of Old and New Testament passages are quoted verbatim.

The Book of Mormon tells the story of a family who left Jerusalem around 600 B.C. Lehi, the father, was a Jewish prophet who had been notified by God that the city was doomed to destruction. Under Lehi's direction, the family, together with some friends and neighbors, built a small ship and sailed eastward. Their probable route was the Arabian Sea, the Indian Ocean, and the South Pacific, for eventually they reached the western coast of America.

The little group established itself in this New World of promise and soon began to expand and multiply. When Lehi died, the group split into two factions, one following Nephi, the youngest son, the other following Laman, the eldest. The Nephites and the Lamanites eventually became hostile to one another, and fighting ensued.

Although there were exceptions on both sides, it appears that the Nephites were a more vigorous people than the Lamanites. The Nephites were industrious, well versed in the arts, and prayed to God for guidance. The Lamanites were often in trouble and became slovenly and idolatrous. They incurred God's displeasure: as a result their skins became dark, and they were reduced to savagery. They were, in fact, forbears of the American Indians.

In brief, the Nephites advanced and the Lamanites declined, and while both groups had an Israelite background, it was no great surprise when Jesus appeared among the Nephites. Indeed, he taught the same things he had taught in Palestine and set up his church in much the same way. However, as the Nephites grew and prospered over the years, they tended to fall away from Christ's teachings. Prophets such as Mormon—who had kept a chronicle of the Nephites—exhorted them to mend their ways, but to no avail. God eventually lost patience with the Nephites and permitted their hereditary enemies, the Lamanites, to prevail.

The final battles took place around the hill Cumorah in A.D. 400, and the Nephites were destroyed as a nation. The last remaining Nephite was Mormon's son, Moroni, who took his father's chronicle, wrote the concluding portion, and buried the entire record—in the form of gold plates—on Cumorah. This was the same Moroni who, as a resurrected personage, divulged the hiding place to Joseph Smith.

The idea of a spiritual bridge between the Old World and the New had a natural appeal for many Americans, especially since there was then much speculation about the origin of the American Indian. And while the account of the Nephites and the Lamanites represents but one small portion of the Book of Mormon, it does illustrate one of the central themes of the book: the cycle of good and evil. Men follow the commandments of God; hence they thrive and prosper. But prosperity leads to pride, and pride leads to selfishness and a rejection of God's ways—hence men fall. To rise again, they must repent and ask His forgiveness.

Over and over again, in a variety of different contexts and with a host of different peoples, the sequence is repeated: from goodness to prosperity, from prosperity to pride and selfishness, from pride and selfishness to downfall, from downfall to repentance. Repentance leads to goodness, and the cycle starts once more. There is little equivocation or obscurity in the Book of Mormon. Good and evil are portrayed with crystalline clarity. This lucidity adds to the appeal of the book.

Doubters and Believers As was mentioned earlier, the golden plates—and the story inscribed thereon—provoked an avalanche of controversy. Critics denounced them as fakes, and Joseph Smith was decried as a mere yarn spinner. If scholars had difficulty with hieroglyphics, how could an uneducated twenty-three-year-old possibly have translated them? The Book of Mormon, furthermore, contains a number of internal errors. The steel sword of Laban is reported as existing in 600 B.C. (1 Nephi 4:9), long before steel was invented. Cows and oxen are reported in the New World about the same time (1 Nephi 18:25), although the first cattle were actually brought from the Old World by Columbus on his second voyage.

Some critics also question the Hebraic origin of the American Indians, since archeological evidence indicates that the Indians are a Mongoloid strain who reached the American continent via the Bering Strait. Leone states that many Mormons seem to have no idea

> that there is an alternative explanation outside *The Book of Mormon* for the peopling and history of the New World before the arrival of Columbus, and that it was not all Nephites and Lamanites as stated in the First and Second Nephi. They are unaware of what the rest of the world has concluded.[7]

Other critics see the Book of Mormon as a not-too-subtle attempt to paraphrase the Bible. They call attention to similarities in name style and wording. The phrase "And it came to pass," for example, appears no less than two thousand times.

Defenders of Mormonism reject all the above arguments in no uncertain terms. They believe that Joseph Smith was a true prophet of God and as such had no need of formal education to translate the golden plates. The Urim and Thummin, as instruments of the Almighty, were all that were necessary.

As for the plates themselves, Mormon supporters point out that no less than eleven witnesses testified—by sworn statement—that they had actually seen the plates. A number of these witnesses later with-

[7]Mark Leone, *Roots of Modern Mormonism* (Cambridge, Mass.: Harvard University Press, 1979), p. 203.

drew from the Mormon Church and renounced their ties completely, *but none ever repudiated their sworn testimony concerning the golden plates.* To this day, every copy of the Book of Mormon contains a facsimile of the sworn statements, together with the eleven signatures.

As far as archeological evidence is concerned, Mormon defenders claim that it is unclear, that the authorities themselves have differing interpretations, and that new discoveries are constantly being made. It is held that, when all the evidence is in, the account contained in the golden plates will be confirmed. The other criticisms—involving word meanings, grammar, and phraseology—are dismissed as inconsequential points that arise whenever a manuscript is processed for publication.

Followers believe strongly that the Book of Mormon is an internally consistent document that has stood the test of time. They feel it is beautifully written, eternally instructive, and a true reflection of the word of God. They accept it—along with the Old and New Testaments—as Scripture. The net result, as Leone states, is that "Mormonism is not a part of traditional Christianity; it is a whole new version."[8]

Formation of the Church

On April 6, 1830, six young men gathered together not far from the hill Cumorah. In addition to Joseph Smith himself, there were his two brothers, Hyrum and Samuel, as well as Oliver Cowdery, Peter Whitmer, and David Whitmer. All had seen the golden plates—they had so testified—and all had been profoundly moved by the inscribed message. Indeed, they were gathered for the purpose of founding a church based on that message. The laws of New York State required a minimum of six members for incorporation, and these were the six. When the meeting opened, Joseph Smith announced that he had received a revelation from God which said, "Behold there should be a record kept among you: and in it thou shalt be called a seer, a translator, a prophet, an apostle of Jesus Christ, an elder of the church through the will of God."

By this revelation, and by the unanimous consent of the original six members, Joseph Smith was acknowledged to be a prophet of God and the undisputed leader of the church. Even today, in routine conversation, Mormons refer to him as the Prophet. It should be men-

[8]Ibid., p. 171.

tioned, however, that the term "Mormon Church" was never adopted, the original designation being simply the Church of Christ. (Outsiders referred to members as "Mormons" or "Mormonites.") A few years later (1838), the present name was made official: the Church of Jesus Christ of Latter-day Saints. ("Latter-day" refers to the Western Hemisphere period of scriptural history.) Members of the church do not mind being called Mormons. They use the name themselves. They are more likely, however, to use terms like "Saints," "Latter-day Saints," or "LDS."

The church grew rapidly—a thousand members in less than a year. It soon became apparent that, being American in both setting and theology, LDS had a natural attraction for many people. Then, too, in this early period the church was blessed with a number of extremely able, vigorous men. In addition to Joseph Smith, a genuinely charismatic leader, there were Oliver Cowdery, Sidney Rigdon, and Parley Pratt. There was also a man named Brigham Young.

Death of the Prophet Mormon growth, however, was accompanied by prolonged and vicious persecution. In New York State, Joseph Smith was arrested several times for disturbing the peace. To escape harassment, the Prophet and his followers moved westward—to Ohio, Missouri, Illinois—but in each state they encountered real trouble. Raids, attacks by mobs, pitched battles—the trail of persecution seemed endless. Joseph Smith himself was assaulted, beaten, and jailed on a number of occasions.

The end came on June 27, 1844, when a mob stormed the jail at Carthage, Illinois, where four Mormon leaders were being held. Willard Richards and John Taylor managed to escape with their lives, but Joseph Smith and his brother Hyrum were brutally shot to death.

The Aftermath—and Brigham Young

Donna Hill reports that Joseph Smith's followers were "shocked, anguished, and outraged by his murder," with the news "hitting like a thunderbolt, crushing the people to earth."[9] The same author notes, however, that in spite of the tragedy,

> the Mormons were later to become exalted by their prophet's martyrdom, as though by a crowning achievement. The official announcement by his church said, "He lived great, and he died great in the eyes of God

[9]Donna Hill, *Joseph Smith: The First Mormon* (Garden City, N.Y.: Doubleday, 1977), p. 5.

and his people, and like most of the Lord's anointed in ancient times, has sealed his mission and his works with his own blood."[10]

The death of the Mormon leader also shocked both the citizens of Illinois and the nation at large. Even the demise of such well-known figures as Ann Lee and John Humphrey Noyes brought nothing like the publicity accorded Joseph Smith. To be sure, the Prophet was brutally murdered, while the others died of natural causes, but the reaction was based on more than that. It was as though the public sensed that—unlike the Shakers, the Oneidans, and scores of others—the Latter-day Saints presaged a major movement.

There were some who thought otherwise. Many outsiders felt that LDS would never survive the death of its leader. And some insiders tried to weaken the movement by forming splinter groups. One faction followed Sidney Rigdon eastward. Another group went with James Strang to Wisconsin and Michigan. Still another followed William Bickerton to West Virginia and Pennsylvania. Not all of these offshoots failed—small groups of Strangites and Bickertonites still exist—but none had any appreciable effect on the health of LDS proper. The only apostate organization to achieve any size and importance was the Reorganized group, which will be discussed later.

In any event, the Church of Jesus Christ of Latter-day Saints not only survived but grew and prospered. The death of Joseph Smith did not result in a bankruptcy of leadership. On the contrary, LDS had any number of able and enthusiastic men. There was, of course, only one Brigham Young.

Born in 1801 at Whitingham, Vermont, Brigham Young reportedly came from the poorest family in town. Instead of going to school, he worked—with his hands. He became a skilled carpenter, painter, and glazier, and—on the side—learned to read and write. He evidenced no special religious leanings until he was twenty-two, when he became a Methodist. A few years later, after reading the Book of Mormon and becoming convinced of its authenticity, he converted to LDS.

In 1832 he met Joseph Smith, and the two had a long talk. From then on, Brigham Young was one of the Prophet's staunchest supporters—and one of Mormondom's most enthusiastic workers. As a carpenter, he helped build temples; as a planner, he laid out whole cities; as a missionary, he achieved a brilliant record in England. His rise within the church was rapid, and following Joseph Smith's death in 1844, he was the dominant figure in LDS for over thirty years. It is difficult to

[10]Ibid., p. 6.

imagine what form Mormonism would have taken without his leadership.

"This Is the Right Place"

After a short—and uneasy—truce, persecution of the Mormons was resumed. The alleged murderers of Joseph Smith were tried but were acquitted, and from then on things went from bad to worse. Mobs attacked Mormon families. LDS temples were set afire. Attacks and counterattacks accelerated. At one time, both sides were using artillery pieces! By the end of 1845, it had become obvious that the Latter-day Saints would have to leave Illinois.

The exodus began on the morning of February 4, 1846, and the going was rough. It took the Saints nearly five months to reach Council Bluffs, Iowa, four hundred miles away. But the Rocky Mountains were still five hundred miles distant—and beyond the mountains was another stretch of a thousand miles, most of it unsettled land.

In the spring of 1847, an advance group of some 150 Mormons, headed by Brigham Young and Heber Kimball, set out to blaze a new path. Their success was startling. Known as the Mormon Trail, the new route was eventually followed by both the Union Pacific Railroad and U.S. Highway 30.

The trailblazers pushed on across the Rockies, and on the morning of July 24, 1847, Brigham Young caught his first sight of the Great Salt Lake Valley. He held up his hand and said, "It is far enough. This is the right place." His followers knew what he meant. Thenceforth, July 24 would be celebrated among the Mormons as Pioneer Day, their greatest holiday.

Miracle of the Gulls One of the stories concerning early Mormon hardships is the so-called miracle of the gulls. The summer of 1849, thanks largely to irrigation, was a good crop year. The vegetation was thick, and the leaves were lush. But just as the Saints were visualizing full storehouses for the winter, hordes of locusts swarmed over the plants and began to devour them. Horrified, the residents tried to beat the insects off with everything at their command. They opened up the irrigation canals to drown the invaders, but for every thousand that were killed, ten thousand more appeared. Finally—after all human effort had failed—the Mormons knelt down beside their crops and prayed to God for help.

Suddenly, in the distance, a dark cloud appeared. It proved to be a large flock of gulls, and for a time the Mormons feared further destruction. But to their unbounded joy, the gulls began to devour the locusts, and soon the danger was over. The story is a true one, and today there is a monument to the gulls in Salt Lake City.

Overseas Efforts It had always been Joseph Smith's feeling that Mormonism needed a strong overseas base, and as early as 1837, an LDS mission had been established in England. The actual flow of converts from Europe to America began shortly afterward, but not until Brigham Young took office did Mormon immigration flourish. During the thirty years of his presidency (1847–1877), tens of thousands of converts arrived in America, nearly all of whom remained loyal to the church.

The chief source of LDS immigration was England and Scandinavia, although some converts were also received from Germany and Switzerland. Mormon attempts in other countries—Italy, Spain, China—failed. There is no doubt, though, that much of Utah today is of Anglo-Scandinavian stock. As Wallace Turner puts it, "A summer's day walk down any street in Salt Lake City's business district shows a constant parade of blonds with blue eyes and skins tanned golden brown under the sun of the high desert."[11]

Polygamy

Once the Salt Lake region was consolidated, the Mormons experienced steady and rapid growth. Like all organizations, they had problems and conflicts. But there was one issue that dwarfed all the others, one issue that almost brought the edifice down. The issue was polygamy, and it is ironic that the very practice that came close to being fatal is the one which, in the public mind, seems interminably linked with Mormonism.[12]

How did the Latter-day Saints come to adopt polygamy in the first place? A number of explanations have been offered, most of them false. It has been suggested that plural marriage was utilized in order to take care of the excess of Mormon females. Census figures indicate, however, that—as in most of the West—the Utah area had an excess of males, not females.

[11]Wallace Turner, *The Mormon Establishment* (Boston: Houghton Mifflin, 1966), p. 69.

[12]Strictly speaking, polygamy refers to plural spouses (wives *or* husbands), while polygyny includes only plural wives. However, writers of the period used the term polygamy when referring to the Mormons, and somehow the term has persisted. To be consistent, therefore, "polygamy" will be used throughout.

It has also been suggested that polygamy was simply a convenient method of satisfying the male sex urge, yet prurient interests can hardly have been paramount. Before a man could take a second wife, he was required to get the permission not only of his bishop but of his first wife. Only by so doing could he be assured of a sanctioned LDS marriage.

Some observers feel that plural marriage was an unsubtle attempt by the church to increase the Mormon birth rate. But this contention is not true either. Polygamous wives, on the average, had fewer children than did monogamous wives.

The Latter-day Saints adopted polygamy for one reason and one reason only. They were convinced that the practice had been ordained by God—as revealed through the Prophet Joseph Smith. Virtually all modern scholars are in agreement on this point.

As a sidelight, Hill makes the following interesting observation:

> Account must be taken also of the Prophet's enormous capacity to love, and of his wish to bind his loved ones to himself forever, in this life, in the millennium, and throughout eternity. He interpreted the Lord's plan for the salvation of men as progression to the state of godhood, in an eternal family union.[13]

Origins While the history of Mormon polygamy contains numerous gaps, the following information has been fairly well documented. Joseph Smith reported that he had received a revelation from God prescribing polygamy. The date of the revelation is unclear. It was *recorded,* however, on July 12, 1843, for on that date the Prophet carefully dictated the revelation to his clerk, William Clayton. The revelation was a lengthy one, but the key portions are as follows:

> If any man espouse a virgin, and desire to espouse another, and the first give her consent, . . . then he is justified; for he cannot commit adultery with that that belongeth unto him and to no one else. . . .
>
> Verily I say unto you, I will reveal more unto you hereafter; therefore, let this suffice for the present. Behold, I am Alpha and Omega. Amen.[14]

There is no indication, however, that the Prophet ever revealed any further word of God on the subject. In less than a year, he was dead. There is evidence which points to the fact that the Principle, as it came to be called, was practiced before 1843, although it seems to have been restricted to high-ranking members of the church—men

[13]Hill, *Joseph Smith,* p. 343.

[14]Joseph Smith, *Doctrine and Covenants* (Salt Lake City: The Church of Jesus Christ of Latter-day Saints, 1974), section 32.

like Parley Pratt, Heber Kimball, Brigham Young, and Joseph Smith himself.

Needless to say, the Principle evoked a good deal of anguish, as can be seen from the following passage:

> To many of Joseph Smith's followers, most of whom were from a New England background in which sexual mores were strict, the commandment to practice plural marriage seemed bitterly hard. Several of his friends confessed that the new tenet brought them close to apostatizing. Brigham Young said that when he heard the revelation, "it was the first time in my life that I desired the grave."[15]

It should be emphasized that in this early period, polygamy was never publicly admitted; indeed, the revelation itself was locked in Brigham Young's desk for many years. Gradually, however, as more and more of the church hierarchy took plural wives, the element of secrecy was lost. When Orson Pratt and Brigham Young made the public announcement in 1852—based on the Prophet's earlier revelation—the Principle had become a more or less open secret.

By this time, of course, the Mormons had "escaped" from the East and the Midwest. Well beyond the Rocky Mountains, they were—or thought they were—safely ensconced in their territorial domain. Church leaders did not expect that the Principle would go unchallenged. They anticipated some intervention by the United States government, but thought that—in the interest of religious freedom—the courts would be on the side of LDS. This was an incorrect assessment.

Nevertheless, for a period of almost fifty years the Latter-day Saints not only practiced polygamy but did so with a fair amount of success. It may well be that this exercise in marital pluralism was the most unusual large-scale experiment in American social history.

The Operation of Polygamy At the time, there were many misconceptions about Mormon polygamy, and some of them still remain. According to the lurid accounts of the eastern newspapers, Mormon patriarchs were simply gobbling up unsuspecting girls in wholesale lots—for lewd and lascivious purposes. And while such charges were obvious nonsense, they did much to inflame public opinion.

The "typical Mormon patriarch" was quite content to have but one wife, for in any group which permits polygamy, most people still practice monogamy. This is because at the marrying ages, males and females are roughly equal in numbers. When there is an excess of one

[15]Hill, *Joseph Smith,* p. 346.

sex, it is usually slight, so that—generally speaking—every plural spouse means that someone else is deprived of matrimony altogether.

What percentage of Mormons practiced polygamy is unknown. The figure doubtless varied over the years, with the peak around 1860. The overall figure—the proportion of Mormon males who ever practiced the Principle—is estimated at 3 percent by LDS. Critics of Mormonism have placed the figure as high as 20 to 30 percent. Most scholarly estimates fall in the neighborhood of 10 percent.

Of the LDS males who were involved in polygamy, a clear majority had but one additional wife, which also ran counter to the public impression. The misconception about numbers arose in part because of the prejudice of certain anti-Mormon elements. But it was also true that there were some LDS males, particularly among the church leadership, who did indeed have a plurality of spouses. Orson Pratt had ten wives; his brother Parley had twelve. John D. Lee had eighteen wives and sixty-five children. Brigham Young had twenty-seven wives and fifty-six children. Heber Kimball had forty-five wives and sixty-eight children. And there were many others. Joseph Smith himself apparently had numerous wives, though the exact number remains in doubt.

A common polygamous practice was for the men to marry sets of sisters, the feeling being that such a procedure would reduce connubial tension. Whatever the reason, Joseph Smith is reported to have married three sets of sisters. Heber Kimball married four sets. John D. Lee married three sisters and also their mother! And so it went.

What about the economic aspect of plural marriage? Was having plural wives (and plural children) an asset or a liability? In many cases, it was a liability. True, an extra wife and children for a Mormon farmer meant that he would have additional help for the farm. But large numbers of Latter-day Saints were not farmers, and even among those who were, there was a point of diminishing returns. A Mormon farmer with twenty wives and fifty children could hardly hope to keep them productively engaged in farming. And with all those mouths to feed . . . Records show clearly that Mormon polygamists were drawn largely from the middle and upper economic brackets.

Celestial Marriage One of the revelatory doctrines promulgated by Joseph Smith and practiced by LDS is *celestial marriage.* According to this concept, there are two distinct types of marriage: one for time, and the other for eternity. The former is regarded as a secular marriage that is broken at the death of either husband or wife. Celestial marriage, on the other hand, serves to "seal" a man and woman not only for time but for all eternity. Such marriages are always solemnized in a Mormon temple and include rites and rituals which are never divulged to non-Mormons. Other types of ceremony—civil or religious—are held to be valid only until death. (Marriages with non-Mormons run counter to LDS policy and are not performed in the temples.)

The point is that celestial marriage dovetailed nicely with polygamy. For example, if a man who had been sealed for time and eternity died before his wife, the latter could—if she desired—marry another man for time only. Some of the women married to Joseph Smith for time and eternity, later (after the Prophet's death) married Brigham Young for time only, even though they bore him children.

It was also possible to marry for eternity rather than time. A woman who had died without ever having married could be sealed for eternity to an LDS male—after her death. The fact that he might already have a legal wife would make no difference, since plural wives were perfectly acceptable.

It should be pointed out that celestial marriage is not a dated concept. It has always been—and still is—an integral part of LDS religion. One Mormon woman puts it as follows:

> The principle of celestial marriage was considered the capstone of the Mormon religion. Only by practicing it would the highest exaltation in the Celestial Kingdom of God be obtained. According to the founders of the Mormon Church, the great purpose of this life is to prepare for the Celestial Kingdom. . . . The tremendous sacrifices of the Mormon people can be understood only if one keeps in mind this basic philosophy.[16]

Affectional Considerations Living arrangements varied among the polygamous families. In some instances, the wives lived with the husband under one roof. In the larger families, however, there were usually separate dwellings for the respective wives and their children. At any rate, a considerate husband was not supposed to show any favoritism. Hypothetically, at least, he was obligated to spend an equal amount of time with (and money on) each wife. In some cases, evidently, the husband would practice "rotation": he would spend one night with each of his spouses.

Although polygamous arrangements may have been onerous for some plural wives, most of them seemed to have adjusted rather well. The wives of Brigham Young, for instance, were devoted to him and

[16]Annie Turner Clark, *A Mormon Mother: An Autobiography* (Salt Lake City: University of Utah Press, 1969), pp. 1, 116. Quoted in Hill, *Joseph Smith,* p. 361.

quite compatible with one another. Susa Young Gates, one of his daughters, writes:

> The wives of Brigham Young lived together without outer friction. They were ladies, and lived their lives as such. The children were never aware of any quarrels, and indeed they could not have been serious or the children would have been aware of them.
>
> None of Brigham Young's wives ever married again after his death, though some were comparatively young women. Mother's love of father . . . and of his memory after his death amounted almost to worship. That all the others felt as did my mother is proved by the way in which they cherished his memory and respected their widowhood.[17]

(There was one exception to the above claim. Ann Eliza, Brigham Young's twenty-seventh wife, was a hellion. She not only sued him for divorce on grounds of cruelty but toured the nation denouncing the entire system of plural marriage.)

The question is sometimes asked whether this sharing of love, as the Gentiles called it, did not have a sexually frustrating effect on the plural wives. In a strictly factual sense, there is very little information on a subject as sensitive as this. The fact that plural wives voiced no complaint along these lines suggests that the problem was not too significant.

It should be kept in mind that during the nineteenth century, American women, both Mormon and non-Mormon, were regarded as having a procreative function. Birth control was by no means accepted in society at large and indeed is still frowned upon by the Mormon Church. The point is that sexual intercourse was probably not considered by most females to be the pleasure-giving activity that it is today. And while there may well have been individual women in the nineteenth century for whom the prevailing climate was sexually frustrating, such women were probably in the minority. In the case of the Latter-day Saints, it is unlikely that these women would have consented to become plural wives.

Marital Adjustment Sex was not the only problem associated with polygamy. Jealousies, economic disputes, child-rearing and in-law conflicts—these too were involved. In a monogamous pairing, for example, there are usually four in-laws, and in-law problems are a well-known factor in marital discord. Where there were two, or six, or ten wives, the parental problem must have been formidable.

Conflicts over child rearing also occurred, especially when the

[17]Susa Young Gates, *The Life Story of Brigham Young* (New York: Macmillan, 1930), pp. 340–41.

wives and children all lived in one house. Children always knew who their real mother was, and they generally bowed to her authority. (The other wives were called aunts.) But with a half-dozen or so aunts in the house, such things as discipline, punishment, and lines of authority must have presented some real problems.

In some cases, also, jealousy did indeed crop up. It was only natural that there would be a certain amount of vying for the husband's attention—and for him to show total impartiality would have required superhuman effort. Conflict apparently occurred when a middle-aged husband took a young woman for his second (or fourth, or seventh) wife.

Culture Conflict All things considered, it is remarkable that polygamous marriages worked as well as they did, for there is no doubt that some mighty problems existed. One of the best accounts of Mormon pluralism is by Kimball Young, a grandson of Brigham Young. Through personal interviews, as well as an examination of journals, diaries, and autobiographies, Young estimated that about half the polygamous marriages were highly successful, a quarter were reasonably successful, and perhaps a quarter had "considerable or severe conflict."

Although there is no satisfactory way to compare these figures with those of monogamous marriages, it does appear that Mormon pluralism not infrequently presented a stern challenge to the good ship of matrimony.

> The real problem was that the difficulties could not be easily settled, because the culture did not provide any standardized ways for handling these conflicts. For the most part, these people genuinely tried to live according to the Principle. But when they applied the rules of the game borrowed from monogamy, such as not controlling feelings of jealousy, they got into real trouble.[18]

The End of Plural Marriage

Mormon polygamists had their share of domestic discord—perhaps a bit more than their share. Given time, however, the system of plural marriage probably could have been made to work. The problems were not insurmountable, and the Saints were a dedicated people. Unfortunately for all concerned, the real difficulties were external rather than internal, and as time went on the situation deteriorated.

[18]Kimball Young, *Isn't One Wife Enough?* (New York: Henry Holt, 1954), p. 209.

It soon became apparent that as far as the outside society was concerned, polygamy was creating a lesion of unhealable proportions.

As portrayed in the Gentile press, Mormonism was a false religion —with many evil connotations. But the target attacked most was polygamy. Over and over and over again, the perfidies and traumas of plural marriage were emblazoned in bold headlines. Some of the stories were factual, but—given the nature of American newspapers —many were the products of reportorial imagination. And as Carl Carmer points out:

> The published "feature stories" found eager readers among Gentile women. The latter wept over the first wife who, on being informed that her husband was bringing a second to the home, climbed through a window and up to the roof, where she sat under the gleaming pattern of western stars until the pitiless cold of a Utah winter stopped the beating of her heart.
>
> Another young spouse, when told that her husband had built a nearby house for a prospective second bride, snatched her rifle from its rack, and for a week or so sent bullets spaced at regular intervals into the honeymoon cottage. This action postponed the contemplated wedding indefinitely.[19]

Such stories clearly tended to inflame public opinion. And when that happens, political reaction is sure to follow. In 1862, President Lincoln signed a bill outlawing polygamy in the territories of the United States, and after the Civil War federal agents began "swarming over Utah." The difficulty was, however, that the agents could not always gain access to church marriage records. Also, Mormon polygamists became adept at scattering and hiding their wives, and—if necessary—themselves.

Brigham Young died in 1877 and was buried in a walnut casket he had designed himself. But even he had not escaped the long arm of the law, having been arrested and jailed on charges of polygamy. However, he was freed after an overnight confinement when he was able to convince the judge that in a *legal* sense, he had only one wife —the first.

After Brigham Young's death, things seemed to go downhill rapidly for the Saints. In 1882, a new federal law provided punishment for anyone found living in "lewd cohabitation," and Mormon leaders found themselves going to jail in droves. During a single year, 1887, some two hundred polygamists were imprisoned.

Still the fight went on, with many Saints building secret passage-

[19]Carl Carmer, *The Farm Boy and the Angel* (Garden City, N.Y.: Doubleday, 1970), pp. 174–75.

ways, hidden rooms, and underground tunnels between houses. Carmer writes that when federal officers appeared, "the 'cohabs' suddenly disappeared into church steeples, haystacks, cornfields, old cellars, or disguised themselves in women's dresses and sunbonnets. The whole countryside was playing a wild game of hide-and-seek."[20] John Taylor, Brigham Young's successor and a devout polygamist, was in office for ten years but had to spend practically all of it in hiding.

To many, it must have seemed as though the conflict between the "cohabs" and the "feds" was a standoff. On the one hand, no matter how many federal agents were sent in—and no matter how many polygamists were brought out—the Latter-day Saints continued to abide by the Principle. This was especially true of the leadership, practically all of whom remained steadfast in their beliefs. On the other hand, it had become clear that the government was prepared to take whatever steps were necessary to obliterate the remaining "relic of barbarism."

The year 1887 marked the beginning of the end of plural marriage, for in that year the Edmunds-Tucker bill was passed. This bill dissolved the church as a corporation and provided for the confiscation of church property. Cost to the Mormon Church was over one million dollars, nearly half of it in cash. And the raids and imprisonments continued. In all, there were 573 convictions for polygamy.

By this time, many Mormons had wearied of the struggle. Then too, LDS leaders—who remained resolute to the end—wanted statehood for Utah, a goal they realized was unattainable so long as polygamy was being practiced.

During 1887, John Taylor died (while still in hiding), and he was succeeded in the church presidency by Wilford Woodruff. In 1890, the Supreme Court upheld the Edmunds-Tucker bill as constitutional, a decision which marked the end of the line for plural marriage. Shortly after the decision was handed down, President Woodruff made the following official pronouncement, known in subsequent years as "the Manifesto."

> Inasmuch as laws have been enacted by Congress forbidding plural marriages, which laws have been pronounced constitutional by the court of last resort, I hereby declare my intention to submit to those laws, and to use my influence with the members of the church over which I preside to have them do likewise. . . .
>
> And I now publicly declare that my advice to the Latter-day Saints

[20]Ibid., p. 181.

is to refrain from contracting any marriage forbidden by the law of the land.[21]

Although the Manifesto caused some internal resentment, both Mormons and non-Mormons were generally glad that the long battle was over. Woodruff's pronouncement was (and is) treated as a revelation. When asked about it, he replied simply, "I went before the Lord, and I wrote what the Lord told me to write." The pronouncement apparently ended the conflict over plural marriage.

Or did it?

Epilogue Woodruff's Manifesto put an end to the open practice of plural marriage, and President Benjamin Harrison granted a pardon to all the imprisoned polygamists. In 1896, Utah was admitted to the Union as the forty-fifth state. Nevertheless, for a decade or so following the Manifesto, a few Mormon leaders continued to take plural wives.

In 1902, Reed Smoot, an LDS official, was elected to the United States Senate. There was opposition to his being seated, however, and during lengthy hearings the facts concerning "secret" polygamy came to light. The Mormon Church, while not condoning plural marriage, had taken no steps to remove those officials who were continuing the practice.

At the final Senate vote, Smoot was confirmed by a narrow margin, and political opposition to Mormon office seekers came to an end. In fact, over the years, any number of ranking government officials have been Mormons. After the highly publicized Smoot hearings, LDS adopted a policy of excommunicating any member known to practice polygamy, a policy that remains in effect today.

Within the Mormon Church, plural marriage is now a dead issue. There is no likelihood that it will ever be resurrected. This is not only because of the threat of excommunication but because the LDS membership itself is antipolygamy. Curiously enough, however, while plural marriage is no longer an issue within Mormondom, it is indeed an issue outside the church. Some polygamists have left LDS rather than give up their pluralistic practices. A fair number of these fundamentalists, as they are called, continue to adhere to the Principle. Their story will be told in a later section.

Looking back on the fifty-year battle over polygamy, one is impelled to question the bitterness on the part of the general public. Why all the rancor? The answer, though perhaps conjecturable,

[21]Smith, *Doctrine and Covenants,* last section.

provides an interesting commentary on nineteenth-century America.

True, there is no doubt that many Gentiles misunderstood both the nature and the extent of plural marriage. Based largely on false newspaper accounts, Mormon polygamy was seen as a rapidly spreading cancer that threatened both marriage and society. And in a period when women were accorded a somewhat higher moral status than they have now, the idea of plural wives was an ethical abomination.

Yet not all readers were taken in by newspaper accounts. Surely there were many thoughtful citizens—then as now—who were able to distinguish fact from propaganda. Even these people, however, seem to have gone along with the tide, for the very idea of plural wives seemed to touch an exposed nerve. People debated the pros and cons of public education, child labor, and women's rights. Even slavery had its defenders. But the subject of plural marriage elicited nothing but public outrage.

Would the same type of clamor have occurred if polygamy had been introduced today rather than 150 years ago? One wonders. Surely, present-day attitudes toward cohabitation are a far cry from those of yesteryear. Perhaps the Latter-day Saints were simply ahead of their time!

We shall never know the answer. What we do know is that the Mormons not only were able to withstand the onslaught, but inside of two generations were able to become a socio-religious organization of major proportions.

Organization of LDS

There is no denying that the Latter-day Saints are still linked with polygamy, and in a sense this is unfortunate, not only because plural marriage is a dead issue but because it draws attention away from the really important aspects of Mormonism. The fact of the matter is that LDS has developed into a most remarkable organization. Family and community involvement, educational policy, organizational structure, missionary work—all are models of effectiveness.

The Hierarchical Rungs The role of the clergy varies greatly from one denomination to the next. Some groups, such as the Quakers and the Amish, have dispensed altogether with professional clergy. Others, including many Protestant denominations and the Roman Catholic Church, have fairly elaborate clerical frameworks. The Mormons are at the upper end of the continuum; that is, they have one of the most complicated—and successful—clerical organizations in America. Every "worthy male" is expected to take his place in the hierarchical priesthood. There are now upwards of a million LDS priests, a figure which far surpasses the number of Roman Catholic priests in the entire world.

Although they are not professional in the sense of being seminarians or receiving pay for their work, it is the priesthood which provides the bones and sinew of present-day Mormonism. Within the priesthood there are two orders, or subdivisions: the Aaronic and the Melchizedek. The Aaronic, or lesser priesthood, is believed by the Saints to have originated when Joseph Smith and Oliver Cowdery received heavenly keys from John the Baptist in 1829. The Melchizedek, or higher order, came about at a later date, when the two men received heavenly keys from the Apostles Peter, James, and John. All Mormon priests trace their ordination back to these two miraculous events.

Both the Aaronic and the Melchizedek orders are subdivided into ranks, and these ranks, or gradations, form a kind of promotional ladder which the Mormon male ascends during his lifetime. Which rung he reaches depends largely on the effort he is willing to put forth in carrying out the Word.

A worthy male starts his priestly career at the age of twelve, when he is admitted to the Aaronic order with the rank of deacon. This is the lowest rank in the priesthood, usually attained a few years after baptism. Chief duties of the deacon include helping at church meetings, collecting fast offerings, and otherwise assisting the higher ranks.

After three years or so as deacon—if all goes well—the boy is promoted to the rank of teacher. This is a kind of apprenticeship, for while teachers do occasionally preach, their primary role is helping their superiors. At about eighteen, the boy advances to the highest rank in the Aaronic order, that of priest. The duty of the priest is "to preach, teach, expound, exhort, and baptize, and administer the sacrament." Leone notes that "whereas the audience in other Christian churches receives meaning declared from the pulpit, every Mormon is the preacher, teacher, exegete, and definer of meaning before an audience of peers, who a moment or a month later may switch positions with him."[22]

If he has performed his duties in the Aaronic order satisfactorily, the boy is ready for the higher order, the Melchizedek, which also has three ranks—elder, seventy, and high priest. Elders are usually or-

[22]Leone, *Roots of Modern Mormonism,* p. 168.

dained in their early twenties and are invested with authority to take charge of meetings, to bestow certain blessings, and to officiate during rites when the high priest is unable to be present.

Seventies are essentially elders who have been chosen to be traveling missionaries, usually for a term of two years. Top rung in the ascending hierarchy is the rank of high priest. Once he has reached this level, there is no higher priestly rank a Latter-day Saint can aspire to. There are, however, any number of administrative and executive positions available—if he has the necessary qualifications. LDS is a huge operation, and its management requires immense effort.

Stakes and Wards The Church of Jesus Christ of Latter-day Saints has two forms of administration, horizontal and vertical. Horizontal, in this context, refers to the various stake and ward organizations, while vertical refers to the overall administrative hierarchy of the church.

The basic horizontal or geographical unit of LDS is the ward, roughly corresponding to the Protestant congregation or the Catholic parish. Wards vary in size from one hundred to eighteen hundred members, with the average being around six hundred. When the number gets much larger than this, the chances are that a division will occur. (Since Mormondom is growing, the number of wards is constantly increasing, the present figure reaching well into the thousands.)

Although each ward contains both priesthood orders—with all the ranks thereof—the ward itself is administered by the bishop. It is he who baptizes and confirms, counsels members, receives contributions, conducts funerals, and so forth. He often gives a prodigious amount of his time, but neither he nor his assistants receive any pay for their work. All Mormons, incidentally, including those at the head of the church, must belong to some ward.

Once a month, each LDS family in the ward is visited by the teachers and deacons for purposes of discussion. Should any spiritual or material needs be detected, the bishop is notified. Most wards also include auxiliary organizations such as the Sunday school, relief society, mutual improvement association, genealogical society, and so on.

A stake—corresponding to the Catholic diocese—is made up of from five to ten wards. Size varies from two thousand to ten thousand members, with the average being around five thousand. At the head is the stake president, who is assisted by two counselors. The president nominates the various ward bishops, holds conferences, and is generally responsible for the smooth functioning of the wards under his jurisdiction. Although his is also an unpaid job, the stake president—like the ward bishop—spends an enormous amount of time on church-related activities.[23]

The General Authorities The vertical, or hierarchical, structure of LDS is more complicated than the horizontal, although its original formulation was simple enough. When the church was founded in 1830, there were but two officers: Joseph Smith was first elder, and Oliver Cowdery was second elder. Little by little, however, the hierarchical structure grew.

At the top of the Mormon establishment is the first president, also known as "prophet, seer, and revelator"—Joseph Smith's original title. The first president holds office for life. Since his mantle of authority is believed to be inherited from the Prophet himself, and as his title "revelator" signifies, the first president is the only member of the church empowered to voice revelations. This power is seldom used, however.

In addition to two presidential assistants, there is also an executive council of twelve apostles, another council of seven members who oversee missionary activities, and a three-member bishopric which looks after the church's business activities. These twenty-five men are often referred to as the general authorities, for together they hold practically all the top LDS offices. Stake and ward officials are under the control of the general authorities.

While the large majority of church leaders—particularly at the stake and ward level—continue their businesses, the general authorities do receive a stipend which enables them to live comfortably. Their assistants are also salaried, as are several hundred clerical and administrative personnel.

Although the general authorities are subject to the approval of the rank-and-file membership—through a "vote" taken at the semiannual conference—the approval is more or less routine. The church makes no pretense of being democratic. The system is theocratic, and authority comes from the top. Indeed, some observers believe that the first president holds more power than any other church leader except the pope.

Participatory Involvement There is no doubt that the organizational structure of LDS is enormously effective. Writing in *Harper's Magazine* at the turn of the century, Richard Ely said, "So far as I can judge

[23]See "What We Can Learn from The Church of Jesus Christ of Latter-day Saints" (Salt Lake City: The Church of Jesus Christ of Latter-day Saints).

from what I have seen, the organization of the Mormons is the most nearly perfect piece of social mechanism with which I have ever, in any way, come into contact, excepting the German army alone."[24]

During the intervening years, this statement has been widely quoted, and in a sense it is unfortunate, for it gives the wrong impression of LDS operations. Mormon discipline and military discipline have little in common. Military discipline operates through the imposition of force; Mormon discipline operates through *voluntary participation.* This is the entire thrust of Mormonism: to get as many members as possible to join in the day-to-day operations necessary to promote God's word as interpreted by the church.

In practice, this participatory involvement—to outsiders, at least—is staggering. Starting at age twelve with the rank of deacon, Mormon males are constantly striving to climb the priestly ladder. There are ward activities and stake activities and temple ceremonies. There are constant visitations by teachers and bishops. Streams of missionaries flow to faraway places, and the conversion rate is high. There are annual and semiannual conferences and visits by the apostles. There are sealings for time and eternity. New religious tracts and publications are constantly being issued. There are weekly social events and Mormon holiday celebrations. There are recreational and musical activities and sporting events. There are a host of subsidiary organizations: women's relief society, young men's and young women's mutual improvement associations, scout troops, the Sunday school union, the genealogical society, the church welfare plan, the Tabernacle Choir, and so on. LDS even has a department of education which, among other things, administers a series of institutes and seminaries. The church also maintains Brigham Young University, founded in 1875.

From the outside, LDS gives the appearance of being a beehive of activity—which in fact it is. (It is no accident that a figure of the beehive, prominently displayed on so many LDS buildings, was chosen to be the state symbol for Mormon Utah.) Both literally and figuratively, Mormons are always on the move. In fact, the Latter-day Saints themselves good-naturedly define a Mormon as "one who is on his way to a meeting, at a meeting, or returning from a meeting."[25]

In addition to the meetings, there are always new jobs to do, new

[24]Richard Ely, "Economic Aspects of Mormonism," *Harper's Magazine,* April 1903, p. 668.

[25]Bruce Campbell and Eugene Campbell, "The Mormon Family," in Charles Mindel and Robert Habenstein, eds., *Ethnic Families in America* (New York: Elsevier, 1976), p. 403.

conversions to make, new challenges to meet. And while the manpower requirements are enormous—it takes hundreds of thousands of dedicated workers to staff the various organizations—the church has never had any recruitment difficulties.

This is not to say that all Latter-day Saints are dedicated. Some young men are considered unworthy and are not accepted into the priesthood. Some adults, of both sexes, are only moderately active, and others (called Jack Mormons) are inactive. But somewhere between one-half and two-thirds of LDS members not only are active, they are hyperactive. This participatory involvement—this hyperactivity—is one of the distinguishing marks of Mormonism.

Primacy of the Family

Another feature of Mormon social organization is the strong emphasis placed on family relations. Whether the family member is young, middle-aged, or old—or even deceased—he is assured a meaningful place in the kin system. Conversely, Latter-day Saints are against those things which they feel are harmful to family life. Premarital and extramarital sex relations are frowned upon, along with abortion, masturbation, indecent language, immodest behavior, birth control, and divorce. While the church mounts no special campaign against these practices, most Mormons seem to have little difficulty abiding by the rules. It is hardly surprising, for example, to learn that Latter-day Saints have comparatively few divorces and a high birth rate.[26]

On an informal basis, the familistic orientation of LDS can be seen in a variety of ways. Whereas most Americans are accustomed to pursuing individualized interests, hobbies, and activities, Mormons tend to participate as families. Their social life is largely a function of church and family. Ward dances, parties, outings, and sporting events are all attended by families and are designed to encourage the intermingling of different age groups. Monday evening is designated as home evening. On this occasion, all members of the household stay home and devote themselves to family recreation, such as singing, games, instrumental music, and dramatics.

The Kin Family Network In view of the stress on family, it is understandable why kinship plays such an important role throughout Mor-

[26]See the discussion in Campbell and Campbell, "Mormon Family," pp. 393 ff. See also Arland Thornton, "Religion and Fertility: The Case of Mormonism," *Journal of Marriage and the Family,* 41 (February 1979): 131–42.

mondom. Brothers and sisters, aunts and uncles, nieces and nephews, grandparents, cousins, in-laws—all maintain an active and enthusiastic kin relationship. During reunions of the kin family network—one of the Saints' favorite summer pastimes—it is not uncommon to see several hundred people in attendance! Special consideration is often shown to direct descendants of pioneer Mormon families, particularly those whose forbears had direct contact with Joseph Smith or Brigham Young.

It should not be thought that their emphasis on family and kinship serves to fragment the Mormon community. On the contrary, every effort is made to extend and apply familistic feelings to the community at large. One has but to attend any of the ward activities to see the closeness and camaraderie involved. The entire social fabric of Mormonism is designed so that "no one feels left out." And in their day-to-day dealings with one another, this same type of we-feeling is evident. Mullen writes:

> Mormons almost always refer to each other as brother or sister. It is Brother Petersen this, or Sister Evans that. A group is composed of brethren, and this word is also applied frequently to the leadership. . . .
>
> To Mormons, there is the feeling that we really are the children of God. . . . Some have one gift and some another; some may be stronger or wiser than others; but each has a duty to help the other. This is the ideal. It may not always be achieved, but Mormons strive for it.[27]

Search for the Dead Before leaving the subject of family, one final observation is in order: the Latter-day Saints' predilection for extending their range of kinship to those long dead. The problem is basically simple. Mormons believe that they themselves are following God's word, as revealed to the Prophet Joseph Smith. But what about those who died without ever hearing the Prophet's revelations?

The answer is also simple. Ancestors who died before the religion was founded in 1830 may be baptized or sealed by proxy. That is, the living person stands in for the deceased during a baptismal or sealing ceremony. The ceremony itself takes place in a Mormon temple, and the deceased is accorded full rites.

Difficulty arises from the fact that, as one goes back in time, (a) the number of ancestors becomes enormous, and (b) they become exceedingly difficult to track down. LDS does not do things halfway, however, with the result that the search

[27]Robert Mullen, *The Latter-day Saints: The Mormons Yesterday and Today* (Garden City, N.Y.: Doubleday, 1966), pp. 27–28.

for ancestry has become one of the major functions of the church.

The Mormon Genealogical Society, an administrative arm of LDS, is located in downtown Salt Lake City. An additional seventeen branches are maintained in other parts of the United States and abroad. The amount of genealogical research undertaken at the various branches is staggering. Vital statistics, census materials, church records, poll books, official documents of all kinds—such things are constantly being microfilmed for use by Mormon (and non-Mormon) researchers.

Some of the figures are hard to grasp. Close to a thousand people a day come to the Mormon Genealogical Society to use the hundreds of microfilm reading machines available. (There is no charge for using either the records or the machines.) The number of temple ceremonies for the dead has now passed the fifty million mark. The number of names on file exceeds ten billion. For some states—and nations—*all the pertinent records have been microfilmed!*

For incomplete areas, the Mormon Genealogical Society dispatches microfilm crews to all parts of the world. During the 1980s, their excursions have included such distant lands as West Africa, Sumatra, and China. In fact, the Mormon collection of Chinese clan genealogies is reported to be the largest outside China![28]

To protect the records from fire or explosion, the negative films are stored in a safe place. Here is Mullen's description of it:

> In Little Cottonwood Canyon, 12 miles into the [Wasatch] mountains from downtown Salt Lake City, there is a solid face of granite from which was taken much of the stone used in the Temple. A narrow mountain road leads to a leveled-off place where one confronts six large concrete portals resembling entrances to a railroad tunnel. If you walk into the main portal and proceed about 150 feet, by which time you are under 800 feet of solid granite, you come across a tunnel, or room, some 402 feet long and 50 feet wide. This is lined in corrugated steel. Between the rough-hewn granite and the exterior of these ten-gauge steel linings has been pumped waterproof concrete. This vast room is the central office for the genealogy records.
>
> You see three huge banklike vault doors. One weighs 15 tons and could withstand almost any known blast. Each door leads to a 350-foot room, extending even farther into the granite mountain. Beyond these rooms is still another. . . .
>
> The vaults have their own self-contained power plant, their own emergency supplies, fresh air filters, and other equipment to endure even a severe atomic attack, which one can only suppose was at the back of the minds of the designers and builders. . . .

[28]*Los Angeles Times Service* report of August 31, 1980.

> Temperature and moisture are controlled for the benefit of the film. Here are the master records of as much of humanity as can be gathered from the vital statistics of nations around the world. The most recent acquisitions, for example, are microfilms of every birth and death in New Zealand since records were kept.
>
> It may surprise some to learn that probably the best records of their family are not in some quiet vestry in the Old World . . . but in the granite fastness of Little Cottonwood Canyon.[29]

The Mormon genealogical collection is doubtless the greatest assemblage of vital records ever housed under one roof. It also appears to be the safest.

Some Mormon Practices

"To us, the greatest day of all time is today." These words, spoken by a former Mormon leader, exemplify LDS philosophy. Few other groups are as present-oriented and as activist as the Latter-day Saints. It is not that they disregard or play down the significance of the hereafter. Their emphasis on genealogy, ancestral baptism, and sealing for time and eternity shows the importance they attach to the next world. But the way they prepare for the next world is to keep religiously active in the present one.

> Mormonism de-emphasizes contemplation, and fosters an activist pragmatism. Children growing up in an orthodox Mormon home will be urged to apply themselves to their studies, to cultivate recreational interests such as music, art, and hobbies, and to apply the rule of moderation to all facets of life.
>
> Regular church attendance is expected, but *speculation about theological problems or the religious answer to modern movements such as existentialism or Freudianism is discounted.* Nothing could be further from the spirit of Mormonism than the Trappist monk—celibate, contemplative, withdrawn from the world.[30]

Group Identification Mormons place great stress on cultural and recreational activities, but in both instances the emphasis is on group rather than individual participation. Team sports, organized recreation, dancing and ballet, orchestral music, choir work, theater—all such activities are felt to have a religious base in the sense that *they enhance group identification.* May writes convincingly on this point:

[29]Mullen, *Latter-day Saints,* pp. 193–94.

[30]William J. Whalen, *The Latter-day Saints in the Modern-Day World* (New York: Day, 1964), p. 213. (Italics added.)

> In contemporary Mormon society there is discernibly greater emphasis on the performing arts than on the visual arts. There is widespread emphasis on group singing, the well-known Mormon Tabernacle Choir being a great source of local pride. Musical ensembles, especially bands, have been widespread among the Mormons since the mid-19th century.
>
> Plays and theatrical productions have also been a favorite cultural activity of the Mormons. . . . Today Salt Lake City supports six professional theater companies, an impressive number for a metropolitan area of 500,000.
>
> Dancing has also been popular since the 19th century, both as a social activity and as a form of creative expression. The city's five dance companies have made Utah a center for dance in the West. Ballet West and the Utah Repertory Dance Theater have a national reputation for excellence.
>
> More individual forms of creative expression have not received the widespread support given to performing arts.[31]

A devout Mormon never forgets that he is a Mormon. The fact that he is helping to carry out God's word reinforces his group identification. Even his *individual* involvements—baptism, tithing, prayer, genealogical research, and certain temple investitures—serve as reinforcement factors.

One of the more interesting of the latter is the issuance of special undergarments. These derive from one of the temple ceremonies called the endowments. When he receives his endowments, a Mormon is issued a special set of underwear, which he is supposed to wear at all times. Originally the temple garments, as they were called, gave the appearance of a union suit. They were made of knit material and covered the body from ankle to neck. Although they are still worn by devout Mormons of both sexes, the undergarments themselves have been shortened in length and modified in appearance. They still contain the embroidered symbols which remind the wearers of their temple obligations.

(A few of the older church members follow the rules literally: they keep at least a part of the fabric touching them at all times. Even when taking a bath, they keep a small portion of the sleeve in contact with the body until fresh undergarments are ready to be worn.)

Word of Wisdom It is a common observation that Mormons do not drink or smoke, a proscription that derives from one of Joseph Smith's revelations:

[31]Dean L. May, "Mormons," in Stephan Thernstrom, ed., the *Harvard Encyclopedia of American Ethnic Groups* (Cambridge, Mass.: Harvard University Press, 1980), pp. 723–24.

> That inasmuch as any man drinketh wine or strong drink among you, behold it is not good. . . .
>
> And again, strong drinks are not for the belly, but for the washing of your bodies.
>
> And again, tobacco is not for the body, neither for the belly, and is not good for man, but is an herb for bruises and all sick cattle. . . .
>
> And again, hot drinks are not for the body or belly.[32]

The revelation is known throughout Mormondom as the Word of Wisdom. Included in the prohibition are tobacco in any form, alcoholic beverages of any kind (including wine and beer), tea, coffee, and soft drinks. LDS has even substituted water for wine in the Sunday communion service.

Although they themselves abstain, Mormons have no objection to drinking or smoking on the part of visitors and outsiders. At the same time, however, "the Word of Wisdom makes Mormons uncomfortable at cocktail parties, coffee breaks, and other such gatherings which serve the rest of American society as important occasions for social interaction."[33]

The Latter-day Saints are convinced they are right, nevertheless, and point to the fact that LDS prohibited smoking long before the surgeon general of the United States and the Royal College of Surgeons affirmed that tobacco was a cancer-causing agent. Mormons are permitted to drink hot chocolate, lemonade, fruit juice, and other noncarbonated beverages.

But does the membership really abstain, abiding by the Word of Wisdom? The answer is yes, all *worthy* Mormons do abstain. Indeed, abstinence is one of the traits most clearly separating the true believer from the Jack Mormon. The Word of Wisdom is looked upon as a commandment. Those who disobey are not considered to be worthy Mormons and are denied admission to the temple—which means they cannot participate in ceremonies involving sealing, baptism of the dead, endowments, and the like.

Tithing In addition to their adherence to the Word of Wisdom, Latter-day Saints have two other practices that should be mentioned. One is tithing; the other is missionary work. Taking them in order, the word *tithing* comes from *tithe,* meaning "one-tenth." In simplest terms, this is exactly what LDS expects: 10 percent of one's income "for the support of the Lord's work." Authority for the tithe comes from a revelation of Joseph Smith in 1838.

[32]Smith, *Doctrine and Covenants,* 89:5.
[33]May, "Mormons," p. 730.

> Those who have been tithed shall pay one-tenth of all their interest annually; and this shall be a standing law unto them forever . . . and all those who gather unto the land of Zion . . . shall observe this law, or they shall not be found worthy to abide among you.[34]

It should be noted that the 10-percent figure is not based on the income that remains after normal living expenses have been deducted; it is a flat 10 percent "off the top." Tithes are collected by the ward bishops and forwarded directly to the general authorities in Salt Lake City, a procedure that also stems from one of the Prophet's revelations.

The membership does not ask—and the general authorities do not disclose—exactly how much money is collected or what happens to it. It appears, however, that the two major expenditures are for missionary work and education, including the support of Brigham Young University.

It is true that all Mormons are not full-tithers. Occasionally, members are permitted to give less than 10 percent and still remain in good standing. Others—the inactive group—may give little or nothing. The typical Mormon, however, not only gives his 10 percent but is quite happy to do so. By being a worthy member, he maintains his place in the Mormon community, he is assured of full temple privileges for himself and his family, and he has the inner security that comes from carrying out the word of the Prophet Joseph Smith.

Missionary Activity As Turner aptly points out, "It is foolish to pick any *one* aspect of this remarkable religion and assert that 'this is its strength.' Yet the temptation is strong . . . to select the missionary program."[35]

Like so many aspects of their religion, the Mormon missionary program is considerably different from that of other groups. It is larger, more vigorous, more youthful, more systematic—and more successful. Latter-day Saints consider it an honor to be missionaries, and many young Mormons look forward to the time when they will be selected. The selection is made by the ward bishop, who forwards a detailed application to the missionary committee in Salt Lake City. The applicant must be young (nineteen or twenty), of good character, and worthy in the eyes of the church. Also he (or his family) must be able to afford the cost, for the expenses incurred during the field work are not borne by LDS.

Either sex may apply, although males outnumber females by a wide

[34]Smith, *Doctrine and Covenants,* section 119.
[35]Turner, *Mormon Establishment,* p. 89.

margin. If an applicant is accepted by the committee, he receives a "call," a letter informing him of his territorial assignment. This may be in the United States or abroad, but in either case the young missionary is expected to stay for the stipulated period of time, usually two years. Before departing for his post, he spends a week or so in Salt Lake City attending a brief training course.

Those who have been approached by Mormon missionaries may wonder how these young people managed to learn so much about Mormonism in so short a time. They are remarkably well versed in their religion, but the fact is that they have been trained in Mormonism all their lives. The short instructional period in Salt Lake City is merely to explain the operational details.

Once they have reached their assigned areas, the young emissaries work hard. It is not at all uncommon for them to put in eight to ten hours a day, seven days a week. They operate in pairs, living together and visiting the homes of potential converts together. They have strict rules of conduct and are not permitted to date during the two-year period.

When they discuss Mormonism with potential converts, the missionaries are sincere but not insistent. They patiently and systematically explain their point of view in accordance with a routine mapped out by LDS authorities. They leave pamphlets and other literature and often make return visits to the same home. The work is occasionally tiring and—like all door-to-door efforts—more than occasionally discouraging. Nevertheless, most missionaries are happy in their assignments. There are some twenty-five thousand of them in the field at any one time, and when their tour is over, memories of their experience will remain with them for the rest of their lives.[36]

Effort and hard work aside, is the missionary effort successful? Indeed it is, in more ways than one. To begin with, the conversion rate is fantastically high. The number of yearly converts is reported to be in the neighborhood of eighty thousand! This is what accounts for much of the phenomenal growth of LDS. Secondly, Mormon missionary efforts have been so successful that in many parts of the world permanent missions have been established. In fact, in Hawaii, Canada, Brazil, England, South Korea, Switzerland, New Zealand, Guatemala, Peru, West Germany, Manila, South Africa, and Sweden, Mormon temples have been erected or are under construction.

The final mark of success of the missionary program relates to the image people have of Mormonism and has nothing to do with conversions. As William J. Whalen observes:

[36]Leone, *Roots of Modern Mormonism,* p. 1.

> The living example of these thousands of young men and women, the cream of Mormonism, postponing their educational, vocational, and even marital plans to serve their church without pay probably exerts a great influence on the Gentile public. . . . Even if they made no converts at all, they would be helping to reshape the image of Mormonism.[37]

Present-day Mormon Problems

All large organizations have problems, and LDS is no exception. In a historical sense, as we have seen, the Mormons have probably had more than their share. That they have managed to resolve most of them is due to good management plus—always—the conviction that God is with them. Of the problems that remain, five seem to merit particular consideration.

The Intellectuals In view of the origin and nature of Mormonism, the church has a special problem with the intellectual element. That is to say, the intellectual is by definition a challenger. He challenges accepted beliefs and tries to apply a so-called rationality to various issues. Through his critical insight, he is able to provide concepts—new ways of looking at things—not obtainable from other sources. The Mormon Church, on the other hand, is based on revelation; it is activist rather than contemplative; it maintains a set of long-cherished beliefs; and, of course, it holds to the view that the Book of Mormon—and the Bible, correctly translated—are literally true. Between LDS and the intellectual members of the church, therefore, there is disagreement.

Other religious groups have the same problem; that is, a reluctance by the intellectual members to accept dogma and literalism. In the case of LDS, however, there is a special consideration. O'Dea puts it as follows:

> Because of the great conviction on the part of Mormons that they are close to a generation especially chosen by God, and that their immediate ancestors talked with God . . . it has been impossible for a middle position to emerge between literalism and liberalism. . . .
>
> The kind of *rapprochement* necessary to satisfy the intellectuals is possible on two bases. The first is to go over to liberalism in theology, which would destroy the basis of the peculiar Mormon claim to legitimacy. The second is to state certain essential articles of faith, adherence to which is necessary for church membership,

[37]Whalen, *Latter-day Saints,* p. 231.

and to leave the rest of the area open to nonliteral interpretation. . . .

But the basic organization of the church, involving as it does the principle of lay leadership, has not produced a specialized corps of theologians who would be professionally prepared to grapple with the problems involved.[38]

Some Mormon leaders acknowledge the problem, while others do not. One of the officials whom I interviewed said, "Oh, I suppose you could call it a problem, but it doesn't amount to too much. I don't think the 'intellectuals,' as you describe them, would feel comfortable in any church. Personally, I think we have more important things to be concerned about."

Women's Liberation LDS does not prohibit their female members from joining the labor force, and indeed Mormon women are to be found in all walks of life, including the professions. At the same time, there is no doubt that—in terms of priorities—the church leaders feel that "women's place is in the home." May writes:

Mormon church leaders, observing changes in societal values which they believe to be destructive to the family, have increasingly advised women to make nurturing children and building a family their first responsibility. The leaders see the women's liberation movement generally and the Equal Rights Amendment (ERA) in particular as causes that divert women from their primary role. The position of the church has undoubtedly influenced Utah's negative response to the ERA.[39]

It should be noted also that while they have their own organization within the church, women are not permitted to ascend the LDS hierarchy. All Mormon leaders, from ward bishop to church president, are —and always have been—male. Some Mormon women have resented their exclusion and have complained bitterly. A few have even been excommunicated, in this respect, for "preaching false doctrine, hurting the church's missionary effort, and undermining church leadership because of their public statements."[40]

The Campbells write that

while many Mormon women might be attracted to elements of the Women's Liberation Movement, some of the women believe it to be anti-child. The importance of children in Mormon life can hardly be overstressed. It is interesting in light of the fact that the Mormons have always encouraged the higher education of their women, that there may

[38]Thomas O'Dea, *The Mormons* (Chicago: University of Chicago Press, 1957), pp. 233–34.

[39]May, "Mormons," p. 729.

[40]Associated Press release of December 6, 1979.

be a fundamental ambivalence in the Mormon subculture about using the full potentials of their women.[41]

This, then, is the problem: although the large majority of Mormon women seem to be quite satisfied with the role accorded them by the church, some are clearly dissatisfied. The Campbells conclude as follows: "To say that the Women's Liberation Movement has had no impact on the Mormon women would be unfair, but to say that it has had a great impact would be an exaggeration."[42]

What the answer is, only time will tell. But it should be noted that blacks formerly had a somewhat similar problem; that is, while they were welcomed into church membership, they were not eligible for the ranks of the priesthood. It took a revelation—reported by church president Spencer W. Kimball on June 9, 1978—to change the rules. Whether a similar change might someday occur regarding the role of women is problematical. Since the Prophet Joseph Smith's death, revelations have been recorded by the church in only three instances: once by Brigham Young when he was guided to Utah; once by Wilford Woodruff when he was commanded to put an end to plural marriage; and once by Spencer W. Kimball, whose revelation indicated that "all worthy male members of the church may be ordained to the priesthood without regard for race or color."

Cultural Insularity Following Joseph Smith's death in Illinois in 1844, the Mormons migrated westward—a murderous thousand-mile trek. They did not make the journey because they wanted to, but because they had to. They were being persecuted. When the Latter-day Saints reached the Great Salt Lake Basin, the area did not belong to the United States but to Mexico. Settlers did not buy the land, for there was no one to buy it from.

It was the Mormons' idea to have the territory set up as an independent state (1849), known as Deseret, the word for honeybee in the Book of Mormon. The plan never materialized, however, and in 1850 the area became known as Utah Territory, under United States jurisdiction. Based on this early history, May comments:

> The Mormons are perhaps the only American ethnic group whose principal migration began as an effort to move out of the United States. Moreover, this migration of the main body of Mormons from Western Illinois to the Rocky Mountains in the late 1840s imprinted upon the group a self-consciousness gained through prior experience in the Midwest. The Mormons have been influenced subsequently by ritual tales

[41]Campbell and Campbell, "Mormon Family," p. 400.
[42]Ibid.

> of privation, wandering, and delivery under God's hand, precisely as the Jews have been influenced by their stories of the Exodus.
>
> A significant consequence of this tradition has been the development of an enduring sense of territoriality that has given a distinctive cast to Mormon group consciousness. . . . Tales of "the exodus" or "the trek" occupy a large place in Mormon folk tradition. Whether or not their ancestors were involved in the migration, most Mormons can recall stories of sacrifice and heroism associated with the experience.[43]

The point is that while the Mormons have no desire today to set up a separate state—or any other kind of territorial separateness—their life-style may be showing signs of cultural insularity. There is no doubt, for example, that the Latter-day Saints take a dim view of the recent trend in American morals. May notes that "pornography, sexual permissiveness, gay liberation, liberal divorce laws, abortion, and women's liberation are opposed by Mormon leaders as threats to family stability."[44] The same author contends that

> Mormon society during the first two-thirds of the 20th century was relatively outward-looking and open to external influence. Since the 1960s, this trend has been reversing and a more defensive attitude similar to that prevailing in the 19th century is developing, partly as a reaction to a perceived disintegration of moral values in the greater society, particularly as they relate to sexual mores and family life.
>
> Perhaps more important, however, a people committed to unity and order as prime social virtues are reacting to what they see as an increasingly chaotic outside world. Over the next few decades, the Mormons, despite an aggressive missionary program and commitment to build a worldwide church, may move toward making even sharper the boundaries dividing their world from that of the Gentiles.[45]

Perhaps so, and—again—only time will tell. But most Mormons apparently do not feel that this so-called cultural insularity poses much of a problem. In answer to my question, one Mormon respondent said simply: "It's no problem. If it were, the church would recognize it as such. Once in a while you hear it mentioned, but that's about all."

The Apostates Over the years, LDS has had its share of trouble with apostates—those who have left the fold. During the nineteenth century, much of the anti-Mormon propaganda could be traced to disgruntled Mormons. Some of the apostates were simply individuals

[43]May, "Mormons," pp. 720–21.
[44]Ibid., p. 729.
[45]Ibid., p. 731.

who became dissatisfied with certain policies of the church. Much more serious, however, were those who, finding themselves unable to accept church doctrine, *defected as a group* in order to pursue their own set of religious beliefs.

A number of such withdrawals occurred after polygamy was officially proclaimed in 1852. The most significant was that of the Josephites, who rejected not only the doctrine of plural marriage but also the leadership of Brigham Young. The Josephites held that church leadership should follow a hereditary line, and that the rightful heir, following Joseph Smith's death, was his son Joseph Smith III.

Organized in 1852, the Josephites grew steadily if not spectacularly, and at the end of the decade proclaimed themselves the Reorganized Church of Jesus Christ of Latter Day Saints, with Joseph Smith III as head. Today the Reorganites are a large, active organization, with some 225,000 members. They make their headquarters at Independence, Missouri, with areas of strength in Kansas City, Los Angeles, and Detroit.[46]

The relationship between LDS and the Reorganites is amicable enough. Indeed, the two groups have much in common, including their founder, Joseph Smith. Like LDS, the Reorganite hierarchy includes a president, twelve apostles, and a quorum of the seventy. The Reorganized church likewise relies on the nonsalaried services of elders and priests for the handling of their local congregations. Most important, perhaps, both LDS and the Reorganites accept the Book of Mormon as divinely inspired. The original manuscript, dictated by Joseph Smith from the controversial golden plates and written in longhand by Oliver Cowdery, is owned by the Reorganized church and kept in a temperature-and-humidity-controlled bank vault in Kansas City.

On the other hand, there is little likelihood that LDS and the Reorganites will bury their differences and unite. The division is too pronounced. In addition to the leadership factor mentioned earlier, the Reorganites do not maintain a volunteer missionary system. Also, they have no secret temple rites of any kind, no endowments, no special undergarments, no sealings, and no celestial marriage. The temples—and the meetings—are open to the public.

[46]As recently as 1981, a collector discovered a 137-year-old document—accepted by both LDS and the Reorganites as authentic—in which Joseph Smith promised that his son Joseph Smith III would succeed his father as church president. Mormon officials announced that the document would have no effect on how church leadership is now transferred ("apostolic succession"). They contend that Joseph Smith, at various times, had designated several different persons to succeed him, but always on the assumption that the church membership would approve the selection (Associated Press report of March 21, 1981).

Although the Reorganites do tithe, their 10 percent is not "off the top" but is computed after normal living expenses have been deducted. The difference between the two kinds of tithes is substantial and goes a long way toward explaining why LDS has grown so much more rapidly than the Reorganized church.

The Reorganites were not the only apostates who seceded as a group. There were the Cutlerites, the Strangites, the Rigdonites, the Bickertonites, and the Hedrickites. Except for the Reorganites, however, none of these groups ever grew to any size. And none of them —including the Reorganites—ever caused the Mormon church any real problem or embarrassment. But there was one group that did.

The Fundamentalists Just as the official adoption of polygamy created a number of schisms within the Mormon Church, the manifesto announcing an *end* to plural marriage had the same effect. Small groups of Mormons—or more accurately, ex-Mormons—have continued to practice plural marriage, even though it is against both the law and the tenets of LDS. These fundamentalists, as they are called, have had the unfortunate effect of prolonging the association between Mormonism and polygamy. Hence it is little wonder that they are denounced by LDS.

After the manifesto was proclaimed, some of the fundamentalists migrated to Mexico, but others stayed in the United States—mainly in the Arizona-Utah-California area—where they have continued their polygamous practices down to the present. Exactly how many fundamentalists there are is not known, since their operations are generally underground. Melissa Merrill, herself a plural wife, places the figure at between twenty and thirty thousand. She goes on to make the interesting contention that "there are probably more living plural marriage in the periphery of the church now than had ever lived it while it was an official practice."[47]

A number of observers—including, perhaps, most LDS members—look upon the fundamentalists as deviants, and of lower socioeconomic status. Fundamentalists themselves say that they come from all walks of life. They also claim to be devout rather than deviant. In point of fact, they seem to be both.

Fundamentalists contend that just before he died in 1887, First President John Taylor called together five of his followers and told them that the practice of polygamy must, at all cost, be retained. His message had great impact on the five men for two reasons: (a) in defense of the Principle, he himself had spent the last years of his life

[47]Melissa Merrill, *Polygamist's Wife* (Salt Lake City: Olympus, 1975), p. 116.

in hiding, and (b) since he was first president of the church at the time, his counsel was assumed to have been based on revelation.

Whatever the rationale, there is no denying that the spark of polygamy is still very much alive—despite the fact that pluralists have long since been cut off from the Mormon Church. The fundamentalists may have some sort of clandestine organization, though not too much is known about it. They have succeeded in publishing a periodical, *Star of Truth,* and every so often newspapers and popular magazines run exposés of their plural marriages. But responsible information is hard to come by.

The reason for our dearth of knowledge is twofold. In the first place, despite their agreement on the Principle, the fundamentalists are not united or organized into one cohesive organization. They are spread over several states and Mexico, and their geographical area encompasses thousands of square miles. A number of different sects, or cults, are involved, most of them quite small. Indeed, many of those who adhere to the Principle do so as individuals; that is, they have no connection with *any* group or organization.

The second reason for the lack of information is that polygamy is illegal, and those involved never know when the authorities will crack down. To circumvent possible court action, most polygamists take but one *legal* wife. Subsequent marriages—and some polygamists are reported to have as many as eleven wives—are performed by some sort of religious officiant, and do not involve a marriage license.[48] Utah, in turn, has made cohabitation a felony—provable merely by the presence of children. (In retaliation, fundamentalists have reportedly planted spies in both LDS and the police departments to warn of impending raids.)

Actually, authorities have been increasingly reluctant to take legal action against the polygamists. For one thing, cohabitation is far from uncommon in society at large, with the public taking a rather tolerant position. For another, there is the welfare problem. The Campbells write as follows:

> If a man practicing polygamy is prosecuted and placed in jail, his wives quit their jobs, and the whole clan goes on welfare. This can have a profound effect on the budgets of local governments, and may be one reason why the practice of polygamy is not likely to die out in the Mormon subculture.[49]

In any case, legal action against polygamists has become more and more infrequent. The last man to be convicted of polygamy left Utah

[48]Ibid., p. 107.
[49]Campbell and Campbell, "Mormon Family," p. 392.

State Prison in 1969, having served a year and a half of a five-year sentence.

Nevertheless, whether or not anyone bothers them, the fundamentalists will continue to be an embarrassment to LDS. The last thing the Mormons want is to continue to be associated with plural marriage. But as long as fundamentalism exists, that association seems inevitable.

The Present Scene

No matter what criterion is used—total membership, rate of growth, wealth, devoutness, education, vigor—the Church of Jesus Christ of Latter-day Saints has an extraordinary record. There is no evidence, furthermore, that its various activities are diminishing, either in scope or tempo.

Business and Financial Interests To say that the Mormon Church is wealthy would be a clear understatement. There are no figures available, but a number of observers—including the *New York Times*—believe that on a per capita basis, LDS is the richest church in the world. It is known, for example, that the church carries hundreds of millionaires on its rolls. A recent Associated Press report indicated that the Mormon Church, with its corporate control, "has revenues of more than three million dollars a day."[50]

Tithing has already been discussed. But in addition to the "off-the-top" 10 percent, each Mormon is expected to contribute another 2 percent more toward the upkeep of the local ward. Total tithing, therefore, is far greater than the contributions in most other churches and has enabled LDS to invest in a number of profitable businesses.

The Mormon Church owns some of the choicest hotels and motels in the West. It owns department stores, insurance companies, radio and television stations, and a newspaper. It has vast real estate holdings, both in the United States and abroad. It owns skyscrapers in such diverse places as Salt Lake City and New York City.

LDS also has a major interest in the United States beet sugar industry. It owns 700,000 acres of Florida ranchland, which means that the church is probably the largest landowner in the state. Additionally, LDS has 100,000 acres of ranchland in Canada and a large sugar plantation in Hawaii. It owns dozens of mills, factories, and stores and hundreds of farms. The church also has large holdings in a number of well-known corporations. And the list of assets could be extended.

[50]Marilyn Warenski, *Patriarchs and Politics* (New York: McGraw-Hill, 1978), p. 82.

LDS is so successful financially that people sometimes overestimate its wealth. Indeed, the church has made its share of economic mistakes. It is not the infallible business colossus it has sometimes been accused of being. Still and all, it has been powerfully successful. This is a safe statement in spite of the fact that no yearly financial statement is issued. The economic prosperity of LDS stems from a generous and enthusiastic tithing system, plus sound business practices. The money generated is used for the maintenance and continued expansion of the church.

Welfare All Mormons are not rich, naturally. Most of them belong to the broad middle class. And, of course, there are some at the lower end of the economic ladder. LDS, however, takes care of its own needy, and the latter seldom have to depend on public relief. The system employed is most effective, for it permits those in need to be helped without drawing on general church revenue.

The program has two main features. First, each stake has one particular welfare project. Some stakes have farms, others have orchards, others have canneries or factories, others raise cattle, and so on. All project-labor is performed without charge by LDS members. Each stake has a quota, and the interchange of commodities takes place on the basis of administrative conferences.

Turner, who studied the distribution system, shows how extensive the program is:

> Peanut butter comes from Houston; tuna from San Diego; macaroni from Utah; raisins from Fresno; prunes from Santa Rosa, California; soup from Utah; gelatine from Kansas City; toothpaste and shaving cream from Chicago; orange juice from Los Angeles; grapefruit juice from Phoenix and Mesa; sugar from Idaho.[51]

The second half of the welfare program involves "fast money" contributed by LDS members. On the first Sunday of the month, each Mormon family skips two meals. The estimated price of the meals is then given as a welfare contribution, most of the money being used for items not obtainable from the exchange program, such as articles of clothing, razor blades, light bulbs, and so forth. Although the fast money collected from each family may not seem like much—perhaps fifteen dollars a month—the LDS welfare program takes in millions of dollars every year by this method.

All the welfare items, both produced and purchased, are stocked in the various bishops' storehouses scattered throughout Mormondom. The storehouses—some 150 of them—resemble fair-sized super-

[51]Turner, *Mormon Establishment,* p. 98.

markets, except that no money changes hands. The needy simply present a written order from the ward bishop, whereupon the necessary supplies are dispensed. (If money is needed, there is a special bishop's fund available.)

Like practically every other aspect of Mormonism, the welfare program is a vigorous undertaking. *It moves.* Large sums of money are collected every month. Farms and factories are ripsaws of activity; supplies stream in and out of the storehouses at a never-ending pace; tens of thousands of needy families are served; priests, bishops, and members of the women's relief society are in constant touch with the recipients. From it all, LDS emerges as a stronger organization.

Some contend that no Mormon ever goes on public relief, and while this may be true in some wards, it is probably not true in all. Also, in spite of the obvious success of its welfare program, it is doubtful whether LDS could handle the need that would arise, say, in the event of a major depression. But then, neither could most other groups. All in all, the Mormon welfare program is one of their more successful undertakings.

Education For some reason, the general public seems unaware that LDS places great stress on education. But the fact is that the Mormons founded both the University of Utah—the oldest university west of the Mississippi—and Brigham Young University.

Whalen makes the following eye-opening statement:

> Traditionally dedicated to education, the Mormon Church boasts that it furnishes a higher percentage of entries in *Who's Who in America* than any other denomination. (The Unitarians may dispute this claim.) The church has produced an army of chemists, agronomists, sociologists, recreation specialists, and educational administrators.
>
> Utah leads the nation in literacy, and in the percentage of its college-age young people actually enrolled in a college or university. LDS itself sponsors the largest church-related university in the country: Brigham Young University, in Provo, Utah.[52]

One of the two major educational efforts of the Latter-day Saints is their system of seminaries and institutes. The seminaries are programs held as supplements to high school, while the institutes are socio-religious centers for Mormon college students. There are well over two thousand institutes and seminaries in the United States and abroad, and at any one time some hundred thousand Mormon youth attend them. These programs are used, Turner points out, "to bridge the critical period of life when young Mormons must make the transition from the blind faith of their childhood to the rea-

[52]Whalen, *Latter-day Saints,* p. 17.

soned acceptance of the faith the church hopes they will achieve."[53]

The second major thrust of the Mormon educational program is in higher education itself. Utah leads the country both in the percentage of college enrollees and in the percentage of college graduates. Latter-day Saints are justifiably proud of this accomplishment and of the fact that they have supplied the presidents for many colleges and universities outside Utah. (The number of eminent men who have been Mormons—corporation heads, scientists, engineers, governors, senators, presidential cabinet members—is too great to attempt even a partial listing.)

Brigham Young University (BYU), of course, is the capstone of the Mormon educational effort. The buildings and campus are magnificent; in fact, having been on a fair share of the campuses in the United States, I would rank Brigham Young at or near the top, in terms of physical plant. In the last thirty years, enrollment has grown from roughly five thousand to twenty-five thousand, making it, as mentioned earlier, the largest church-related university in the nation. There are no mortgages, even though the university receives no financial aid from the federal government. Practically all the money comes from LDS and LDS members, principally from tithing.

Tuition at BYU is remarkably low—less than $1,000 a year! The low figure again points up the importance of tithing. As elsewhere in Mormondom, tithing supplies fuel for the machinery.

BYU is primarily an undergraduate institution, though it does offer a doctorate in twenty fields. The large majority of the student body are Mormons, and they come from all fifty states as well as sixty-nine foreign countries. Interestingly enough, in a religious sense the campus is organized into stakes and wards, just as in Mormondom at large. It might also be mentioned that student attire is noticeably conservative; for example, no beards, no dungarees.

Why the Mormon stress on education? The impetus can be traced to a revelation of Joseph Smith at Kirtland, Ohio, in 1833: "The Glory of God is intelligence, or, in other words, light and truth." This motto, encircling a figure of a beehive, can be seen on BYU literature and letterheads.

The Outlook

During World War I, LDS had a membership of approximately half a million. At the outbreak of World War II, the number had risen to around a million. Today, total membership is approaching five million!

[53]Turner, *Mormon Establishment,* p. 123.

A decade or so ago, there were—worldwide—fifteen Mormon temples (for rituals such as the endowments, baptisms, and sealings). Today there are thirty-seven such temples built or under construction. In fact, there are now stakes and wards in all fifty states. LDS membership is also increasing sharply in a number of foreign countries.

There is nothing secret about this phenomenal rate of increase. The Mormon Church grows because it wants to grow. The Latter-day Saints maintain not only a high birth rate but a high conversion rate.[54] The same avenues of growth are open to other groups but are seldom used in conjunction with one another. The Hutterites and the Old Order Amish, for instance, have exceptionally high birth rates, but their conversion figures are near zero.

The upshot is that if the present rate of growth continues—as it gives every indication of doing—the Church of Jesus Christ of Latter-day Saints will be adding about a million new members every decade! True, not all of the membership is active, but the ratio of active to inactive is probably higher than in most other denominations.

The Latter-day Saints have had more than their share of problems. They have been criticized for not assimilating, for not caring enough about the larger community. They have been troubled by apostates and plagued by polygamy. They have been rebuked because of their position on women. And they have been condemned by other denominations for stealing their members.

In the early days, of course, persecution was rampant. Time after time, in state after state, entire Mormon settlements were forced to flee. LDS leaders were jailed, and substantial amounts of church property were confiscated. Despite the many problems, however, both old and new, the long-term vitality of the movement has remained unimpaired. If anything, the tempo has accelerated. The fact is that Mormonism is more than a religion or a set of theological beliefs. For most of its members, it is a whole way of life.

SELECTED READINGS

Arrington, Leonard, and Bitton, Davis. *The Mormon Experience.* New York: Knopf, 1979.

Barlow, Brent. "Notes on Mormon Interfaith Marriages." *Family Coordinator,* 26 (April 1977): 143–50.

Campbell, Bruce, and Campbell, Eugene. "The Mormon Family." In *Ethnic*

[54]Thornton, "Religion and Fertility," pp. 131–42.

Families in America, ed. by Charles Mindel and Robert Habenstein, pp. 379–412. New York: Elsevier, 1976.

Carmer, Carl. *The Farm Boy and the Angel.* Garden City, N.Y.: Doubleday, 1970.

Clark, Annie Turner. *A Mormon Mother: An Autobiography.* Salt Lake City: University of Utah Press, 1969.

Ensign. Published monthly by the Church of Jesus Christ of Latter-day Saints, 50 E. North Temple St., Salt Lake City, Utah.

Gates, Susa Young. *The Life Story of Brigham Young.* New York: Macmillan, 1930.

Hill, Donna. *Joseph Smith: The First Mormon.* Garden City, N.Y.: Doubleday, 1977.

Leone, Mark. *Roots of Modern Mormonism.* Cambridge, Mass.: Harvard University Press, 1979.

May, Dean L. "Mormons." In the *Harvard Encyclopedia of American Ethnic Groups,* ed. by Stephan Thernstrom, pp. 720–31. Cambridge, Mass.: Harvard University Press, 1980.

Melton, J. Gordon. *The Encyclopedia of American Religions.* 2 vols. Wilmington, N.C.: Consortium Books, 1979.

Merrill, Melissa. *Polygamist's Wife.* Salt Lake City: Olympus, 1975.

Mullen, Robert. *The Latter-day Saints: The Mormons Yesterday and Today.* Garden City, N.Y.: Doubleday, 1966.

O'Dea, Thomas. *The Mormons.* Chicago: University of Chicago Press, 1957.

Porter, Blaine. *Selected Readings in the Latter-day Saint Family.* Dubuque, Iowa: Brown, 1963.

Stegner, Wallace. *The Gathering of Zion.* New York: McGraw Hill, 1964.

Taylor, Samuel W. *Rocky Mountain Empire.* New York: Macmillan, 1978.

Thornton, Arland. "Religion and Fertility: The Case of Mormonism." *Journal of Marriage and the Family,* 41 (February 1979): 131–42.

Turner, Wallace. *The Mormon Establishment.* Boston: Houghton Mifflin, 1966.

Wallace, Irving. *The Twenty-Seventh Wife.* New York: New American Library, 1961.

Warenski, Marilyn. *Patriarchs and Politics.* New York: McGraw-Hill, 1978.

Whalen, William J. *The Latter-day Saints in the Modern-Day World.* New York: Day, 1964.

Wilkinson, Ernest, and Skousen, W. C. *Brigham Young University: A School of Destiny.* Provo, Utah: Brigham Young University Press, 1976.

Yorgason, Laurence M. *Preview on a Study of the Social and Geographical Origins of Early Mormon Converts, 1830–1845.* Master's thesis, Brigham Young University, 1974.

SEVEN

THE HUTTERITES

"The Hutterites are quite possibly the world's finest practicing sociologists."[1] So says John Bennett, and he knows whereof he speaks, for he has studied the group over a period of many years. In fact, of the scores of communistic groups that have appeared on the North American scene, the Hutterian Brethren are far and away the most successful. Most of the others have either changed their economic orientation or are defunct. Amana, Zoar, New Harmony, Ephrata, Oneida, Brook Farm, Aurora—the list of communistic failures goes on and on. The Hutterites have not only succeeded but are truly in a class by themselves.

The story of their success is interesting, for as Bainton points out, "Socially radical groups tend either to die out by the second or third generation, or else to survive by dropping the radical features."[2] The Hutterites obviously have done neither, and the whys and wherefores are the subject of the present chapter.

Persecution: The Hutterian Burden

The Hutterites have been in existence for more than 450 years and in one way or another have been persecuted throughout their entire history. Hard working, honest, devout, and friendly, they have nevertheless aroused the enmity of their neighbors in both the Old World and the New. The reasons for this ill will, furthermore, derive from the very nature of their religion. The long-term persecution of the Brethren, however oppressive, was not entirely unpredictable.

To begin with, the Hutterites are Anabaptists, and their historical persecution begins shortly after the founding of the Anabaptist move-

[1]John Bennett, "Social Theory and the Social Order of the Hutterian Community," *Mennonite Quarterly Review,* 1 (April 1977): 293.

[2]Roland Bainton, introduction to Leonard Gross, *The Golden Years of the Hutterites* (Scottdale, Pa.: Herald Press, 1980), p. 15.

ment in January 1525. On this date, a number of religious scholars—notably Conrad Grebel, George Blaurock, and Felix Mantz—gathered in Zurich to discuss matters of faith. Finding nothing in Scripture to support child baptism, they thereupon rejected the concept altogether, and to affirm their belief, Conrad Grebel rebaptized George Blaurock and several other adults. On this unheralded occasion, the Anabaptist movement had its inception.

Although they considered themselves a Christian sect, the Anabaptists were dissatisfied with the Protestant Reformation. In addition to adult baptism, for example, they believed strongly in the separation of church and state. They refused to take oaths or to bear arms. They believed in the right of the individual to worship as he saw fit. And they believed in the supremacy of the human conscience.

As a result of these beliefs, the Anabaptists were branded as heretics by both Protestant and Catholic groups. They were persecuted by the followers of Martin Luther and Ulrich Zwingli on the one hand and by the Jesuits on the other. Yet they refused to abandon any of their principles. In fact, over the years their convictions became stronger. Today the three groups which comprise the Anabaptists—Amish, Mennonites, and Hutterites—have solidified their beliefs and gained a fair measure of respect for their unswerving devoutness.

Origin of the Hutterites The Hutterites have been persecuted not only because they are Anabaptists but because they are Hutterites. The starting date for the group, which they acknowledge, is 1528. On this date, a group of Anabaptist refugees, fleeing to central Moravia (now Czechoslovakia), decided to pool their resources. According to the Old Hutterian Chronicle, cloaks were spread on the ground, and the men—mainly of Swiss, German, and Austrian (Tyrolean) extraction—"deposited all their worldly goods."

This symbolic action is understood by modern Hutterites to be the actual beginning of communal ownership. From 1528 to the present, the Hutterian Brethren have continually followed the practice of having "all things common." By so doing, they feel that they are following God's word as exemplified by the original Christian Church. The practice of communalism sets the Brethren apart from other Anabaptist groups and explains why the Hutterites have experienced even more persecution than the other Anabaptist bodies.

Jacob Hutter, Co-leader Oddly enough, Jacob Hutter—whose name the Hutterites bear—did not appear on the scene until some time after the Hutterites were formed. An Anabaptist minister from the Tyrol, Hutter was a brilliant organizer. Traveling from the Tyrol to Moravia with his own flock of refugees in 1529, he found the Moravian congregations in disarray. There were factions and dissensions, and some of the Brethren were becoming disenchanted with communal living.

In short order, he proceeded to weld the factions together, reinstate the practice of strict communalism, and instill a sense of mission into the various groups. Jacob Hutter's efforts were so successful that he was named leader of the Brethren in 1533. Interestingly, the name Hutterites was given them—over their strong objections—by their enemies. Today they accept the term, although they prefer "Brethren" or "Hutterian Brethren."

What kind of person was Jacob Hutter? Unfortunately, not too much is known about the man. His date of birth is unknown, though he was probably born between 1475 and 1500. The name Hutter (Huter) means "hatter," and his original occupation seems to have been hat making. It is believed that he had some schooling, for he spoke well and presumably had an understanding of mathematics and geography.

The man whose name the Hutterites bear was a man of strong will and exceptional courage. On a visit to the Tyrol early in 1536, he was captured and imprisoned by his enemies. Despite inhuman tortures, he refused to recant, and in February he was burned at the stake. After three years as leader, he had become a martyr.

Jacob Hutter was not a charismatic leader in the same sense as John Humphrey Noyes, Joseph Smith, or Father Divine. All of these men were able to move their followers by the spiritual power of their personalities. There is no evidence of Jacob Hutter having done so. His forte was in organizing and solidifying, rather than in creating and inspiring. Before he appeared on the scene, the Brethren were disintegrating. He rallied the group and designed the institutional structure. These traits—courage, organization, solidarity—came to be woven into the life-style of the Brethren.

Peter Rideman, Co-leader Following the death of Jacob Hutter in 1536, Hans Amon became head of the church, and upon his death in 1542, Peter Rideman—one of Hutter's former assistants—assumed leadership. While Jacob Hutter may—or may not—be overrated as a church leader, Peter Rideman has probably been underrated.

Born in Silesia (now central Poland), Rideman was a helmsman of the first order. Unshakable in his religious convictions (he spent a total of nine years in various jails for his heretical beliefs), Rideman was also an organizer and a disciplinarian. A tall man with a resonant voice, he set down hard and fast rules and was able to make them stick. He pulled dissident factions together and expanded the work begun by Jacob Hutter.

The effectiveness of Peter Rideman's leadership can perhaps be measured by the growth in church membership. During his regime, the Brethren grew from a few straggling groups to dozens of well-populated communities. In fact, for several decades after his death (1556), Hutterite colonies continued to grow until—by 1600—there were probably around twenty-five thousand Hutterites in eighty different communities. As Gross concludes, "The period of peace and prosperity that the Hutterites enjoyed during the latter half of the sixteenth century was later looked upon as the Golden Years."[3]

One reason for Peter Rideman's sustained influence was that he was such a prolific writer. He wrote dozens of epistles, hymns, and articles of faith setting forth the Hutterian viewpoint. Originally penned in longhand and laboriously copied, most of the writings were eventually published. Over the years, they came to be accepted as standard doctrinal sources. Today, for example, Peter Rideman's 266-page *Rechenschaft* (Account of Our Religion, Doctrine, and Faith), written in prison, is considered the Hutterites' most important book, with the exception of the Bible.

However one assesses the relative contributions of Jacob Hutter and Peter Rideman, it is obvious that these two men were the top leaders. The movement might have survived without one of them, but not without both.

The Road to Russia

Following the Jacob Hutter–Peter Rideman era, it was apparent that the Hutterites would not only survive but grow. At the same time—as every Hutterite who has ever lived knows—persecution was never farther away than the nearest hill or county. If not this year, then the next . . .

Sure enough, the outbreak of war between Austria and Turkey in 1593 found the Brethren under attack from both sides. Heavy taxation was followed by plundering, looting, and killing. They fled eastward from Moravia to Translyvania and Slovakia, where they tried to live inconspicuously. But it was not to be. Whereas once they had numbered in the tens of thousands, relentless persecution had cut their ranks to a few hundred.

In 1770, the "last exodus" took place, and 123 Brethren settled in the Ukraine, with a promise of toleration from the Russian government. The promise included freedom of religion, exemption from mili-

[3]Ibid., p. 31.

tary service, and—irony of ironies—permission to practice communal living. Eventually, other small groups of refugees followed. However, although the Brethren enjoyed a century's respite in Russia, the movement failed to recapture its former vigor.

In 1870, the czarist government withdrew its guarantee of toleration. All schools were brought under government supervision, and a new nationalization policy went into effect. Shortly afterward, a compulsory military conscription act was passed, and the Hutterites knew that the time had come for yet another exodus.

To the New World

In 1873, two Hutterian men traveled to North America on an exploratory mission. They returned with a highly favorable report, and the following year the mass exodus from Russia began. Between 1874 and 1877, some eight hundred Brethren—the entire Hutterite population—immigrated to the United States. Of this number, approximately half had not been practicing communal living. In America, the noncommunal group continued living as individual families, eventually joining the Mennonites.

The remaining four hundred, in actuality, form the basis of the present account: these men and women were the bedrock Hutterites. Their ancestors had been pursued and persecuted throughout eastern Europe: the Tyrol, Moravia, Hungary, Slovakia, Bohemia, Transylvania, Wallachia, the Ukraine. They were imprisoned and brutally tortured, slain by the thousands and tens of thousands, whole communities wiped out, generation after generation. And these four hundred were all that remained. They would be persecuted and imprisoned in America, too. And—once again—the large majority would be forced to leave. But it was a safe bet that the Hutterian Brethren would survive. Historically, culturally, and genetically, the odds must have been on the order of a thousand to one in their favor.

All four hundred settled in South Dakota in three different colonies, each named after its leader—hence the Schmiedeleut, the Dariusleut, and the Lehrerleut. *Leut* simply means "group" or "people," and while the number of colonies in North America has grown considerably, each colony continues to identify with one of the original three *Leut*. This means that, for most purposes, the Hutterites are divided into three branches. They maintain friendly relations, but each *Leut* has its own council of elders, each differs in terms of minor customs and rituals, and there is little or no intermarrying among the three.

At any rate, between the time of their settlement and World War

I, the Hutterian Brethren grew and prospered. Membership increased from four hundred to around seventeen hundred. The number of colonies, or *Bruderhofs,* grew from three to seventeen. Crops were good, land was plentiful, and the future seemed bright. Unfortunately, battle clouds were on the horizon, and so far as the Hutterites were concerned, war carried with it a special kind of trouble.

The United States' entry into World War I brought the "special trouble" in a hurry. Because of their refusal to serve in the armed forces or buy war bonds, Hutterites were met by hostility on all sides. Various *Bruderhofs* found their property burned and their livestock stolen. Since the law made no clear-cut provision for conscientious objectors, a number of young Hutterian men were drafted and confined to army guardhouses. The climax came in 1918 when four young Brethren were sent to Alcatraz, where they were beaten and starved. Transferred to Fort Leavenworth, two of the young men died because of maltreatment.

All this was too much for the Hutterites. After lengthy discussion and much anguish (and no satisfaction from Washington), they decided that the time had come to leave the country. As soon as arrangements were made with the Canadian government—which granted them immunity from the draft—the Brethren embarked on yet another exodus. With the exception of a single *Bruderhof* in South Dakota, all the Hutterian colonies immigrated to the Canadian provinces of Alberta and Manitoba. Their American property had to be sold at a substantial loss.

The Modern Period In the aftermath of World War I, there arose a more tolerant attitude toward conscientious objectors, and U.S. law was changed accordingly. Also, during the Depression of the 1930s there was a need to build up deserted farmlands, and local laws were modified to extend tax privileges. The upshot was that a number of the *Bruderhofs* moved back to the United States.

During World War II, the Brethren were treated more equitably. Although a few chose jail, most of the young men were sent to civilian work camps (United States) or assigned to forestry service (Canada). Could it be, after 450 years of apprehension and suffering, that Hutterian persecution has finally ended? The Brethren think not. They think that only the form has changed, that in the modern era the instruments of torture and imprisonment have been replaced by a more subtle and effective method: the legal prohibition.

During the 1940s, legislation was passed in Alberta forbidding or restricting the sale of land to Hutterites. In the 1950s, Manitoba also passed restrictive legislation, the Brethren agreeing to limit the number of *Bruderhofs* per municipality to two. About the same time, South Dakota passed a law which prohibited any of the existing *Bruderhofs* from adding to their acreage. The formation of new colonies was not outlawed, however.

Today, in both the United States and Canada, the Hutterites face a variety of legal obstacles aimed at inhibiting their expansion. Whether at the township, county, or state (province) level, these pressures have become so serious that practically all the *Bruderhofs* now employ legal advisors.

The Brethren themselves are philosophical about the matter. They realize that to be a Hutterite means to live in the shadow of the past. At the same time, they are keenly aware of the mutual-aid factor. As one Hutterite minister explained to an outsider: "The stronger the pressures are upon us, the stronger we become. In your life, you stand alone. In ours, there are many to help lift up a fallen brother."[4]

Organization of the *Bruderhof*

The Hutterian Brethren are a miraculous combination of past and present. The language they speak is a virtually extinct Tyrolean dialect. Their attire is much the same as it was four hundred years ago. Their social and economic organization is similar to that of the old Moravian *Bruderhof.* Periodic conflicts with the outside serve to remind them of their agonizing history.

Yet the Brethren are not smothered by the past. In their daily routine, they live very much in the present. As a matter of fact, although they are guided by their history in everything they do, they have made some highly successful adjustments to modern living. For example, in the late 1920s—after much discussion—they decided to add automotive equipment to their list of acceptable items. Today, trucks, tractors, and farm machinery are an integral part of Hutterian economy. The Brethren also permit the use of electricity for certain purposes, and in this sense they have made a more effective economic adjustment than the Old Order Amish—who have rejected both the automobile and electric power.

Leadership The Hutterian system operates not through written rules and regulations but through custom and tradition. In each *Bruderhof,* responsibility for maintaining this tradition—and for adminis-

[4]William A. Allard, "The Hutterites, Plain People of the West," *National Geographic* (July 1970): 112.

tering the colony itself—is vested in a council of five or six men: the minister, the business manager, the farm boss, the German teacher, and one or two other members elected by the male congregation. Council members enjoy no special privileges. On the contrary, they normally work harder than most other members.

The minister (also called the first minister, or *Diener am Wort*) is generally looked upon as the principal leader of the *Bruderhof.* He is obviously the spiritual head of the group, but he is also the secular head. Because of this dual role, he can—and often does—involve himself in practically any phase of community life. He disseminates information, interprets doctrine, settles disputes, administers punishment, keeps travel records, checks on council members, and otherwise acts as "shepherd of the flock."

As minister, of course, he conducts the regular religious services, as well as weddings, funerals, and baptisms. Theoretically, he refers controversial or weighty matters to the council, although his course of action depends to some degree on the man himself. Some ministers have more natural leadership qualities than others. Hutterite society frowns on strong personalities, however, and an overly dominant individual would be unlikely to reach the top position. In a number of *Bruderhofs,* the minister performs a regular agricultural or mechanical job in addition to his duties as *Diener am Wort.*

The number two man in the *Bruderhof* hierarchy is the business manager (also called the householder, or colony steward). His is a rather arduous job, for he not only must oversee all the colony's business enterprises but is expected to pitch in and help whenever needed. In a typical *Bruderhof,* the business manager can be seen consulting with the farm boss and the cattle man, supervising and visiting in the workshops, checking with the pig man and the duck man, discussing menus with the cook, and so on. The business manager also keeps the financial records of the colony, signs checks, and handles most of the commercial transactions with the outside.

Since the mainstay of the Hutterian economy is agriculture, it is not surprising that the number three man in the hierarchy is the farm boss. He decides what crops are to be sown, when the land should be cultivated, when seeding and harvesting should occur, and so on. He, too, is expected to work in the fields as well as supervise and make decisions.

The German teacher occupies a special place in the *Bruderhof.* He not only teaches German but is in charge of disciplining the children. And since Hutterian discipline includes corporal punishment, the German teacher—figuratively and literally—is an imposing figure.

Additionally, he often serves as colony gardener and in some *Bruderhofs* fulfills the role of second minister.

The minister, business manager, and farm boss are automatically members of the council. The German teacher is usually a member, but the other two members of the council can be anyone from the sheep man to the assistant carpenter. All members are elected and in the last analysis are responsible to the colony at large—or at least to its male members, since women do not vote. The organizational system thus includes checks and balances.

For example, the council is elected, but if members do not fulfill their duties properly they can be deposed, although this is infrequent. The council also formulates policy, but the really important matters are expected to be brought before the entire *Bruderhof.* In practice, therefore, while the council serves as a board of governors, its implicit function is to reflect the will of the colony. As might be imagined —given the Hutterian outlook on life—many of the basic *Bruderhof* decisions are preceded by long discussion. The goal is to arrive at a consensus rather than to "win" through block voting. Most of the time, the system works.

Council members are normally elected for a lifetime, so it is true, as outsiders contend, that the *Bruderhof* tends to be dominated by the aged. This is quite in keeping with the Hutterian way of life. After all, the Brethren are a conservative people, and aged members are the ones most likely to maintain the conservative position on various issues. It is no accident that, unlike society at large, the Hutterites show great respect for their older members. In fact, if two equally qualified candidates are being considered for elective office, the chances are that the older one will receive the larger number of votes.

However, Hutterian society is not totally static. Old members do resign or die, and younger ones are elected to take their place. Moreover, retirement policy is much more liberal than in society at large. After age forty-five, the amount of work a Hutterite does is pretty much a matter of individual choice. And while a few old-timers may be reluctant to give up the reins, they have been steeped in the philosophy of group primacy. Some gentle nudging by the younger men is usually sufficient to make an oldster step down. Out of deference and respect, however, the nudging will probably not occur until the older person is clearly unable to fulfill his duties.

A final method whereby young men move ahead is the process of "fission" or "branching." Hutterian Brethren do not believe in or practice birth control of any kind. As a consequence, their population grows rapidly, and the *Bruderhofs* are constantly dividing. Each division means a new colony; each new colony means a new council. So while the Hutterian leadership is clearly weighted in favor of age, there is just enough vertical mobility to give the younger men a reasonable chance of attaining responsible positions.

Although the entire Hutterite system is based on preventing any one person—or group of persons—from attaining too much power, the minister is clearly the most important person in the *Bruderhof.* He can, and often does, set both the religious and secular tone for the entire colony. Perhaps because of this fact, the *Diener am Wort* is chosen on a basis different from that of the other council members.

While the business manager, farm boss, German teacher, and others are elected by a simple majority, the minister—in the Hutterian view—is selected with God's help. Although the specific procedures vary among the *Leut,* the minister is generally chosen by a combination of regular *Bruderhof* voting plus the voting of ministers from other colonies. The names of candidates with the most votes are then placed in a hat, and the one drawn out is the new minister.

Just as each *Bruderhof* has a minister, each of the three *Leut*—Schmiedeleut, Dariusleut, and Lehrerleut—has a bishop, or *Vorsteher.* And once a year, all the ministers and business managers of the *Leut* gather to discuss current problems. (The only organization involving all three *Leut* is the United Hutterian Brethren Church, which was set up to present a unified front in negotiating with the Canadian government.)

Living Arrangements Home and family are important to most people, and the Hutterites are no exception. At the same time, family does not have the same meaning among the Brethren that it does in society at large. When a Hutterian uses the pronoun "we," he refers not to his family but to the *Bruderhof.* Similarly, the contention that a man's home is his castle would find little support among the Brethren. Hutterites not only do not knock before entering each other's residences, they drop in unannounced at all hours! As they see it, seclusion by individual families might lead to a lessening of overall group loyalty. The *Bruderhof* itself, therefore, is designed to discourage family privacy.

The actual buildings, numbering about fifty per *Bruderhof,* are well planned. The creamery is next to the cattle stable; the duck pen is by the lake; fuel tanks and machine shops are near the garage; and so on. Grouped around the communal dining hall are four to six residence halls. These are perhaps best described as a cross between a dormitory and an apartment. That is, while there are several families to a building, each family has its own quarters with a separate entrance.

Most apartments contain a living room and two or more bedrooms, depending on number of children. The rooms are comfortably furnished, though by modern standards they are anything but fancy. Most of the furniture is homemade. Style and decor vary somewhat from one *Bruderhof* to the next, but the conservative colonies will not have such things as wallpaper, mirrors, pictures, or curtains. Indeed, most Hutterites continue to use the old-fashioned outhouse!

Because of communal dining arrangements, there are no kitchens in any of the apartments. Most of the community kitchens, however, are quite modern and include refrigerators, freezers, large bake ovens, and electric mixers. Mealtime, incidentally, is a quasi-religious activity. Men are seated at one long table, women at another. (Children have their own dining hall.) Each meal begins and ends with a prayer. Like the Shakers, Hutterites eat their food in silence, and an attitude of solemnity prevails. The Brethren also eat quickly, a typical meal taking less than ten minutes to complete. Afterward, each member carries his dishes to the kitchen, and the tables are cleared.

Neither the Amish nor the Hutterites maintain separate buildings for their church services. The Amish, it will be remembered, hold Sunday services in their homes on a rotating basis. In the *Bruderhof,* services are normally held in the school, although on certain occasions the dining hall is utilized. To the Brethren, the place of worship is unimportant. What matters is what goes on in the human heart.

The Hutterian Way of Life

The basic tenets of Hutterian faith have not changed since the days of Jacob Hutter and Peter Rideman. They are: (a) adult baptism, (b) rejection of oaths, (c) pacifism, (d) economic communism, and (e) nonassimilation. These tenets are all self-explanatory, with the possible exception of the last.

As used by sociologists, the term *assimilation* refers to the absorption of one population group by another, where the end result is a blending of culture traits. The so-called melting pot in America has boiled unevenly, some groups becoming assimilated much faster than others. The Hutterites, of course, would fall at the lower end of any assimilation scale, for their religion demands that they remain apart. Referring to the *Bruderhof,* for example, the Brethren often say, "You are either in the ark, or you are not in the ark," the implication being that only those in the ark will achieve eternal life.[5] In any case, most of their colonies, both in the United States and Canada, are located some distance away from towns and major highways. The Hutterians have no desire to be in the limelight or jeopardize their separatist status.

By the same token, the Brethren have not been totally immune to the forces of assimilation. Time has succeeded in chipping away a small portion of their separatist domain. That is, while Hutterites do in fact live within the *Bruderhof,* they are probably having more contact with the world than ever before. Of necessity, they must deal with lawyers and government officials. They patronize hospitals and health centers. They exchange goods and services with the outside world. Also, the Hutterites are friendly people. Although their social life is largely restricted to their own or neighboring colonies, outside visitors are always welcomed, and over the years some of the Brethren have formed friendships with members of the "out-group."

Conservatism The five tenets listed above represent the major rungs on which the Hutterian ladder of life is based. By following them, the Brethren believe they are following God's path—which has not changed in 450 years. The details, however, are something else, and these the Hutterites have had to work out for themselves. The principle followed has been that of *nondisruptive change;* that is, acceptance of only those changes which are compatible with a fundamentalist view of the Bible and an agrarian style of life. In practice, this means that the Hutterian Brethren are one of the two or three most conservative groups in North America.

Hutterian clothes are plain. Men's work garb is not much different from that of neighboring farmers, but the female attire is clearly distinctive. It is quite similar to that worn in sixteenth-century Europe and includes an ankle-length skirt, separate bodice, long apron, low-heeled black shoes, and the familiar polka-dot head scarf. Practically all of the clothing (and underclothing) of both sexes is homemade, each woman doing the necessary sewing for her own family.

Personal adornments—makeup or any kind of jewelry—are taboo. Married men traditionally wear beards, although the beards are noticeably shorter than the Amish variety. While cameras and picture taking are supposed to be taboo, some Hutterites raise no real objection when outsiders snap their pictures. Smoking, gambling, dancing, and card playing are prohibited in all the colonies. Hutterites are not

[5]It is not uncommon for the Brethren to compare the *Bruderhof* to Noah's ark. For an excellent account, see John A. Hostetler, *Hutterite Society* (Baltimore: Johns Hopkins Press, 1974), pp. 153 ff.

abstemious, however. On special occasions—such as weddings and holidays—they drink beer and wine. In fact, they often make their own wine. The drinking is moderate, done largely by the men. There is no drunkenness or alcoholism.

While the Brethren prohibit what they consider useless frills and adornments, they are surprisingly modern in their use of certain appliances and housewares. Practices vary among the colonies, but such things as telephones, electric shavers, linoleum floors, stainless-steel ranges, sewing machines, and electric grills are now being used in many of the *Bruderhofs.* Predictably, innovations accepted in one colony have a habit of spreading to others.

Commercial amusements such as movies, shows, concerts, and sporting events are *verboten* in all the *Leut.* Even within the *Bruderhof,* entertainment—as the term is commonly used—has a limited connotation. Parties, games for young people, musical instruments, radios, record players, home films, television—such things are considered too worldly. Hutterites read to a fair extent, but their reading is confined largely to daily newspapers, farm journals, religious works, and German Mennonite literature.

The chief form of recreation for Hutterites everywhere is visiting, and in this respect they are like the Amish. Within the *Bruderhof,* visiting is more or less continual, members thinking nothing of dropping in at all hours. Hutterites are ready conversationalists, and there is usually a good deal of joking, teasing, and banter. Visiting also takes the form of journeying to other colonies, and since some of the trips are overnight they represent highlights in the Hutterian social calendar.

One reason for their restricted recreational fare is that the Brethren have a demanding work schedule. Theirs is an agrarian economy, after all, and this—plus the fact that there are so many children—means that both men and women are kept busy from the time the rising bell sounds at 6:15 A.M. until the time of the evening meal at 7:00 P.M. The work schedule itself, coordinating as it does the various age and sex groupings, is a veritable masterpiece. The day is divided into small time-segments, everyone is kept busy, and—from all reports—time seems to pass quickly.

Health Practices Despite their general conservatism, Hutterites are decidedly health-conscious. They are particular about their diet. Most of their food—milk, vegetables, meat, and poultry—is home-grown. They do almost all their own baking. If they have doubts about the adequacy of their menus, they do not hesitate to call in nutrition experts.

The Brethren keep regular hours. Their meals are served on time, in accordance with the work schedule. And because of the lack of interruption, members are more or less assured of a good night's sleep.

Medical and dental services are an integral part of the Hutterian program, and the per capita cost for doctors, dentists, and opticians is considerable. The sick and the infirm are cared for in the *Bruderhof* and are allowed to eat in their own apartments. The seriously ill are permitted to select their own doctors and hospitals. (Some of the Brethren have patronized the Mayo Clinic.) On the whole, researchers report that the physical health of the Hutterites is very good indeed.

In the sphere of mental health, the Hutterian Brethren also come off rather well. There is virtually no suicide, drug addiction, or drunkenness. Sexual problems are almost unheard of. And several surveys have reported a good overall adjustment pattern. There have been cases of serious mental disorders, but even these cases are often handled effectively within the framework of the *Bruderhof.*

The Economy

The Hutterian economy is a paradox. On the one hand, the Brethren are not entrepreneurs. The very idea of "buying low and selling high" is against their religion. As Peter Rideman put it, over four centuries ago, "We allow none of our number to do the work of a trader or merchant, since this is a sinful business. The wise man saith, 'As a nail sticketh fast between door and hinge, so doth sin stick close between buying and selling.' "[6]

On the other hand, there is no denying that the Hutterites—in their own way—employ some sound business practices. They buy astutely. They understand market values. They are frugal in their consumption practices, yet they do not hesitate to invest in the latest farm equipment. They are resourceful in their use of manpower. They pay cash for whatever they purchase, and they buy in wholesale quantities—which means that they generally pay the lowest prices.

There is no secret to the economic success of the Hutterites. On the contrary, their system is quite explicit. It is based on three pillars, each of which forms a part of their religion: hard work, communism, and agriculture.

[6]Peter Rideman, *Account of Our Religion, Doctrine, and Faith,* trans. Kathleen E. Hasenberg (London: Hodder and Stoughton, 1950), pp. 126–27.

The Concept of Work Work is a built-in part of the Hutterian lifestyle. For an able member not to work would be a sin. In practice, there is no such thing as a lazy Hutterite, just as there is no such thing as a nonreligious Hutterite.

Since the Brethren look upon work not as a disagreeable chore but as a positive expression of the communal way of life, the *Bruderhof* often appears to be a beehive of activity. Because of this, outsiders sometimes get the impression that the Brethren shun leisure activities in favor of work, but this is not true.

When the men finish their assigned tasks ahead of time, they gather in the shops and gab—much the same as other farmers. The women can usually be heard talking and laughing as they set about their household duties. In the last analysis, however, Hutterian recreation is something that occurs as an adjunct to work, never as a substitute for it.

Hutterians raise a fairly wide variety of crops, keeping members busy throughout the year. However, like farmers everywhere, the Brethren are busier in summer than in winter. During the cold months, therefore, jobs are reassigned. Farm hands work in the machine shop, the gardener takes on the duties of carpenter, equipment is overhauled, new buildings are constructed, and so on.

During an extremely slack season, or if a new colony is in financial need, Hutterites will sometimes "work out" for wages. Conversely, when they need extra labor they have been known to hire outside help. Such practices are rather rare, however. Hutterian Brethren feel most comfortable when they are surrounded by their own kind.

Communism Economic communism pervades the entire *Bruderhof;* it is the cement that binds the group together. As the Brethren practice it, communism is not simply an agreement to abolish private property and share the wealth but is an ingrained part of their religion, and they go to great lengths to make the system work. To practice communism in the midst of capitalist culture is no easy task—and the Hutterites know it.

The Brethren begin by rejecting the concept of private property. To a Hutterite, property is something to be used, not owned. It follows, then, that there is no such thing as affluence within the *Bruderhof.* It is true that the Brethren buy the best types of farm machinery and use various labor-saving devices. But these are *Bruderhof* properties and as such are presumed to further the group cause. As for individual aggrandizement, the Hutterites will have none of it.

The Hutterian economic system is all-inclusive. The Brethren raise most of their own food; make their own clothes, including shoes; build their own buildings; and make most of their own furniture. They supply practically all of their own labor. They are not 100-percent self-sufficient, but they are reasonably close to it. They no longer make their own sugar or grind their own flour. They also purchase a variety of farm machinery. If necessary, however, most colonies could survive on their own.

Generally speaking, Hutterian consumption practices are austere. The Brethren eat well, are clothed adequately, and their living quarters are sufficient for their needs, but they have very few luxuries. A recurrent theme in Hutterian culture is the necessity to reject the temptations of the secular world. This willingness on the part of the individual to live austerely accounts for much of the success of the colony as a whole.

Since they live in the midst of a capitalistic society, and since they carry on economic transactions with that society, how do the Hutterites handle money matters? The answer is fairly simple. The colony maintains a common bank account in a commercial bank, and the proceeds from all sales are deposited in the account. Bills are paid through checks signed by the business manager, although other members are sometimes authorized to make small cash purchases.

Individual Hutterites receive no salary or income of any kind. All their needs are filled by the *Bruderhof.* The only exception is a small monthly allowance for personal use. The amount varies from one colony to another, but for adults it probably does not exceed five dollars a month.[7]

Since they receive no salaries, individual Hutterites pay no income taxes, although the *Bruderhof* is taxed. Conversely, the Brethren receive no governmental benefits such as social security, disability payments, old-age pensions, and Medicare.

Agriculture Although the type of farming practiced by a particular *Bruderhof* depends somewhat on climate, water supply, type of soil, and other conditions, the various colonies—both in the United States and Canada—are basically alike. *They are all agricultural communes.* Hutterites believe they were meant by God to till the soil, and this belief permeates their entire way of life.

The agricultural operations of the Hutterian Brethren are considered superior to those of their neighbors. This is the opinion of both Hutterites and non-Hutterites, and the reasons are not hard to find. The Brethren employ the latest methods, they use the most modern

[7]David Flint, *The Hutterites: A Study in Prejudice* (Toronto: Oxford University Press, 1975), p. 24.

machinery, they have a reliable work force to call upon as needed, and they have had over four centuries of experience. Also, in their own minds at least, they have God on their side.

The farm boss plays a major role in all agricultural operations. Although major decisions are generally made by the group, the farm boss is responsible for the work assignments, the tempo of the work, the schedule for planting and harvesting, and the like. He is considered the technical expert on farming. A good farm boss reads the farm journals and obtains up-to-date information from commercial companies. He understands such things as market values, cost-price ratios, and the efficiency of labor-saving machinery.

Some colonies specialize in wheat and rye, others in feed grains and fodder. Nearly all have sizeable holdings in pigs and cattle. Chickens and eggs—and more recently, turkeys—are also profitable endeavors, some of the *Bruderhofs* having flocks of twenty-five thousand or more birds. Ducks and geese are another Hutterian favorite, and in order to provide a suitable habitat, most of the farms have a creek or other body of water.

Gelassenheit

Gelassenheit is rich in meaning, and for this reason the term is difficult to define. It has been described as "self-surrender," "yielding absolutely to God's wishes," "brotherly love," and "renouncing all selfish actions." Whatever its definition, only by understanding *Gelassenheit* can an outsider comprehend the smooth and highly successful operation of Hutterian communities.

To live and work closely with the same people day in and day out, sharing everything, requires a never-ending concentration of effort. This is facilitated by *Gelassenheit.* For example, although some jobs are obviously more important than others, the Brethren do not think of them in this light. Within the *Bruderhof,* positions have no high or low status, which would imply inequality. Indeed, one of the basic goals of Hutterian society is the *elimination* of social-status differentials. While they have not entirely succeeded, the Brethren have certainly minimized the prestige factor.

Over and over again in Hutterite literature, the cooperative theme is stressed: all members putting aside personal preference and working for the good of the group. In effect, this is *Gelassenheit*—submission to the will of God.

There are many manifestations of this togetherness, or group primacy. For instance, all members of the *Bruderhof* wear the same kind of clothes. They live in similar buildings and eat the same food. They have the same philosophy of life. They sing and pray together.

Hutterites rarely travel very far from the *Bruderhof,* and when they do—as on a business trip—they are glad to get back. Defections are also rare. Of those who do leave, most eventually return to the fold.

Within the colony itself, there are naturally differences of opinion. But there is seldom an argument—and almost never any shouting, cursing, or fighting. The Brethren tend to settle all differences through quiet conversation, group discussion, and consensus. Leaders do not really try to persuade followers; instead, they try to get all members to participate and share in the decision-making process. The end result, in most instances, is truly a group decision. However, if an individual member disagrees with the final verdict, he is nevertheless expected to bow to the group will—for the group will is God's will, or *Gelassenheit.*

As Peter Rideman put it long ago, "God worketh only in surrendered men."[8]

Sacred vs. Secular Society

Just as *Gelassenheit* is a religious rather than a secular concept, so the *Bruderhof* is a sacred rather than a secular society. A *sacred society* to sociologists is

> one that sees all its customs and institutions as being of divine origin. Misfortunes are generally explained as the result of the breaking of divine law. . . . Although man often makes a distinction between the things that are sacred and those that are not, the distinction is not too great in the sacred society. Religion is a pervasive, every-day affair that regulates law, marriage, moral obligations, taking of food, planting and harvesting, and all the multitudinous aspects of culture.[9]

A *secular society,* on the other hand,

> can have its religious rituals and mores, but most social arrangements are thought of as simply the practical ways of meeting the material problems of life. Laws and rules are made by legislatures, not by the divine will of God.[10]

[8]Rideman, *Account of Our Religion,* p. 86.

[9]Elbert Stewart and James Glynn, *Introduction to Sociology* (New York: McGraw-Hill, 1971), pp. 215–16.

[10]Ibid.

As far as Hutterian belief is concerned, Hostetler and Huntington state that "absolute authority resides in a single supernatural being, an omnipotent God, who created the universe and placed everything in a divine order and hierarchy. All events are ordered of God, and nothing happens without the knowledge of God."[11] To the Hutterites, religion is the most important thing in the world. It is more important than the family, the *Bruderhof,* even the individual himself.

To take one striking example: from the time he is a few months old, a Hutterian child's hands are held together in a position of prayer just prior to each feeding. By the time he is *one year old,* the child voluntarily prays before every meal—a procedure he will follow for the rest of his life.

The Brethren believe not only that man is born in sin, but that sinfulness persists. It is only by repentance and submission to God's will that salvation—in the next world—can be attained. Existence on earth is thus looked upon as a temporary journey, with eternal life being attained only after death. Self-surrender *(Gelassenheit),* rather than self-development, is the key to this attainment.

In addition to actually living his religion through such concepts as *Gelassenheit* and communality, the individual Hutterite also finds spiritual enrichment through a profusion of formal religious services. Grace is said before every meal; a regular—though shortened—service is held every evening; lengthy church services are held every Sunday; and special services take place on holidays, as well as during weddings, funerals, and baptisms.

Sunday, as it is throughout Christendom, is the heart of the religious program. For the morning service, men wear their best clothes, and women don their "Bible dresses." The minister leads the hymns, reads the sermon, and makes the necessary announcements. The sermons, incidentally, are age-old. All were written during the early persecutions and have been passed down ever since.

It should also be mentioned that the Hutterites employ no missionaries of any kind. They will explain their point of view to anyone who makes a serious inquiry but will not actively proselytize. One of their favorite biblical quotations is, "A city that is set on a hill cannot be hid" (Matt. 5:14). In spite of the quotation, however, the Brethren gain very few converts.

[11]John Hostetler and Gertrude Enders Huntington, *The Hutterites in North America* (New York: Holt, Rinehart and Winston, 1967), pp. 15 ff.

Gemeinschaft vs. Gesellschaft

It is no secret that the individual Hutterite tends to have a somewhat passive personality. He "self-surrenders" his own desires for the welfare of the group. Creativity and individuality are sacrificed in favor of the communal concept. Acquisitiveness is constantly played down. Theoretically, therefore, conformity should be high, deviance low. In practice, this is exactly what happens. Within the *Bruderhof,* crime and delinquency, divorce and desertion, violence, suicide, alcoholism, drug addiction, sexual problems, and the like are exceedingly rare. Exceptions do occur, of course, and the Brethren handle them in true Hutterian fashion: gently and with a minimum of fuss.

Why are the Hutterian social controls so effective? Basically, the *Bruderhof* is a *Gemeinschaft* rather than a *Gesellschaft* type of social structure. A term first used by the German sociologist Ferdinand Tonnies, *Gemeinschaft* refers to a community characterized by face-to-face relationships, where members and their families are well known to one another, and where standards and traditions are local rather than national. *Gesellschaft,* on the other hand, refers to a societal rather than a communal type of social organization, where people are not well known to one another, where relationships are impersonal and contractual, and where laws and regulations assume major importance. The point is that Hutterian conformity is based on the interplay between conscience and fear of rejection, an interplay which is possible only within a *Gemeinschaft* type of social structure.

Much of a Hutterian youngster's training is devoted to the development of conscience. Ideas of right and wrong are drummed in from all sides, so that by the time he reaches baptismal age his conscience ("feeling scared inside when you do wrong") is finely honed. And since his entire life has been molded by *Gemeinschaft* relationships, even a mild threat of rejection by the group is likely to bring about the necessary penitence. This is what makes Hutterian punishment —ludicrously mild by *Gesellschaft* standards—so consistently effective.

Let us take a few examples, starting with the less-serious offenses. For minor transgressions, a simple admonition or a heart-to-heart talk by one of the Brethren may be all that is necessary. If this is ineffective, the errant member will probably receive a visit from the minister. This is perhaps the most common method of social control and is generally sufficient to rectify the situation. Typical offenses in this category would be smoking, keeping a radio, argumentative behavior, or wearing improper clothing.

For more serious offenses, admonition by the minister is followed by the transgressor's standing before the congregation at the close of church service and asking for their forgiveness. Offenses in this category would include dishonesty, fighting, or openly disruptive behavior.

For the gravest of offenses, such as the misappropriation of funds or the flagrant disregard of colony rules, a kind of isolation is imposed. Hutterites call this form of punishment *den Frieden nehmen* (taking away the peace), and it corresponds to the Amish *Meidung.* It involves a temporary suspension of church membership: the errant member eats alone, sleeps alone in a separate room, and may not communicate with other *Bruderhof* members, including his own family. He is not reinstated until he shows the proper repentance.

Banishment—the permanent expulsion of a member from the colony—is the ultimate form of punishment and is almost unheard of in most Hutterite areas.

Most offenses are minor—drinking, smoking, possessing a musical instrument—and most involve young, unbaptized men. (About the only infractions involving females are things like using makeup or wearing a too-colorful kerchief.) If a serious offense is committed by a council member, he is ordinarily removed from office. There is no lasting retribution, however, and after a period of good behavior, he may be reelected to a responsible position.

For all intents and purposes, the crimes that are considered really serious by society at large—shooting, murder, rape, arson—do not exist in the Hutterite world.

Commitment

The reader may wonder at this point—in view of the rather obvious success of the Hutterites—why the *modern communal movement* has been characterized by failure. During the 1960s and 1970s, communes of all sizes, shapes, and descriptions seemed to sprout overnight. The total number probably ran into the thousands. But by the 1980s, nearly all had succumbed. Why? Although there are many reasons, one stands out: the matter of *commitment.* This is an exceedingly important point, and Kanter has written as follows:

> The problem of commitment is crucial. Since the commune represents an attempt to establish an ideal social order within the larger society,

> it must vie with the outside for the members' loyalties. It must ensure high member involvement despite external competition without sacrificing its distinctiveness or ideals. It must often contravene the earlier socialization of its members in securing obedience to new demands. It must calm internal dissension to present a united front to the world. The problem of securing total and complete commitment is central.[12]

The point is that the Hutterian Brethren are deeply committed to their venture, and their social and religious organization reflects this commitment. Since they have a greater "investment" in the undertaking, their economic policy, roles, assignments, operational procedures, social control—these and other elements of communal living are carefully mapped out. Most "modern" communes, on the other hand —lacking the necessary commitment—were deficient in these areas, hence their demise.

Male and Female Roles: The Hutterian Anachronism

Female emancipation has no place in the Hutterian scheme of things. Anachronistic or not, the Hutterite world is a man's world. It always has been and probably always will be.

Within the *Bruderhof,* women do not hold office or serve on the council. Strange as it may seem to us, they are not even permitted to vote. When a difference of opinion arises and a group discussion is called for, it is the men who do the discussing and the deciding, not the women. The latter are "excused" from all business meetings. In the dining hall, women sit at their own tables. At church services, they sit in their own section.

All business dealings between the *Bruderhof* and the larger community are transacted by men. Women are not allowed to drive vehicles. When a young couple get married, they always make their new home at the boy's *Bruderhof* rather than the girl's. And when a colony becomes too large and decides to branch, the decision as to when, where, and how is made solely by men.

No matter how distasteful the thought may be to outsiders, the Brethren feel that this is the natural order of things: the old over the young, the parent over the child, the husband over the wife. Peter Rideman, whose authority the Hutterites accept without question, is clear on this point.

[12]Kanter, *Commitment and Community,* p. 65.

> We say, first, that since woman was taken from man—and not man from woman—man hath lordship but woman weakness, humility, and submission. Therefore, she should be under the yoke of man and obedient to him. . . .
>
> The man on the other hand, should have compassion on the woman . . . and in love and kindness go before her and care for her; and faithfully share with her all that he hath been given by God.[13]

The last paragraph is significant, for Rideman did not intend the male-female relationship to be entirely one-sided. Male leadership was to be balanced by responsibilities and obligations. In practice, that is precisely how the Hutterian Brethren look upon sex roles.

Men are polite and considerate of women's feelings. Husbands are more than willing to help out around the house and are happy to relieve their wives of the heavier tasks. Instances of the husband's bathing the young children or assisting with the toddlers are probably more common in the *Bruderhof* than in society at large. Though barred from voting, Hutterian women make their wishes known to their husbands, and one suspects their influence is considerable.

Division of Labor Division of labor in the *Bruderhof* is much more pronounced than in the larger society, with men having one set of duties and women another. The positions of minister, assistant minister, farm boss, and German teacher are always filled by men. All the agricultural jobs are handled by men, although women occasionally assist. All craft work, such as that of the carpenter, shoemaker, machinist, and electrician, is performed by males. The field hands and laborers are also males, though in some colonies women do the painting.

In keeping with their traditional roles, women are responsible for food preparation, kitchen maintenance, gardening, clothes making, and child care. Some of these tasks are more involved—and more important—than they sound. Clothing manufacture, for example, is fairly complicated. Being farmers, Hutterian males are hard on clothes, and all apparel must be sturdy. The women purchase the fabric in wholesale lots and distribute it to the various households. Most wives have sewing machines, and all clothing is made at home.

Cooking is also a major undertaking; in fact, it is so important that the job of head cook is in the managerial category and is an elected position. The *Bruderhof* thrives on fresh food and home cooking. Mixes, canned goods, and other store-bought items are much less in evidence than in the average home.

[13]Rideman, *Account of Our Religion,* pp. 98–99.

Hutterian women work hard and take pride in what they do. On the whole, they do not seem to resent being kept out of the managerial positions. They feel, rather, that they can make their influence felt in other ways. Whatever resentment there might be, furthermore, would probably be sublimated in the light of the prevailing *Gelassenheit.* At the same time, by keeping women in a subservient position, the *Bruderhof* is depriving itself of an enormous amount of talent. This is indeed the Hutterian anachronism.

Child Rearing

Hutterite children are treated with a combination of love and kindness on the one hand and firmness and punishment on the other. The system works and is one of the most successful parts of the entire Hutterian program.

Babies are loved and welcomed, not only by the immediate family but by the entire *Bruderhof.* They are the center of attention, and even young children delight in holding them. By the age of two months, however, the socialization process has begun: the child's will must be broken and *Gelassenheit* developed. For example, although the infant is constantly coddled and pampered, when it is time for meals or church he is left alone in his crib. He soon learns that he cannot disrupt the community schedule. He learns that the same things are done, at the same time, day after day, year after year.

During the first two or three years, the conditioning process is largely home-centered. Toilet training starts at an early age, as soon as the child is able to sit up. In fact, the entire sequence of child development—toilet training, walking, weaning, and so forth—starts early and is fairly strict. Children are also taught not to fight or use bad language. They are encouraged to love all *Bruderhof* members and are warned about the dangers of greed and private property.

Like children everywhere, Hutterian youngsters do not always obey; indeed, they disobey a fair amount of the time. Unlike other children, however, Hutterite youth are expected to pay for their transgressions—and payment is likely to be in the form of corporal punishment. Thick leather straps are commonplace in Hutterian dwellings. But whether by strap, by willow switch, or by hand, corporal punishment starts early and is used frequently. How effective it is is anybody's guess—it certainly does not stop the youngsters from misbehaving. On the other hand, when coupled with other aspects of child training, corporal punishment seems to help develop *Gelassenheit.*

Young Hutterians do not appear to resent the whippings and spankings. Boys are punished more frequently than girls, but neither sex shows any long-lasting effects. Oddly enough, the punishment meted out is not always consistent with the "crime." Sometimes the child is strapped, while at other times—for the same offense—he is merely reprimanded. But again, if Hutterian adults are unpredictable in this respect, the youth take it all in stride. Corporal punishment is part of the culture pattern, and its use, consistent or otherwise, is accepted by the entire *Bruderhof.*

Contrary to the belief of many outsiders, Hutterite children do not lead an overly restricted existence. They can pretty much roam at will within the colony, and small bands of children can usually be seen cavorting in or around the various buildings. However, they are expected to start work at a much earlier age than other children. Boys from ten to fifteen can often be seen assisting adults in planting and harvesting, animal feeding, and occasionally even in tractor operations. Girls of the same age are required to help with household tasks, to baby-sit, and to assist in the communal kitchen.

By age fifteen, Hutterite boys and girls are expected to put away childish things and assume the transitional role of young adult. They no longer attend school, play with the children, or perform the routine chores assigned to children. They take their place in the adult dining hall and do adult work. It is not unusual, for example, for a seventeen-year-old boy to be given responsibility for the operation and maintenance of a tractor. A girl will now take her regular turn in the kitchen—cooking, baking, and preparing food. Both sexes also begin the courtship process that leads to marriage. Before turning to this subject, however, a word about the Hutterian school system.

Kindergarten The Hutterian Brethren had kindergartens as early as the sixteenth century, and it seems likely that the *Kleinschul* (small school) fulfills the same functions today as it did then: (a) to free the mothers for other duties, and (b) to introduce the child to the group life he will henceforth follow.

Entering the *Kleinschul* at two-and-a-half to three, the Hutterian youngster is taught hymns, prayers, and nursery rhymes. He learns obedience to adults other than his parents; he learns to adjust to his peers; and he is rewarded for passive, peaceful behavior rather than for assertion or aggression. In this sense, kindergarten serves as one of the first steps in the indoctrination process, a fact which the Brethren make no attempt to hide.

The *Kleinschul* operates on a regular school-year calendar, with few vacations. The children arrive after breakfast and in some colonies stay until after supper. Kindergarten mothers are usually chosen from among the older women in the *Bruderhof,* one practice being to rotate the job from day to day. Whoever is in charge, though, is given complete authority over the children, and while the relationship is usually a pleasant one, the kindergarten mother on occasion will use the willow switch or the strap.

The English School There is a widespread belief that Hutterites are opposed to education, but this is not really the case. The Brethren want their children to learn English, to understand basic arithmetic, and to be able to read and write without difficulty. What they object to are: (a) sending their children away from the *Bruderhof* to attend school, (b) exposing their children to the worldly influences encountered in a typical public school, and (c) forcing Hutterite youth to take courses which have no relevance to communal farm life.

These objections, of course, run counter to compulsory school laws, and over the years there have been conflicts between government forces and various colonies. Both sides have made accommodations, however, and for the time being, at least, the issue has been resolved. In brief, the school board supplies the teacher (and pays his salary), and the Hutterites supply the school, which is located in the *Bruderhof.* This system permits the Brethren to comply with the law and at the same time enables them to retain control over the children and—to some extent—over the teacher.

Theoretically, the English school poses a real threat to the *Bruderhof.* Coming in contact with youth during their formative years, the school might be expected to act as a wedge, a divisive force within the colony. Hutterites are well aware of this threat and go to some lengths to counteract it. The minister, for example, explains Hutterian policy to the new teacher. The latter is encouraged to take strict disciplinary measures in the classroom and not to introduce things which are against the Hutterite religion, such as radios, movies, and television.

On the other hand, the Brethren make little attempt to interfere with educational practices per se or with the curriculum. In fact, most of the colonies go out of their way to make things pleasant for the teacher, by supplying him or her with low-cost food and housing, giving presents, assuring privacy, providing transportation, and so on. Teachers are reportedly quite fond of the Hutterian Brethren, and the relationship is generally good.

Perhaps the most remarkable thing about the English school is not its influence, but its *lack* of influence. Hutterian children learn their lessons as well as anyone else, but despite their exposure to an outsider for eight years, they remain convinced that their own way of life is best.

The German School Unlike the English school, the German school has been a Hutterite landmark for many centuries and was first mentioned in the Great Chronicle of 1533. While all Hutterian youth must attend both schools, the German school is considered the more important. It is normally held in the English school building for an hour or two at the beginning of the day, and again at the end. This positioning—whereby the German school surrounds or encapsulates the English school—is deliberate and is aimned at counteracting the English school's influence.

The German school has two major functions: to teach German and to provide a formal introduction to the Hutterian way of life. German teaching involves German-language readers, copying lessons, and application of rote memory. The children also learn the elements of Hutterian history. However, the school is not divided into grades or levels. No child is promoted, and no one is kept back. Each child progresses at his own pace. Slow learners are given extra help, and the more intelligent children are encouraged to read additional material at home. Direct academic competition in the classroom is not permitted.

Indoctrination of the Hutterian life-style, really the main function of the German school, is a never-ending process that calls for genuine pedagogical skill on the teacher's part. Children are taught how to behave in church, in front of visitors, and on trips to town. They are taught to show proper respect for the aged and are admonished over and over again to share everything. Throughout the various teachings and parables runs a central theme: self-surrender to the will of God.

The German teacher himself is looked upon as a combination of kindly shepherd and stern disciplinarian. His effectiveness often depends on the extent to which he can combine the two qualities. Nevertheless, as the *Bruderhof*'s chief disciplinarian, he usually keeps the strap close at hand. Should other methods fail—persuasion, threats, scolding, reprimand—the German teacher will not hesitate to use the "enforcer." As Paul Gross says: "One of the first tasks, is to teach growing children to do the things they are supposed to do whether they like it or not; and to avoid doing those things which they should not do, no matter how pleasant they may seem.[14]

[14]Paul S. Gross, *The Hutterite Way: The Inside Story of the Life, Customs, Religion, and Traditions of the Hutterites* (Saskatoon, Saskatchewan: Freeman, 1965), p. 70.

Courtship and Marriage

During the Russian period, Hutterite marriages were arranged by colony leaders, but this practice was discontinued in North America. Hutterian youth choose their own mates, though their choice is much more restricted than our own. Hutterites must (a) marry other Hutterites, and (b) marry within the same *Leut.* (Marriages among the Schmiedeleut, the Dariusleut, and the Lehrerleut have taken place on occasion, but they rarely occur today.)

Within the *Leut,* marriages may be between people of the same colony or different colonies. The latter type, however, are much more common, since within a given *Bruderhof* so many of the young people are likely to be brothers, sisters, or cousins. Even when they are not, they tend to *feel* that they are related. Indeed, in some colonies, *most of the members have the same surname!* In his study of Pincher Creek Colony, for example, David Flint writes:

> Most of the people in this colony are surnamed Gross—although not all of them are closely related. There is also one Reid and one Hofer family. . . . Because of the closely knit nature of the sect, there are only about twenty different surnames among all the Hutterites in the world.
>
> Most of the names are German or Tyrolean, and seven—Walter, Gross, Hofer, Wurz, Mendel, Mueller, and Wollman—date back to their first communities in 16th-century Czechoslovakia. Other common names are Waldener, Kleinsasser, Stahl, and Decker. Historically minded Hutterites are interested in genealogy and have records whereby nearly every family can trace its ancestry back to the 1500s.[15]

Hutterian boys and girls marry at a slightly older age than outsiders (baptism is usually not until age twenty or later), and both parental and colony consent are required. This is seldom withheld, however, and only about 1 percent of the Hutterites remain single.

Although Hutterian youths are expected to date a variety of partners, they probably have less overall dating experience than other young people. For a specific courtship to last three or four years is not at all unusual. During this period, the boy and girl may see each other only once or twice a month.

Physical attractiveness, while certainly not ignored, is played down. The term "sex appeal," for instance, is not part of the Hutterian vocabulary. Rather, such traits as industriousness, reliability, and cooperativeness are stressed.

With regard to specific courtship behavior—necking, petting, "making out," or whatever the term—no ready data are available.

[15]Flint, *Hutterites,* p. 6.

Such activity undoubtedly occurs. It is extremely unlikely, however, that it occurs with anything like the frequency found on the outside. For one thing, the Hutterian Church frowns on premarital sex, and Hutterites of all ages take their religion seriously. For another, Hutterian youth simply do not have much privacy. They do not have their own automobiles and do not normally go to town by themselves. Even within the *Bruderhof*—where knocking on doors is not part of the culture pattern—opportunities for privacy are limited.

Needless to say, when they set their minds to it, courting couples can always find ways to be alone, and the adults are usually understanding. If a courting couple are "missing" for an hour or so, nothing is said. Prolonged absences, however, would not be tolerated. All in-all, premarital sex is not now, and never has been, a major problem in any of the colonies.

The Wedding Some courtships are longer than others, but all the successful ones terminate in engagement and marriage. The engagement period is short, often only a week or so in duration. The wedding itself is a fairly elaborate affair. If there are two colonies involved, the ceremony and festivities take place in the groom's colony.

Generally held on a Sunday, the wedding service is similar to that found in Protestant churches. The minister performs the ceremony, vows are taken by the bride and groom, prayers are said, and the couple are pronounced man and wife. In keeping with the ban on jewelry, neither an engagement ring nor wedding band is used.

After the ceremony, there is an elaborate meal, replete with wine and wedding cake. Songs are sung, children play games, old folks reminisce, relatives exchange news, and courting couples court. Weddings, clearly, are among the happiest of Hutterite occasions. They are also—'twas ever thus—a lot of work. The women must start preparations days in advance. Indeed, because of the work involved, a *Bruderhof* will sometimes hold three, four, or even five weddings simultaneously, thus cutting down on the amount of preparation.

There is no such thing as a honeymoon among the Hutterites. Following the services, bride and groom move directly into their apartment, ready to begin their new life. Between the engagement and wedding ceremonies, however, friends and relatives will have given them a variety of small presents—an alarm clock, table lamp, dishes, soap, bed linen, and the like.

How do husband and wife get along? Although we have no empirical research studies on the matter, most observers report a high level of marital satisfaction among the Hutterites. There is little quarreling or bickering. Sexual maladjustment seems unknown. Divorce and desertion rates are practically zero. Children are loved and welcomed. Old folks are cared for and respected. The husband is the "boss," but while the system is patriarchal, it is not authoritarian. All things considered, marriage is one of the strong features of Hutterian life.

Population Policy

Basic to any understanding of the Hutterian Brethren is the realization that they do not practice birth control. Period. Condoms, diaphragms, intrauterine devices, the pill, even the rhythm method—all are taboo. Outsiders sometimes feel that the reason for this is that Hutterite parents do not have to support their own children, and that if they did, there would be fewer of them. But this is false. The real reason for the ban on birth control is religious, not economic. "Natural intercourse" between spouses has always been an ingrained part of the Hutterian religion. The point is not even debated.

It is taken for granted that when a Hutterite girl marries, she will commence to have babies—as God intended—and that she will continue to have babies until God dictates otherwise. Pregnant wives, a common sight in the *Bruderhof,* are given no special consideration. Most of them keep right on working up to the time of childbirth, believing that work will make the child stronger.

Hutterian insistence on following the biblical injunction to "be fruitful and multiply" has had remarkable demographic consequences. Their birth rate is nearly unequaled—45.9 per thousand population versus 16.2 for the United States as a whole. To put it in nondemographic terms, the Hutterian Brethren average better than ten children per family! And because the Hutterites are health-conscious and spend a good bit of time and money on medical care, their death rate is less than half that of the United States—4.4 per thousand versus 8.9.

The combination of high birth rate and low death rate has resulted in a phenomenal rate of natural increase; in fact, the Hutterian Brethren may be the fastest-growing population in the world, doubling their numbers every seventeen years!

These figures are not mere statistics but represent what has actually been happening to the Hutterian population. Four hundred Brethren came to the United States in 1875 to form their first colonies. Their numbers are now approaching thirty thousand. In little more than a hundred years, their population has doubled six times!

One aspect of Hutterite fertility may be unique: the tendency of the women to bear children right up to the time of menopause. Demographic studies indicate that at ages forty to forty-four, Hutterite women have a higher birth rate than the women of such countries as France, Sweden, and the United States *during their maximum fertility period, twenty-four to twenty-nine.* Demographers have commented on this phenomenon. Is it possible, they ask, that during the hundreds of years of inbreeding, the Brethren have developed a biological strain with a higher fertility potential (fecundity) than the rest of mankind?

If it were not for their taboo on premarital sex plus their somewhat later age at marriage, the Hutterites might well have reached the maximum possible rate of human fertility. As it is, their rate of increase is so high that it colors virtually every phase of colony life. The chief problem, of course—one that recurs with relentless regularity—is simply what to do with all the people.

Branching To take care of their burgeoning population, the Hutterian Brethren have obviously had to increase their landholdings. This could have been done (a) by enlarging the size of existing colonies, or (b) by forming new colonies. The Hutterites have chosen (b), and in spite of considerable opposition by local and state governments, they have been remarkably successful. Starting with but three *Bruderhofs* in South Dakota in the 1874–1877 period, the Brethren now have some 250 colonies scattered over North Dakota, South Dakota, Montana, Minnesota, Washington, Alberta, Saskatchewan, and Manitoba.

Branching or fission, as it is called, is a complicated and time-consuming process. Money must be raised, a several-thousand-acre site selected, new buildings erected, crops planted, livestock and farm machinery transported. The parent colony must also decide which people will go and which will stay. The actual moving of the people—together with clothing, furniture, and belongings—is the last step in an arduous process.

Plans for branching are discussed several years prior to the actual move. Maximal size of a colony is about 150 people. The Brethren know from experience that when numbers exceed this figure, there will not be enough managerial jobs to go around. Some of the young men become dissatisfied, and cliques and factions tend to form.[16] Also, as the *Bruderhof* goes beyond the 150 mark, per capita return

[16]See John Bennett, "Frames of Reference for the Study of Hutterian Society," *International Review of Modern Sociology,* 6 (Spring 1976): 23–39.

from the agricultural enterprise may diminish, since it is difficult to increase productivity without increasing acreage. At any rate, since there are sound social and economic reasons for branching at 150, and since it takes roughly fifteen years for a colony to reach this number—assuming a starting figure of 75—plans for fission are begun any time after the tenth year.

The initial problem is to find a new site close enough to the parent colony so that assistance can be accepted, but far enough away so that independence can be achieved. The ideal distance is considered to be twenty-five to fifty miles, although other considerations are involved, such as water supply, topography, type of soil, rainfall—and price. The last is especially important, for as land prices have risen, the cost of branching has become increasingly expensive—so expensive, in fact, that some colonies now hire a commercial agent to do their land buying.

While the land is being purchased and cultivated and the living quarters constructed, the parent colony must work out the details of actually dividing itself. Accordingly, two lists are drawn up—by the minister and the second minister—for the consideration of the membership. The lists are presumably impartial, and while some personal preference is permitted—especially on the part of older people—each list contains a minister, business manager, farm boss, chicken man, carpenter, machinist, and so on.

Who goes and who stays is sometimes not known until a day or two ahead of time. In some colonies everyone packs and gets ready to move. (Trucks are borrowed from nearby colonies for this purpose.) At the last moment, the two lists are placed in a hat. The one withdrawn by the minister is the one that moves. And as the trucks roll out with the "branchers," those remaining unpack their belongings.

Hutterian colonies are never really "rich" in a strictly economic sense. The money they accumulate must be spent every fifteen years or so in the development of a new *Bruderhof.* True, the older colonies have an easier time of it than the newer ones, but with such a phenomenally rapid population growth, fission is always just around the corner. This means that austerity is more or less a recurrent theme.

The Brethren do not complain. They know that much of their income goes, not to make life easier for themselves, but to expand the Hutterian way of life. The individual Hutterite, in other words, is quite content to make whatever personal sacrifice is necessary for the good of the *Bruderhof.* The *Bruderhof* makes the same kind of sacrifice for the good of the *Leut.* As the Hutterian Brethren see it, this is the natural order of things.

Relations with the Outside

What is the current relationship between Hutterites and the surrounding community? Are the Brethren integrating in any real sense of the word? Is the attitude of outsiders softening, or are the old hostilities still apparent? These are questions on which observers are divided. Even the Hutterites disagree on the matter. For the fact is that the evidence points in both directions.

On the one hand, there is no doubt that some traditional antagonisms remain. When Hutterites settle in an area, there is sometimes resentment on the part of the local people. There is a fear that the Brethren will tend to dominate an area, or at least that they will not contribute to its economic well-being. Hutterites are condemned for their communism, their quaint customs, their refusal to fight for their country, their apartness and clannishness, and their reluctance to participate in the civic affairs of the community.

The Brethren are also criticized for their rejection of higher education, their insistence that only they are following in God's footsteps, and their insatiable demand for more land. Several states and provinces have laws restricting Hutterian landholdings. Additionally, the Brethren have had their property stolen and their buildings set on fire. Their homes have been vandalized. They have been cheated and overcharged. They have been ridiculed, harassed, beaten, and treated unfavorably in the press.

No wonder some Hutterites are wary of their neighbors and suspicious of all outsiders. The world beyond the *Bruderhof* is looked upon as a veritable pitfall. To such Brethren, a good neighbor is one who is neither seen nor heard. In some colonies, small children cry and flee at the sight of approaching strangers.

Yet there is another side to the story. Mistreatment of the Hutterites is not typical. It happens all too often, but for every such tale, there are many more involving friendship and reciprocity between the Brethren and their neighbors. Communities are coming to realize that Hutterites are honest and hardworking, that they can help the local economy and generally upgrade the area.

Little by little, the Hutterian Brethren are taking more of an interest in civic matters. They have supplied men and machinery to help fight fires, clear roads, fix fences, and dam overflowing rivers. They have set up repair-service facilities for local farmers, donated money to nearby hospitals, given food to the needy. They have shared their agricultural and mechanical expertise with their neighbors. They have visited—and been visited by—nearby farmers and in a few cases have even established lasting friendships. All in all, a reasonably encouraging picture.

The Hutterian Paradox There is one final point—alluded to earlier—that bears repetition. In spite of their long history of mistreatment and persecution, Hutterites tend to be friendly individuals. This is the Hutterian paradox. The individual Hutterite knows—in his bones, perhaps—that outsiders cause trouble. Yet in his heart he feels friendly and desires the interactive rewards that characterize true friendship. He is pulled in two directions: he must live apart, for his religion demands it, but by so doing, he knows that some enmity will probably befall him. So, while the Hutterite is spontaneously open and friendly, he is at the same time inwardly wary. He is reluctant to establish real friendship in the outside world because he lacks confidence in that world.

Naturally, there are great differences in this respect, among both individuals and colonies. Most of the *Bruderhofs* have made workable accommodations with their neighbors, although there are still some flareups. At the present time, however, no colony is surrounded by the bitterness and hostility that characterized, say, the World War I period.

Conflicts over Hutterian land acquisition will doubtless recur from time to time. Individual acts of harassment will also continue, though probably on a reduced basis. But the important point is that accommodation—in both the United States and Canada—seems to be working. There is no incarceration and no bloodshed.

Real assimilation, of course, will never take place, because of the Hutterite religion. Nor will the Brethren yield on those issues which might weaken that religion. Such issues would include higher education, popular entertainment, conspicuous consumption, and other manifestations of "worldliness." If, in his steadfastness, the Hutterite is forced to suffer hardship and indignities, he is prepared to pay the price, for he has no doubt that his religion is more important than himself.

Disruptive Factors

All groups have problems, and the Hutterites are no exception. In addition to persecution and harassment, they have a variety of internal problems. This may be surprising to some readers, for the Hutterians do not advertise their troubles. On the contrary, they generally keep them under cover. Nevertheless, they exist, and in some cases they are serious.

To begin with, the Hutterite religion acts as a kind of common denominator, above which no member is supposed to rise. Terms like achievement, status, and prestige are deliberately avoided. Individual aptitudes which might lead, say, to accomplishments in the arts and sciences are not only played down—they are stamped out. To be a Hutterite means to bow to the group will, but not all members can do this. Some leave the *Bruderhof* to seek fulfillment on the outside. While the number of such cases is small, the problem itself is one which the Brethren will probably never solve.

A more common cause of defection is internal strife. Despite the fact that *Gelassenheit* is generally successful, disputes between individuals do occur. Cliques and factions also arise. Indeed, not all the colonies are on good terms with one another, although to the outside world the Brethren generally present a united front. The point is that when factionalism within a *Bruderhof* cannot be resolved, there may be only two solutions. One is branching, the other is for the dissidents simply to leave the colony and sever all ties with the church.

Factionalism occurs for a number of reasons. There may be an insufficient number of managerial jobs to satisfy the men of the colony. Cliques may form on the basis of family lines. Members may feel that they have been unjustly accused of wrongdoing. Leaders may be accused of favoritism. Dissatisfaction may arise over the handling of young people. And so on.

Young people are a special problem. Since baptism seldom occurs before age twenty, it is more or less expected that they will take some liberties prior to that age: smoke cigarettes on the sly, listen to clandestine radios, sneak off to town, and so forth. The difficulty is that once they succumb to temptations on the outside, young people sometimes refuse to return to the *Bruderhof.* Some stay away for years, only to return and resume their Hutterian practices. Others never return, and while the percentage is small, the problem of restive youth is another that likely will never be solved.

A more serious internal problem is that of leadership. Hutterites tend to be suspicious of dominant personalities and strong leaders. Such traits are difficult to reconcile with *Gelassenheit,* or self-surrender. At the same time, the social system as practiced within the *Bruderhof* calls for intelligent, firm, and resourceful leadership, particularly on the part of the minister and the business manager. When these men falter or make poor judgments, the *Bruderhof* is in for trouble.

Hutterian leaders, however, have no real authority other than that vested in them by the male membership. If they do not satisfy that membership, they can be replaced. Major decisions, furthermore, are voted on. As a consequence, the top men often find themselves in an anomalous position. On the one hand, they lead; on the other, they follow. On the one hand, they make decisions; on the other, they must strive for consensus. Such an exacting position is more than some men can stand, and they have resigned—though in most other walks of life they would have made topnotch leaders.

In some colonies, of course, there are simply not enough men with leadership ability to man the top positions. If the scarcity should affect the posts of minister and business manager, the *Bruderhof* may become unstable and liable to recall; that is, the *Leut* may rule that the entire membership must return to the parent colony and a new complement be sent out to replace them. If replacement is not feasible, the malfunctioning colony may simply be dissolved, and in a few instances this has actually happened.

Population and Expansion From the long-range view, the most serious and persistent problems facing the Hutterites are population increase and land acquisition. The difficulties mentioned above—factionalism, nonconformity of youth, leadership failure, and the like—do not have a pronounced effect on the overall Hutterian movement. Such problems are not so radically different from those experienced by other groups. Population control, however, is another matter.

More population means more mouths to feed. More mouths mean more food. And more food means more land. Then the process starts all over again—more people, more food, more land. Under the Hutterian system, there is no way to stop the cycle. Their religion forbids any kind of birth control; socioeconomically, each colony must divide when its numbers reach 150. The result is a genuine population explosion.

With a doubling of numbers every seventeen years, the Brethren are growing at a rate that alarms their neighbors. Already there have been a variety of laws aimed at restricting Hutterian land acquisition. In effect, people are saying, "We must pass such laws. We cannot sit back and let the Hutterites gobble up all the land." To which the Brethren answer, "We are doing no more—and no less—than what God put us on earth to do."

The implications of the problem are difficult to grasp. Is it conceivable that Hutterian growth will continue at its present rate? Will their population—currently in the neighborhood of thirty thousand—actually reach sixty thousand during the 1990s? Will the number of colonies increase to well over four hundred? Will the Hutterites really acquire a million new acres of land by then?

Currently, there is still enough unused land in North America to prevent the problem from reaching the acute stage. Sooner or later, however, the issue must be met head on. When that time comes, no one can predict what will happen. Meanwhile, the Brethren will go right on, doing no more—and no less—than they were put on earth to do.

The Hutterites: Success, and Yet . . .

There is no doubt that the Hutterites have compiled a remarkable success story. For more than four hundred years, they have shown a sense of resilience and an adaptation that is virtually unequaled. Moreover, their future looks bright. Their membership loss is low, despite their rather austere way of life. (Most observers put their defection rate at around 2 percent.) A major reason for this is their feeling of belonging and at-homeness within the *Bruderhof.* In the Hostetler survey, for instance, when Hutterite adults were asked, "How many close friends would you say you had?" most of the respondents said they had several hundred![17]

Interestingly enough, however, some observers feel that "prosperity" may prove to be the Hutterians' greatest threat. Bennett writes that

> When the colony as a whole has enjoyed considerable success in sales of farm products, there is temptation to indulge in more consumer goods, or for individual Brethren to scheme to obtain private shares. . . . Affluence is, in fact, the greatest evil of the system, and it is one that Hutterites, in their increasing economic success, have had difficulty controlling.[18]

Cultural as well as economic prosperity is involved. In Canada, for example, the government has set aside millions of dollars "to give to minority group organizations for their own cultural purposes." Flint continues as follows:

> Does multi-culturalism actually threaten groups like the Hutterites? The Hutterites would say that it does. Good times can bring the greatest danger to the Brethren, in the form of subtle and hard-to-resist temptations.
>
> Paradoxically, they are wary of those who do not persecute them, for tolerance is but a step toward encroachment by the outside world, and, eventually, assimilation. Hutterites, then, can never escape the dilemma

[17]Hostetler, *Hutterite Society,* p. 246.
[18]Bennett, "Frames of Reference," p. 29.

of co-existing with the world from which they have chosen to withdraw.[19]

Only time will tell whether the Hutterites will continue in the footsteps of Jacob Hutter and Peter Rideman, or whether they will be "killed by kindness." On the record, there is probably no real cause for concern. The Brethren have met—and overcome—vastly greater dangers.

SELECTED READINGS

Allard, William A. "The Hutterites, Plain People of the West." *National Geographic* (July 1970): 98–125.

Bainton, Roland. Introduction to Leonard Gross, *The Golden Years of the Hutterites.* Scottdale, Pa.: Herald Press, 1980.

Bennett, John. "Frames of Reference for the Study of Hutterian Society." *International Review of Modern Sociology,* 6 (Spring 1976): 23–39.

———. "Social Theory and the Social Order of the Hutterian Community." *Mennonite Quarterly Review* (April 1977): 292–307.

Flint, David. *The Hutterites: A Study in Prejudice.* Toronto: Oxford University Press, 1975.

Friedmann, Robert. "Peter Rideman: Early Anabaptist Leader." *Mennonite Quarterly Review,* 44 (January 1970); 5–44.

Gross, Leonard. *The Golden Years of the Hutterites.* Scottdale, Pa.: Herald Press, 1980.

Gross, Paul S. *The Hutterite Way: The Inside Story of the Life, Customs, Religion, and Traditions of the Hutterites.* Saskatoon, Saskatchewan: Freeman, 1965.

Hostetler, John A. *Hutterite Society.* Baltimore: Johns Hopkins Press, 1974.

———. "Hutterites." In *Harvard Encyclopedia of American Ethnic Groups,* ed. by Stephan Thernstrom, pp. 471–73. Cambridge, Mass.: Harvard University Press, 1980.

———, and Huntington, Gertrude Enders. *The Hutterites in North America.* New York: Holt, Rinehart and Winston, 1967.

Kanter, Rosabeth Moss. *Commitment and Community: Communes and Utopias in Sociological Perspective.* Cambridge, Mass.: Harvard University Press, 1972.

Kephart, William. *The Family, Society, and the Individual.* Boston: Houghton Mifflin, 1980. See pp. 108–57.

Khoshkish, A. "Decision-Making Within a Communal Setting: A Case Study of Hutterite Colonies." *International Review of Modern Sociology,* 6 (Spring 1976): 41–55.

[19]Flint, *Hutterites,* p. 146.

Lewis, Russell E. "Controlled Acculturation Revisited: An Examination of Differential Acculturation and Assimilation Between the Hutterian Brethren and the Old Order Amish." *International Review of Modern Sociology,* 6 (Spring 1976): 75–83.

Peters, Victor. *All Things Common: The Hutterian Way of Life.* Minneapolis: University of Minnesota Press, 1965.

———. "The Process of Colony Division Among the Hutterians: A Case Study." *International Review of Modern Sociology,* 6 (Spring 1976): 57–64.

"Pockets of High Fertility in the United States." *Population Bulletin* (November 1968): 26–44.

Pratt, William F. "The Anabaptist Explosion." *Natural History Magazine,* 78 (February 1969): 12–24.

Thernstrom, Stephan, ed. *Harvard Encyclopedia of American Ethnic Groups.* Cambridge, Mass.: Harvard University Press, 1980.

Waldrer, Jakob. "Diary of a Conscientious Objector in World War I." *Mennonite Quarterly Review* (January 1974): 73–111.

Zablocki, Benjamin. *The Joyful Community.* Baltimore: Penguin, 1971.

INDEX